# Quantum-Inspired Intelligent Systems for Multimedia Data Analysis

Siddhartha Bhattacharyya
*RCC Institute of Information Technology, India*

A volume in the Advances
in Computer and Electrical
Engineering (ACEE) Book Series

Published in the United States of America by
    IGI Global
    Engineering Science Reference (an imprint of IGI Global)
    701 E. Chocolate Avenue
    Hershey PA, USA 17033
    Tel: 717-533-8845
    Fax: 717-533-8661
    E-mail: cust@igi-global.com
    Web site: http://www.igi-global.com

Library of Congress Cataloging-in-Publication Data

Names: Bhattacharyya, Siddhartha, 1975- editor.
Title: Quantum-inspired intelligent systems for multimedia data analysis /
  Siddhartha Bhattacharyya, editor.
Description: Hershey, PA : Engineering Science Reference, [2018] | Includes
  bibliographical references.
Identifiers: LCCN 2017037441| ISBN 9781522552192 (hardcover) | ISBN
  9781522552208 (ebook)
Subjects: LCSH: Multimedia data mining. | Artificial intelligence. | Quantum
  logic.
Classification: LCC QA76.9.D343 Q365 2018 | DDC 006.7--dc23 LC record available at https://
lccn.loc.gov/2017037441

This book is published in the IGI Global book series Advances in Computer and Electrical Engineering (ACEE) (ISSN: 2327-039X; eISSN: 2327-0403)

British Cataloguing in Publication Data
A Cataloguing in Publication record for this book is available from the British Library.

All work contributed to this book is new, previously-unpublished material.
The views expressed in this book are those of the authors, but not necessarily of the publisher.

For electronic access to this publication, please contact: eresources@igi-global.com.

# Advances in Computer and Electrical Engineering (ACEE) Book Series

ISSN:2327-039X
EISSN:2327-0403

Editor-in-Chief: Srikanta Patnaik, SOA University, India

## MISSION

The fields of computer engineering and electrical engineering encompass a broad range of interdisciplinary topics allowing for expansive research developments across multiple fields. Research in these areas continues to develop and become increasingly important as computer and electrical systems have become an integral part of everyday life.

The **Advances in Computer and Electrical Engineering (ACEE) Book Series** aims to publish research on diverse topics pertaining to computer engineering and electrical engineering. **ACEE** encourages scholarly discourse on the latest applications, tools, and methodologies being implemented in the field for the design and development of computer and electrical systems.

## COVERAGE

- Algorithms
- Digital Electronics
- Circuit Analysis
- Computer Architecture
- Sensor Technologies
- Electrical Power Conversion
- Optical Electronics
- Computer Hardware
- Power Electronics
- VLSI Design

IGI Global is currently accepting manuscripts for publication within this series. To submit a proposal for a volume in this series, please contact our Acquisition Editors at Acquisitions@igi-global.com or visit: http://www.igi-global.com/publish/.

# Titles in this Series

*For a list of additional titles in this series, please visit:*
*https://www.igi-global.com/book-series/advances-computer-electrical-engineering/73675*

*For an entire list of titles in this series, please visit:*
*https://www.igi-global.com/book-series/advances-computer-electrical-engineering/73675*

701 East Chocolate Avenue, Hershey, PA 17033, USA
Tel: 717-533-8845 x100 • Fax: 717-533-8661
E-Mail: cust@igi-global.com • www.igi-global.com

*I would like to dedicate this book to my father, Late Ajit Kumar Bhattacharyya, my mother, Late Hashi Bhattacharyya, and my beloved wife, Rashni.*

# Editorial Advisory Board

# Table of Contents

**Chapter 9**

# Detailed Table of Contents

    *Deeksha Kaul, VIT University, India*
    *Harika Raju, VIT University, India*
    *B. K. Tripathy, VIT University, India*

In this chapter, the authors discuss the use of quantum computing concepts to optimize the decision-making capability of classical machine learning algorithms. Machine learning, a subfield of artificial intelligence, implements various techniques to train a computer to learn and adapt to various real-time tasks. With the volume of data exponentially increasing, solving the same problems using classical algorithms becomes more tedious and time consuming. Quantum computing has varied applications in many areas of computer science. One such area which has been transformed a lot through the introduction of quantum computing is machine learning. Quantum computing, with its ability to perform tasks in logarithmic time, aids in overcoming the limitations of classical machine learning algorithms.

    *Sandip Dey, OmDayal Group of Institutions, India*
    *Siddhartha Bhattacharyya, RCC Institute of Information Technology,*
       *India*
    *Ujjwal Maulik, Jadavpur University, India*

Quantum computing has emerged as the most challenging field of research in efficient computation. This chapter introduces a novel quantum-inspired ant colony optimization technique for automatic clustering. This chapter presents an application of this proposed technique to the automatic clustering of real-life gray-scale image data sets. In contrary to the other techniques, the proposed one requires no previous knowledge of the data to be classified. It finds the optimal number of clusters of the data by itself. The Xie-Beni cluster validity measure has been employed as the objective function for clustering purpose. Effectiveness of the proposed technique is exhibited on four real-life gray-scale images. Superiority of the proposed technique is established over its counterpart with respect to various aspects, which include accuracy, stability, computational time and standard errors. Finally, a statistical supremacy test, called unpaired two-tailed t-test, is conducted between them. It shows that superiority in favor of the proposed technique is established.

## Chapter 3

Sunanda Das, University Institute of Technology, India
Sourav De, Cooch Behar Government Engineering College, India
Siddhartha Bhattacharyya, RCC Institute of Information Technology,
India

In this chapter, a quantum-induced modified-genetic-algorithm-based FCM clustering approach is proposed for true color image segmentation. This approach brings down the early convergence problem of FCM to local minima point, increases efficacy of conventional genetic algorithm, and decreases the computational cost and execution time. Effectiveness of genetic algorithm is tumid by modifying some features in population initialization and crossover section. To speed up the execution time as well as make it cost effective and also to get more optimized class levels some quantum computing phenomena like qubit, superposition, entanglement, quantum rotation gate are induced to modified genetic algorithm. Class levels which are yield now fed to FCM as initial input class levels; thus, the ultimate segmented results are formed. Efficiency of proposed method are compared with classical modified-genetic-algorithm-based FCM and conventional FCM based on some standard statistical measures.

## Chapter 4

Subhrajit Sinha Roy, Global Institute of Management and Technology,
India
Abhishek Basu, RCC Institute of Information Technology, India
Avik Chattopadhyay, University of Calcutta, India

In this chapter, hardware implementation of an LSB replacement-based digital image watermarking algorithm is introduced. The proposed scheme is developed in spatial domain. In this watermarking process, data or watermark is implanted into the cover image pixels through an adaptive last significant bit (LSB) replacement technique.

The real-time execution of the watermarking logic is developed here using reversible logic. Utilization of reversible logic reduces the power dissipation by means of no information loss. The lesser power dissipation enables a faster operation as well as holds up Moore's law. The experimental results confirm that the proposed scheme offers high imperceptibility with a justified robustness.

## Chapter 5

Pankaj Pal, RCC Institute of Information Technology, India
Siddhartha Bhattacharyya, RCC Institute of Information Technology, India
Nishtha Agrawal, RCC Institute of Information Technology, India

A method for grayscale image segmentation is presented using a quantum-inspired self-organizing neural network architecture by proper selection of the threshold values of the multilevel sigmoidal activation function (MUSIG). The context-sensitive threshold values in the different positions of the image are measured based on the homogeneity of the image content and used to extract the object by means of effective thresholding of the multilevel sigmoidal activation function guided by the quantum superposition principle. The neural network architecture uses fuzzy theoretic concepts to assist in the segmentation process. The authors propose a grayscale image segmentation method endorsed by context-sensitive thresholding technique. This quantum-inspired multilayer neural network is adapted with self-organization. The architecture ensures the segmentation process for the real-life images as well as synthetic images by selecting intensity parameter as the threshold value.

## Chapter 6

Kalyan Mahata, Government College of Engineering and Leather Technology, India
Rajib Das, Jadavpur University, India
Subhasish Das, Jadavpur University, India
Anasua Sarkar, Jadavpur University, India

Computer science plays a major role in image segmentation and image processing applications. Despite the computational cost, PSO evaluated QCA approaches perform comparable to or better than their crisp counterparts. This novel approach, proposed in this chapter, has been found to enhance the functionality of the CA rule base and thus enhance the established potentiality of the fuzzy-based segmentation domain with the help of quantum cellular automata. This new unsupervised method is able to detect clusters using 2-dimensional quantum cellular automata model based on PSO evaluation. As a discrete, dynamical system, cellular automaton explores uniformly interconnected cells with states. In the second phase, it utilizes a 2-dimensional cellular automata to prioritize allocations of mixed pixels among overlapping land cover areas. The authors experiment on Tilaya Reservoir Catchment on Barakar River. The clustered regions are compared with well-known PSO, FCM, and k-means methods and also with the ground truth knowledge. The results show the superiority of the new method.

## Chapter 7

*Pankaj Pal, RCC Institute of Information Technology, India*
*Siddhartha Bhattacharyya, RCC Institute of Information Technology,*
*India*

In this chapter, the authors propose the true color image segmentation in real-life images as well as synthetic images by means of thresholded MUSIG function, which is learnt by quantum-formulated self-supervised neural network according to change of phase. In the initial phase, the true color image is segregated in the source module to fragment three different components—red, green, and blue colors—for three parallel layers of QMLSONN architecture. This information is fused in the sink module of QPSONN to get the preferred output. Each pixel of the input image is converted to the corresponding qubit neurons according to the phase manner. The interconnection weights between the layers are represented by qubit rotation gates. The quantum measurement at the output layer destroys the quantum states and gets the output for the processed information by means of quantum backpropagation algorithm using fuzziness measure.

## Chapter 8

*Debanjan Konar, Sikkim Manipal Institute of Technology, India*
*Suman Kalyan Kar, Sikkim Manipal Institute of Technology, India*

This chapter proposes a quantum multi-layer neural network (QMLNN) architecture suitable for handwritten character recognition in real time, assisted by quantum backpropagation of errors calculated from the quantum-inspired fuzziness measure of network output states. It is composed of three second-order neighborhood-topology-based inter-connected layers of neurons represented by qubits known as input, hidden, and output layers. The QMLNN architecture is a feed forward network with standard quantum backpropagation algorithm for the adjustment of its weighted interconnection. QMLNN self-organizes the quantum fuzzy input image information by means of the quantum backpropagating errors at the intermediate and output layers of the architecture. The interconnection weights are described using rotation gates. After the network is stabilized, a quantum observation at the output layer destroys the superposition of quantum states in order to obtain true binary outputs.

**Chapter 9**

    *Raul Valverde, Concordia University, Canada*
    *Beatriz Torres, University of Quebec in Outaouais, Canada*
    *Hamed Motaghi, University of Quebec in Outaouais, Canada*

NeuroIS uses tools such as electroencephalogram (EEG) that can be used to measure high brainwave frequencies that can be linked to human anxiety. Past research showed that computer anxiety influences how users perceive ease of use of a learning management system (LMS). Although computer anxiety has been used successfully to evaluate the usability of LMS, the main data collection mechanisms proposed for its evaluation have been questionnaires. Questionnaires suffer from possible problems such as being inadequate to understand some forms of information such as emotions and honesty in the responses. Quantum-based approaches to consciousness have been very popular in the last years including the quantum model reduction in microtubules of Penrose and Hameroff. The objective of the chapter is to propose an architecture based on a NeuroIS that collects data by using EEG from users and then use the collected data to perform analytics by using a quantum consciousness model proposed for computer anxiety measurements for the usability testing of a LMS.

# Preface

Multimedia data, both in discrete and continuous forms, exhibit varied degrees of uncertainties and imprecision, which cannot be handled by the conventional computing paradigm. The situation becomes more severe when it comes to deal with multidimensional data to name the true color images (which exhibit a wide variety of color content in the entire color gamut) and the video data which includes elements of synchronization apart from the curse of dimensionality.

Of late, the soft computing paradigm, which has proven to be efficient in handling uncertainties, has been successfully put to use to deal with this problem. However, it is also a proven fact that these soft computing tools and techniques often fall short in offering a formidable solution to the problems inherent therein. Hence, scientists have come up with the hybridization of the soft computing tools to give rise to more robust and failsafe solutions. Typical examples include the rough-fuzzy, neuro-fuzzy, neuro-fuzzy-genetic architectures to name a few.

So much so forth, in their attempt to yield more time efficient solutions, the recent trend of computing takes off to the quantum inspired domain, where every information is represented in the form of qubits, thus entailing massive parallelism by dint of the properties inherited from the quantum mechanics. Quantum computing stems from the principles of quantum mechanics and is now conjoined with the hybrid soft computing paradigm to give rise to the quantum inspired intelligent computing paradigm which provides better time efficient solutions taking the help of the massive parallelism due to the principles of superposition between the constituent basis states.

This book looks to discuss and address the difficulties and challenges that are encountered in the field of multimedia data processing using the state-of-the art quantum inspired computational intelligent tools and techniques. The editor will seek chapters that address the challenging propositions of multimedia information processing using the most recent intelligent paradigms in the form of quantum inspired versions of swarm intelligence, neural networks, deep learning to name a few.

The present volume would come to the benefits of several categories of students and researchers. At the students' level, this book can serve as a treatise/reference book for the special papers at the master's level aimed at inspiring possibly future researchers. Newly inducted PhD aspirants would also find the contents of this book useful as far as their compulsory coursework are concerned. At the researchers' level, those interested in interdisciplinary research would also be benefited from the book. After all, the enriched interdisciplinary contents of the book would always be a subject of interest to the faculties, existing research communities and new research aspirants from diverse disciplines of the concerned departments of premier institutes across the globe. This is expected to bring different research backgrounds (due to its cross-platform characteristics) close to one another to form effective research groups all over the world. Above all, availability of the book should be ensured to as much universities and research institutes as possible through whatever graceful means it may be.

The book comprises nine well versed chapters dealing with the recent research trends in the topic under consideration.

In Chapter 1, the authors discuss the use of quantum computing concepts to optimize the decision making capability of classical machine learning algorithms. Machine learning, a subfield of artificial intelligence, implements various techniques to train a computer to learn and adapt to various real-time tasks. With the volume of data exponentially increasing, solving the same problems using classical algorithms becomes more tedious and time consuming. Quantum computing has a wide variety of applications in many areas of computer science. One such area which has been transformed a lot through the introduction of quantum computing is machine learning and artificial intelligence. Quantum computing, with its ability to perform tasks in logarithmic time, aids in overcoming the limitations of classical machine learning algorithms.

Quantum computing has also emerged as the most challenging field of research in efficient computation. Chapter 2 introduces a novel quantum inspired ant colony optimization technique for automatic clustering. This chapter presents an application of this proposed technique to the automatic clustering of real life gray scale image data sets. In contrary to the other techniques, the proposed one requires no previous knowledge of the data to be classified. Somewhat, it finds the optimal number of clusters of the data by itself. The Xie-beni cluster validity measure has been employed as the objective function for clustering purpose. Effectiveness of the proposed technique is exhibited on four real life gray scale images. Superiority of the proposed technique is established over its counterpart with respect to various aspects, which include accuracy, stability and computational time, Standard errors. Finally, a statistical supremacy test, called unpaired two-tailed t-test has conducted between them, the shows that superiority in favor of the proposed technique is established.

In Chapter 3, a quantum induced modified genetic algorithm based FCM clustering approach is proposed for true color image segmentation. This approach brings down the early convergence problem of FCM to local minima point, increases efficacy of conventional genetic algorithm and decreases the computational cost and execution time. Effectiveness of genetic algorithm is tumid by modifying some features in population initialization and crossover section. To speed up the execution time as well as make it cost effective and also to get more optimized class levels some quantum computing phenomena like qubit, superposition, entanglement, quantum rotation gate are induced to modified genetic algorithm. Class levels which are yield now fed to FCM as initial input class levels thus the ultimate segmented results are formed. Efficiency of proposed method are compared with classical modified genetic algorithm based FCM and conventional FCM based on some standard statistical measures.

In Chapter 4, a hardware implementation of an LSB replacement based digital image watermarking algorithm has been introduced. The proposed scheme is developed in spatial domain. In this watermarking process, data or watermark is implanted into the cover image pixels through an adaptive last significant bit (LSB) replacement technique. The real time execution of the watermarking logic is developed here using reversible logic. Utilization of reversible logic reduces the power dissipation by means of no information loss. The lesser power dissipation enables a faster operation as well as holds up the Moore's law. The experimental results confirm that the proposed scheme offers high imperceptibility with a justified robustness.

A method for gray scale image segmentation is presented in Chapter 5 using a quantum inspired self-organizing neural network architecture by proper selection of the threshold values of the multilevel sigmoidal activation function (MUSIG). The context sensitive threshold values in the different positions of the image are measured based on the homogeneity of the image content and is used to extract the object by means of effective thresholding of the multilevel sigmoidal activation function guided by the quantum superposition principle. The neural network architecture uses fuzzy theoretic concepts to assist in the segmentation process. The authors propose a gray scale image segmentation method endorsed by context sensitive thresholding technique. This quantum inspired multilayer neural network is adapted with self-organization. The architecture ensures the segmentation process for the real-life images as well as synthetic images by selecting intensity parameter as the threshold value.

Computer science has major role in image segmentation and image processing applications. Despite the computational cost, PSO evaluated QCA approaches perform comparable to or better than their crisp counterparts. This novel approach, proposed in Chapter 6, has been found to enhance the functionality of the CA rule base and thus enhance the established potentiality of the fuzzy based segmentation domain with the help of Quantum Cellular Automata. This new unsupervised method is able to detect clusters using 2-Dimensional Quantum Cellular Automata model based on PSO evaluation. As a discrete, dynamical system, cellular automaton explore of uniformly interconnected cells with states. In the second phase, we utilize a 2-dimensional cellular automata to prioritize allocations of mixed pixels among overlapping land cover areas. We experiment our method on Tilaya Reservoir Catchment on Barakar River. The clustered regions are compared with well-known PSO, FCM and K-Means methods and also with the ground truth knowledge. The results show the superiority of our new method.

In Chapter 7, the authors propose the true color image segmentation in real life images as well as synthetic images by means of thresholded MUSIG function which is learnt by quantum formulated self-supervised neural network according to change of phase. In the initial phase the true color image is segregated in the source module to fragment three different components are red, green and blue colors for three parallel layers of QMLSONN architecture. This Information is fused in the sink module of QPSONN to get the preferred output. Each pixel of the input image is converted to the corresponding qubit neurons according to the phase manner. The interconnection weights between the layers are represented by qubit rotation gates. The quantum measurement at the output layer destroys the quantum states and gets the output for the processed information by means of quantum backpropagation algorithm using fuzziness measure.

Chapter 8 proposes a Quantum Multi-Layer Neural Network (QMLNN) architecture suitable for hand written character recognition in real time, assisted by quantum back-propagation of errors calculated from the quantum inspired fuzziness measure of network output states. It is composed of three second order neighborhood topology based inter-connected layers of neurons represented by qubits known as input, hidden and output layers. The QMLNN architecture is a feed forward network with standard quantum back-propagation algorithm for the adjustment of its weighted inter-connection. QMLNN self-organizes the quantum fuzzy input image information by means of the quantum back-propagating errors at the intermediate and output layers of the architecture. The interconnection weights are described using rotation gates. After the network is stabilized, a quantum observation at the output layer destroys the superposition of quantum states in order to obtain true binary outputs.

NeuroIS uses tools such as Electroencephalogram (EEG) that can be used to measure high brainwave frequencies that can be linked to human anxiety. Past research showed that computer anxiety influences how users perceive ease of use of a learning management system (LMS). Although computer anxiety has been used successfully to evaluate the usability of LMS, the main data collection mechanisms proposed for its evaluation has been questionnaires. Questionnaires suffer from possible problems such inadequate to understand some forms of information such as emotions and honesty in the responses. Quantum based approaches to consciousness have been very popular in the last years including the quantum model reduction in microtubules of Penrose and Hameroff. The objective of Chapter 9 is to propose an architecture based on a NeuroIS that collects data by using EEG from users and then use the collected data to perform analytics by using a quantum consciousness model proposed for computer anxiety measurements for the usability testing of a LMS.

The aim of the book is to bring a broad spectrum of artificial intelligence and its applications under the purview of multimedia information processing so that it is able to trigger further inspiration among various research communities to contribute in their respective fields of applications thereby orienting these application fields towards faithful understanding of multimedia data. Once the purpose, as stated above, is achieved a larger number of research communities may be brought under one umbrella to ventilate their ideas in a more structured manner. In that case, the present endeavor may be seen as the beginning of such an effort in bringing various intelligent research applications in multimedia data processing close to one another.

*Siddhartha Bhattacharyya*
*RCC Institute of Information Technology, India*

# Chapter 1
# Quantum–Computing–Inspired Algorithms in Machine Learning

**Deeksha Kaul**
*VIT University, India*

**Harika Raju**
*VIT University, India*

**B. K. Tripathy**
*VIT University, India*

## ABSTRACT

*In this chapter, the authors discuss the use of quantum computing concepts to optimize the decision-making capability of classical machine learning algorithms. Machine learning, a subfield of artificial intelligence, implements various techniques to train a computer to learn and adapt to various real-time tasks. With the volume of data exponentially increasing, solving the same problems using classical algorithms becomes more tedious and time consuming. Quantum computing has varied applications in many areas of computer science. One such area which has been transformed a lot through the introduction of quantum computing is machine learning. Quantum computing, with its ability to perform tasks in logarithmic time, aids in overcoming the limitations of classical machine learning algorithms.*

DOI: 10.4018/978-1-5225-5219-2.ch001

# INTRODUCTION

Quantum is a Latin word for amount and in modern understanding means the smallest possible discrete unit of any physical property such as energy, matter. The quantum science is often intimidating due to unfamiliarity with the discipline, even though it is the backbone of many of today's major state-of-the-art technologies ranging from lasers to semiconductors devices. However, quantum computing is quickly gaining popularity and has found many applications in real time scenarios. Even though applying the ideologies of quantum mechanics to computer science may feel like a sophisticated task, the science has already moved past its theoretical stage as confirmed by the latest researches.

The exciting aspect of quantum computational intelligence is that its fundamentals integrate the principles of both computer science and quantum physics. As pointed out by Feynman, in the early eighties, simple simulations of quantum mechanics on a classical computer appear to require a simulation overhead which is exponential with respect to the size of the system and the simulated time.

Presently, computers in theory (Turing machines) as well as in practice (Personal Computers) are based on classical physics i.e. the state of ON or OFF. Nevertheless, as indicated by modern quantum physics, the world behaves quite differently i.e. between the states of ON and OFF.

And as such, quantum systems exhibit a superposition of various states lying in [0, 1], at any point of time, and exhibit the effects of interference during its evolution. Moreover, in quantum systems due to the theory of entanglement, a particle loses its individuality which results in remote effects. The discipline of quantum computation aims to investigate and enhance the computational power and other performance based aspects of computers based on quantum-mechanical principles. The idea is to obtain alternative quantum algorithms that give better computational results as opposed to classical solutions of the problem. Genetic quantum algorithms and their applications in combinatorial optimisation problems is discussed in (Han and Kim, 2000). A study of cognitive radio decision engine based on quantum genetic algorithm is discussed in (Zhao, Zheng and Shang, 2007).

Instead of storing information as 0s or 1s as done in conventional computers, a quantum computer stores the information as qubits which can store the state of 0 or 1 or a superposition of both at the same time. The fast and powerful quantum computation has been realized by various quantum effects such as quantum superposition, entanglement and quantum tunnelling enabling quantum computers to examine and exploit the fusion of qubits concurrently which do not necessarily follow the binary nature of computing.

While conventional computers encode information into bits and can only perform discrete binary calculations, quantum computers use as spin directions of electrons or polarization orientations of a photon to encode information. These quantum-mechanical states might represent a 1 or a 0, or combination of both or a value lying somewhere in between 1 and 0. The edge that a quantum computer has over a classical computer is that it can perform arbitrary reversible computations on a set of numbers simultaneously, which is impossible for a classical computer. It also has the ability to produce interference between various states. This interference property helps a quantum computer to outperform a classical computer of same size. Although a quantum computer uses only a single processing unit, it can perform numerous operations in parallel. The approach adopted by quantum computing is entirely dissimilar to that of classical computing. A map connecting various locations is an appropriate analogy for explaining this dissimilarity. As an example, solving optimization problems can be thought of as trying to find the shortest distance between two locations. Every possible solution is mapped to this distance, and the cost of travelling that path is the cost of the solution for the problem. The aim is to find an optimal solution which gives the least cost of traversing the corresponding path. Classical computers employing classical algorithms can only "walk over this map". Quantum computers on the other hand can tunnel through the map making it faster to find the shortest path.

The D-Wave processor used by quantum computers helps in finding the cheapest solution among all possible optimal solutions. The computation is much faster than in case of a classical computer and provides a vast number of optimal solutions. This gives the user the optimal solutions along with various alternative solutions.

D-Wave, a Canadian company announced in 2010 that it had begun the production of the world's first commercial quantum computer, which was based on theoretical work done at MIT. It has been observed that Quantum computers have faster problem solving capability in comparison to the classical computers and there is a case when it works exponentially faster. In 2013, a consortium including Google and NASA bought one of D-Wave's machines. In fact, a group of Google researchers released a paper claiming that in their experiments, a quantum algorithm running on their D-Wave machine was 100 million times faster than a comparable classical algorithm. The Google researchers' paper focused on two algorithms; simulated annealing and quantum annealing.

Simulated annealing is one of the premier optimization methods that is used today. It was invented in the early 1980s by direct analogy with what happens when people anneal metals, which is a 7,000-year-old technology. You heat the metal up, the atoms are all jiggling around randomly, and as you slowly cool it down, the atoms are more and more likely to go somewhere that will decrease the total energy.

In the case of an algorithm, you have a whole bunch of bits that start flipping between 1 and 0 willy-nilly, regardless of what that does to the solution quality. And then as you lower the "temperature," a bit becomes more and more unwilling to flip in a way that would make the solution worse, until at the end, when the temperature is zero, a bit will only go to the value that keeps the solution going straight downhill — toward better solutions.

The main problem with simulated annealing, or for that matter with any other local-search method, is that you can get stuck in local optima. If you're trying to reach the lowest point in some energy landscape, you can get stuck in a crevice that is locally the best, but you don't realize that there's a much lower valley somewhere else, if you would only go up and search. Simulated annealing tries to deal with that already: When the temperature is high, then you're willing to move up the hill sometimes. But if there's a really tall hill, even if it's a very, very narrow hill — just imagine it's a big spike sticking out of the ground — it could take you an exponential amount of time until you happen to flip so many bits that you happen to get over that spike. In quantum mechanics, we know that particles can tunnel through barriers (This is the language that the physicists use, which is a little bit misleading). In an important paper, Farhi, Goldstone and Guttmann published in 2002, when all of them were at MIT, showed that if a barrier is really a tall thin spike, then quantum annealing can give you an exponential speedup over classical simulated annealing. Classical annealing is going to get stuck at the base of that spike for exponential time, and quantum annealing is going to tunnel over it and get down to the global minimum in polynomial time.

In the current model of the D-Wave chip, there are 1,000 or so qubits [quantum bits], but they're organized into clusters of eight qubits each. The qubits within each cluster are very tightly connected to each other, and between clusters there are only weaker connections. I think that this is the best evidence we've had so far for quantum tunnelling behaviour, at least at the level of the eight-bit clusters.

The main way that they got an advantage over simulated annealing in these results was by taking advantage of the fact that quantum tunnelling — or anything that correlates all the qubits within the cluster — can flip all the bits within each cluster at the same time, whereas simulated annealing is going to try flipping the bits one by one, then see that that's not a good idea, then flip them all back, and not realize that by flipping all eight of them, you could get something better.

The case has now clearly been made that whatever the D-Wave device is doing, it's something that can tunnel past this eight-qubit barrier. Of course, that still doesn't mean that you're doing anything faster than you could do it classically. However, even though quantum Monte Carlo has the same asymptotic performance, the constant is way, way better for the D-Wave machine. The constant is about 100 million times better.

## Quantum Computing

Quantum computing has emerged as a trending field in computer science and has sparked intensive research work over the last decade. It takes its foundations from the fundamentals of quantum physics. The ability of quantum computers to perform various tasks in parallel on a single processor reduces the algorithmic complexity and enhances the efficiency of various optimization problems. According to authors (Dong et al, 2008) due to inexistence of powerful quantum computers, it has been suggested to implement quantum algorithms on traditional computers or integrate them with existing classical algorithms to decrease complexity of algorithms. Some researchers (Shon et al, 2008) mention Knapsack problem, travelling salesman problem, N-queens problem and image segmentation as some example of successfully implemented combinations of classical algorithms and quantum computing principles.

Quantum processing is the range of study concentrated on creating innovations in view of the standards of quantum hypothesis, which clarifies the nature and conduct of energy and matter on the quantum (nuclear and subatomic) level. Evolution of a quantum computer, if feasible, would stamp a jump forward in registering ability far more prominent than that from the abacus to the present day supercomputer, with billion-fold improvement in performance. The quantum computer, taking after the laws of quantum mechanics, would increase gigantic processing power through the capacity to be in various states, and to perform operations utilizing all conceivable stages concurrently.

Some of the major renowned research laboratories working in the field of quantum computing are MIT, IBM, Oxford University, and the Los Alamos National Laboratory. Paul Benio, working at Argonne National Labs, in 1981, laid down the basic components of quantum computing. He conjectured a classical computer operating with quantum mechanical standards. Yet, it is for the most part acknowledged that David Deutsch of Oxford University gave the basic impulse for quantum computing research. In 1984, while at a computational theory conference he started to ponder about the likelihood of constructing a computer that was solely based on quantum rules. With this, the race started to endeavour his thoughts. In any case, before we dive into what he began, it is beneficial to observe the foundation of the quantum world. For a good account of computational intelligence theory one can refer the book (Engilbrecht, 2007).

## Quantum Theory

Max Planck's presentation in the German Physical Society, in which he introduced the idea of "quanta", encouraged the development of quantum theory in 1900.

Improvements facilitated by various researchers over the following thirty years prompted the cutting edge comprehension of quantum hypothesis.

## The Essential Elements of Quantum Theory

1.   Energy, similar to matter, comprises of discrete units called quanta, as opposed to exclusively as a consistent wave.
2.   Basic particles of energy and matter, contingent upon the conditions, may carry on like either particles or waves (duality).
3.   The movement of basic particles is intrinsically arbitrary, and, therefore, capricious.
4.   The simultaneous estimation of two interdependent entities, such as the position and momentum of a basic molecule, is unpreventably awed; the more precise measurement of one value, lesser the precision in the measurement of the other value.

## Further Developments of Quantum Theory

Niels Bohr proposed the Copenhagen understanding of quantum hypothesis, which declares that a molecule is whatever it is measured to be i.e. a wave or a molecule. However it can't be expected to have specific properties, or even to exist, until it is measured. To put it plainly, Bohr was saying that objective reality is not in existence. This gives rise to the principle known as superposition which is based on the fact that a state of any particle cannot fully known as it may be present in various possible states at the same time.

To delineate this hypothesis, we can utilize the well-known and fairly remorseless similarity of Schrodinger's Cat. To begin with, we place a living cat in a thick lead box. At this stage, we are quite sure that the cat is alive. Then we toss in a vial of cyanide and seal the container. After doing this, now we don't know whether the cat is alive or dead or whether the cyanide case has been damaged by the cat. This situation of not knowing whether the cat is alive or dead illustrates the principle of superposition as proposed in quantum law. Superposition is lost only when we tear open the container to check the condition the cat that is whether it is alive or dead. The second elucidation of quantum hypothesis is the multiverse or numerous universes hypothesis. It holds that when a potential exists for any particle be in any state, the universe of that particle transmutes into a progression of parallel universes equivalent to the quantity of conceivable states in which that the particle can exist, with every universe containing a one of a kind single conceivable state of that particle.

Besides, there is an instrument for association between these universes that by one means or other grants all states to be attainable somehow and for every conceivable state to be influenced in some way. Stephen Hawking and the late Richard Feynman are among the elite scientists who have communicated an inclination for the numerous universes hypothesis. Whichever contention one picks, the rule that, somehow, one molecule can exist in various states opens up significant ramifications for computing.

In (Blaise et al, 2004) a realizable architecture is proposed, using one-dimensional transmission line resonators to reach the strong coupling limit of cavity quantum electrodynamics in superconducting electrical circuits. The vacuum Rabi frequency for the coupling of cavity photons to quantized excitations of an adjacent electrical circuit (qubit) can easily exceed the damping rates of both the cavity and the qubit. The proposed circuits therefore provide a simple and efficient architecture for solid-state quantum computation, in addition to opening up a new avenue for the study of entanglement and quantum measurement physics with macroscopic objects.

## Comparison of Classical and Quantum Computing

Traditional computing depends, at its definitive level, on standards communicated by Boolean variable based math, working with a (for the most part) 7-mode logic gate guidelines, however it is conceivable to exist simply with three modes (which are AND, NOT, and OR). Information must be handled in a select binary state anytime i.e. in the state of 0/1 or on/off or true/false.

These quantities are paired (binary) digits, or bits. Generally, the transistors and capacitors which are the basic building blocks of a computer are understood to be only in one state at any point of time. While the time that the every transistor or capacitor require be either in 0 or 1 preceding exchanging states is presently quantifiable in billionths of a moment, there is still a restrain with reference to how rapidly these gadgets can be done to switch state. As we advance to smaller and quicker circuits, we start to achieve the physical potential of materials and the limit for traditional laws of physics. Past this, the quantum world assumes control, which opens a potential as extraordinary as the difficulties that are displayed. Contrastingly, the Quantum computers can work with a two-mode logic gate: XOR and a mode we'll refer to as QO1, which has the capacity to change 0 into a superposition of 0 and 1. This is something which is out of the capabilities of conventional computing.

In a quantum computer, various fundamental particles for example, electrons or photons can be utilized (achievement has likewise been accomplished with ions), with either their charge or polarization going about as a portrayal of 0 as well as 1. Each of these particles is known as a quantum bit, or qubit, the nature and conduct of these particles frame the premise of quantum processing. Superposition and entanglement lay the fundamentals of quantum physics and further quantum computations. Short dephasing times pose one of the main challenges in realizing a quantum computer. Different approaches have been devised to cure this problem for superconducting qubits, a prime example being the operation of such devices at optimal working points, so-called "sweet spots." In (Koch et al, 2007) a new type of superconducting qubit called the "transmon" is introduced. Unlike the charge qubit, the transmon is designed to operate in a regime of significantly increased ratio of Josephson energy and charging energy. The transmon benefits from the fact that its charge dispersion decreases exponentially with, while its loss in anharmonicity is described by a weak power law. As a result, we predict a drastic reduction in sensitivity to charge noise relative to the Cooper pair box and an increase in the qubit-photon coupling, while maintaining sufficient anharmonicity for selective qubit control. Our detailed analysis of the full system shows that this gain is not compromised by increased noise in other known channels.

## Superposition

An electron in a magnetic field is analogous to a qubit in quantum computation. There are primarily two states of electron spin. Spin-up state in which the electron's spin is in alignment with the magnetic field and spin-down state in which the electron's spin is opposite to the magnetic field. A pulse of energy is applied to change the spin of electron from one state to another is achieved. This pulse can be obtained from a laser. Let us assume that 1 unit of laser energy is required to change the state of electron spin. Yet, imagine a scenario in which we just utilize a large portion of a unit of laser energy and totally seclude the particle from all outside influences? As indicated by quantum law, the particle then enters a superposition of states, in which it carries on as though it were in both states at the same time. In such a scenario, each qubit represents a superposition of both 0 and 1 resulting in $n^2$ calculations using only n qubits.

A quantum computer comprised of 500 qubits would have a potential to do 2500 calculations in a single step. This is an exponential increase efficiency of computation which cannot be achieved even by classical computers that claim parallel processing using multiple processors.

These particles collaborate with each other by means of quantum entanglement. Entangled particles, (for example, photons, electrons, or qubits) that have communicated at a certain point hold an association and can be entangled with each other in sets of two, in a procedure known as correlation . Knowing the spin state of one entangled particle - up or down - permits one to conclude that the spin of its partner is the other way. Even more surprising is the fact that, due to the occurrence of superposition, the corresponding particle does not have a single spin value before being estimated, but rather is concurrently in both a spin-up and spin-down state. The spin state of the particle being estimated is chosen at the point of estimation and furthermore, conveyed to the associated particle, which at the same time expect the inverse spin direction to that of the particle under consideration.

This is a genuine phenomenon (referred to it as "spooky action at a distance" by Einstein), the system of which cannot, as of now, be clarified by any hypothesis - it just should be taken as given. Quantum entanglement permits qubits that are isolated by vast separations to interface with each other quickly (not restricted to the speed of light). Regardless of how incredible the separation between the connected particles, they will remain entangled. Working in collaboration, quantum superposition and entanglement create an exponentially enhance computing power. While in case of a conventional computer, 2-bit register can store only one out of the four possible binary configurations (00, 01, 10, or 11) at a point of time, since each qubit holds two values, a 2-qubit register in a quantum computer can store all four possibilities at the same time. In the event that more qubits are included, the expanded limit is extended exponentially.

## Quantum Programming

Maybe considerably more captivating than the sheer energy of quantum processing is the capacity that it offers to compose programs in a totally new manner. For instance, a quantum computer could integrate a programming arrangement that would be along the lines of "take every one of the superpositions of all the earlier calculations" - something which is insignificant with a conventional computer PC - which would allow to a great degree quick methods for taking care of certain mathematical problems, for example, factorization of huge numbers, one such case which we examine further.

There have been two striking triumphs hitherto with quantum programming. The first happened in 1994 by Peter Shor (now at ATT Labs) who built up a quantum formula that could systematically factorize extensive numbers. It fixates on a framework that utilizes number hypothesis to measure the recurrence of a substantial number series. The other crucial discovery occurred with Lov Grover of Bell Labs in 1996, with a very rapid algorithm that is established to take the least time for traversing through disorganised databases. The algorithm is so effective as it requires roughly N square root (where N is the aggregate number of components) traverses to find the coveted outcome, rather than a hunt in conventional computing, which by and large needs N/2 seeks.

## The Problems, and Some Solutions

The various advantageous of quantum computing sounds promising, yet there are huge impediments still to be overcome. Few of the issues with quantum processing are as follows:

### Interference

During the calculation period of a quantum computation, the smallest unsettling influence in a quantum framework (say a stray photon or wave of EM radiation) causes the quantum calculation to fall, a procedure known as de-coherence. A quantum computer must be completely secluded from all outer impedance amid the calculation stage. Few achievements have been accomplished with the utilization of qubits in intensive magnetic field, with the utilization of ions. Experimental results showing how a quantum superposition of charge states can be prepared in the simplest superconducting island circuit, namely super conducting box are reported in (Bouchiat et al, 1998).

### Error Correction

As quantum systems cannot be completely secluded, it has been found very difficult to develop error correction algorithms for quantum processing. Qubits are not computerized bits of information; accordingly they can't utilize traditional (and extremely effective) error correction, such as the triple redundant strategy. As quantum processing is very specific, error correction becomes very crucial as even a minute error in estimation can lead to collapsing of the entire system. There has been significant advance around this field, with an error rectification formula built up that uses 9 qubits (1 computational and 8 restorative). Presently, there is an algorithm which was successfully built by IBM that uses only 5 qubits (1 computational and 4 restorative).

### Yield Recognition

Closely identified with the over two, recovering yield information after a quantum computation is in complete risk of ruining the information. In a case of a quantum computer with 500 qubits, we have a 1 in 2500 shot of watching the correct yield in the event that we measure the yield. Along these lines, what is required is a technique to guarantee that, as soon as all estimations are mentioned and the examination of values happens, the scrutinized value will map to the right answer.

But the main question here which arises is that by which method can the desired output be achieved? It has been accomplished by Grover with his database exploring numeration that depends on the extraordinary "wave" appearance of the expected curl intrinsic in quantum computers that guarantees, once all computations are completed, the demonstration of estimation will witness the quantum state decoherer into the right answer.

Despite the fact that there are numerous issues to be resolved, the discoveries over the most recent decade, particularly in the recent 3 years, have made the possibility of pragmatic quantum processing feasible, yet there is much open deliberation with respect to whether this can be made into reality within the next decade or will it take another 100 years to achieve this. Nevertheless, the potential that this innovation presents is pulling in colossal enthusiasm from both the administration and the private part. Military applications are using brute force techniques to crack encryptions keys, while regular private experiments run from DNA demonstrating to complex material science examination. It is this potential that is quickly overcoming the obstructions to this innovation, yet whether all hindrances can be overcome, and when, is still an open question.

## Why Quantum Computing

We all are aware of the splendid theoretical outcomes in quantum processing: factoring of numbers is exponentially quicker and unranked search is speedier by quadratic order than any known traditional formulation. However, aside from the known cases, finding a use of quantum processing is a test. Planning a decent quantum formulation is a challenging assignment though it does not obtain from the challenges of quantum mechanics. Or maybe, the issue lies in our desires: a quantum computation must be speedier, computationally less mind boggling than any known established algorithm to the same reason.

The latest advances in quantum processing demonstrate that machine learning may very well be the correct field of utilization. As machine learning typically comes down to a type of multi-variable optimization, it deciphers straightforwardly to quantum annealing and adiabatic quantum processing. This type of learning has officially exhibited outcomes on real quantum equipment, yet endless challenges are present to make the technique scale higher. Nevertheless, we should not be restrict ourselves to adiabatic quantum computers. In reality, we scarcely require broadly useful quantum PCs: the challenge of learning is much more limited. Henceforth different algorithms in quantum data processing and quantum mechanics are promising for discovering.

Quantum computing tomography is helpful for regression analysis as it can identify an unknown function within well laid down symmetry and physical boundaries. A valuable level of abstraction can be obtained from quantum neural systems which use the random execution of qubits. Moreover, there is an incredible flexibility in executing such systems: optical frameworks, atomic magnetic reverberation, and quantum points have been recommended. Quantum equipment devoted to machine learning may progress toward becoming reality substantially quicker than a universally useful quantum computer.

## QUANTUM INSPIRED COMPUTATIONAL INTELLIGENCE TECHNIQUES

Quantum computing is a field that has recently gained popularity. It is believed that by applying certain principles of quantum mechanics like entanglement, superposition and quantum tunnelling can help overcome certain performance issues that cannot be dealt with using classical computing techniques. These quantum mechanics inspired techniques when used in collaboration with computational intelligence as shown in (Dunjko, Taylor and Briegel, 2016), can be used to solve many engineering problems. Quantum computing tries to implement the classical computing methods using quantum physics concepts, being inspired by the theory of reversible computing. There are various techniques that apply the ideas of quantum mechanics to improve the computation power and reduce the computation complexity. Following are the techniques that we will be discussing in detail:

- Quantum inspired Neural Networks
- Quantum inspired Fuzzy logic
- Quantum inspired evolutionary methods

### Quantum Inspired Neural Networks

Quantum inspired neural network (QNN) alludes to NN models, depending on standards based on Quantum Mechanics which could be classified into two categories. The class of QNN which expressly employs ideas from Quantum Computing is still at theoretical level only, as it requires a useful Quantum Computer to be realized. Scientists have suggested models where the neuron behaves like a quantum bit and quantum associative memory (QAM). Another class incorporates models of organic NN explaining the incredible performance of natural brains by utilizing ideas from Quantum mechanics and quantum computing.

Quantum version of a neural network a wave function is represented by a neurons, entanglement by learning rule, coherence de-coherence by evolution of weights as provided in (Ezhov and Ventura, 2000) and (Kak, 1995). More optimized use of resources in case of quantum algorithms as opposed to classical algorithms provided motivation for development of quantum neural networks. Moreover, quantum neural networks do not require evolution of quantum computers for implementation, but can be just as easily implemented using traditional computers. In early 90s (Matsuda, 1993) suggested using discreet integer values or continuous real values rather than just binary values in Neural Networks for solving optimization problems without getting stuck in local minima. He observed that the computation time, along with the number of neurons, is much less as compared to that in conventional methods. In (Meng and Gong, 2010) suggested a Multi-Agent Reinforcement based Neural Network model inspired by Quantum Computational Multi-Agent Systems. Each neuron, according to this model, would compute in parallel to reduce time, increase the computation efficiency and optimize the learning process.

## Quantum Inspired Fuzzy Logic

Majority of the research associated with developing new processing platform is based on quantum computing and fuzzy sets. The uncertainty in these theories greatly differs from the uncertainty involved in classical probability theory. The similarities between fuzzy set theory and quantum mechanics can be exploited to implement them in collaboration.

The authors (Rigatos, Gerasimov and Tzafestas, 1998) replaced serial matrix operations by single step quantum addition or subtraction operations which greatly increased the processing speed of the algorithm. The use of fuzzy bits to represent the superposition among crisp values is suggested in (Hannachi and Hirota, 2005). A fuzzy Q bit model was also developed for implementation of Quantum Associative Memory Learning. A wave function was formulated for Fuzzy C-means algorithm. Integration of FCM with an unsupervised quantum inspired clustering algorithm was observed to help overcome issues faced by traditional clustering algorithms while classifying complex data. A major difference between fuzzy and quantum logic using a concept called "Square root of Not" is discussed in (Kreinovich et al, 2008).

## Quantum Inspired Evolutionary Techniques

Now-a-days a lot of optimization and design problems are being solved using biologically inspired algorithms as shown in (Vlachopiannts, Sohn and Kwang, 2008) and (Han and Kim, 2001). These algorithms are inspired by the typical biological or natural activities taking place around us. They help us build approximate solutions for complex NP-hard problems which cannot be solved in polynomial time using general classical algorithms. Different methods which differ in the execution and efficiency are being applied depending on a specific issue belonging to a particular domain.

To overcome the different deficiencies in the traditional evolutionary strategies, scientists have started to merge the classical algorithms with quantum idea to perform effective parallel computations. We can generate the best results in terms of efficiency if such algorithms are run on quantum computer rather than a traditional one because in the latter there would be too much of resource consumption. Therefore, the idea of developing quantum inspired evolutionary algorithms (Zhang, 2011; Cruz et al, 1998) for traditional computers originated instead of creating quantum methods for quantum computer.

The quantum-inspired evolutionary techniques draw their major principles from two major sub-groups of computer science which are quantum computing and evolutionary computing. Contrary to "genuine" quantum techniques, the considered algorithms don't require a practical quantum computer for their proficient execution. Rather, these methods utilize the advantage of extra level of arbitrariness roused by ideas and standards drawn from quantum mechanical frameworks, for example, qubits, impedance or superposition of states.

## LEARNING THEORY AND DATA MINING

Machine learning is all about data processing algorithms and computational complexity. The field of data mining shares the principles of machine learning but the emphasis is on something else. The goal much like machine learning is to identify patterns in data of huge size. Aside from that we can say that data mining is a cross-disciplinary field that borrows it's techniques from many related concepts. For example, pattern analysis is done through various machine learning algorithms, performance analysis techniques are borrowed from statistics and for information retrieval, pre-processing and visualization it relies on the concepts of database management. Data mining, as it includes all kinds of extensive information processing, has more applications in real time scenarios as opposed to machine learning itself. We can even say that data mining is a field that applies the principles and techniques of machine learning to achieve its goals. Whereas the field of machine learning simply focuses on supervised or unsupervised learning algorithms that help a computer learn and predict from data without being implicitly programmed. While machine learning can be used for data mining, data mining also uses other techniques along with or on top of machine learning. Roughly stating, database management and machine learning are two of the basic concepts that data mining relies on. Database offers information administration strategies, while machine learning offers information examination procedures. Real time data comes from numerous sources like business, science, sensors, media, surveillance, etc. The main objective of data mining is to make sense of this extensive data and draw conclusions.

## Machine Learning Using Classical Approaches

Machine Learning is the sub-field of computer science that reviews techniques to provide for machines the capacity to learn from past involvement. Common tasks in machine learning incorporate the capacity to predict the class (known as classification) or some unobserved characteristics (regression) of an object based on a few perceptions in supervised learning, or the capacity to discover some hidden structure from the information (clustering) in unsupervised learning. Generally, in machine learning techniques, a machine is trained through a learning algorithm that takes as information a training dataset. This dataset is thought to be hundred percent classical, implying that it contains "classical" perceptions about "traditional" objects. Deep quantum networks for classification are proposed in (Zhou, Chen and Wang, 2010). A proposal for fuzzy neural network model based on quantum clustering is presented in (Sup and Hao, 2009).

Generally, the learning is done through detailed analysis of existing datasets to make a training model. A typical framework cannot deal with extensive calculations over large datasets and with information size is expanding every single day, the acquired model ought to be adjusted likewise. Implementing distributed computing using big data technologies as discussed in (Chandler, 2016) is one way to achieve that. Big data (Ali, 2017) refers to the data that is beyond the storage and processing capabilities of a traditional computer. This data can come from numerous sources and can be in structured, semi-structured or unstructured form. Use of big data reduces storage cost, provides powerful multicore processors and reduces delay by connecting computer clusters through a high speed network. Furthermore, big data employs machine learning techniques as discussed in (Vamanan, 2015) to perform advanced analysis, partitions and clusters resources dynamically as per requirement and provides affordable storage and computing power by making use of cloud.

## Quantum Inspired Machine Learning

Quantum machine learning algorithms mostly employ some version of Grover's algorithm. These mostly include unsupervised learning algorithms like k-medians, hierarchical clustering, etc. Grover algorithm is a search algorithm for unordered sets performs faster than a classical search algorithm's theoretical computational speed limits by quadratic order. This increase in efficiency can even be exponential if the input and output formats are also quadratic. When used in collaboration with classical computing, reading the conventional data or specifying class membership means the algorithm already has a linear time complexity which leaves scope for only polynomial increase in performance speed.

Principles of quantum mechanics can be directly applied to machine learning algorithms that work for classical computers. These algorithms, though not quantum, still incorporate the principles of superposition and entanglement. Such algorithms are called 'quantum like learning algorithms'.

Computational intelligence (Engilbrecht, 2007) is an area that aims to find solutions to optimizations through algorithms which are inspired by biological systems. Some such examples are neural networks, ant colony optimization, swarm intelligence etc. Since quantum like learning algorithms can somewhat relate to natural phenomenon, they are also related to computational intelligence. For example, quantum neural networks employ the principle of superposition to store the class membership details of data points. Similarly, simulated quantum annealing utilizes tunnelling property to overcome the issue of being stuck in local minima. Feed forward neural networks are used for fuzzy classification and their capacity is computed in (Purushothaman and Karayiannis, 2006).

## Quantum Information Theory

Quantum information theory generalizes the concepts of classical information theory to quantum systems. One of the basic measures of classical information theory is Entropy, which quantifies the extent of uncertainty which predicting the value of a random variable. Classical systems employ Shannon Entropy:

$$H(X) = -\sum_x P(X = x) \log P(X = x) \tag{1}$$

When applied to quantum systems, Von Neumann Entropy is used to quantify randomness:

$$S(\rho) = -tr(\rho \log(\rho)) \tag{2}$$

Here, $\rho$ is the density matrix. For any matrix, a function definition applies on its spectral decomposition. Decomposition of the density matrix $\rho$ is as follows:

$$\rho = \sum_i \lambda_i \mid i \rangle \langle i \mid \tag{3}$$

$$\text{i.e. } S(\rho) = \sum_k \langle k \mid \left( \sum_i \lambda_i \log \lambda_i \mid i \rangle \langle | \right) \mid k \rangle \tag{4}$$

Von Neumann Entropy of a pure state is zero and that of a mixed state is always more than zero. Bipartite pure states are entangled if and only if there reduced density matrix is a mixed matrix. Thus, von Neumann Entropy is a good measure of entanglement in reduced state.

Quantum distinguishability is a property of quantum information systems. Theoretically, differentiating between two bit sequences in case of classical computing seems simple enough. Same cannot be said for quantum state unless they are orthogonal. Generally, two states, say $\rho$ and $\sigma$ are orthogonal, projective measurements are not possible and we must rely on Positive Operator Value Measures (POVM). Hence we use fidelity to measure the distinguishability between two states. For pure states, fidelity measures the similarity between the two states. This can be related to the concept of cosine similarity that is commonly used in machine learning. Fidelity on two states is defined as:

$$F(\rho, \sigma) = tr\left[\sqrt{\sqrt{\rho}\sigma\sqrt{\rho}}\right] \tag{5}$$

## Grover's Algorithm

Grover's algorithm locates a component in an unordered set quicker than that is possible for conventional methods by quadratic order. The searched component defines a function: the function returns true on a component if it turns out to be the component being searched. Grover's algorithm makes internal calls to a specialist that notifies the exact value of this function, that is, whether or not the membership is valid for a specific occurrence. The objective is then to utilize the smallest conceivable number of applications of the oracle to find all components that test true.

Suppose, the data has N instances with $n = \log(N)$ bits to represent each entry. We apply Hadamard Transformation on $|0\rangle^{\otimes n}$ to obtain the equal superposition state

$$|\psi\rangle = \frac{1}{\sqrt{n}}\sum_{x=0}^{n-1}|x\rangle \tag{6}$$

Then we apply the Grover's Diffusion Operator on this state $O\left(\sqrt{N}\right)$ times. This operator, G, consists of the following steps:

- Apply the oracle O.
- Apply the Hahamard Transformation $H \otimes n$
- Perform a conditional phase shift on states with an exception of $|0\rangle$:

$$\left|x\right\rangle \rightarrow -(-1)^{\delta_{x0}}\left|x\right\rangle \tag{7}$$

- Apply the Hadamard transform $H \otimes n$ again.

The combined effect of the above steps is:

$$H^{\otimes n}\left(2\left|0\right\rangle\left\langle 0\right| - I\right)H^{\otimes n} = 2\left|\psi\right\rangle\left\langle\psi\right| - I \tag{8}$$

Where $\left|\psi\right\rangle$ is equal superposition state in equation (6). Thus Grover operator can be written as:

$$G = \left(2\left|\psi\right\rangle\left\langle\psi\right| - I\right)O. \tag{9}$$

## Support Vector Machine With Grover's Search

In a basic quantum support vector machine, if the parameters of cost function are discretized, we can perform an exhaustive search in cost space based on a modification of Grover's search algorithm as discussed by the authors (Durr and Hoyer, 1996). Since we do not depend on any algorithm like gradient descent, the objective function can be non-convex as provided in (Denchev et al, 2012). This ability to handle non-convex objective function is strength of quantum SVM as it helps with better generalization performance.

Since adiabatic quantum optimization is suitable for non-convex optimization, it would be worth formulating SVM as quadratic unrestricted binary optimization, suitable for an adiabatic quantum computer. Such a formulation leaves calculating the kernel matrix untouched, and has $O(N^2d)$ complexity. Although the search process has a reduced complexity, calculations will be dominated by generating the kernel matrix.

Due to lack of any restrictions on the rate of convergence of the gradient descent in the optimization phase of SVM, it is difficult to establish the extent of improvement in performance after using the Grover's algorithm. The bottleneck in this formulation remains the $O(N^2d)$ complexity of calculating the kernel matrix. If we make use of quantum input and output states, we can achieve an exponential speedup over classical algorithms. Using the least squares formulation of support vector machines, the self-analysis of quantum states will solve the matrix inversion problem, and the overall complexity becomes $O(\log(Nd))$.

# ERROR CORRECTION AND FAULT TOLERANCE

In the beginning of classical computing, errors were a very common occurrence, memory-errors, errors in transferring bits over network, incorrect implementations of instructions etc. Nowadays the machines are a great deal more dependable, but we likewise have more efficient "error correction and detection techniques" for errors, specifically error correcting codes. Such codes take a string of information and encode it in a bigger string (called "code words"), increasing the amount of redundancy so that a little part of error on the code word will not have the capacity to diminish the alter the encoded information.

## Error Correction Using Classical Approaches

Detecting and correcting errors in case of classical systems is done by applying redundancy. The easiest method for employing this is by storing the data repeatedly and - if these duplicates are later found to deviate - simply take the predominating value. For example, assume we duplicate a bit three times. Furthermore, assume that a noisy error distorts the three-piece state with the goal that one piece is equivalent to zero however the other two are equivalent to one. In the event that we expect that distortion errors independently occur with a probability of p. It is no doubt that the error is a one bit distortion and the transmitted message is three ones. It is conceivable that a two bit distortion happens and the transmitted message is equivalent to three zeros, yet this result highly improbable.

## Quantum Inspired Error Correction

In a classical system, information is encoded in the form of bits and we assume that an error due to bit flip may occur at any time with a flip probability 'p'. One of the classical solutions to this bit flip error is to use the 3-bit code. Here the encoded information stores three duplicated copies of the original information. After the transfer of data over a channel, the information is retrieved based on majority voting. Assuming out of three, one bit was flipped and the remaining two have the same value x, we conclude the sent value was x.

## Quantum Error Correction: 3-Qubit Code

Assume the information is encoded in qubit state $| \psi = \alpha | 0 + \beta | 1$. The idea is to encode the information onto three qubits as $| \Psi = \alpha | 000 + \beta | 111$. Now $| \Psi$ will be an entangled state. After all the bits have been independently affected, error diagnosis and correction should be done. Let us assume the error is in the first bit.

i.e. $|\Psi = \alpha\,|\,100 + \beta\,|\,011$

Now we apply the CNOT gate. The output of the CNOT gate is:

$|\Psi = \alpha\,|\,110 + \beta\,|\,011$

Then continue to apply the CNOT gate and obtain states

$|\Psi = \alpha\,|\,111 + \beta\,|\,011 \to |\Psi = \alpha\,|\,011 + \beta\,|\,111$

Finally we apply Toffoli gate which assumes the first qubit as target and the remaining qubits as control. We obtain:

$|\Psi = \alpha\,|\,0 + \beta\,|\,1$

Since the first qubit is still $|\,0$ we say that the error has been corrected.

## IMAGE SEGMENTATION

The method of classifying a computerized image into various regions or groups of pixels is known as image segmentation. Partitioning of an image is done in such a manner such that the objects which possess the same colour and texture are grouped together. Adjoining partitions are quite dissimilar when compared with same features. The output of image segmentation is segmenting the image into partitions where the pixels of same partitions have same characteristics with respect to colour, intensity and size.

### Image Segmentation Using Classical Approaches

Image segmentation plays a very crucial role in any computer vision techniques or methods (Pappas, 1992). It aims to segment a low-level picture into homogenous partitions. It can also be used as an initial stage for many high-level processes pattern matching, object recognition or scenery depiction (Huang et al, 2011). Numerous algorithms have been formulated to carry out image segmentation which can be broadly classified into four categories.

1.   **Histogram Based Approach:** Depending upon the intensity of colour in an image, the pixels are partitioned using image histogram. Usually K-means is one of the most prevalent approaches to carry out this task.

2.   **Edge Based Approach:** Pixels demonstrating significant shift in their intensity levels are extricated and afterwards connected with contours that demonstrates to object limits. These methodologies offer low processing cost yet they show genuine challenges in fixing the proper limits and delivering constant contours which are one-pixel wide in width.

3.   **Region Based Approach:** Its goal is to classify regions which satisfy a threshold condition for it to be called homogenous. The prevalent methods in this approach are pyramidal methods and region growing but one of the major problems with these algorithms is that they may end up over-segmenting the image.

4.   **Split/Merge Approach:** It intends to resolve the issue of over-segmentation by methods of a two-stage computation. The primary stage segments the actual picture into homogeneous areas. In the second phase it tries to improve the segmentation by combining adjacent areas which are judged sufficiently comparable.

The issues concerning image segmentation have been dealt as single-objective case, i.e. every choice depends on the assessment of just a single expression which may add up a group of goals that are by and large clashing. But image segmentation can also be dealt as multi-objective optimization case whose goal is to arrive at a group of feasible solutions. The assessment is done in parallel with respect to two unique characteristics: intra-region homogeneity and inter-region heterogeneity. The intention of examining image segmentation as a multi-objective issue depends on our knowledge that howsoever good the quality of image segmentation output, there might be a problem in presenting this result to high-level process which might have a difficulty in extracting and processing the data present in the image. Thus, having diverse segmentation outputs may permit considering the image distinctively in the further stages. This will be more profitable if the cutting edge parallel computing potential outcomes are utilized.

## Quantum Inspired Approach for Image Segmentation

Split and merge algorithm is adopted for performing image segmentation using quantum computing inspired approaches as discussed in (Talbi, Batouche and Draa, 2007).In the first stage splitting is done through k-means algorithm as this algorithm has proved to work faster than other methods such as fuzzy c-means. The output of this first phase will be k number no clusters where pixels within each cluster will have same characteristics.

Since it is not a necessity that pixels belonging to a cluster should be adjacent to each other, we need to utilize the k-means result to search for the distinctive areas whose number is much larger than k. Due to the distortion and keeping in mind the end goal to diminish the look up space, the smaller regions are separated out and joined with the adjacent regions that have the similar colorimetric values. The threshold is set at 10 pixels i.e. a region containing less than 10 pixels is removed. Toward the finish of this stage, we have N edges and R regions.

The subsequent image apportioning is considered as feed in for this multi-objective quantum propelled transformative formulation. The goal of this approach is to come up with a group of non-dominating partitions. Every partitioning result is acquired through consolidating some neighbouring locales. Just three quantum chromosomes are utilized in this method where each chromosome is made up of N qubits. Here every qubit depicts the edge parting the segments.

The essential state $|0\rangle$ connotes that the edge is taken out, i.e. the two areas isolated at first by that edge will be merged while the essential state $|1\rangle$ connotes that the edge is kept up.

At first, the chromosomes are created arbitrarily and solution represented by string of N ones is only solution present in the group of non-ruled solutions. Later, 4 operations are applied in a cyclic manner. Quantum interference forms the first stage where each qubit is allowed to move towards the associated bit value in one of the non-commanded solutions. This solution has the least Euclidean distance when measured from the derived solution of chromosome. A unary quantum operator is utilized to perform quantum interference which results in a transformation whose angle is function of $\alpha i$ and $\beta i$.

The second operation comprises of a quantum transformation which performs for some qubits, as indicated by the transformation rate, a change between their $\alpha i$ and $\beta i$ values. That will switch the probabilities of having the number 0 and 1 while applying estimation.

In the third stage, an estimation is applied on each chromosome to transform it from one solution to all those which are part of superposition. One of the obstacles observed in pure quantum systems is that estimation ruins the superposition of states which is overcome in this model. As this algorithm runs on classical computer it is possible to work with all the feasible solutions present in the superposition for the latter stages. 3 binary solutions are obtained from 3 quantum chromosomes towards the end of this stage.

In the last and final stage, updation of non-dominated solutions takes place by first examining them, on basis of their intra-region homogeneity and the inter-region heterogeneity, and then comparing them with the remaining non-dominated solutions. A new solution dominating an existing non-dominated solution will replace it from the set and is any solution is found to be not dominated by any other solutions then it will be placed in the non-dominated solutions set.

The results obtained indicate that this approach is far more efficient and powerful than the classical algorithm. The two major reasons accounting for is are: First, the search space reduces drastically when the solutions are encoded in quantum bits so a single chromosome can represent all the feasible solutions at any particular time and secondly search stability is reinforced by the utilization of quantum inference. Here we can conclude that quantum based algorithms are the most well suited techniques which can be applied to image segmentation problems.

## CONCLUSION

In this chapter, a detailed study on literature has been discussed on how quantum computing is inspiring and transforming various machine learning algorithms to produce exponentially better results than the classical techniques in wide range of areas such as big data, artificial intelligence, speech and object recognition, error correction, secure communication and image classification etc. We have discussed how quantum principle of superposition and entanglement optimizes machine learning algorithms. Also, some quantum versions of classical machine learning algorithms can be easily implemented on traditional computers and do not require the sophisticated quantum computers. These quantum techniques have exponentially increased the processing power of these classical algorithms. We also saw how according to the no-cloning theorem of quantum theory, communication via qubits is more secure than via traditional units of communication (bits). Quantum techniques also improve image segmentation process by drastically reducing the search space and increasing the stability of the algorithm. Although the principle of superposition significantly reduces the computation time, increasing the efficiency, it yields a set of feasible results leading to ambiguity about the correct result. This leaves scope for future improvement in identifying the accurate solution.

## REFERENCES

Ali, R. (2017). Quantum Computing in Big Data, Computer and Information Technology (CIT). *IEEE International Conference*. DOI: doi:10.1109/CIT.2016.79

Blais, A., Huang, R-S, Wallraff, A., Girvin, S.M., & Schoelkopf, R.J. (2004). Cavity quantum electrodynamics for superconducting electrical circuits: An architecture for quantum computation. *Phys. Rev., 69.*

Bouchiat, V., Vion, D., Joyez, P., Esteve, D., & Devoret, M. H. (1998). Quantum coherence with a single Cooper pair. *Physica Scripta. T, 76*(1), 165–170. doi:10.1238/Physica.Topical.076a00165

Chandler, D. L. (2016). *A new quantum approach to big data.* MIT News Office.

Cruz, A. V. A., Vellatco, M. M. B., & Pacheco, M. A. C. (1998). Quantum inspired evolutionary algorithm for numerical optimization. Academic Press.

Denchev, V. S., Ding, N., Vishwanathan, S., & Neven, H. (2012). Robust classification with adiabatic quantum optimization. *Proceedings of the 29 th International Conference on Machine Learning,* 1-8.

Dong, D., Chen, C., Li, H., & Tarn, T.-J. (2008). Quantum Inspired Reinforcement. *IEEE Transactions on Systems, Man, and Cybernetics. Part B, Cybernetics, 38*(5), 1207–1220. doi:10.1109/TSMCB.2008.925743

Dunjko, V., Taylor, J. M., & Briegel, H. J. (2016). Quantum-Enhanced Machined Learning. *Physics Review Letters, 117*(13).

Durr, C., & Hoyer, P. (1999). *A quantum algorithm for finding the minimum.* arXiv:quant-ph/9607014

Engilbrecht, A. P. (2007). *Computational Intelligence: An Introduction* (2nd ed.). John Wiley. doi:10.1002/9780470512517

Ezhov, A., & Ventura, D. (2000). Quantum neural networks. In N. Kasabov (Ed.), Future directions for intelligent systems and information science (pp. 213–234). Academic Press. doi:10.1007/978-3-7908-1856-7_11

Han, K. H., & Kim, J. H. (2000). Genetic quantum algorithm and its application to combinatorial optimization problem. *Proceedings of the 2000 Congress on Evolutionary Computation, 2,* 1354–1360. doi:10.1109/CEC.2000.870809

Han, K. H., & Kim, J. H. (2001). Analysis of Quantum-Inspired Evolutionary Algorithm. *Proceedings of the 2001 International Conference on Artificial Intelligence,* 727–730.

Hannachi, M. S., & Hirota, K. (2005). Fuzzy set representation of quantum logic (1-valued) automata. *International symposium on computational intelligence and intelligent informatics,* 14-16.

Huang, Y., Huang, K., Tao, D., & Tan, T. (2011). Enhanced Biologically Inspired Model for Object Recognition. *IEEE Transactions on Systems, Man, and Cybernetics*, *41*(6), 1668–1680. doi:10.1109/TSMCB.2011.2158418 PMID:21768049

Kak, S. (1995). On quantum neural computing. *Information Sciences*, *83*(3-4), 143–160. doi:10.1016/0020-0255(94)00095-S

Koch, J., Yu, T. M., Gambetta, J., Houck, A. A., Schuster, D. I., Majer, J., ... Schoelkopf, R. J. (2007). Charge-insensitive qubit design derived from the Cooper pair box. *Physical Review A.*, *76*(042319), 1–19.

Kreinovich, V., Kohout, L. J., & Kim, E. (2008). "Square root of Not": A major difference between fuzzy und quantum logics. *Annual meeting of the North American fuzzy information processing society*, 1-5. doi:10.1109/NAFIPS.2008.4531327

Matsuda, S. (1993). Quantum neurons and their implications. Proceedings of international joint conference on neural networks, 2, 1610–1613.

Meng Q & Gong C (2010). Web information classifying and navigation based on neural network. *2nd international conference on signal processing systems*, 2, V2-431-V2-433.

Pappas, T. E. (1992). An adaptive clustering algorithm for image segmentation. *INEE Trans. On Signal Processing*, *40*(4), 901–914. doi:10.1109/78.127962

Purushothaman, G., & Karayiannis, N. B. (2006). On the capacity of feed forward neural networks for fuzzy classification, J. *Applied Functional Analysis*, *1*, 9–32.

Rigatos, G. G., & Rzafestas, S. G. (2006). Quantum learning for neural associative memories. *Fuzzy Sets and Systems*, *157*(13), 1797–1813. doi:10.1016/j. fss.2006.02.012

Sup, J., & Hao, S. (2009). Research of fuzzy neural network model based on quantum clustering. *2nd international workshop on knowledge discovery and data mining*, 133-136.

Talbi, H., Batouche, M., & Draa, A. (2007). A Qantum - Inspired Evolutionary Algorithm for Multi-objective Image Segmentation, International Journal of Mathematical. *Physical and Engineering Sciences*, *1*(7), 109–114.

Vamanan, R. (2015). Quantum computing for big data analysis. *Indian Journal of Science*, *14*(43), 98–104.

Vlachopiannts, S. G., & Lee, K. Y. (2008). Quantum-inspired evolutionary algorithm for real and reactive power systems. *Power Systems. IEEE Transactions on, 23*(4), 1627–1636.

Wittek, P. (2014). *Quantum Machine Learning: What Quantum Computing Means to Data Mining.* Academic Press.

Zhang, G. (2011). Quantum-inspired evolutionary algorithms: A survey and empirical study. *Journal of Heuristics, 17*(3), 303–351. doi:10.1007/s10732-010-9136-0

Zhao, Z., Zheng, S., & Shang, J. (2007). A study of cognitive radio decision engine based on quantum genetic algorithm. *Wuli Xuebao, 56*, 6760–6766.

Zhou, S., Chen, Q., & Wang, X. (2010). Deep quantum networks for classification. *20th International conference on international conference on pattern recognition*, 2885–2888.

## KEY TERMS AND DEFINITIONS

**Computational Intelligence:** Computational Intelligence provides a way for computers to perform like human beings.

**Linear Operator:** It is a function from one vector space to another that preserves the operations of vector addition and scalar multiplication. By preserving we mean the image of sum of two vectors is equal to the sum of their images and by preserving scalar multiplication we mean that the image of a scalar multiple of a vector is equal to the scalar multiple of the image of the vector.

**Linear System:** A linear system is a mathematical model of a system based on the use of a linear operators defined over it.

**Machine Learning:** It is the process that deals with how we create computer programs that improve with experience.

**Magnetic Field:** A magnetic field is a force field that is created by moving electric charges (electric currents) and magnetic dipoles, and exerts a force on other nearby moving charges and magnetic dipoles.

**Qubit:** It is a bit of quantum information in parallel to the classical bit.

**Superposition Principle:** It states that for all linear systems, the net response caused by two or more stimuli is the sum of the responses that would have been caused by each stimulus individually.

**Transistors:** These are semiconductor devices having three connections and with rectification as well as amplification capabilities.

# Chapter 2
# Quantum–Inspired Automatic Clustering Technique Using Ant Colony Optimization Algorithm

**Sandip Dey**
*OmDayal Group of Institutions, India*

**Siddhartha Bhattacharyya**
*RCC Institute of Information Technology, India*

**Ujjwal Maulik**
*Jadavpur University, India*

## ABSTRACT

*Quantum computing has emerged as the most challenging field of research in efficient computation. This chapter introduces a novel quantum-inspired ant colony optimization technique for automatic clustering. This chapter presents an application of this proposed technique to the automatic clustering of real-life gray-scale image data sets. In contrary to the other techniques, the proposed one requires no previous knowledge of the data to be classified. It finds the optimal number of clusters of the data by itself. The Xie-Beni cluster validity measure has been employed as the objective function for clustering purpose. Effectiveness of the proposed technique is exhibited on four real-life gray-scale images. Superiority of the proposed technique is established over its counterpart with respect to various aspects, which include accuracy, stability, computational time and standard errors. Finally, a statistical supremacy test, called unpaired two-tailed t-test, is conducted between them. It shows that superiority in favor of the proposed technique is established.*

DOI: 10.4018/978-1-5225-5219-2.ch002

## 1. INTRODUCTION

Clustering is defined as segregating an unlabeled data set into groups of similar objects. Each group is known as "cluster". The objects in one cluster are similar between themselves, whereas these objects possess dissimilarity to the objects of any other groups. Formally, clustering can be defined as follows:

$$S = \bigcup_{k=1}^{m} C_k \qquad (1)$$

where, $C \subset S$, $C = \{C_1, C_2, \ldots, C_m\}$ and $C_k \cap C_j = \phi$ for $k \neq j$. Subsequently, any object exactly lies in only one $C_k$ where, $k \in \{1, 2, \ldots, m\}$. From the last few decades, cluster analysis has been used in various fields successfully. These fields include engineering (e.g., electrical and mechanical engineering, machine learning, pattern recognition, artificial intelligence and so on), social sciences (e.g., psychology, sociology, and education), computer sciences (e.g., image segmentation, web mining, textual document collection), medical sciences (e.g., psychiatry, biology, microbiology and pathology), earth sciences (e.g., geology, geography, and remote sensing) and economics (e.g., marketing and business) . In the literature, a number of different clustering algorithms have been introduced for various applications (Jain, 1999; Bakhshi, 2012).

The concept of Quantum Computing (QC) has been emerged by exploiting the principles of quantum mechanical phenomena. To research in this area is probably the most demanding and challenging task of twenty-first century. The behavior of QC can be described by the Schrödinger equation (Han, 2002). Quantum bits (qubits) are the smallest unit in QC. Superposition of states is a very important feature of QC where two states are combined in the fashion of linear superposition satisfying some probabilistic criteria. Unlike classical computer, the state space becomes $n$-dimensional for an $n$-qubits QC. Hence, this exponential growth of the state space makes QC perform exponentially faster compared to its classical computer (conventional computer). Like this computer, QC also possesses different quantum logic gates, called Q-gate which operates on a small number of quantum bits. Some popular examples of these quantum logic gates are CNOT, Hadamard gate and rotation gate (Hey, 1999) to name a few.

Quantum computer is much faster than its counterpart in terms of computational capability (Han, 2002). Richard Feynman discovered that the limitation of the computational capability of conventional computers can be overcome successfully with the use of quantum effect (Talbi, 2004). QC can possess its inherent parallelism capability, which in turn makes algorithms to execute exponentially faster compared to others (Talbi, 2006 ; Reiffel, 2000). The use of QC was proved to be very effective to run such algorithms which may require larger solution space. These days, this technique is successfully and efficiently used to solve different complex optimization problems. In the literature, some popular quantum algorithms are Grover's database search algorithm (Grover, 1996) and Shor's quantum factoring algorithm (Shor, 1996).

Meta-heuristic algorithms can be referred to as strategies that can be utilized to guide the search procedure. In these algorithms, the search space is efficiently explored in order to find optimal solutions. This is a non-deterministic technique that can be used both for solving simple problems and the problems having complex learning processes. Quantum-Inspired meta-heuristic algorithms are designed by using the basic principles of QC in the meta-heuristic framework. Compared to the existing clustering algorithms, the proposed algorithm necessitates no previous knowledge of image data set for classification. Rather, it finds the optimal number of clustered dataset "on the run."

The rest of this paper is arranged as follows. Section 2 describes the basics of quantum computing. Section 3 discusses the representation scheme of basic quantum computing. A brief theory of a popular meta-heuristic, called ant colony optimization is described in Section 4. In Section 5, a detailed discussion on clustering validity measures are given. The details about some popular cluster index methods are also flourished in this section. The proposed technique is described in Section 6. The experimental results of the proposed technique along with its comparable classical counterpart are presented in Section 7. Some valuable concluding remarks are presented in Section 8.

## 2. QUANTUM COMPUTING BASICS

A quantum computer is basically a device which employs quantum mechanical phenomena for performing computations and manipulation of data. The properties of QC result in faster computation for quantum computer compared to its classical counterpart. The basic characteristics of QC are discussed below.

## a. Dirac's Notation

The state of any quantum system can be described in a complex Hilbert space (Mcmohan, 2008). In quantum system, Hilbert space is symbolized by the notation $H$. The utility of the "bra-ket" notation is very noteworthy for describing quantum mechanics. The "bra-ket" notation was introduced by Paul Dirac. The "ket" vector, its hermitian conjugate, "bra" and the "bra-ket" notation are generally symbolized as seen in Table 1 (Mcmohan, 2008).

*Table 1.*

| Name | Notation |
|------|----------|
| Ket | $\lvert \psi \rangle$ |
| Bra | $\langle \phi \rvert$ |
| bracket | $\langle \phi \vert \psi \rangle$ |

It can be noted that, the "bracket" is molded by combining the above vectors ("bra" and "ket"). Theoretically, a quantum system is expressed by the following

$$\lvert \psi \rangle = \sum_k c_k \varphi_k \tag{2}$$

where, $\lvert \psi \rangle$ represents a wave function described in Hilbert space. $\varphi_k$ are the basic states of the quantum system and $c_k$ are complex numbers satisfying the following relation

$$\sum_k c_k^2 = 1 \tag{3}$$

## b. Quantum Bit

The concept of a quantum bit or in short qubit is analogous to the concept of bit, used in classical computer. A qubit is a memory element for QC, which is used to store information for QC (Hey, 1999). The "bra-ket" notation is used to represent quantum bit (Araujo, 2008). A quantum bit can hold the states "0" and "1". It can also holds both of these two states in superposed form. In QC, these states are denoted by l0> and l1> respectively, where,

$$\lvert 0 \rangle = \begin{bmatrix} 1 \\ 0 \end{bmatrix} \text{ and } \lvert 1 \rangle = \begin{bmatrix} 0 \\ 1 \end{bmatrix} \tag{4}$$

The superposition of these state vectors are represented by

$$|\psi\rangle = \alpha|0\rangle + \beta|1\rangle \tag{5}$$

Here, $\alpha$ and $\beta$ are complex numbers satisfying the relation (*quantum orthogonality*) given by

$$|\alpha|^2 + |\beta|^2 = 1 \tag{6}$$

The probability to measure $|0\rangle$ and $|1\rangle$ are given by $|\alpha|^2$ and $|\beta|^2$, respectively. For a quantum system having *n* number of qubits, the basis of the state space is given by $\underbrace{|000\cdots0\rangle}_{n\ qubits}, \underbrace{|000\cdots1\rangle}_{n\ qubits}, \cdots, \underbrace{|111\cdots1\rangle}_{n\ qubits}$. Let $\xi$ be the angle which is used to define qubit phase. It can be defined as follows

$$\xi = \arctan\left(\beta\Big/\alpha\right) \tag{7}$$

The dot product of $\alpha$ and $\beta$ is given by (Araujo, 2008).

$$d = \alpha.\beta \tag{8}$$

## c. Quantum Gate

A *quantum gate* or sometimes called *quantum logic gate* is a simple quantum circuit, which operates on a small number of qubits. These gates are analogues for quantum system (computers) to the logic gates for conventional computers. By nature, these gates are reversible. Mostly, these quantum gates operate on spaces of one/two quantum bits. Some popular quantum gates are NOT gate, Controlled NOT, Hadamard gate, rotation gate to name a few (Hey, 1999; Araujo, 2008). One basic feature of quantum gates is that it only accomplishes unitary operations (Dey, 2017; Dey, 2016; Dey, 2010; Dey, 2015).

Let $U$ be the unitary operator. For this unitary operator, adjoint of $U$ must be equal its corresponding inverse operation, i.e., $U^+ = U^{-1}$. Moreover, it satisfies the relation given by

$$UU^+ = U^+U = I \tag{9}$$

Again, let $H$ be a Hermitian operator. In quantum mechanics, most operators are Hermitian in nature. An operator $\left(A\right)$ is called Hermitian, if it holds the relationship given by, $A^+ = A$. The unitary operator shares a relationship with Hermitian operator, as given by the subsequent equation

$$U = e^{iHt} \qquad\qquad (10)$$

## d. Quantum Register

A collection of quantum bits is normally known as quantum register. The size of a quantum register is calculated by the size of quantum bits used in operation. A quantum register having $n$ qubits is presented below

$$\underbrace{\left|1\right\rangle \otimes \left|1\right\rangle \otimes \cdots \otimes \left|0\right\rangle \left|1\right\rangle}_{n \; quantum \; bits} \equiv \underbrace{\left|11\cdots 01\right\rangle}_{n \; bits} \equiv \left|EDN\right\rangle \qquad\qquad (11)$$

where, EDN is called equivalent decimal number and $\otimes$ is referred to as the tensor product (Dey, 2014; Dey, 2014a; Dey, 2014b).

## e. Quantum Entanglement

Quantum entanglement is as an interesting characteristic of quantum states. It can be coined as a quantum mechanical phenomenon which ensures that the quantum states containing more than one object are described with respect to one another, even though the particular objects may be partially separated. The correlation can exist between dissimilar qubits. It ensures that if one qubit is in the $\left|0\right\rangle$ state, the other will be in the $\left|1\right\rangle$ state. Entanglement can be computed, changed, and even sanitized if required (Bhattacharyya, 2011; Dey, 2016a; Dey, 2016b).

## f. Quantum Coherence and Decoherence

The idea of coherence and decoherence are similar to linear superposition of the basic states. When two states are in superposed form, coherence exists between the participating basic states. There is always a constant phase relationship between these states. Likewise, decoherence occurs when the aforementioned phase relationship is destroyed. When decoherence occurs, probability for collapsing the state $|0\rangle$ is measured as $|\alpha|^2$ and same for the state $|1\rangle$, it is $|\beta|^2$ (Dey, 2013; Dey, 2013a; Dey, 2013b).

## 3. QUANTUM INSPIRED DEPICTION

A quantum inspired algorithm (Han, 2002 ; Araujo, 2008) may use different kinds of mechanisms for its representation. This may include symbolic representation, numerical representation, or also binary representation (Hinterding, 1999). For example, in a quantum inspired evolutionary algorithm, proposed by Han *et al.*, a probabilistic representation using quantum bits has been employed for developing the algorithm (Han, 2002). In quantum inspired algorithm, a quantum bit or a qubit individual comprising of a number of quantum bits, can be represented as follows.

**Representation 1:** In QC, a quantum bit can be represented using the complex numbers $(\alpha, \beta)$ as follows

$$r_1 = \begin{bmatrix} \alpha \\ \beta \end{bmatrix} \tag{12}$$

where, $\alpha$ and $\beta$ satisfies equation $(6)$. Geometrically, let $\theta$ be the angle measured between $\alpha$ and $\beta$, then $\cos(\theta) = |\alpha|$ and $\sin(\theta) = |\beta|$ so that equation $(6)$ is satisfied, since (Han, 2002)

$$\left[\cos(\theta)\right]^2 + \left[\sin(\theta)\right]^2 = 1 \tag{13}$$

**Representation 2:** A qubit individual can be defined as a collection of numbers (say, $q$) of qubit string. This can defined as follows

$$s = \begin{bmatrix} \alpha_1 & \alpha_2 & \alpha_3 & \cdots & \alpha_q \\ \beta_1 & \beta_2 & \beta_3 & \cdots & \beta_q \end{bmatrix} \tag{14}$$

Each $\alpha_i$ and $\beta_i$ must satisfy the relation given by $|\alpha_i|^2 + |\beta_i|^2 = 1$ for $i = 1, 2, \ldots, q$.

Hence, capability of storing information can be increased by using the superposition principle of QC, since number of states is combined together as a single individual unit. Let a qubit individual comprises three qubits $(q = 3)$ as follows:

$$u = \begin{bmatrix} \dfrac{1}{\sqrt{2}} & -\dfrac{1}{\sqrt{2}} & \dfrac{\sqrt{3}}{2} \\ \dfrac{1}{\sqrt{2}} & \dfrac{1}{\sqrt{2}} & \dfrac{1}{2} \end{bmatrix} \qquad (15)$$

From equation $(14)$, the states can be formed as

$$t = -\left(\dfrac{\sqrt{3}}{4}\right)|000\rangle - \left(\dfrac{1}{4}\right)|001\rangle + \left(\dfrac{\sqrt{3}}{4}\right)|010\rangle + \left(\dfrac{1}{4}\right)|011\rangle - \left(\dfrac{\sqrt{3}}{4}\right)|100\rangle - \left(\dfrac{1}{4}\right)|101\rangle$$

$$+ \left(\dfrac{\sqrt{3}}{4}\right)|110\rangle + \left(\dfrac{1}{4}\right)|111\rangle \qquad (16)$$

From equation $(16)$, it can be shown that there are 8 states namely, $\underbrace{|000\rangle}_{3\ qubits}, \underbrace{|001\rangle}_{3\ qubits}, \ldots, \underbrace{|111\rangle}_{3\ qubits}$ having probabilities 3/16, 1/16, 3/16, 1/16, 3/16, 1/16, 3/16 and 1/16 respectively. One $q$-individual can represent these 8 states as a single unit (Han, 2002 ; Araujo, 2008).

## 4. OVERVIEW OF ANT COLONY OPTIMIZATION

Ant Colony Optimization (ACO) is a population based probabilistic meta-heuristic optimization technique, proposed by Dorigo et al. in the year of 1996 (Dorigo, 1996). In ACO, the basic activities of real ants are imitated in a variety of ways to find the solutions of different optimization problems. In real scenario, ants search food for sustaining their existence. So, they travel here and there for searching food. In this process, a number of paths are traversed by them. At every path, they spurt a chemical (pheromone) from their bodies. The smell of pheromone instigates them to exchange information among themselves to trace food source. In this way, they discover shortest path between their nest and the nearest food source. It is obvious that most number of ants is attracted to follow those particular paths where more amount of pheromone is squirted. This mutual understanding of real ants motivated a number of scholars to develop several algorithms to solve combinatorial optimization problems (Parpinelli, 2002).

## 5. CLUSTERING VALIDATION MEASURES

In this section, the fundamental theories of some validation measures, are discussed. The validation measures usually depend on the criteria given below (Tan, 2005; Zhao, 2002).

- **Compactness:** It describes the closeness of objects in a cluster. There are many measures available, which can be used to calculate cluster compactness on the basis of variance. Lower variance shows better compactness. Likewise, there exist several measures, which can be introduced to evaluate the cluster compactness on the basis of distance.
- **Separation:** It describes the dissimilarity of a cluster from other cluster. For instance, pairwise distances between the cluster centers or sometimes pairwise minutest distances between objects in various clusters are extensively used as the measure of separation. Occasionally, density based measures are also used in some cases.

Some popular validity indexes are described below.

1. **Silhouette Index ($S$):** This cluster index assesses the performance of any clustering algorithm by evaluating the pairwise difference of within and between cluster distances. Additionally, the value of this index need to be maximized to find the optimal cluster number of a clustering algorithm (Rousseeuw, 1987). Formally, Silhouette index is defined as follows.

$$S = \frac{1}{cn} \sum_{j} \left[ \frac{1}{n_j} \sum_{y \in C_j} \frac{\{b(y) - a(y)\}}{\max\{b(y), a(y)\}} \right] \tag{17}$$

where, $cn$ represents number of clusters, $c_j$ is the $j$-th cluster, $n_j$ denotes the number of objects in $C_j$.

The values of $a(y)$ and $b(y)$ are defined by

$$a(y) = \frac{1}{(n_j - 1)} \sum_{z \in C_j, y \neq z} d(y, z) \text{ and } b(y) = \min_{k, k \neq j} \left[ \frac{1}{n_k} \sum_{z \in C_j} d(y, z) \right] \tag{18}$$

$d(y, z)$ is the distance between $y$ and $z$.

2. **Calinski-Harabasz Index (*CH*):** This cluster index evaluates the average of within and between cluster sums of squares (Calinski, 1974). Formally, Calinski-Harabasz index is defined as follows.

$$CH = \frac{\sum_j n_j d^2 (c_j, c) \Big/ (cn - 1)}{\sum_j \sum_{y \in C_j} d^2 (y, c_j) \Big/ (n - cn)} \tag{19}$$

where, $cn$ is the number of clusters, $c_j$ is the $j$-th cluster, $n_j$ represents the number of objects in $C_j$ and $c$ denotes the center of the data set.

3. **Dunn Index (*D*):** This is one of most popular cluster validity index proposed by Dunn (Dunn, 1974). This index classifies clusters which are basically well separated and compact. The objective of this index is therefore maximizing the inter-cluster distance and minimizing the intra-cluster distance. The formal definition of Dunn index is given below

$$D = \min_j \left[ \min_k \left\{ \frac{\min_{y \in C_j, z \in C_k} d(y, z)}{\max_i \left( \max_{y, z \in C_i} d(y, z) \right)} \right\} \right] \tag{20}$$

where, $d(y, z)$ is the distance between $y$ and $z$. $c_i, c_j, c_k$ represent $i$-th, $j$-th and $k$-th cluster respectively.

4. ***I* Index $\left( I_j \right)$:** This is one of the more recent cluster validity index, proposed by U. Maulik and S. Bandyopadhyay (Maulik, 2002). This index is basically a combination of three different terms, as given by

$$I_j = \left[ \frac{1}{j} \times \frac{F_1}{F_j} \times D_j \right]^p \tag{21}$$

where, $F_j$ represents the intra-cluster distance, which is defined by $F_j = \sum_{i=1}^{j} \sum_{z \in C_i} \| z - y_i \|$ and $D_j$ is called the inter-cluster distance by $D_j = \max_{i,k=1}^{j} \| y_i - y_k \|$. $y_i$ denotes the center of cluster of $C_i$. p is an natural number (chosen by the author). The optimal number of clusters is determined by maximizing $I_j$ as given by equation $(21)$.

5. **Davies-Bouldin Index** $(DB)$**:** Davies and Bouldin introduced a popular cluster validity index, called Davies- Bouldin index in 1979 (Davies, 1979). In this index, similarities between each cluster, say $C_i$, with other clusters are determined first, thereafter the utmost value is allocated to $C_i$. The $DB$ index is the average of such cluster similarities. The optimal clusters are determined by minimizing this index value. The formal definition of $DB$ index is given by

$$DB = \frac{1}{cn} \sum_j \max_{k, k \neq j} \left[ \left\{ \frac{1}{n_j} \sum_{y \in C_j} d(y, c_i) + \frac{1}{n_k} \sum_{y \in C_k} d(y, c_k) \right\} \Big/ d(c_j, c_k) \right] \tag{22}$$

where, $cn$ denotes number of clusters, $c_j, c_k$ are the $j$-th and $k$-th cluster, $n_j, n_k$ denotes the number of objects in $C_j$ and $C_k$, respectively. $d(y, c_i)$ is the distance between $y$ and $c_i$.

6. **The Xie-Beni Index** $(XB)$**:** For this cluster validity index, the inter-cluster separation and intra-cluster compactness are required to be determined. Inter-cluster separation is calculated by minimizing the square of distance between cluster centers, whereas the intra-cluster compactness is determined by evaluating the mean square distance value between each data object and its corresponding cluster center. (Xie, 1991). To find the optimal cluster number,

one needs to maximize the $XB$ value. Formally, the Xie-Beni index is defined as follows

$$XB = \frac{\left[\sum_j \sum_{y \in C_j} d^2\left(y, c_j\right)\right]}{\left[n.\min_{k, k \neq j} d^2\left(c_j, c_k\right)\right]} \tag{23}$$

where, $n$ denotes the number of objects in the data set, $d\left(y, c_i\right)$ is the distance between $y$ and $c_i$ and $d^2\left(c_j, c_k\right)$ is the distance between the $j$-the and $k$-th cluster centers.

7. **R-Squared** $\left(RS\right)$: R-squared is introduced to measure the unlikeness of clusters. Basically,

it finds the degree of homogeneity between different groups. The values of $RS$ may varies from 0 to 1. The value '0' indicates that there is no significant difference among the clusters whereas '1' tells that there must have significant difference among the clusters (Sharma, 1996; Halkidi, 2001). Formally, $RS$ index is defined as follows.

$$RS = \frac{\left[\sum_{y \in D} \|y - c\|^2 - \sum_j \sum_{y \in C_j} \|y - c_j\|^2\right]}{\sum_{y \in D} \|y - c\|^2} \tag{24}$$

8. **RMSSDT:** Root-mean-square standard deviation or shortly, RMSSTD is a popular validity cluster index which indicates the variance of the clusters. RMSSTD measures the homogeneousness of the clusters. This index identifies the homogenous groups. Better clustering is obtained by lowering the RMSSTD value (Sharma, 1996). The formal definition of RMSSTD is given by

$$\text{RMSSTD} = \left[\frac{\sum_j \sum_{y \in C_j} \|y - c_j\|^2}{\sum_j \left(n_j - 1\right)}\right]^{1/2} \tag{25}$$

## 6. PROPOSED ALGORITHM

In this section, a novel quantum inspired automatic clustering technique using ant colony optimization (QIACACO), is proposed. The proposed approach has been deigned to find the optimum number of clusters from gray scale images. The detailed description of the proposed technique is illustrated herewith.

The proposed technique is designed in such a way that it can be efficiently employed to find the optimum number of clusters from any real life gray scale images. At initial, pixel intensity values are randomly selected from the input image to create the population ($P$) of $n$ number of strings. Then, the concept of QC is used to apply a real encoding scheme to each pixel in $P$, which produces creates $P^+$. Next, each element of $P^+$ is passed through a popular QC feature, called quantum orthogonality, which produces $P^{++}$. Then, the input data are being normalized between 0 &1. Next, the cluster centers are randomly chosen and activated from each of the participating string of $P$. Thereafter, the distance between each cluster center and data point is calculated, the shortest distance is recorded. The data point is kept into the corresponding cluster ($C_r$). The proposed technique has been run for $G$ number of generations. At each generation, $P$ is updated using the pheromone matrix, $\tau$ as follows.

1. For each $i \in P^{++}$ do
2. For all $j^{th}$ position in $i$ do
3. If $\left(rand > \varsigma\right)$ then // $\varsigma$ =priory defined number

$$P^{++}_{ij} = \arg \max \tau_{ij}$$

4. Else

$$P^{++}_{ij} = rand$$

5. End if
6. End for

Thereafter, pheromone matrix $\left(\tau\right)$ is updated at each generation as follows.

1. For each $i \in P^{++}$ do
2. For all $j^{th}$ position in $i$ do
3. $\tau_{ij} = \rho\tau_{ij} + (1 - \rho)b_s$ // $b_s$ = string having best index value

39

4.   End for
5.   End for

The brief summary (step wise) of the proposed technique is presented below.

**Step 1:** Initially, a population *(P)* of *n* number of strings is being generated by choosing pixel intensity values from gray scale image at random. The length of each string has been selected as *m*.

**Step 2:** Using the principle of QC, each member in *P* is encoded with real number between 0 & 1. Let it be called, $P^+$.

**Step 3:** From each string, randomly selected elements are activated separately to create its cluster centers.

**Step 4:** Data points (pixel intensities values) of input image are normalized between 0 & 1. Let it produce $D^+$.

**Step 5:** Each element of $P^+$ is undergone through a feature of QC called, *quantum orthogonality* Let it be called, $P^{++}$.

**Step 6:** Create the pheromone matrix, $\tau$. Note that, $\tau$ has the identical dimension as *P*.

**Step 7:** For *t*=1 to *G* do

**Step 8:** For each data point in $D^+$, compute its distance from each individual active cluster centers of each participating string.

**Step 9:** Assign each data point to the corresponding cluster center which possesses least distance from the data point. Let it creates cluster, $C_r$.

**Step 10:** The cluster centers are updated using step 3 if $C_r$ contains two or less number of data points.

**Step 11:** Using $C_r$, apply a cluster validity index as fitness function to measure the quality of clustering.

**Step 12:** Save the quality index value and the corresponding number of clusters for each string.

**Step 13:** Use $\tau$ to update *P*.

**Step 14:** Update the pheromone matrix, $\tau$.

**Step 15:** Save the global best quality index value $\left(\vartheta\right)$ and number of clusters $\left(\nu\right)$ among all participating strings.

**Step 16:** Repeat steps 2, 3 & 5.

**Step 17:** End for

**Step 18:** The optimum number of clusters and the corresponding cluster validity index values are reported.

## a. Complexity Analysis

The worst case time complexity of the proposed technique is analyzed herewith. The step by step description of this technique is presented in this section.

**Step 1:** The time complexity to create initial population is $O(n \times m)$, where $n$ and $m$ are the population size and length of string, respectively.

**Steps 2:** For real encoding using the concept of QC, time complexity becomes $O(n \times m)$.

**Steps 3:** For performing this step, time complexity becomes $O(n \times m)$.

**Steps 4:** To perform this normalization process, time complexity turns into $O(S)$, where $S$ is the size of the data set.

**Steps 5 &6:** For accomplishing these two steps, again time complexity becomes $O(n \times m)$.

**Steps 7-11:** To evaluate steps 8 &9, time complexity for each step becomes $O(S \times n \times m)$. As in step 10, cluster centers is updated (for number of data points less than or equal to 2) using step 3, if required. So, to perform this step, time complexity becomes $O(n \times m)$. As given in step 11, a cluster validity index is applied as fitness function to measure the quality of clustering. So, the time complexity turns into $O(S)$.

**Steps 13 &14:** The population $(P)$ and the pheromone matrix are updated using the steps discussed above. To evaluate these two steps, time complexity for performing each of them becomes $O(n \times m)$.

**Steps 16:** Steps 2, 3 & 5 are repeated in this step. So, to perform each of the step, time complexity becomes $O(n \times m)$.

The proposed technique is run for $G$ number of generations. Hence, considering the whole scenario, the overall time complexity turns out to be $O(S \times n \times m \times G)$.

## 7. EXPERIMENTAL RESULTS

In this paper, a novel quantum inspired automatic clustering technique using ant colony optimization technique, is proposed. This technique is designed in such a way that it can be efficiently used to find optimal number of clusters $(n_c)$ from each data set. For this purpose, a popular cluster validity index called, Davies-Bouldin index $\left(DB\right)$ has been used as fitness function. The proposed technique has been executed for a predefined number of times and maximizes $DB\left(n_c\right)$ (as given in equation $\left(22\right)$) to get optimal solutions.

## a. Data Sets Used

To perform experiment, a number of real-life gray scale images, each of dimensions $256 \times 256$, have been used as data sets. The normalized values of pixel intensities of these images are used as the data points for experimental purpose. The original test images are shown in Figure 1.

*Figure 1. Original test images (a) Cameraman, (b) Car, (c) Shoppingcart and (d) House*

(a) Cameraman

(b) Car

(c) Shoppingcart

(d) House

## b. Parameter Specification for the Participating Algorithms

As the comparative study, the proposed technique has been compared with its classical counterpart (ACACO). The parameters used for experimental purpose have been tuned for a number of times to get best possible outcomes (for both of the techniques). The parameter settings of these two techniques are presented in Table 2.

In Table 2, $G$ indicates the number of generation that the proposed and compared techniques are executed. $S$ represents the population size. $\varsigma$ is the priory defined number, used to update the population using pheromone matrix.

## c. String Representation Scheme

A novel qubit encoded scheme has been introduced to create the population of strings. Let us assume that a particular string in the population has $p$ number of cluster centroids.

Generally, a cluster centroid might have $q$-dimensional data points. The chromosome representation scheme is presented in Figure 2.

From Figure 2 it can be depicted that the participating string is designed with $p$ qubits in the form of cluster centroids. Assuming that in a quantum bit, $\alpha_i$ for $1 \leq i \leq p$ is produced at initial. Thereafter, a popular property of QC, called *quantum orthogonality* is applied for each quantum bit to form $\beta_i$, $1 \leq i \leq p$. Out of these

*Table 2. Parameter specification of the proposed technique and its classical counterpart.*

| QIACACO | ACACO |
|---|---|
| Number of Generation: $G=80$<br>Size of the population: $S=20$<br>Priory defined number: $\varsigma =0.6$ | Number of Generation: $G=2000$<br>Size of the population: $S=20$<br>Priory defined number: $\varsigma =0.6$ |

*Figure 2. String representation scheme in the proposed technique*

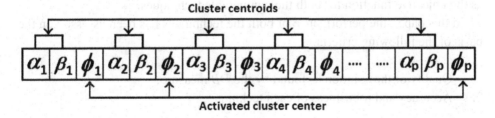

$p$ cluster centroids, $r$ $(1 \leq r \leq p)$ of them are activated based on a probability criterion given by $p_r \geq |\beta|^2$ where, $p_r \in [0,1]$ is the predefined probability value. The activated cluster centers $\phi_i, 1 \leq i \leq p$ are set to 1.

## d. Fitness Function

In the proposed technique, a renowned cluster validity index, known as Davies-Bouldin index $(DB)$ (Davies, 1979) is used as the objective function to find the optimal number of clusters. To find this optimal value, $DB$ measure has to be minimized. As the data point, the normalized values of four real life gray scale images have been used. So, the fitness function used for evaluating the proposed technique can be depicted as

$$f = DB_k (e) \tag{26}$$

where, $DB_k$ is the value of $DB$ measure of $k$-th string. Hence, minimization of $f$ leads to the optimum number of clusters.

## e. Simulation Approach

In this paper, a novel quantum inspired technique for automatic clustering has been introduced. In this paper, the data set comprises four real-life gray-scale images. The pixel intensity values have been normalized between 0 and 1 for the experimental purpose of the proposed technique. The proposed QIACACO is designed to efficiently find optimal number of clusters $(n_c)$ from each input image (data points). A well-known cluster validity index called, $DB$ measure has been introduced as objective function for experimental purpose. QIACACO maximizes this measure to find optimal solution. For the purpose of comparative study, QIACACO has been compared with its classical counterpart, called ACACO in various facets. In case of classical technique, the activation of cluster centers are done on the basis of a predefined cut-off value (selected value= 0.5). The $DB$ measure has been employed as the objective function for both the comparable techniques.

In this paper, the performance of both the techniques has been assessed on the basis of the following criteria.

1. Quality of the solution as found by the $DB$ measure;
2. Accuracy and robustness of each technique;

3.   A statistical superiority test, called unpaired *t*-tests;
4.   Derivation of standard error; and
5.   Time required for computation (in seconds).

The proposed QIACACO and its counterpart have been executed for 30 different runs using the data points stated above. Five representatives among the most promising solutions have been presented in Table 3.

The accuracy and stability among the participating techniques have been established by determining the mean and standard deviation of fitness measure over different runs. The corresponding results have been reported in Table 3. It can be clearly observed that QIACACO possesses better values in terms of mean and standard deviation of fitness as compared to its classical counterpart. Hence, the proposed technique outperforms other with respect to accuracy and stability.

*Table 3. Five representative favorable outcomes of the data set for QIACACO and ACACO*

| QIACACO | | | | | | | | | | | |
|---|---|---|---|---|---|---|---|---|---|---|---|
| Cameraman | | | Car | | | Shoppingcart | | | House | | |
| S. No. | $n_c$ | $XB(n_c)$ | S. No. | $n_c$ | $XB(n_c)$ | S. No. | $n_c$ | $XB(n_c)$ | S. No. | $n_c$ | $XB(n_c)$ |
| 1 | 2 | 0.03572 | 1 | 2 | 0.04494 | 1 | 3 | 0.06838 | 1 | 3 | 0.060787 |
| 2 | 2 | 0.03573 | 2 | 2 | 0.04497 | 2 | 3 | 0.07002 | 2 | 3 | 0.062276 |
| 3 | 2 | 0.03574 | 3 | 2 | 0.04510 | 3 | 2 | 0.07197 | 3 | 3 | 0.062821 |
| 4 | 2 | 0.03576 | 4 | 2 | 0.04511 | 4 | 2 | 0.07205 | 4 | 3 | 0.063283 |
| 5 | 2 | 0.03578 | 5 | 2 | 0.04532 | 5 | 2 | 0.07218 | 5 | 3 | 0.065121 |
| ACACO | | | | | | | | | | | |
| Cameraman | | | Car | | | Shoppingcart | | | House | | |
| S. No. | $n_c$ | $XB(n_c)$ | S. No. | $n_c$ | $XB(n_c)$ | S. No. | $n_c$ | $XB(n_c)$ | S. No. | $n_c$ | $XB(n_c)$ |
| 1 | 2 | 0.03574 | 1 | 2 | 0.04493 | 1 | 2 | 0.07195 | 1 | 3 | 0.062993 |
| 2 | 2 | 0.03577 | 2 | 2 | 0.04494 | 2 | 2 | 0.07205 | 2 | 4 | 0.064405 |
| 3 | 2 | 0.03636 | 3 | 2 | 0.04498 | 3 | 2 | 0.07299 | 3 | 3 | 0.064826 |
| 4 | 2 | 0.03651 | 4 | 2 | 0.04503 | 4 | 2 | 0.07237 | 4 | 3 | 0.067219 |
| 5 | 2 | 0.03695 | 5 | 2 | 0.04542 | 5 | 2 | 0.07242 | 5 | 2 | 0.067354 |

The superiority among these techniques has also been assessed by determining standard error (SE) for the data set. The outcome of standard error has been reported in Table 4, which undoubtedly proves the dominance of the proposed technique over its counterpart.

A statistical superiority test, called two-tailed $t$–test has been conducted at 5% confidence level to check whether the $p$-value less than 0.05 or not (Flury, 1997). Any value less than this cut-off point is said to be significant and the alternative hypothesis would be accepted. The results of $t$-test amongst these two techniques are reported in Table 5.

Superiority among the participating techniques has also been evaluated in terms of executional times ($t$) (in seconds) between these two techniques. The results have been reported in Table 6, which clearly shows that the proposed technique outperforms other. Finally, it should be mentioned that the experiments have been conducted in MATLAB on a Intel (R) Core (TM) i3 2.53GHz CPU, with a 256-kB cache and a 2-GB main memory in Windows 7 environment.

*Table 4. Mean $(\mu)$ and standard deviation $(\sigma)$ of QIACACO and ACACO*

| QIACACO | | | | | | | |
|---|---|---|---|---|---|---|---|
| Cameraman | | Car | | Shoppingcart | | House | |
| $\mu$ | $\sigma$ | $\mu$ | $\sigma$ | $\mu$ | $\sigma$ | $\mu$ | $\sigma$ |
| 0.0358 | 0.0001 | 0.0451 | 0.0003 | 0.0657 | 0.0035 | 0.0668 | 0.0031 |
| ACACO | | | | | | | |
| Cameraman | | Car | | Shoppingcart | | House | |
| $\mu$ | $\sigma$ | $\mu$ | $\sigma$ | $\mu$ | $\sigma$ | $\mu$ | $\sigma$ |
| 0.0445 | 0.0129 | 0.0626 | 0.0340 | 0.0830 | 0.0177 | 0.0764 | 0.0206 |

*Table 5. Standard Error (SE) of QIACACO and ACACO for the data set*

| Data Set | QIACACO | ACACO |
|---|---|---|
| Cameraman | 0.000045 | 0.002971 |
| Car | 0.000072 | 0.007804 |
| Shoppingcart | 0.000808 | 0.004063 |
| House | 0.000719 | 0.004734 |

*Table 6. Results of two-tailed (unpaired) t-test between QIACACO and ACACO for the data set*

| Data Set | Two-Tailed $p$ Value | Significance |
|---|---|---|
| Cameraman | 0.004847 | Extremely significant |
| Car | 0.027312 | Significant |
| Shoppingcart | 0.000115 | Extremely significant |
| House | 0.046688 | Significant |

*Table 7. Best Executional time (t) of QIACACO and ACACO for the data set*

| Data Set | QIACACO | ACACO |
|---|---|---|
| Cameraman | 2.35 | 14.03 |
| Car | 2.15 | 14.14 |
| Shoppingcart | 4.01 | 21.48 |
| House | 8.85 | 18.44 |

## 8. CONCLUSION

In this paper, a novel ACO-based quantum inspired technique (QIACACO) has been introduced for automatic clustering of image data sets. The foremost feature of the proposed technique is that without having any prior knowledge, it can efficiently and automatically finds the optimal number of clusters of the given data set. Experiments have been conducted for the sake of finding optimal number of clusters of a data set using Xie-beni cluster validity measure as the objective values. The effectiveness of the proposed technique has been proved with regard to optimal number of clusters, its fitness measure, computational time, mean, standard deviation of the fitness measure, and finding standard errors. Finally, an unpaired two-tailed t-test has been conducted to prove the superiority of QIACACO compared to the other one. It has been proved that the proposed technique outperforms other in all respects.

As a scope of future research, quantum inspired automatic technique in multi-objective flavor (Saha, 2011) can also be designed.

## REFERENCES

Araujo, T., Nedjah, N., & Mourelle, L. (2008). Quantum-Inspired Evolutionary State Assignment for Synchronous Finite State Machines. *Journal of Universal Computer Science*, *14*(15), 2532–2548.

Bakhshi, M., Feizi-Derakhshi, M., & Zafarani, E. (2012). Review and Comparison between Clustering Algorithms with Duplicate Entities Detection Purpose. *International Journal of Computer Science & Emerging Technologies, 3*(3), 108-114.

Bhattacharyya, S., & Dey, S. (2011). An Efficient Quantum Inspired Genetic Algorithm with Chaotic Map Model based Interference and Fuzzy Objective Function for Gray Level Image Thresholding. *Proceedings of 2011, International Conference on Computational Intelligence and Communication Systems*, 121-125. doi:10.1109/CICN.2011.24

Bhattacharyya, S., Dutta, P., Chakraborty, S., Chakraborty, R., & Dey, S. (2010). Determination of Optimal Threshold of a Gray-level Image Using a Quantum Inspired Genetic Algorithm with Interference Based on a Random Map Model. *Proceedings of 2010 IEEE International Conference on Computational Intelligence and Computing Research*, 422-425.

Calinski, T., & Harabasz, J. (1974). A dendrite method for cluster analysis. *Communications in Statistics, 3*(1), 1–27.

Davies, D., & Bouldin, D. (1979). A cluster separation measure. *IEEE PAMI, 1*(2), 224–227. doi:10.1109/TPAMI.1979.4766909 PMID:21868852

Deutsch, D., & Jozsa, R. (1992). Rapid Solution of Problems by Quantum Computation. *Royal Society of London Proceedings Series, 439*(1907), 553–558.

Dey, S., Bhattacharyya, S., & Maulik, U. (2013). Chaotic Map Model based Interference Employed in Quantum Inspired Genetic Algorithm to Determine the Optimum Gray Level Image Thresholding. Global Trends in Intelligent Computing Research and Development, 68-110.

Dey, S., Bhattacharyya, S., & Maulik, U. (2013a). Quantum Inspired Meta-heuristic Algorithms for Multi-level Thresholding for True Colour Images. *Proceedings of IEEE INDICON*, 1–6.

Dey, S., Bhattacharyya, S., & Maulik, U. (2014). Quantum inspired genetic algorithm and particle swarm optimization using chaotic map model based interference for gray level Image thresholding. *Swarm and Evolutionary Computation, 15*, 38–57. doi:10.1016/j.swevo.2013.11.002

Dey, S., Bhattacharyya, S., & Maulik, U. (2014a). Quantum Inspired Automatic Clustering for Multilevel Image Thresholding. *Proceedings of International Conference On Computational Intelligence and Communication Networks (ICCICN 2014)*, 247– 251.

Dey, S., Bhattacharyya, S., & Maulik, U. (2014b). Quantum Behaved Multi-objective PSO and ACO Optimization for Multi-level Thresholding. *Proceedings of International Conference On Computational Intelligence and Communication Networks (ICCICN 2014)*, 242– 246.

Dey, S., Bhattacharyya, S., & Maulik, U. (2014c). New Quantum Inspired Tabu Search for Multilevel Colour Image Thresholding. *Proceedings of 8th International Conference On Computing for Sustainable Global Development (INDIACom-2014)*, 311–316.

Dey, S., Bhattacharyya, S., & Maulik, U. (2015). Quantum Behaved Swarm Intelligent Techniques for Image Analysis: A Detailed Survey. In Handbook on Research on Swarm Intelligence in Engineering. IGI Global.

Dey, S., Bhattacharyya, S., & Maulik, U. (2016). New quantum inspired meta-heuristic techniques for multi-level colour image thresholding. *Applied Soft Computing, 46*, 677–702. doi:10.1016/j.asoc.2015.09.042

Dey, S., Bhattacharyya, S., & Maulik, U. (2016a). Quantum Inspired Multi-objective SA for Bi-level Image Thresholding. In Quantum Inspired Computational Intelligence: Research and Applications. Morgan Kaufmann.

Dey, S., Bhattacharyya, S., & Maulik, U. (2016b). Optimum Gray Level Image Thresholding using a Quantum Inspired Genetic Algorithm. In Handbook of Advanced Research on Hybrid Intelligent Techniques and Applications. IGI Global.

Dey, S., Bhattacharyya, S., & Maulik, U. (2017). Efficient quantum inspired meta-heuristics for multi-level true colour image thresholding. *Applied Soft Computing, 56*, 472–513.

Dey, S., Saha, I., Bhattacharyya, S., & Maulik, U. (2013b). New Quantum Inspired Meta- heuristic Methods for Multi-level Thresholding. *Proceedings of 2013 International Conference on Advances in Computing, Communications and Informatics (ICACCI)*, 1236-1240.

Dey, S., Saha, I., Bhattacharyya, S., & Maulik, U. (2014). Multi-level Thresholding using Quantum Inspired Meta-heuristics. *Knowledge-Based Systems, 67*, 373–400. doi:10.1016/j.knosys.2014.04.006

Dorigo, M., Maniezzo, V., & Colorni, A. (1996). The ant system: Optimization by a colony of cooperating agents, *IEEE Trans. Syst. Man Cybernet. – Part B, 26*(1), 29–41. doi:10.1109/3477.484436 PMID:18263004

Dunn, J. (1974). Well separated clusters and optimal fuzzy partitions. *Journal of Cybernetics*, *4*(1), 95–104. doi:10.1080/01969727408546059

Grover, L. (1996). A fast quantum mechanical algorithm for database search. *Proceedings of 28th ACM symposium on Theory of Computing*, 212–219. doi:10.1145/237814.237866

Halkidi, M., Batistakis, Y., & Vazirgiannis, M. (2001). On clustering validation techniques. *Journal of Intelligent Information Systems*, *17*(2-3), 107–145. doi:10.1023/A:1012801612483

Han, K., & Kim, J. (2002). Quantum-Inspired Evolutionary Algorithm for a Class Combinational Optimization. *IEEE Transactions on Evolutionary Computation*, *6*(6), 580–593. doi:10.1109/TEVC.2002.804320

Hey, T. (1999). Quantum computing: An introduction. Computing & Control Engineering Journal, 10, 105–112.

Hinterding, R. (1999). Representation, constraint satisfaction and the knapsack problem. *Proceedings of 2008 Congress on Evolutionary Computation*, *2*, 1286–1292. doi:10.1109/CEC.1999.782591

Jain, A. K., Murty, M. N., & Flynn, P. J. (1999). Data clustering: A review. *ACM Computing Surveys*, *31*(3), 264–323. doi:10.1145/331499.331504

Kim, M., & Ramakrishna, R. S. (2005). New indices for cluster validity assessment. *Pattern Recognition Letters*, *26*(15), 2353–2363. doi:10.1016/j.patrec.2005.04.007

Kim, Y., Kim, J., & Han, K. (2006) Quantum-inspired Multiobjective Evolutionary Algorithm for Multiobjective 0/1 Knapsack Problems. *Proceedings of 2006 IEEE Congress on Evolutionary Computation, Sheraton Vancouver Wall Centre Hotel*, 16–21.

Maulik, U., & Bandyopadhyay, S. (2002). Performance evaluation of some clustering algorithms and validity indices. *IEEE PAMI*, *24*(12), 1650–1654. doi:10.1109/TPAMI.2002.1114856

Mcmohan, D. (2008). *Quantum computing explained*. Hoboken, NJ: John Wiley & Sons, Inc.

Parpinelli, R., Lopes, H., & Freitas, A. (2002). Data mining with an ant colony optimization algorithm. *IEEE Transactions on Evolutionary Computation*, *6*(4), 321–332. doi:10.1109/TEVC.2002.802452

Reiffel, E., & Polak, W. (2000). *An Introduction to Quantum Computing for Non-Physicists*. arxive.org.quant-ph/9809016v2.

Rousseeuw, P. (1987). Silhouettes: A graphical aid to the interpretation and validation of cluster analysis. *Journal of Computational and Applied Mathematics, 20*(1), 53–65. doi:10.1016/0377-0427(87)90125-7

Saha, I., Maulik, U., & Plewczynski, D. (2011). A new multi-objective technique for differential fuzzy clustering. *Applied Soft Computing, 11*(2), 2765–2776. doi:10.1016/j.asoc.2010.11.007

Sharma, S. (1996). *Applied multivariate techniques*. New York: John Wiley & Sons, Inc.

ShorP. (1998). *Quantum computing*. Available: http://east.camel.math.ca/ EMIS/ journals/ DMJDMV/ xvolicm/ 00/Shor.MAN.html

Talbi, H., Draa, A., & Batouche, M. (2004). A New Quantum-Inspired Genetic Algorithm for Solving the Travelling Salesman Problem. *Proceedings of IEEE International Conference on Industrial Technology (ICIT'04), 3,* 1192–1197 doi:10.1109/ICIT.2004.1490730

Talbi, H., Draa, A., & Batouche, M. (2006). A Novel Quantum-Inspired Evolutionary Algorithm for Multi-Sensor Image Registration. *The International Arab Journal of Information Technology, 3*(1), 9–15.

Tan, P.-N., Steinbach, M., & Kumar, V. (2005). *Introduction to Data Mining*. Addison-Wesley Longman, Inc.

Test images. (n.d.). Available: http://www.math.tau.ac.il/~turkel/images.html. (Accessed on 15-Jan-2007)

Xie, X. L., & Beni, G. (1991). A validity measure for fuzzy clustering. *IEEE PAMI, 13*(8), 841–847. doi:10.1109/34.85677

Xie, X. L., & Beni, G. (1991). A validity measure for fuzzy clustering. *IEEE PAMI, 13*(8), 841–847. doi:10.1109/34.85677

Zhao, Y., & Karypis, G. (2002). Evaluation of hierarchical clustering algorithms for document datasets. *Proceedings of CIKM,* 515–524.

## ADDITIONAL READING

Atkins, M., & Mackiewich, B. (1998). Fully Automatic Segmentation of the Brain in MRI, *Proceedings of 1998. IEEE Transactions on Medical Imaging, 17*(1), 98–107. doi:10.1109/42.668699 PMID:9617911

Bezdek, J. C. (1981). *Pattern Recognition with Fuzzy Objective Function Algorithms.* New York: Plenum. doi:10.1007/978-1-4757-0450-1

Boyarsky, A., & G'ora, P. (2010). A random map model for quantum interference. *Communications in Nonlinear Science and Numerical Simulation, 15*(8), 1974–1979. doi:10.1016/j.cnsns.2009.08.018

Chiou, Y. C., & Lan, L. W. (2001). Theory and methodology genetic clustering algorithms [EJOR]. *European Journal of Operational Research, 135*(2), 413–427. doi:10.1016/S0377-2217(00)00320-9

De, S., Bhattacharyya, S., & Dutta, P. (2010a). Efficient Gray Level Image Segmentation Using An Optimized MUSIG (OptiMUSIG) Activation Function, *International Journal of Parallel. Emergent and Distributed Systems, 26*(1), 1–39. doi:10.1080/17445760903546618

Dey, S., Bhattacharyya, S., & Maulik, U. (2014). Quantum inspired genetic algorithm and particle swarm optimization using chaotic map model based interference for gray level Image thresholding. *Swarm and Evolutionary Computation, 15*, 38–57. doi:10.1016/j.swevo.2013.11.002

Dey, S., Bhattacharyya, S., & Maulik, U. (2016). New quantum inspired meta-heuristic techniques for multi-level colour image thresholding. *Applied Soft Computing, 46*, 677–702. doi:10.1016/j.asoc.2015.09.042

Dey, S., Bhattacharyya, S., & Maulik, U. (2017). Efficient quantum inspired meta-heuristics for multi-level true colour image thresholding. *Applied Soft Computing, 56*, 472–513. doi:10.1016/j.asoc.2016.04.024

Dey, S., Saha, I., Bhattacharyya, S., & Maulik, U. (2014). Multi-level Thresholding using Quantum Inspired Meta-heuristics. *Knowledge-Based Systems, 67*, 373–400. doi:10.1016/j.knosys.2014.04.006

Doelken, M., Stefan, H., Pauli, E., Stadlbauer, A., Struffert, T., Engelhorn, T., ... Doerfler, A. (2008). Hammen. T. 1H-MRS profile in MRI positive-versus MRI negative patients with temporal lobe epilepsy. *Seizure, 17*(6), 490–497. doi:10.1016/j.seizure.2008.01.008 PMID:18337128

Flury, B. (1997). *A First Course in Multivariate Statistics*. Berlin, Germany: Springer-Verlag. doi:10.1007/978-1-4757-2765-4

Gonzalez, R. C., & Woods, R. E. (2002). *Digital Image Processing*. Prentice Hall.

Halkidi, M., Batistakis, Y., & Vazirgiannis, M. (2001). M. On clustering validation techniques. *Journal of Intelligent Information Systems*, *17*(2/3), 107–145. doi:10.1023/A:1012801612483

Jain, K. (1989). *Fundamentals of Digital Image Processing*. Upper Saddle River, NJ: Prentice-Hall.

Jawahar, C., Biswas, P., & Ray, A. (1997). Investigations on Fuzzy Thresholding Based On Fuzzy Clustering. *Pattern Recognition*, *30*(10), 1605–1613. doi:10.1016/S0031-3203(97)00004-6

Krishna, K., & Murty, M. N. (1999, June). Genetic *K*-means algorithm. *IEEE Transactions on Systems, Man, and Cybernetics*, *29*(3), 433–439. doi:10.1109/3477.764879 PMID:18252317

Kuo, R. J., Liao, J. L., & Tu, C. (2005). Integration of ART2 neural network and genetic *K*-means algorithm for analyzing web browsing paths in electronic commerce. *Decision Support Systems*, *40*(2), 355–374. doi:10.1016/j.dss.2004.04.010

Niblack, W. (1986). *An Introduction to Image Processing* (pp. 115–116). Englewood Cliffs, NJ: Prentice-Hall.

Sauvola, J., & Pietaksinen, M. (2000). Adaptive document image binarization. *Pattern Recognition*, *33*(2), 225–236. doi:10.1016/S0031-3203(99)00055-2

Zhang, Y. (1996). A survey on evaluation methods for image segmentation. *Pattern Recognition*, *29*(8), 1335–1346. doi:10.1016/0031-3203(95)00169-7

## KEY TERMS AND DEFINITIONS

**Ant Colony Optimization:** A basic meta-heuristic optimization that is inspired by real ants to build its search strategy.

**Clustering:** Clustering is a popular technique that is applied to divide given data into some clusters. The data in each set must share some common feature.

**Quantum Computing:** Quantum computing can be described as a technique that uses the principles of quantum physics.

**Quantum-Inspired Meta-Heuristic Algorithms:** The basic features of quantum computing are embedded in popular meta-heuristic frameworks to build hybrid algorithms called quantum-inspired meta-heuristics.

**Xie-Beni Measure:** It is a cluster validity index that is utilized as the quality measure in clustering algorithm.

# Chapter 3
# True Color Image Segmentation Using Quantum-Induced Modified-Genetic-Algorithm-Based FCM Algorithm

**Sunanda Das**
*University Institute of Technology, India*

**Sourav De**
*Cooch Behar Government Engineering College, India*

**Siddhartha Bhattacharyya**
*RCC Institute of Information Technology, India*

## ABSTRACT

*In this chapter, a quantum-induced modified-genetic-algorithm-based FCM clustering approach is proposed for true color image segmentation. This approach brings down the early convergence problem of FCM to local minima point, increases efficacy of conventional genetic algorithm, and decreases the computational cost and execution time. Effectiveness of genetic algorithm is tumid by modifying some features in population initialization and crossover section. To speed up the execution time as well as make it cost effective and also to get more optimized class levels some quantum computing phenomena like qubit, superposition, entanglement, quantum rotation gate are induced to modified genetic algorithm. Class levels which are yield now fed to FCM as initial input class levels; thus, the ultimate segmented results are formed. Efficiency of proposed method are compared with classical modified-genetic-algorithm-based FCM and conventional FCM based on some standard statistical measures.*

DOI: 10.4018/978-1-5225-5219-2.ch003

## INTRODUCTION

True color image segmentation always be a highly research oriented field as it is treated in the fields of vision, medical image processing, biometric measurements etc for the purpose of detection, face recognition, tracking of an object. Image segmentation is the process to partition an image into some non disjoint regions by groupifying the pixels having same characteristics such as intensity, homogeneity, texture etc. A true color image contains much more information than a gray scale image as a color image convey much more features than gray scale image. The underlying data of a true color image deal with the information in primary color components viz Red(R), Green(G) and Blue(B) and also their admixtures. So a proper segmentation algorithm always be needed for more perfect and accurate result, otherwise it may be happened that after segmentation a new color component may be generated which does not belong to the original true color image.

Different classical and soft computing based techniques are used for segmentation purpose. Classical techniques are categorized into three categories: feature space based segmentation, image domain based segmentation and graph based segmentation. Thresholding, region growing and merging, edge detection, clustering are popularly used some classical segmentation techniques. On the other hand, soft computing techniques have been manifested for the solution of control problems. Fuzzy Logic, artificial neural network, genetic algorithm are three components of soft computing techniques. Fuzzy logic mainly deals with the problem of imprecision and uncertainty, artificial neural network used for learning and adaptation and GA is opted for optimization problem. By using classical segmentation techniques, uncertainties may be arrived as segmentation results if incomplete, imprecise and/or ambiguous information used as input data, overlapping boundaries between classes are present and extracting features and relations among them are indefinite. Soft computing techniques deal with these kinds of problems and produce more convenient result.

Fuzzy C-Means (FCM) [Bezdek, 1981] clustering, a soft clustering technique, is widely used for image segmentation. It follows the rule of fuzzy set theory [Zadeh, 1965]. Though it is more efficient than many other clustering techniques but it also has some deficiencies like it may be stuck into local minima point unless to reach global maxima point; second at the very first time cluster centres are initialized by the programmer; and third it is only applied to hyper spherical structured clusters. Incorporating different evolutionary algorithms like GA [Goldberg, 1989], PSU [Mekhmoukh, 2015] into FCM above stated problems can be solved. Evolutionary algorithms produce global optimal solutions which will be gone to FCM as input data. Though this kind of hybrid algorithm produces optimal solutions but they take high computational time.

High computational time indicates usage of large amount of electronic circuits. From Moore's law, it is known that electronic circuits loss their efficiency and computing ability in day to day fashion. So after some more years later it may be happened that to compute the same algorithm much more circuits will be needed which will be become obviously cost effective. To decrease the computational cost as well as computational time and also to get more accurate and competent results, quantum computing [Mcmohan, 2008] concept is evolved and induced to classical methods. It sustains some properties of quantum mechanics like qubit, superposition, entanglement, orthogonality, quantum rotational gate etc.

In this chapter a Quantum induced Modified Genetic Algorithm (QIMfGA) based FCM algorithm is proposed for true color image segmentation. Here a modified genetic algorithm is applied to FCM to overcome the problem of stucking to local minima. Modified Genetic Algorithm (MfGA) [Das, 2016] indicates some modifications done in population initialization and crossover part of GA, which enhance efficacy of traditional GA. The above stated quantum properties are now incorporated to modified GA as a result computational time is decreased and the output class levels generated by quantum induced modified GA are more optimal than conventional version. The resultant class levels are now employed to FCM as initial input class levels which yield more accurate and competent segmented result. This QIMfGA based FCM algorithm is applied on two true color test images Lena and Peppers and all the results are compared with both classical MfGA based FCM and conventional FCM methods using three evaluation metrics $\rho$ [De, 2012], $F'$ [Borosotti, 1998] and $Q$ [Borosotti, 1998]. The comparison leads to the conclusion that our proposed method efficiently segment true color images than both classical MfGA based FCM and conventional FCM methods.

This chapter is formed in the following manner. A literature review is given here where different eminent works are presented. After that a brief description of FCM, Genetic algorithm and quantum computing concept are stated. Then it proceeds to proposed methodology, comparison based experimental results and lastly to the conclusion.

## LITERATURE REVIEW

Segmentation is an important image processing technique which helps to analyze an image automatically. Different classical and non classical segmentation approaches are proposed to segment true color images in [Gonzales, 2002]. Bhattacharyaa [Bhattacharyaa, 2011] presented a survey paper where different segmentation techniques are discussed for color images. Thresholding is one of the most popular image segmentation techniques, used by many researchers. A multilevel thresholding approach has been applied to a color image to extract the information of the main object from its background and others object [Kulkarni, 2012]. A modified watershed algorithm has been conducted to true color images [Rahman, Islam, 2013]. In this article, to overcome the problem of over segmentation, an adaptive masking and thresholding approach are applied to each plane of color images, before merging them to final one. A multilevel thresholding method combined with data fusion technique applied to color images for segmentation purpose which increased information quality and produced more reliable segmented output [Harrabi and Braiek, 2012]. A morphological gradient based active contour model is used for color image segmentation [Anh, 2011]. Here, the proposed model extract the edge map direct from color images without losing the color characteristics and this provides good region and edge information as an active contour without re-initialization. Tan and Isa [Tan, 2011] proposed a histogram thresholding based FCM algorithm where thresholding methods used to determine the class levels for color images and those are employed to FCM. Mao et al. [Mao, 2009] used region growing and ant colony algorithms to segment color image. In this article, based on the similar intensity value, edge information and spatial information, seeds are first automatically selected. Then applying ant colony technique, the regions are merged maintaining the homogeneity property. In article [Verma, 2011], a single seeded region growing technique is adopted for true color image segmentation. To decrease the computational cost and execution time, a new region growing formula is formulated and Otsu's thresholding method is used here as the stopping criteria. A meta-heuristics algorithm is introduced for color image segmentation in [Preetha, 2014]. Segmentation has done based on seed region growing. Primarily the seeds are chosen by Cuckoo search method. Tao *et al.* [Tao, 2007] proposed a method where mean shift segmentation and normalized cut are used in a combined manner. Mean shift algorithm is applied to color image to store the discontinuity characteristics and after that n-cut algorithm are applied to those region to get global optimized clusters. An automatic color image segmentation using adaptive grow cut algorithm is proposed by Basavaprasad *et al.* [Basavaprasad, 2015]. Chen and Ludwig [Chen, 2017] proposed a Fuzzy C- regression model for color image segmentation. It considered spatial information and applied to the hyperplaned cluster. Chaabane *et al.* [Chaabane, 2015] used a feature based modified FCM clustering technique to segment color images. In first stage, statistical features and fuzzy clustering technique are integrated to obtain the segmented image; after that these segmented results are merged over different channel based on some combination rule. Dong *et al.* [Dong, 2005] evolved a segmentation technique where both supervised and unsupervised techniques are used. SOM and simulated anneling are used to achieve color reduction and color clustering respectively for segmentation. After that supervised learning is applied to get the ultimate segmented result. In another article [Arumugadevi,

2016] features of color images are employed to FCM to get the class levels which are fed to the feed forward network to get segmented results. The parallel optimized multilevel sigmoidal (ParaOptiMUSIG) activation function in connection with the multilevel self-organizing neural network (MLSONN) is introduced for the true color image segmentation [De, 2010, 2012]. In this method, the genetic algorithm is applied to generate the ParaOptiMUSIG activation function. This algorithm is also applied for multi objective function without confining within the single objective function. De *et al.* [De, 2013] proposed NSGA II based ParaOptiMUSIG activation function incorporating the multi-criterion to segment the color images. GA in combination with the weighted undirected graph is employed to segment the color images [Amelio, 2013]. Krishna *et al.* [Krishna, 2015] proposed a new approach for color image segmentation where texture and color features are applied to Sequential Minimal Optimization-Support Vector Machine (SMO-SVM). A soft rough FCM is used here to train the SMO-SVM classifier for segmentation purpose. A new approach is introduced where modified GA and FCM are combined to get more optimal solution [Das, 2016]. Class levels generated by Modified GA are employed to FCM to overcome the convergence problem of FCM. Modifying the population initialization part and crossover section of GA with the use of a new weighted mean and new crossover probability formula, more optimal results are found.

Though the hybrid systems give more reliable results but computational cost and execution time are also extended. To overcome this problem quantum characteristics are incorporated to different conventional or classical methods in different research articles. To solve TSP problem in minimum computational time quantum computing concept is merged with GA [Talbi, 2004]. Here a lookup table is maintained for rotational angel. A quantum based PSO algorithm is used for color image segmentation [Nebti, 2013]. A multiobjective quantum inspired evolutionary algorithm [Li, 2014] is applied to SAR images to get more optimal segmented results in less time. A quantum inspired tabu search algorithm is applied to color image for multilevel thresholding in [Dey, 2014]. Dey *et al.* [Dey, 2013] incorporate quantum computing phenomena to particle swarm algorithm and differential evolutionary algorithm. These quantum versions are used for multilevel thresholding of color images.

## FUZZY C-MEANS CLUSTERING

To make clustering concept more convenient, Fuzzy C-Means clustering (FCM) technique was introduced by Dunn [Dunn, 1973] in 1973 and improved by Bezdek [Bezdek, 1981] in 1981. It is actually a classification based unsupervised clustering algorithm works on the principle of fuzzy set theory [Zadeh, 1965]. The main aim of this algorithm is to minimize the objective function with respect to the cluster centre *Centre*$_i$ and the membership function $U$. The membership matrix $U$ denotes the belongingness of each data point in each cluster as here one data point resides more than one cluster. The data points, belong to the same cluster, have higher membership value with respect to that cluster and others have lower membership value. Clusters are formed based on the Euclidean distance between each data point and cluster centre. By iteratively updating its cluster centre and membership function this algorithm reaches to its goal. Suppose $X=\{x_1,x_2,x_3,...,x_N\}$ is a set of $N$ number of unlabeled data patterns having $f$ number of features which are allowed to partition in C number of clusters. Now this can be done by updating membership function $U_i$ and cluster centre *Centre*$_i$ using the following formula:

$$U_{ik} = \frac{1}{|| x_k - Centre_i ||^{\frac{2}{m-1}} \Big/ \sum_{C=1}^{j} || x_k - Centre_j ||^{\frac{2}{m-1}}} , \quad 1 \le k \le N, 1 \le i \le C \tag{1}$$

where $U_{ik}$ denotes the degree of membership of $x_k$ in i$^{th}$ cluster and $m$ represents the degree of fuzziness which is greater than 1.

The cluster centroids are calculated by the following formula:

$$Centre_i = \frac{\sum_{k=1}^{N}(U_{ik})^m x_k}{\sum_{k=1}^{N}(U_{ik})^m}, 1 \le i \le C \tag{2}$$

## GENETIC ALGORITHM

Genetic Algorithm, a heuristics search method, provides global optimal solution in large, complex and multimodal problem space. This method forged the idea of natural evolution procedure. In GA a fixed population size is maintained throughout the method. This method starts by random generation of individuals which are called chromosomes. Quality of each individual is manipulated using fitness value. Using three genetically inspired operation selection, crossover and mutation, better solutions are produced.

A chromosome is made of a set of genes which are noting but the values of cluster centroids and a set of chromosomes are created a population pool. Each chromosome

*Figure 1. Graphical representation of Gene, Chromosome and Population*

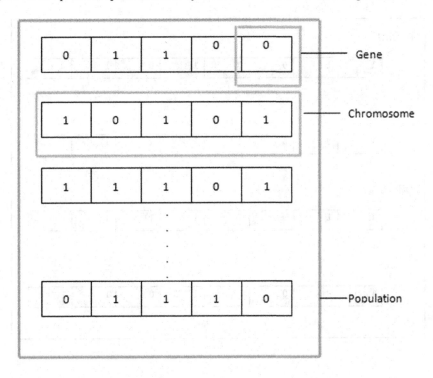

*Figure 2. Single Point Crossover*

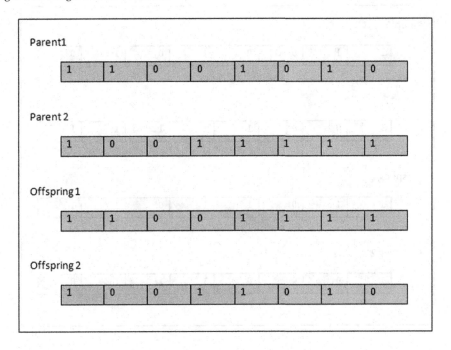

*Figure 3. Two Point Crossover*

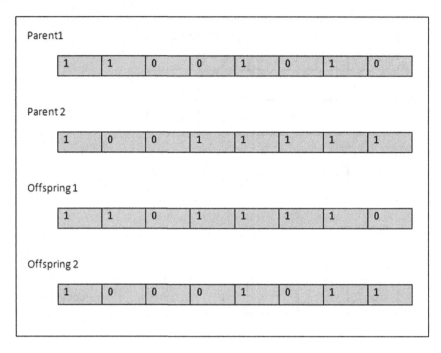

*Figure 4. Multi Point Crossover*

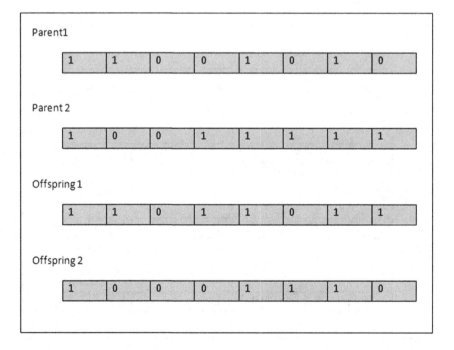

*Figure 5. Mutation*

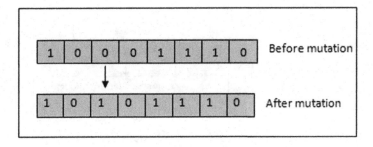

actually represents solution of the problem space, having some properties. These solutions are altered and mutated using the crossover and mutation probability to produce the global optimized solution. Crossover is occured between two or more selected candidate solutions. This selection can be done using different selection procedures like Roulette wheel selection, Rank selection, Tournament selection, Boultzman selection etc. There are also different types of crossover techniques e.g. single point crossover, two point crossover, uniform crossover. Next to the crossover operation, mutation is applied to child solution to make it more fitted.

## QUANTUM COMPUTING CONCEPT

Now-a-days, quantum computing plays a vital role in different research area. Different conventional methods accomplished their jobs in efficient manner; hybrid systems enhance efficiencies of those conventional methods. But, though the hybrid system provides more accurate and effective results than conventional methods, it takes huge computational time. High computation indicates usage of more computational circuits. Again from Moore's law it can be said that the number of transistors per square inch on integrated circuits would double in every 18 months. So whatever amount of electronic circuits are used today for one program, in future the same program will need more electronic circuits, which leads to the problem of high computational cost. From this point of view Quantum Computing has been evolved by American computer engineer Howard Aiken in 1947. It works on the principle of quantum mechanics and follows some properties like qubit, orthogonality, entanglement, rotational gate etc. When these properties are embedded into the classical methods, within the minimum time period a high quality of output is generated.

In quantum computing the smallest information bit is known as *qubit*. Where classical computers deal with bit, represents by 0 or 1, in quantum computing a single qubit can be represented by 0 or 1 or any linear superposition of both states. If

*Figure 6. Flow Diagram of Genetic Algorithm*

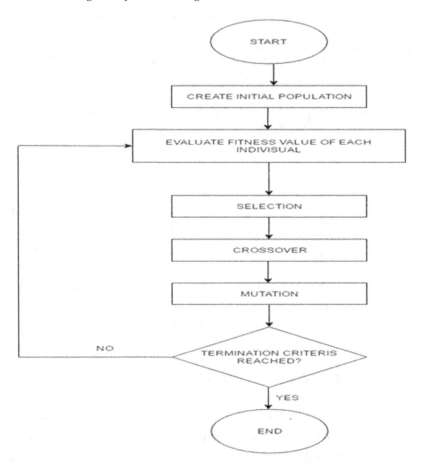

a sphere has been taken as consideration then in classical computing bits are resided either of two poles of sphere but in quantum computing qubit can be any point of the sphere. When qubit system is applied to classical computers, to represents states of an *n-qubit* system it requires the storage of $2^n$ complex coefficient, where classical computers represent states by only n- bit. So it can be said that using less energy quantum computing can store more information than classical computing. A qubit can be represented as

$$| \psi \rangle = \alpha | 0 \rangle + \beta | 1 \rangle \tag{3}$$

where, $| 0 \rangle$ denotes "ground state" and $| 1 \rangle$ is known as "excited state" and $\alpha, \beta$ are complex numbers follow the quantum orthogonality property, presented as

$$\alpha^2 + \beta^2 = 1 \qquad\qquad (4)$$

Another property of quantum computing is *quantum entanglement*. In this property quantum states are highly correlated to each other so that it is hardly differentiable. It is a tensor product of states given as

$$| \vartheta_1 \rangle \otimes | \vartheta_2 \rangle .$$

Quantum measurement is the procedure where entangled states are converted to its corresponding single state. From equation 3, it can be stated that to transform the function $| \psi \rangle$ in a single state $| 0 \rangle$ and $| 1 \rangle$ have the probability of $\alpha^2$ and $\beta^2$ respectively.

Quantum gates [Nielsen, 2002] are reversible in nature. They are represented by unitary matrices. Different types of quantum gates are used like Hadamard gate [Maitra,2005], Pauli-X gate (= NOT gate), Pauli-Y gate, Pauli-Z gate, Square root of NOT gate ($\sqrt{\text{NOT}}$), Phase shift gates, Swap gate, Square root of Swap gate, Controlled gates, Toffoli gate [Muthukrishnan, 1999], Fredkin gate [Lee, 2010]. In this article quantum rotational gate is used which is defined as

$$\begin{pmatrix} \alpha'_i \\ \beta'_i \end{pmatrix} = \begin{pmatrix} \cos\theta_i & -\sin\theta_i \\ \sin\theta_i & \cos\theta_i \end{pmatrix} \begin{pmatrix} \alpha_i \\ \beta_i \end{pmatrix} \qquad\qquad (5)$$

where $(\alpha_i, \beta_i)$ and $(\alpha'_i, \beta'_i)$ are the $i^{th}$ qubit before and after updating; and $\theta_i$ denotes the rotation angle between $\alpha_i$ and $\beta_i$ .

## DIFFERENT QUALITY EVALUATION METRICS

Quality evaluation metrics are different statistical mathematical formulas which apply to the output result to verify the efficiency of the applied method. It measures the quality of output segmented image after applying different segmentation on an image. In this article three quality evaluation metrics, one correlation coefficient ($\rho$) and two empirical measures($F'(I)$ and $Q(I)$) are defined which show the goodness of segmented result.

## Correlation Coefficient (ρ)

It is a standard measure metric which measures the degree of similarity between original and segmented image [De, 2012]. This is defined as

$$\rho = \frac{\frac{1}{n^2}\sum_{i=1}^{n}\sum_{j=1}^{n}(X_{ij}-\overline{X})(Y_{ij}-\overline{Y})}{\sqrt{\frac{1}{n^2}\sum_{i=1}^{n}\sum_{j=1}^{n}(X_{ij}-\overline{X})^2}\sqrt{\frac{1}{n^2}\sum_{i=1}^{n}\sum_{j=1}^{n}(Y_{ij}-\overline{Y})^2}} \tag{6}$$

where $\overline{X}$ stands for mean of the original image and $\overline{Y}$ stands for mean of the segmented image. As the $\rho$ value of the segmented image increases, the quality of the segmentation enhances. $X_{ij}$, $1 \leq i, j \leq n$ and $Y_{ij}$, $1 \leq i, j \leq n$ are the original and the segmented images respectively, each of dimensions n×n.

## F′(I)

It is another evaluation function which is introduced by Borosotti *et al.* [Borosotti, 1998].

$$F'(I) = \frac{1}{1000S_M}\sqrt{\sum_{u=1}^{max\,area}[N(u)]^{1+\frac{1}{u}}\sum_{Re=1}^{N}\frac{e_{Re}^2}{\sqrt{S_{Re}}}} \tag{7}$$

where, $N$ is the number of segmented regions, $S_M$ represents the area of an original image, *maxarea* represents the area of the largest region in the segmented image, $N(u)$ refers to the number of regions in the segmented image having an area of exactly u. $e_{Re}^2$ defines the squared color error of region $Re$ and is presented as

$$e_{Re}^2 = \sum_{v\in(R,G,B)}\sum_{px\in RE_{Re}}(C_v(px) - C_v(\widehat{RE_{Re}}))^2 \tag{8}$$

Here, $RE_{Re}$ signifies the number of pixels placed in region *Re*. $C_v(\widehat{RE_{Re}})$ is the average value of feature *v* (Red, Green or Blue) of a pixel *px* in region *Re* and is given by

$$C_v(\widehat{RE_{\text{Re}}}) = \frac{\sum_{px \in RE_{\text{Re}}} C_v(px)}{S_{\text{Re}}} \tag{9}$$

where, $C_v(px)$ denotes the value of component $v$ for pixel $px$.

## Q(I)

It is another evaluation function proposed by Borosotti *et al.* [Borosotti, 1998]. It is actually modified version of $F'(I)$.

$$Q(I) = \frac{1}{1000S_M} \sqrt{N} \sum_{\text{Re}=1}^{N} \left[ \frac{e_{\text{Re}}^2}{1 + \log S_{\text{Re}}} + \left( \frac{N(S_{\text{Re}})}{S_{\text{Re}}} \right)^2 \right] \tag{10}$$

where, $N(S_{Re})$ stands for the number of regions having an area $S_{Re}$.

## PROPOSED METHODOLOGY

In this article, a quantum induced modified genetic algorithm based FCM algorithm is proposed for true color image segmentation. FCM suffers with some difficulties which are described before. Quantum induced Modified Genetic algorithm is added to FCM to solve the convergence problem of FCM. In case of FCM, initial cluster centroids play a very important role. If they are not defined properly then the algorithm may stuck to the local minima point which hampers the ultimate segmented result.

Despite of superiority of GA, a modified genetic algorithm (MfGA) [Das, 2016] is introduced to enhance the efficacy of GA. In MfGA, population initialization and crossover part are modified to some extent which increases optimality of GA. In case of GA, when chromosomes are created by randomly selecting their cluster centroids, then perhaps the difference between two cluster centroids are too small that these are not considered as different cluster. To bring down this situation a weighted mean formula is formulated in MfGA. In crossover section, fixed crossover probability is modified in that way that the probability varies at every iteration. Crossover probability indicates the ratio that how many couples are chosen for mating purpose. As in GA a fixed crossover probability is used so when good chromosomes are mated with bad chromosomes there is a possibility that good chromosomes are not stored in population pool for next generation. So in MfGA, crossover probability is formulated in that manner that at each iteration crossover probability is decreased as iterations are increased. Selection and mutation sections are same in both GA and MfGA. After running the method optimal class levels are generated which are fed to FCM for ultimate result. Though MfGA provides more optimal results than GA but it takes huge computational time. To remit this computational time as well as cost quantum computing concept is added to MfGA.

Here the proposed methodology is applied to true color images. A true color image consists of three color components viz *Red(R), Green (G) and Blue (B)*. So it is the first job to segregate *R, G, B* as different color components. Now this QIMfGA based FCM algorithm is applied to each plane to get the output. A brief description of this proposed algorithm is given here. After decomposing the image into three color planes, the population pool *P* is generated for each plane i.e. population pool for red, population pool for green and population pool for blue. Now the procedure is applied to each population pool simultaneously. This population pool is generated using the weighted mean formula of MfGA. Each chromosome contains a set of centroids which are actually the pixel intensity values. Now as per the rule of quantum computing these intensity values are randomly converted to the any real number between 0 and 1 thus create the population *P′*. Applying quantum orthogonality property to population *P′* we get another population called *P″*. Afterwards quantum rotational gate is embedded to *P″* for quick convergence and the ultimate population $P^+$ is evolved. Now selection, crossover and mutation are applied to $P^+$. After compilation of first iteration the child solutions are spawned which are added to the parent solution and create population *P′* for next generation maintaining the fixed population size. Again from *P′*, *P″* and $P^+$ are formed and the same procedure is iterated for certain time. After completion of QIMfGA near-optimal solutions are produced which are employed to FCM as initial input cluster centres thus the desired segmented output is get. As this method is applied to *R, G, B* planes differently so the segmented output is also produced for three planes differently. So as a last step the three segmented results are merged and the final true color segmented output image is formed. The total procedure in step by step manner is demonstrated below:

## Quantum Inspired MfGA (QIMfGA) Based FCM Algorithm

### Input

1. Number of segment
2. Size of population
3. Number of iterations
4. Maximum crossover probability and minimum crossover probability
5. Mutation probability
6. Error

## Procedure

**Step 1:** At the very first step a true color image is to be decomposed into *R, G, B* three color components. Now the following steps are applied to each color plane separately.

**Step 2:** After segregating the image, population pool is created for each plane. Here to segment an image into *N* partitions, *N+1* number of initial class levels which are actually pixel intensity values, are randomly selected. Afterwards using the weighted mean formula ultimate *N* number of class levels are generated. Following this concept a set of chromosomes is produced called population pool *P* for each plane. The weighted mean defined as

$$N_i = \frac{\sum_{j=L_i}^{L_{i+1}} f_j * I_j}{\sum_{j=L_i}^{L_{i+1}} f_j} \tag{11}$$

where $L_i$ and $L_{i+1}$ are the temporary class levels, $f_j$ is the frequency of the $j^{th}$ pixel and $I_j$ denotes pixel intensity value of $j^{th}$ pixel.

**Step 3:** Each pixel intensity value of each chromosome is now encoded with the real number between 0 and 1, and formed new population *P′*.

**Step 4:** In population *P′*, quantum orthogonality property is applied to create population *P″*.

**Step 5:** For quick convergence, lastly quantum rotational gate is induced to each chromosome of population *P″*; and final population *P⁺* is generated for further processing.

**Step 6:** The method propagates by manipulating the fitness values based on some fitness functions, and based on those fitness values better fitted chromosomes are selected using Roulette-wheel selection method for crossover and mutation operations.

**Step 7:** Crossover is happened based on crossover probability. Here crossover probability depends on the maximum and minimum crossover probability and is decreased as the iterations are increased. It can be defined as

$$C_p = C_{max} - \frac{C_{max} - C_{min}}{Iteration_{max} - Iteration_{current}} \tag{12}$$

where $C_{max}$ and $C_{min}$ are the maximum and minimum crossover probability; and *Iteration*$_{max}$ and *Iteration*$_{current}$ indicate maximum and present iteration number.

**Step 8:** After crossover, the child solutions are passed to the mutation part where they are mutated according to mutation probability.

**Step 9:** Now the mutated child solutions are mixed with parent solution and create the population $P'$.

**Step 10:** For a certain time of iteration, this algorithm follows the step 4 to step 9 and after that the optimized result is produced.

**Step 11:** This optimized class levels are now employed to FCM as the initial class levels thus get the desired segmented output.

**Step 12:** The desired segmented output for each color component are now merged and formed the final true color segmented image.

## EXPERIMENTAL RESULT AND ANALYSIS

Segmentation results of true color images using Quantum induced modified genetic algorithm (QIMfGA) based FCM algorithm are demonstrated in this section. Two true color test images viz Lena and Peppers with size of 256 X 256 are used here for segmentation purpose. Though the segmentation results are taken for different number of clusters but here results are presented only for $K= \{6, 8\}$ clusters. Experimental results of both classical MfGA based FCM and conventional FCM are also presented in this section. Those results are compared with respect to their efficiency based on three quality measure metrics $\rho$, $F'$ and $Q$.

*Figure 7. Original color image (a) Lena (b) Peppers*

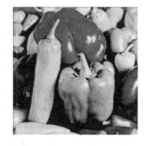

 (a)                    (b)

In initial phase it is needed to define value of some constant terms which play important role in the proposed method. GA considers a fixed population size, a crossover probability and also a mutation probability throughout the method. A population of 50 is considered here as fixed population size. Unlike GA, in MfGA a maximum and minimum crossover probability is used, as in MfGA the crossover probability varies with respect to iteration. In this methodology maximum and minimum crossover probability is applied as 0.9 and 0.5 respectively, based on which the present crossover probability for that instance of iteration is manipulated. After crossover the child solutions are taken part in mutation operation to make them more fitted. Mutation are committed based on mutation probability which is considered here as 0.01. After the mutation better solutions are evolved and mixed up with previous parent solution but maintain their population size. After certain iterations the ultimate class levels are generated which are employed to FCM as initial class levels thus the ultimate segmented results are formed.

Segmented result of color image of Lena based on three measurement functions $\rho$, $F'$ and $Q$ are demonstrated in Table 1, Table 2 and Table 3 respectively. Those tables are structured in that manner that the first column defines the number of segment, second column indicates methods which are applied to test color image, third and forth column present serial number and class levels of corresponding applied method, respectively and lastly the fitness value is presented. These methods are applied to the test images many times but only three good results are presented in this section. The best result obtained by any process for each number of segments are highlighted by boldfaced.

The mean and standard deviation are evaluated for each algorithm based on each fitness functions and are reported in Table 4. The mean computational time for FCM is also presented in the same table. It is known that if initial class levels of FCM are defined properly then FCM easily reaches to its goal. In this table the mean time indicates that, in minimum time span FCM meets to its goal using the proposed methodology than both classical MfGA based FCM and conventional FCM methods.

If a comparison is done between proposed methodology and both classical MfGA based FCM and conventional FCM methods, then it will be seen that fitness value as well as mean time of proposed method are better than the other two methods. This indicates that the class levels generated by QIMfGA always be better than other two methods so that when it is employed to FCM, the ultimate result is more convenient in respect of fitness value and computational time.

The same procedures are applied on Peppers image. The class boundaries along with their fitness value based on fitness function of $\rho$, $F'$ and $Q$ for each algorithm applied on that image are reported in Table 5, Table 6 and Table 7 respectively. Good results for each method are enlightened.

*Table 1. Class boundaries and evaluated segmentation quality measures, ρ by different algorithms for different classes of Lena image.*

| # Segments | Algorithm | # | Class Levels | Fit val |
|---|---|---|---|---|
| 6 | Conventional FCM | 1 | **R={ 89, 110,152, 181, 208, 219}** <br> **G={ 24, 65,98, 126, 153, 196}** <br> **B={ 57, 78, 99, 111,152, 181}** | **0.9623** |
| | | 2 | R={ 90, 116,152, 181, 208, 233} <br> G={ 21, 64,95, 120, 153, 196} <br> B={ 60, 78, 110, 121,152, 181} | 0.9326 |
| | | 3 | R={ 90, 116,152, 181, 208, 233} <br> G={ 24, 63,95, 126, 150, 196} <br> B={ 57, 78, 99, 121,152, 181} | 0.9320 |
| | MfGA based FCM | 1 | R={ 93, 130,170, 198, 218, 238} <br> G={ 24, 63,95, 126, 153, 196} <br> B={ 57, 78, 99, 121,152, 181} | 0.9806 |
| | | 2 | R={ 92, 125,152, 190, 213, 233} <br> G={ 21, 63,95, 126, 153, 196} <br> B={ 57, 78, 99, 121,152, 181} | 0.9768 |
| | | 3 | **R={ 90, 116,152, 181, 208, 233}** <br> **G={ 24, 63,95, 126, 153, 196}** <br> **B={ 57, 78, 99, 121,152, 181}** | **0.9832** |
| | Proposed | 1 | **R={93, 126, 170, 188, 219, 233}** <br> **G={24, 63, 95, 126, 154, 196}** <br> **B={56, 78, 99, 123, 152, 181}** | **0.9898** |
| | | 2 | R={91, 130, 170, 192, 211, 238} <br> G={25, 63, 98, 126, 158, 196} <br> B={57, 81, 99, 121, 152, 181} | 0.9874 |
| | | 3 | R={93, 130, 170, 198, 219, 238} <br> G={24, 63, 95, 126, 154, 196} <br> B={57, 78, 101, 121, 149, 181} | 0.9859 |

*continued on following page*

*Table 1. Continued*

| #<br>Segments | Algorithm | # | Class Levels | Fit val |
|---|---|---|---|---|
| 8 | Conventional FCM | 1 | R={86,106,138,168,188,205,222,239}<br>G={20,43,67,92,114,135,164,198}<br>B={55,73,90,106,121,139,161,185} | 0.9126 |
| | | 2 | R={86,106,138,165,182,201,220,241}<br>G={18,43,65,92,110,135,164,196}<br>B={54,72,89,104,120,138,160,185} | 0.9257 |
| | | 3 | **R={83,101,128,155,178,202,221,239}**<br>**G={20,43,69,92,114,135,164,198}**<br>**B={55,73,90,105,121,139,161,185}** | **0.9543** |
| | MfGA based FCM | 1 | R={83,101,128,155,178,202,221,239}<br>G={20,43,68,92,114,135,164,198}<br>B={45,63,79,95,112,128,156,183} | 0.9815 |
| | | 2 | **R={81,101,129,155,175,202,221,239}**<br>**G={20,43,67,92,114,135,164,198}**<br>**B={55,73,90,105,121,139,161,185}** | **0.9824** |
| | | 3 | R={83,101,128,155,178,202,221,239}<br>G={20,43,67,92,114,135,164,198}<br>B={45,63,79,95,112,128,156,183} | 0.9792 |
| | Proposed | 1 | **R={81,100,128,159,178,202,221,239}**<br>**G={20,44,67,91,119,135,164,198}**<br>**B={45,63,79,95,112,128,156,189}** | **0.9876** |
| | | 2 | R={83,101,134,155,178,202,221,239}<br>G={20,46,67,92,114,135,164,198}<br>B={45,63,83,98,112,128,156,185} | 0.9864 |
| | | 3 | R={84,101,128,155,178,202,221,239}<br>G={21,43,70,92,114,135,164,198}<br>B={45,63,80,95,112,128,156,183} | 0.9861 |

*Table 2. Class boundaries and evaluated segmentation quality measures, **F′** by different algorithms for different classes of Lena image.*

| # segments | Algorithm | # | Class Levels | Fit val |
|---|---|---|---|---|
| 6 | Conventional FCM | 1 | R={ 89, 110,150, 179, 218, 236} | 326547.42 |
| | | | G={ 24, 64,95, 125, 150,198} | |
| | | | B={ 57, 79, 101, 121,152, 181} | |
| | | 2 | **R={ 91, 116,152, 181, 210, 233}** | **254791.34** |
| | | | **G={ 25, 63,95, 125, 153, 196}** | |
| | | | **B={ 52, 70, 99, 120,152, 186}** | |
| | | 3 | R={ 90, 118,156, 181, 210, 233} | 289325.74 |
| | | | G={ 24, 63,95, 126, 153, 196} | |
| | | | B={ 59, 80, 99, 121,152, 181} | |
| | MfGA based FCM | 1 | **R={ 90, 116,152, 181, 208, 233}** | **58484.59** |
| | | | **G={ 24, 63,95, 125, 153, 196}** | |
| | | | **B={ 57, 80, 101,121,152, 181}** | |
| | | 2 | R={ 91, 116,154, 181, 208, 231} | 75358.72 |
| | | | G={ 21, 63,95, 128, 153, 196} | |
| | | | B={ 58,78, 99, 120,152, 181} | |
| | | 3 | R={ 90, 116,153, 181, 209, 230} | 66751.31 |
| | | | G={ 24, 63,95, 126, 153, 196} | |
| | | | B={ 57, 79, 99, 120,151, 181} | |
| | Proposed | 1 | R={40, 78, 111, 145, 183, 236} | 43698.47 |
| | | | G={38, 68, 98,128, 158, 192} | |
| | | | B={21, 56, 89, 122, 165, 210} | |
| | | 2 | R={93, 130, 171, 198, 219, 238} | 45744.65 |
| | | | G={24, 63, 95, 126, 154, 196} | |
| | | | B={57, 78, 101, 121, 152, 181} | |
| | | 3 | **R={92, 130, 172, 198, 219, 238}** | **39778.79** |
| | | | **G={24, 63, 90, 126, 156, 198}** | |
| | | | **B={57, 78, 99, 121, 152, 181}** | |

*continued on following page*

*Table 2. Continued*

| # segments | Algorithm | # | Class Levels | Fit val |
|---|---|---|---|---|
| 8 | Conventional FCM | 1 | R={86,106,139,168,190,205,222,239}<br>G={20,43,67,92,114,135,164,198}<br>B={45,63,79,95,112,128,156,183} | **987636.25** |
| | | 2 | R={81,102,139,162,188,206,220,238}<br>G={21,46,65,93,111,135,165,190}<br>B={57,72,86,106,120,138,161,185} | 1270489.10 |
| | | 3 | R={83,100,128,152,178,202,221,240}<br>G={20,43,69,92,114,135,162,198}<br>B={54,71,91,105,122,139,161,185} | 1025394.78 |
| | MfGA based FCM | 1 | R={86,106,126,138,168,188,220,239}<br>G={20,43,68,93,114,136,199,165}<br>B={45,68,79,95,111,128,156,183} | 332122.96 |
| | | 2 | R={86,106,138,168,188,205,222,239}<br>G={20, 45, 68,93,115,136, 199,165}<br>B={55,73,90,106,121,139,161,185} | 394524.47 |
| | | 3 | R={87,106,138,168,189,205,222,239}<br>G={21,43,68,93,115,136,166,201}<br>B={55,73,90,106,121,139,161,185} | **316578.63** |
| | Proposed | 1 | R={88,110,138,168,187,205,222,242}<br>G={21,43,68,96,115,136,167,199}<br>B={54,73,90,106,121,141,163,185} | **146789.25** |
| | | 2 | R={86,106,138,168,188,205,220,239}<br>G={20,45,68,93,114,136,166,199}<br>B={55,73,90,106,121,139,161,187} | 254789.69 |
| | | 3 | R={86,106,138,168,188,208,222,238}<br>G={20,43,68,93,119,136,161,199}<br>B={52,73,98,106,121,139,161,185} | 298772.72 |

*Table 3. Class boundaries and evaluated segmentation quality measures, **Q** by different algorithms for different classes of Lena image.*

| # segments | Algorithm | # | Class Levels | Fit val |
|---|---|---|---|---|
| 6 | Conventional FCM | 1 | R={ 89, 110,150, 181, 218, 233} <br> G={ 24, 63,95, 125, 150,198} <br> B={ 57, 79, 100, 121,152, 181} | 25315.77 |
| | | 2 | **R={ 91, 116,152, 181, 208, 233}** <br> **G={ 25, 63,95, 126, 153, 196}** <br> **B={ 52, 70, 99, 120,152, 181}** | **21973.64** |
| | | 3 | R={ 90, 115,156, 181, 210, 233} <br> G={ 24, 63,95, 126, 153, 196} <br> B={ 57, 78, 99, 121,152, 181} | 26977.81 |
| | MfGA based FCM | 1 | R={ 90, 116,152, 181, 208, 233} <br> G={ 24, 63,95, 126, 153, 196} <br> B={ 57, 80, 99, 121,152, 181} | 9299.335 |
| | | 2 | **R={ 90, 116,154, 181, 208, 231}** <br> **G={ 24, 63,95, 128, 153, 196}** <br> **B={ 57, 78, 99, 120,152, 181}** | **8973.337** |
| | | 3 | R={ 90, 116,153, 181, 209, 230} <br> G={ 24, 63,95, 126, 153, 196} <br> B={ 57, 78, 99, 121,152, 181} | 9555.05 |
| | Proposed | 1 | **R={40, 78, 111, 145, 183, 236}** <br> **G={38, 68, 98,128, 158, 192}** <br> **B={21, 56, 88, 122, 165, 210}** | **6459.53** |
| | | 2 | R={93, 130, 170, 198, 219, 238} <br> G={24, 63, 95, 126, 154, 196} <br> B={57, 78, 99, 121, 152, 181} | 7473.59 |
| | | 3 | R={92, 130, 172, 198, 219, 238} <br> G={24, 63, 90, 126, 156, 198} <br> B={57, 78, 99, 121, 152, 181} | 6648.63 |

*continued on following page*

*Table 3. Continued*

| #<br>segments | Algorithm | # | Class Levels | Fit val |
|---|---|---|---|---|
| 8 | Conventional FCM | 1 | R={86,106,138,168,188,205,222,239}<br>G={20,43,67,92,114,135,164,198}<br>B={45,63,79,95,112,128,156,183} | 70869.63 |
| | | 2 | R={81,102,139,162,188,206,220,238}<br>G={21,42,65,93,114,135,165,199}<br>B={54,72,86,106,120,138,161,185} | 84254.32 |
| | | 3 | **R={83,100,128,152,178,202,221,240}**<br>**G={20,43,69,92,114,135,162,198}**<br>**B={54,73,90,105,121,139,161,185}** | **69701.27** |
| | MfGA based FCM | 1 | **R={86,106,126,138,168,188,222,239}**<br>**G={20,43,68,93,114,136,199,165}**<br>**B={45,63,79,95,112,128,156,183}** | **45944.56** |
| | | 2 | R={86,106,138,168,188,205,222,239}<br>G={20, 43, 68,93,115,136, 199,165}<br>B={55,73,90,106,121,139,161,185} | 50472.78 |
| | | 3 | R={86,106,138,168,188,205,222,239}<br>G={20,43,68,93,115,136,166,199}<br>B={55,73,90,106,121,139,161,185} | 51976.51 |
| | Proposed | 1 | **R={87,110,138,168,187,205,222,242}**<br>**G={21,43,68,96,115,136,167,199}**<br>**B={54,73,90,105,121,141,161,185}** | **35679.23** |
| | | 2 | R={86,106,138,168,188,205,220,239}<br>G={20,45,68,93,114,136,166,199}<br>B={55,73,90,106,121,139,161,185} | 39543.87 |
| | | 3 | R={86,106,138,168,188,208,222,238}<br>G={20,43,68,93,118,136,161,199}<br>B={52,73,95,106,121,139,161,185} | 38453.16 |

*Table 4. Different algorithm based mean and standard deviation using different types of fitness functions and mean of time taken by different algorithms for Lena image.*

| Fit. fn. | # segments | Algorithm | Mean ± Std. Div. | Mean time |
|---|---|---|---|---|
| $\rho$ | 6 | Conventional FCM | 0.9510±0.0173 | 00:02:22 |
| | | MfGA based FCM | 0.9850±0.0011 | 00:01:58 |
| | | **Proposed** | **0.9874±0.0015** | **00:01:46** |
| | 8 | Conventional FCM | 0.9237±0.0144 | 00:02:57 |
| | | MfGA based FCM | 0.9831±0.0023 | 00:02:43 |
| | | **Proposed** | **0.9865±0.0009** | **00:02:01** |
| $F'$ | 6 | Conventional FCM | 273668.44±104648.48 | 00:02:39 |
| | | MfGA based FCM | 66674.73±9941.64 | 00:02:23 |
| | | **Proposed** | **43297.81±8716.32** | **00:01:51** |
| | 8 | Conventional FCM | 3275837.43±4373796.89 | 00:03:10 |
| | | MfGA based FCM | 404902.11±119179.93 | 00:02:48 |
| | | **Proposed** | **222546.40±67476.67** | **00:02:12** |
| Q | 6 | Conventional FCM | 16551.48±6437.06 | 00:02:40 |
| | | MfGA based FCM | 8830.74±654.32 | 00:02:05 |
| | | **Proposed** | **6972.52±314.87** | **00:01:51** |
| | 8 | Conventional FCM | 85576.15±13697.8 | 00:02:53 |
| | | MfGA based FCM | 51898.67±8452.06 | 00:02:41 |
| | | **Proposed** | **39273.63±5439.23** | **00:02:06** |

In Table 8, mean and standard deviation of fitness value for each algorithm are demonstrated. Mean time has taken by those algorithms are also reported here. If the accounted results are taken as consideration then it will be cleared that the proposed methodology outperforms than classical MfGA based FCM and conventional FCM.

*Table 5. Class boundaries and evaluated segmentation quality measures, ρ by different algorithms for different classes of Peppers image.*

| # segments | Algorithm | # | Class Levels | Fit val |
|---|---|---|---|---|
| 6 | Conventional FCM | 1 | R={45, 87, 118, 147, 176, 201} | 0.9190 |
| | | | G={10, 48, 96, 143, 178, 206} | |
| | | | B={7,42, 62, 92, 132, 184} | |
| | | 2 | R={45, 87, 118, 147, 176, 201} | 0.8964 |
| | | | G={10, 48,96, 143, 178, 206} | |
| | | | B={5, 39, 70, 92, 132, 184} | |
| | | 3 | **R={45, 87, 118, 147, 176, 201}** | **0.9197** |
| | | | **G={9, 52, 96, 143, 178, 206}** | |
| | | | **B={8, 39, 70, 92, 132, 184}** | |
| | MfGA based FCM | 1 | R={90, 116, 152, 181, 208, 233} | 0.9814 |
| | | | G={24, 63, 95, 126, 153, 196 } | |
| | | | B={57, 78, 99, 121, 152, 181} | |
| | | 2 | R={42, 87, 120, 147, 175, 200} | 0.9837 |
| | | | G={15, 48, 99, 142, 178, 206} | |
| | | | B={8,39, 70, 92, 131, 185} | |
| | | 3 | **R={45, 87, 118, 147, 176, 201}** | **0.9850** |
| | | | **G={10, 48, 96, 143, 178, 206}** | |
| | | | **B={8,39, 70, 92, 132, 184}** | |
| | Proposed | 1 | R={45, 88, 118, 150, 176, 200} | 0.9865 |
| | | | G={10, 48, 96, 145, 178, 204} | |
| | | | B={8,42, 70, 93, 132, 184} | |
| | | 2 | **R={45, 87, 116, 147, 176, 201}** | **0.9889** |
| | | | **G={10, 49, 96, 141, 178, 206}** | |
| | | | **B={8, 39, 73, 92, 132, 189}** | |
| | | 3 | R={45, 87, 118, 147, 176, 201} | 0.9878 |
| | | | G={10, 48, 96, 143, 178, 208} | |
| | | | B={6, 42, 70, 92, 132, 185} | |

*continued on following page*

79

*Table 5. Continued*

| # segments | Algorithm | # | Class Levels | Fit val |
|---|---|---|---|---|
| 8 | Conventional FCM | 1 | R={41, 80, 110, 129, 150, 172, 192, 208}<br>G={5, 32, 54, 90, 126, 159, 184, 208}<br>B={6, 30, 44, 67, 86, 109, 147, 191} | 0.9289 |
| | | 2 | **R={42, 79, 111, 129, 152, 172, 198, 203}**<br>**G={5,33,54,91,125,159,184,208}**<br>**B={5,30,43,63,80,108,147,191}** | **0.9436** |
| | | 3 | R={42,81,109,129,155,172,198,209}<br>G={5,33,54,91,125,160,184,208}<br>B={5,30,44,69,80,108,147,191} | 0.9164 |
| | MfGA based FCM | 1 | **R={40,77,108,127,148,170,190,207}**<br>**G={5,32,53,90,125,159,184,208}**<br>**B={6,35,51,74,91,115,193,152}** | **0.9841** |
| | | 2 | R={41,79,110,129,150,171,192,208}<br>G={5,32,53,90,125,159,184,208}<br>B={5,29,43,67,86,109,147,191} | 0.9833 |
| | | 3 | R={41,80,110,129,151,172,192,208}<br>G={5,32,53,90,125,159,184,208}<br>B={5,30,44,68,86,109,148,191} | 0.9812 |
| | Proposed | 1 | R={42,78,110,127,148,171,190,207}<br>G={5,32,53,93,125,163,185,208}<br>B={6,37,51,74,89,115,193,152} | 0.9873 |
| | | 2 | R={40,77,108,127,148,170,190,207}<br>G={5,32,53,90,125,159,184,208}<br>B={6,35,51,74,91,118,193,152} | 0.9879 |
| | | 3 | **R={42,77,108,129,148,170,190,209}**<br>**G={5,32,51,90,125,159,184,208}**<br>**B={8,35,51,74,90,115,193,155}** | **0.9884** |

80

*Table 6. Class boundaries and evaluated segmentation quality measures, **F′** by different algorithms for different classes of Peppers image.*

| # segments | Algorithm | # | Class Levels | Fit val |
|---|---|---|---|---|
| 6 | Conventional FCM | 1 | R={ 45, 89, 110, 150, 166, 198 }<br>G={8, 49, 98, 143, 178, 206}<br>B={ 6, 41, 64, 91, 132, 184} | 493779.18 |
| | | 2 | **R={ 48, 85, 118, 147, 176, 199 }**<br>**G={10,59, 91, 140, 178, 202}**<br>**B={ 8, 41, 70, 92, 132, 184}** | **214505.86** |
| | | 3 | R={ 48, 75, 111, 147, 176, 198 }<br>G={10, 51, 98, 143, 178, 200}<br>B={ 8, 41,78, 92, 132, 184} | 476584.74 |
| | MfGA based FCM | 1 | **R={45, 87, 118, 147, 176, 201}**<br>**G={10, 48, 96, 143, 178,206}**<br>**B={8, 39, 70, 92, 132, 184}** | **36987.49** |
| | | 2 | R={49, 83, 120, 147, 178, 200}<br>G={10, 48, 96, 143, 206, 178}<br>B={8, 39, 70, 92, 132, 184} | 45896.87 |
| | | 3 | R={48, 87, 118, 147, 176, 201}<br>G={10, 51,96, 143,187, 208 }<br>B={6, 41, 69, 92, 132, 184} | 54256.52 |
| | Proposed | 1 | **R={51, 89, 120, 147, 176, 201}**<br>**G={10, 48, 96, 143, 179,208}**<br>**B={8, 39, 71, 92, 132, 185}** | **21547.91** |
| | | 2 | R={45, 87, 118, 145, 176, 202}<br>G={11, 48, 96, 143, 178,206}<br>B={7, 39, 70, 92, 132, 184} | 26797.79 |
| | | 3 | R={45, 89, 118, 147, 178, 201}<br>G={10, 51, 96, 143, 181,206}<br>B={7, 39, 10, 92, 132, 184} | 31687.54 |

*continued on following page*

81

*Table 6. Continued*

| # segments | Algorithm | # | Class Levels | Fit val |
|---|---|---|---|---|
| 8 | Conventional FCM | 1 | **R={40,80,112,129,155,172,192,208}**<br>**G={6,35,55,98,132,163,187,209}**<br>**B={6,38,52,76,91,115,152, 193}** | **1270489.09** |
| | | 2 | R={41,79,110,130,150,172,192,208}<br>G={6,35,56,98,132,187,163,209}<br>B={5,37,52,71,91,112,152, 199} | 2976124.94 |
| | | 3 | R={41,79,110,129,150,169,192,208}<br>G={4,34,54,97,130,187,163,209}<br>B={6,35,52,74,91,115,152, 193} | 2457839.24 |
| | MfGA based FCM | 1 | **R={41,79,110,129,150,171,208, 192}**<br>**G={5,34,55,95,130,162,186,209}**<br>**B={6,35,51,74,90,152,115,193}** | **413654.65** |
| | | 2 | R={41,79,110,129,150,172,192,208}<br>G={5,34,125,90,53,184,159,208}<br>B={5,31,45,69, 110,123,148,191} | 453259.44 |
| | | 3 | R={41,79,110,150,129,152,172,208}<br>G={5,33,54,92,127,160,185,208}<br>B={5,31,44,68,86,110,191,148} | 513697.46 |
| | Proposed | 1 | **R={41,81,110,129,150,171,208, 192}**<br>**G={5,34,52,95,131,167,186,209}**<br>**B={6,35,49,74,90,152,116,193}** | **298534.74** |
| | | 2 | R={41,79,111,129,150,171,198,208}<br>G={5,34,55,98,130,162,186,209}<br>B={6,35,51,74,90,152,115,193} | 312599.66 |
| | | 3 | R={45,80,110,131,150,171,208, 192}<br>G={5,34,55,95,130,162,186,209}<br>B={6,35,44,67,87,115,149,193} | 371675.49 |

*Table 7. Class boundaries and evaluated segmentation quality measures,* **Q** *by different algorithms for different classes of Peppers image.*

| # segments | Algorithm | # | Class Levels | Fit val |
|---|---|---|---|---|
| 6 | Conventional FCM | 1 | R={ 45, 89, 110, 150, 166, 198 }<br>G={8, 48, 96, 143, 178, 206}<br>B={ 6, 39, 64, 90, 132, 184} | 31566.56 |
| | | 2 | R={ 48, 85, 118, 147, 176, 201 }<br>G={10, 58, 90, 140, 178, 202}<br>B={ 8, 41, 70, 92, 132, 184} | 32759.42 |
| | | 3 | **R={ 48, 75, 111, 147, 176, 198 }**<br>**G={10, 48, 98, 143, 178, 200}**<br>**B={ 8, 39, 76, 92, 132, 184}** | **26457.05** |
| | MfGA based FCM | 1 | **R={45, 87, 118, 147, 176, 201}**<br>**G={10, 48, 96, 143, 178,206}**<br>**B={8, 39, 70, 92, 132, 184}** | **9546.87** |
| | | 2 | R={49, 83, 120, 147, 178, 200}<br>G={10, 48, 96, 143, 206, 178}<br>B={8, 39, 70, 92, 132, 184} | 9854.54 |
| | | 3 | R={45, 87, 118, 147, 176, 201}<br>G={10, 48,96, 143,187, 208 }<br>B={6, 40, 70, 92, 132, 184} | 10443.71 |
| | Proposed | 1 | R={51, 89, 120, 147, 176, 201}<br>G={10, 48, 96, 143, 179,208}<br>B={8, 39, 71, 92, 132, 185} | 7964.61 |
| | | 2 | **R={45, 87, 118, 145, 176, 202}**<br>**G={11, 48, 96, 143, 178,206}**<br>**B={8, 39, 70, 92, 132, 184}** | **7818.24** |
| | | 3 | R={45, 87, 118, 147, 178, 201}<br>G={10, 51, 96, 143, 181,206}<br>B={7, 39, 10, 92, 132, 184} | 8158.46 |

*continued on following page*

*Table 7. Continued*

| # segments | Algorithm | # | Class Levels | Fit val |
|---|---|---|---|---|
| 8 | Conventional FCM | 1 | **R={40,80,112,129,155,172,192,208}**<br>**G={6,38,55,98,132,163,187,209}**<br>**B={6,35,52,76,91,115,152, 193}** | **38569.22** |
| | | 2 | R={41,79,110,130,150,172,192,208}<br>G={6,38,56,97,132,187,163,209}<br>B={5,35,52,71,91,112,152, 195} | 39320.89 |
| | | 3 | R={41,79,110,129,150,169,192,208}<br>G={4,34,54,97,130,187,163,209}<br>B={6,35,52,74,91,115,152, 193} | 38628.41 |
| | MfGA based FCM | 1 | R={41,79,110,129,150,171,208, 192}<br>G={5,34,55,95,130,162,186,209}<br>B={6,32,51,74,90,152,115,193} | 33285.41 |
| | | 2 | **R={41,79,110,129,150,172,192,208}**<br>**G={5,32,125,90,53,184,159,208}**<br>**B={5,31,45,69, 110,123,148,191}** | **31316.45** |
| | | 3 | R={41,79,110,150,129,152,172,208}<br>G={5,33,54,92,127,160,185,208}<br>B={5,31,44,68,86,110,191,148} | 33654.86 |
| | Proposed | 1 | R={41,81,110,129,150,171,208, 192}<br>G={5,34,52,95,131,167,186,209}<br>B={6,35,49,74,90,152,116,193} | 29766.79 |
| | | 2 | **R={41,79,111,129,150,171,208, 192}**<br>**G={5,34,55,98,130,162,186,209}**<br>**B={6,35,51,74,90,152,115,193}** | **28497.41** |
| | | 3 | R={45,80,110,131,150,171,208, 192}<br>G={5,34,55,95,130,162,186,209}<br>B={6,35,44,67,87,115,149,193} | 31657.55 |

The segmented output results for each method according to fitness functions and class levels is reported here. Figure 8 presents the color segmented image of Lena for 6 segments based on fitness function $\rho$. Here the first row shows the segmented result by conventional FCM, second row represents segmented image by MfGA

*Table 8. Different algorithm based mean and standard deviation using different types of fitness functions and mean of time taken by different algorithms for Peppers image.*

| Fit. fn. | # segments | Algorithm | Mean ± Std. Div. | Mean time |
|---|---|---|---|---|
| ρ | 6 | Conventional FCM | 0.9098±0.0111 | 00:01:46 |
| | | MfGA based FCM | 0.9835±0.0054 | 00:01:24 |
| | | **Proposed** | **0.9869±0.0023** | **00:01:09** |
| | 8 | Conventional FCM | 0.9289±0.0329 | 00:02:51 |
| | | MfGA based FCM | 0.9826±0.0017 | 00:02:25 |
| | | **Proposed** | **0.9879±0.0043** | **00:02:02** |
| F′ | 6 | Conventional FCM | 316707.31±190897.43 | 00:02:06 |
| | | MfGA based FCM | 44909.88±6770.82 | 00:01:56 |
| | | **Proposed** | **26750.14±3717.35** | **00:01:24** |
| | 8 | Conventional FCM | 2313022.28±730888.96 | 00:03:12 |
| | | MfGA based FCM | 492546.95±76658.40 | 00:02:51 |
| | | **Proposed** | **326238.85±31805.60** | **00:02:06** |
| Q | 6 | Conventional FCM | 39094.12±29621.6 | 00:02:06 |
| | | MfGA based FCM | 10256.26±3028.12 | 00:01:56 |
| | | **Proposed** | **8074.45±2201.54** | **00:01:12** |
| | 8 | Conventional FCM | 39260.52±10019.85 | 00:03:08 |
| | | MfGA based FCM | 33894.33±2601.31 | 00:02:49 |
| | | **Proposed** | **27701.33±2809.64** | **00:02:04** |

based FCM and third row indicates segmented image by QIMfGA based FCM. In the same manner segmented images of Lena for 8 segment based on fitness function $Q$ are depicted in Figure 9.

In Figure 10 and Figure 11, 6-class levels and 8-class levels segmented result for Peppers image are depicted based on $F'$ and $Q$ as fitness functions respectively.

*Figure 8. 6-class segmented 256 × 256 Lena image with the class levels obtained by (a-c) FCM (d-f) MfGA based FCM (g-i) QIMfGA based FCM algorithm of three results of Table 1 with ρ as the quality measure.*

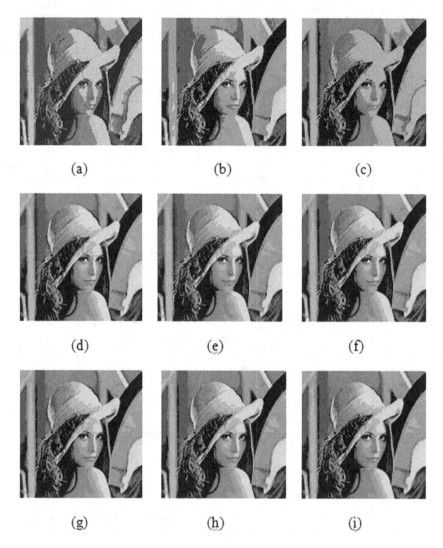

(a)  (b)  (c)

(d)  (e)  (f)

(g)  (h)  (i)

From those images it is clear that proposed algorithm is better than the classical MfGA based FCM and conventional FCM.

A statistical one way ANOVA analysis is also deduced here for each test images. This test ensures that rejection of null hypothesis. One way ANOVA test is actually

*Figure 9. 8-class segmented 256 × 256 Lena image with the class levels obtained by (a-c) FCM (d-f) MfGA based FCM (g-i) QIMfGA based FCM algorithm of three results of Table 3 with Q as the quality measure.*

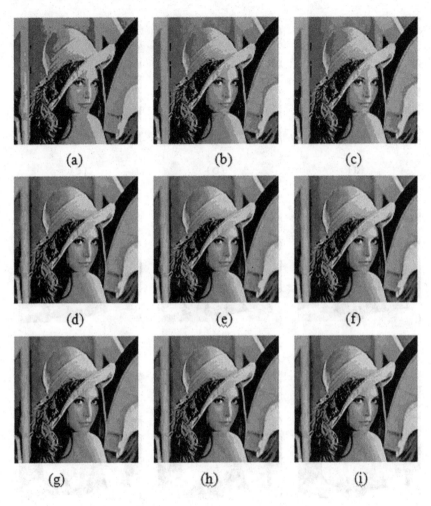

analyze statistical difference between more than two independent group mean. If the value of F is greater than value of $F_{crit}$ then it reject the null hypothesis. If the Table 9 and Table 10 are considered, then it will be clearly shown that $F > F_{crit}$ which indicates that they reject null hypothesis that means the group means are different and independent. In this analysis 5% significance level is used.

*Figure 10. 6-class segmented 256 × 256 Peppers image with the class levels obtained by (a-c) FCM (d-f) MfGA based FCM (g-i) QIMfGA based FCM algorithm of three results of Table 6 with F' as the quality measure.*

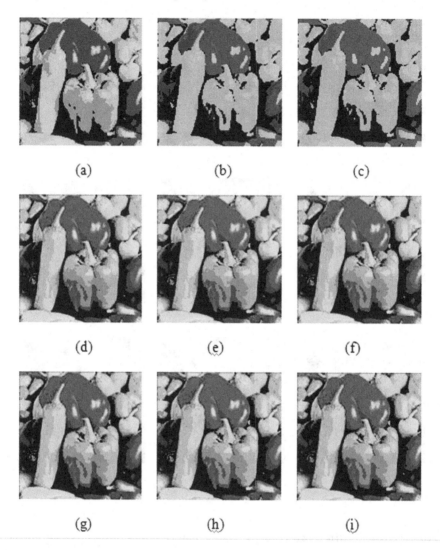

(a)  (b)  (c)

(d)  (e)  (f)

(g)  (h)  (i)

## CONCLUSION

A quantum induced modified genetic algorithm (QIMfGA) based FCM clustering approach is discussed here for segmentation of true color images. This method has

*Figure 11. 8-class segmented 256 × 256 Peppers image with the class levels obtained by (a-c) FCM (d-f) MfGA based FCM (g-i) QIMfGA based FCM algorithm of three results of Table 7 with Q as the quality measure.*

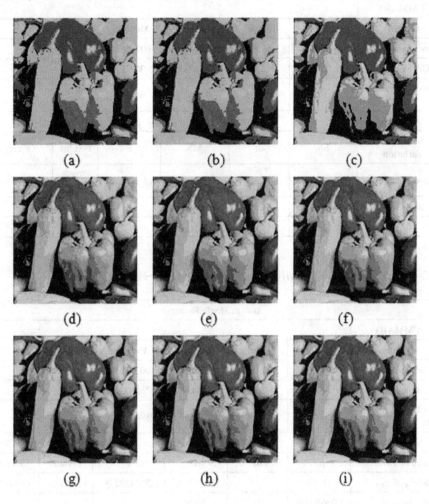

been compared with its classical counterpart and also with conventional FCM. In this article class levels for different number of segments based on different fitness functions are reported. The convergence time of FCM for each method are also shown here. Considering all accounted results, one can concluded that after incorporating quantum concepts into classical methods the results are changed in drastic manner. Quantum version is not only efficient by its fitness value but it also effectively

*Table 9. Single ANOVA analysis based on for ρ for Lena image*

| Anova: Single Factor | | | | | | |
|---|---|---|---|---|---|---|
| **SUMMARY** | | | | | | |
| **Groups** | **Count** | **Sum** | **Average** | **Variance** | | |
| Conventional FCM | 10 | 9.2367 | 0.92367 | 0.00020968 | | |
| MfGA based FCM | 10 | 9.8311 | 0.98311 | 5.0677E-06 | | |
| QIMfGA based FCM | 10 | 9.8655 | 0.98655 | 8.9611E-07 | | |
| **ANOVA** | | | | | | |
| **Source of Variation** | **SS** | **df** | **MS** | **F** | **P-value** | **F crit** |
| Between Groups | 0.024996139 | 2 | 0.012498069 | 173.867367 | 3.786E-16 | 3.354130829 |
| Within Groups | 0.001940835 | 27 | 7.18828E-05 | | | |
| Total | 0.026936974 | 29 | | | | |

*Table 10. Single ANOVA analysis based on for Q for Peppers image*

| Anova: Single Factor | | | | | | |
|---|---|---|---|---|---|---|
| **SUMMARY** | | | | | | |
| **Groups** | **Count** | **Sum** | **Average** | **Variance** | | |
| Conventional FCM | 10 | 392605.29 | 39260.529 | 100397451.1 | | |
| MfGA based FCM | 10 | 338943.35 | 33894.335 | 6766814.343 | | |
| QIMfGA based FCM | 10 | 277013.35 | 27701.335 | 7894109.613 | | |
| **ANOVA** | | | | | | |
| **Source of Variation** | **SS** | **df** | **MS** | **F** | **P-value** | **F crit** |
| Between Groups | 669214202 | 2 | 334607101 | 8.724452278 | 0.001195 | 3.354131 |
| Within Groups | 1.036E+09 | 27 | 38352792 | | | |
| Total | 1.705E+09 | 29 | | | | |

reduces execution time which makes it cost effective. From all stated and presented facts and figures it is concluded that the proposed methodology qualitatively and quantitatively is more superior to its classical approach and conventional FCM for true color image segmentation.

# REFERENCES

Amelio, A., & Pizzuti, C. (2013). A Genetic Algorithm for Color Image Segmentation. In A. I. Esparcia-Alc'azar (Eds.), *EvoApplications, LNCS 7835* (pp. 314–323). Verlag Berlin Heidelberg. doi:10.1007/978-3-642-37192-9_32

Anh, N. T. L., Kim, S. H., Yang, H. J., & Lee, G. S. (2013). Color Image Segmentation using Morphological Gradient based Active Contour Model. *International Journal of Innovative Computing, Information, & Control, 9*(11), 4471–7784.

Arumugadevi, S., & Seenivasagam, V. (2016). Color Image Segmentation Using Feedforward Neural Networks with FCM. *International Journal of Automation and Computing, 13*(5), 491–500. doi:10.1007/s11633-016-0975-5

Bezdek, J. C. (1981). *Pattern Recognition with Fuzzy Objective Function Algorithms.* New York: Plenum. doi:10.1007/978-1-4757-0450-1

Bhattacharyaa, S. (2011). A Brief Survey of Color Image Preprocessing and Segmentation Techniques. *Journal of Pattern Recognition Research, 1*(1), 120–129. doi:10.13176/11.191

Borsotti, M., Campadelli, P., & Schettini, R. (1998). Quantitative evaluation of color image segmentation results. *Pattern Recognition Letters, 19*(8), 741–747. doi:10.1016/S0167-8655(98)00052-X

Chaabane, S. B., Bouchouicha, M., & Fnaiech, F. (2015). *A Hybrid Technique for Color Image Segmentation: Application to the Fire Forest Images. International Journal of Scientific Engineering and Research.*

Chen, M., & Ludwig, S. A. (2017). *Color Image Segmentation Using Fuzzy C-Regression Model.* Advances in Fuzzy Systems.

Das, S., & De, S. (2016). Multilevel Color Image segmentation using Modified Genetic Algorithm (MfGA) inspired Fuzzy C-Means Clustering. *Second International Conference on Research and Computational Intelligence and Communication Networks (ICRCICN), 1,* 78-83. doi:10.1109/ICRCICN.2016.7813635

De, S., Bhattacharyya, S., & Chakraborty, S. (2010). True color image segmentation by an optimized multilevel activation function. *IEEE International Conference on Computational Intelligence and Computing Research,* 545-548. doi:10.1109/ICCIC.2010.5705833

De, S., Bhattacharyya, S., & Chakraborty, S. (2012). Color image segmentation using parallel OptiMUSIG activation function. *Appl. Soft Comp. J., 12*(10), 3228–3236. doi:10.1016/j.asoc.2012.05.011

De, S., Bhattacharyya, S., & Chakraborty, S. (2013). Color Image Segmentation by NSGA-II based ParaOptiMUSIG Activation Function. *IEEE International Conference on Machine Intelligence Research and Advancement*, 105 - 109. doi:10.1109/ICMIRA.2013.27

Dey, S., Bhattacharyya, S., & Maulik, U. (2013). Quantum inspired meta-heuristic algorithms for multi-level thresholding for true colour images. *2013 Annual IEEE Conference on India Conference (INDICON)*, 1-6. doi:10.1109/INDCON.2013.6726024

Dey, S., Bhattacharyya, S., & Maulik, U. (2014). New quantum inspired tabu search for multi-level colour image thresholding. *2014 IEEE International Conference on Computing for Sustainable Global Development (INDIACom)*, 311-316. doi:10.1109/IndiaCom.2014.6828150

Dong, G., & Xie, M. (2005). Color Clustering and Learning for Image Segmentation Based on Neural Networks. *IEEE Transactions on Neural Networks*, *16*(4), 925–936. doi:10.1109/TNN.2005.849822 PMID:16121733

Dunn, J. C. (1973). A Fuzzy Relative of the ISODATA Process and Its Use in Detecting Compact Well-Separated Clusters. *Journal of Cybernetics*, *3*(3), 32–57. doi:10.1080/01969727308546046

Goldberg, D. E. (1989). *Genetic Algorithm in Search Optimization and Machine Learning*. New York: Addison-Wesley.

Gonzalez, R. C., & Woods, R. E. (2002). *Digital image processing*. Upper Saddle River, NJ: Prentice Hall.

Harrabi, R., & Braiek, E. B. (2014). Color image segmentation using a modified Fuzzy C-Means technique and different color spaces: Application in the breast cancer cells images. *2014 1st International Conference on Advanced Technologies for Signal and Image Processing (ATSIP)*, 231-236.

Krishna, R. V. V., & Kumar, S. S. (2015). Color Image Segmentation using Soft Rough Fuzzy-C-Means Clustering and SMO Support Vector Machine. *An International Journal on Signal & Image Processing*, *6*(5), 49. doi:10.5121/sipij.2015.6504

Kulkarni, N. (2012). Color Thresholding Method for Image Segmentation of Natural Images, *I.J. Image. Graphics and Signal Processing*, *1*(1), 28–34. doi:10.5815/ijigsp.2012.01.04

Lee, J., Huang, X., & Zhu, Q. (2010). Decomposing Fredkin Gate into Simple Reversible Elements with Memory. *International Journal of Digital Content Technology and its Applications*, *4*(5).

Li, Y., Feng, S., Zhang, X., & Jiao, L. (2014). SAR image segmentation based on quantum-inspired multiobjective evolutionary clustering algorithm. *Information Processing Letters*, *114*(6), 287–293. doi:10.1016/j.ipl.2013.12.010

Maitra, A., & Parashar, P. (2005). *Hadamard type operations for qubits.* arXiv:quant-ph/0505068v1

Mao, X., Zhang, Y., Hu, Y., & Binjie, S. (2009). Color Image Segmentation Method Based on Region Growing and Ant Colony Clustering. *Intelligent Systems, GCIS*, *09*. doi:10.1109/GCIS.2009.344

Mcmohan, D. (2008). *Quantum computing explained.* Hoboken, NJ: John Wiley & Sons.

Mekhmoukh, A., & Mokrani, K. (2015). Improved Fuzzy C-Means based Particle Swarm Optimization (PSO) initialization and outlier rejection with level set methods for MR brain image segmentation. *Computer Methods and Programs in Biomedicine*, *122*(2), 266–281. doi:10.1016/j.cmpb.2015.08.001 PMID:26299609

Menon, P. S., & Ritwik, M. (2014). A Comprehensive but not Complicated Survey on Quantum Computing. *2014 International Conference on Future Information Engineering*, *10*, 144 – 152. doi:10.1016/j.ieri.2014.09.069

Muthukrishnan, A. (1999). *Classical and Quantum Logic Gates: An Introduction to Quantum Computing.* Quantum Information Seminar, Rochester Center for Quantum Information.

Nebti, S. (2013). Bio-Inspired Algorithms for Color Image Segmentation. *International Journal of Computers and Applications*, *73*(18).

Nielsen, M. A., & Chuang, I. L. (2002). *Quantum Computation and Quantum Information.* Cambridge University Press.

Preetha, M. M. S. J., Suresh, L. P., & Bosco, M. J. (2015). Cuckoo Search Based Color Image Segmentation Using Seeded Region Growing. In C. Kamalakannan, L. Suresh, S. Dash, & B. Panigrahi (Eds.), Power Electronics and Renewable Energy Systems (Vol. 326). New Delhi: Academic Press. doi:10.1007/978-81-322-2119-7_154

Rahman, H., & Islam, R. (2013). Segmentation of color image using adaptive thresholding and masking with watershed algorithm. *2013 International Conference on Informatics, Electronics & Vision (ICIEV)*. doi:10.1109/ICIEV.2013.6572557

Talbi, H., Draa, A., & Batouche, M. (2004). A New Quantum-Inspired Genetic Algorithm for Solving the Travelling Salesman Problem. *2004 IEEE International Conference on Industrial Technology*, *3*, 1192-1197.

Tao, W., Jin, H., & Zhang, Y. (2007). Color Image Segmentation Based on Mean Shift and Normalized Cuts. *IEEE Transactions on Systems, Man, and Cybernetics, Part B (Cybernetics)*, *37*(5), 1382 – 1389. doi: 10.1109/TSMCB.2007.902249

Verma, O. P., Hanmandlu, M., Susan, S., Kulkarni, M., & Jain, P. K. (2011). A Simple Single Seeded Region Growing Algorithm for Color Image Segmentation using Adaptive Thresholding. *2011 International Conference on Communication Systems and Network Technologies (CSNT)*. doi:10.1109/CSNT.2011.107

Zadeh, L. A. (1965). Fuzzy sets. *Information and Control*, *8*(3), 338–353. doi:10.1016/S0019-9958(65)90241-X

## KEY TERMS AND DEFINITIONS

**Cluster:** Data having homogeneous characteristics form a group called a cluster.

**Clustering:** It is a segmentation technique that groups the objects in such a manner that objects of the same group are more similar than objects residing in other groups.

**FCM:** It is a soft clustering technique used for segmentation purpose. It works on the principle of fuzzy set theory.

**Genetic Algorithm:** It is a probabilistic technique used to achieve optimal solutions for large problem space. It imitates working procedures of natural evolution.

**Quantum Computing:** It makes the direct use of quantum mechanics principle on data to get more reliable output.

**Segmentation:** In this process a set of non-homogeneous data are partitioned in non-overlapping homogeneous data sets.

**Statistical Measure:** It provides some mathematical formulas that are used to assess the quality of the output image.

# Chapter 4
# Hardware Implementation of a Visual Image Watermarking Scheme Using Qubit/Quantum Computation Through Reversible Methodology

**Subhrajit Sinha Roy**
*Global Institute of Management and Technology, India*

**Abhishek Basu**
*RCC Institute of Information Technology, India*

**Avik Chattopadhyay**
*University of Calcutta, India*

## ABSTRACT

*In this chapter, hardware implementation of an LSB replacement-based digital image watermarking algorithm is introduced. The proposed scheme is developed in spatial domain. In this watermarking process, data or watermark is implanted into the cover image pixels through an adaptive last significant bit (LSB) replacement technique. The real-time execution of the watermarking logic is developed here using reversible logic. Utilization of reversible logic reduces the power dissipation by means of no information loss. The lesser power dissipation enables a faster operation as well as holds up Moore's law. The experimental results confirm that the proposed scheme offers high imperceptibility with a justified robustness.*

DOI: 10.4018/978-1-5225-5219-2.ch004

## INTRODUCTION

New age digital data communication offers easy access over data processing. So, Data security is essential to put off illegitimate copying or forgery attempts over transmission channel. The increasing consumer number proportionally causes a huge data augmentation which is easily performed in digital domain. But the possessor demands a copyright protection to their belongings multimedia data so that the information remains tenable. Thus the copyright protection has become a challenging research point in this rapidly developing multimedia communication domain. A good number of secured data transmission methods are invented in terms of cryptography, steganography, digital watermarking etc. during last few decades.

In cryptography the message itself converted into a distinct and unreadable form and transmitted through a secret channel. Cryptographic systems are unable to provide enough protection and reliability for data authentication. Moreover the cryptographic techniques are not reversible in nature which causes data loss. Steganography is a point to point data transmitting process where the message is made imperceptible in a cover object. The message may have nothing to do with the cover as the cover is required only to serve the purpose of concealment. On the other hand digital watermarking is the process to embed a unique code (may be in form of text or image or any multimedia object), said watermark into a cover object to make an assertion on it. Being offering a one-to-many communication without any type of secret channel or encryption, watermarking is preferred for copyright protection.

A good number of digital watermarking algorithms have been developed to reach the maximum rate of efficiency in terms of three exigent qualities of – robustness, imperceptibility and payload capacity. The software logic level development for insertion process can be performed in spatial or frequency domain. Though the frequency domain provides robustness, spatial domain is chosen for effective real time hardware implementation.

Field programmable gate array (FPGA) is one of the most intended tools for hardware execution but the more alarming issue of modern VLSI industry is power dissipation. The exponential growth of transistors within an IC causes generation of heat which results into information loss. Therefore supporting the pace of Moore's law has become gradually more complicated over modern systems. The solution was received from the new age quantum computation. The development of quantum hardware also defines the hardware software co-simulation. This quantum computation can be performed through Reversible circuits of which logic operations theoretically ensure zero percent computational sate data loss and thus the inputs could be recovered from the outputs. This property can be fully utilized in designing the hardware architecture of an effective watermarking embedding and extracting model with minimum power dissipation.

## DIGITAL WATERMARKING

Watermarking is the process of inserting a mark into a multimedia object to make an assertion on the owner or the originality of the object. The use of watermark is an old age art. It began after a little time span of invention of paper manufacturing procedure. At that time, to manufacture paper, a semi liquid mixture of fiber and water is poured in a frame of mesh and distributed throughout the frame to give a proper shape and finally by applying pressure leaving off the water the fiber is cohered. In the wet fiber a picture or text can be impressed from a negative and it left a permanent mark on the paper – fibers when the fibers compressed and dried. As by water vaporization the mark is manufactured, it is called 'watermark', Mohanty, S.P. (1999).

In another discussion, it is noted that the watermarking mechanism was first invented about 700 years ago in Fabriano Itally, Kutter M. (1999). In this mechanism to label an article in an invincible manner a portion of the article was made slightly thin. The thinner location of the particular article could be perceived by looking at it when it is held against a strong light source. As the thinner portion looked like watery area on the article, it was called watermark.

The ancient age watermark embedding process cannot sustain for the first-rate growth of modern communication technology with multimedia objects. Now a day the cover object may be audio, video, image or text which is mostly preferred in a form of digital signal. Another multimedia object should be formed as a unique mark i.e. the watermark to embed into the cover object.

## Basic Operations of Digital Watermarking

Throughout the discussion, authors have chosen image as the multimedia objects to be used as cover or watermark for better comparison as most of the works have been developed using image and any image can be represented through a 2-D matrix form. Any type of digital watermarking process principally consists of three operational blocks –

1. Watermark Insertion Block
2. Transmission Block or Channel
3. Watermark Extraction Block

As shown in Figure 1, in the insertion block the data or watermark is injected to the cover image and the watermarked image is generated. The watermark image is transmitted over the communication channel and at the receiving end an extraction block is required. It recovers the watermark bits and reconstructs the watermark to

*Figure 1. General Block Diagram of Water Encoder & Extractor*

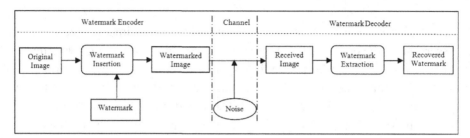

judge the novelty by comparing with the original one. During transmission, signal processing attacks or noise can affect the cover as well as the watermark. Thus in the time of embedding a watermark, it is desired to achieve the maximum robustness as well as energy. In maximize the signal energy designer should try to decrease the error rate.

## Applications and Classifications of Digital Watermarking

The application domain of digital watermarking expands as follows:

- **Copyright Protection:** The most distinct application of digital watermarking is copyright protection. As lots of multimedia objects are exchanged over insecure network every time, the copyright protection has become a vital issue. Because of availability of the images through internet, these will be used without payment of royalty. So, watermark acting as an ownership mark can restrain the redistribution of the object.
- **Content Protection:** If content (like library manuscript) stamped with a robust and visible watermark, it will indicate the ownership original. So, the content can be made available through the internet and be distributed more freely and publicly.
- **Content Labeling:** Watermark may carry more information about the object like quality, manufacturer's description etc. This is known as content labeling.
- **Authentication:** In some applications like ATM cards, ID cards, Credit cards etc., the ownership of the contain has to be verified. This quarry can be solved by embedding a watermark and in addition by providing the owner with a private key to access the message.
- **Evidence of Ownership:** Invisible watermarking may also used in copyright protection. Here it plays a roll of ownership evidence. That means the seller's watermark in the object proves that the public object is property of the seller

not produced illegally or without payment of royalties by copying or editing the object.

- **Misappropriation Detection:** It may occur that someone bought a fee generating object from a license owner and sell these objects in cheap or free of cost, keeping of the revenue license owner. This type of fraudulent business can be restrained by invisible watermarking.
- **Tamper Detection:** By using the Fragile Watermarks any type of tampering on the object where the water mark was embedded, can be detected. Because, it tampering happened, the watermark will be degenerated or distorted.
- **Trustworthy Detection:** Invisible watermarking may also use in a trustworthy camera to indicate the images have been originally captured by the camera not produced by editing or falsifying any scene. Actually, at the time of capturing a picture an invisible watermark is embedded into the picture.
- **Digital Fingerprinting:** To justify the owner of as content, or to detect any alternation of object store in a digital library, it is used. Because for each party or object there should be a unique fingerprint.
- **Broadcast Monitoring:** It mainly helps the advertising companies to verify whether the advertisement broadcasted on T.V. or Radio appeared for the right duration or not.
- **Source Tracking:** Is another application of Digital Watermarking.

The dilate application field of digital watermarking has categorized this process in several ways.

1. According to the human perception watermarking can be classified in two types-
   a. **Visible**: It is used mainly in purpose of identification of the owner. It always robust in nature.
   b. **Invisible**: It is used for authentication and copyright protection. This section may further be divided into two types such as- Robust, Fragile.
2. Working domain of digital watermark is divided in two types-
   a. **Spatial Domain**: In this technique randomly, selected pixels are modified.
   b. **Frequency Domain**: In frequency domain secret data is embedded into the best frequency portions of the protected image.
3. According to application water marking is also of two types, which are-
   a. **Source Based**: Used for ownership identification
   b. **Destination Based**: Used to trace buyer in case of illegal reselling.

Now, invisible watermarking it is preferred that the aesthetic magnificence of the cover image should not affected by the mark. But these two properties are opposing to each other. Moreover, to obtain a better visual transparency, payload should be reduced. To overcome this trade off a number of watermarking algorithms have been developed during last few decades.

A software algorithm deals with the challenges in terms of imperceptibility, robustness and payload capacity. Whereas in case of hardware implementation of the algorithms, the main considerations are power dissipation, energy, speed and space efficiency. In the recent years, the reversible logic has obtained immense interest in low power VLSI design because of their capability to trim down the power dissipation with a high-speed computation. Moreover, in reversible computation, the process is allowed to run both in forward and backward path i.e. the inputs can be generated from the outputs. Thus, the authors have employed reversible logic technique in hardware implementation of the proposed watermarking scheme.

## LITERATURE SURVEY

Paper watermark was first brought up in Italy in late 13th century paper watermark was first introduced in Italy to be a symbol of design, class recognition and ownership proof. Very soon this technique spread over whole Europe, Emery, O. (1958), Weiner J. and Mirkes K. (1972). The paper watermarking technique is utilized in protecting legal papers, postage stamps, currencies whole over the world till now, Jaseena K.U. et al. (2011). But the concept of digital or electronic watermarking was first invented by Tanaka et al. (1990) and it was brought into use by Tirkel et al. (1993). Since that time, digital watermarking started putting on preferences as a copyright protection tool. As discussed in the earlier section, the efficiency or acceptance of any digital watermarking scheme can be measured generally through three qualities– Imperceptibility, Robustness and Payload capacity. These three features are contradictory to each other Liu N et al. (2006) & Juergen S. (2005) and a number of methods have been developed to deal with these tradeoffs among them. The watermarking techniques, developed in several ways, can be categorized principally in two domains. One is the spatial domain where the cover image pixels are directly modified by the watermark, Lin P-L, (2001), Megalingam, R.K. (2010), Mukherjee D.P. (2004) & Mohanty Saraju P. et al. (2006). And another one is frequency domain where data embedding is performed after converting the cover and watermark images into frequency domain. The frequency domain transfer operation may be performed using different transforms like discrete wavelet transform, Lalitha (2013), discrete cosine transform (DCT), Patra J. C. et al. (2010), discrete Fourier transform (DFT), Ming Li Dong (2012) etc. Although the frequency domain offers a better robustness with respect to the spatial domain techniques, but when imperceptibility is given higher preference, the spatial domain practices result superior. Moreover for real time implementation spatial domain is preferred again for its less computational cost and easy to implement feature Grgic Mislav (2009) & Maity S. P. (2009).

In this section a concise review on some recent trade of digital watermarking techniques is provided. Khandare S., and Shrawankar U. (2015) proposed a digital image watermarking algorithm for secured and classified data transmission which works on bit depth plane. The system is consists of two processes. At first the image is translated into classified information through maximum likelihood categorization and fuzzy logic. In the later process the classified image is got copyright protected by means of watermarking. Xiang-yang et al. (2015) developed a robust digital watermarking scheme based on local polar harmonic transform. The watermark inserted through this algorithm, can sustain against several signal processing noises as well as geometric distortions. Moreover the watermark does not cause any visual distortion for this embedding process. A comprehensive sensing method based watermarking method was introduced by Hong, L. et al. (2016), where the original image is encrypted with the sensing process. A Scalar-Costa algorithm is involved here to implant the watermark into the encrypted image. The study of the practice confirms supremacy in terms of robustness and hiding capacity. Hu Hwai-Tsu & Ling-Yuan Hsu (2016) used mixed modulation to develop a blind digital image watermarking scheme. Here watermark embedding is executed through Quantization index modulation and Relative modulation. This is basically a discrete cosine transfer domain based algorithm. For the transfer coefficients with small estimation differences, the relative modulation is activated for the watermark implanting process. If the estimation variation surpasses the preset boundary threshold the Quantization index modulation is drawn on. To close down the concept of verification via password, Wioletta and Ogiela (2015) projected a bimodal biometric validation based digital image watermarking scheme. In this technique a fingerprint along with iris biometrics is considered as watermark and embedded into a sovereign region of the cover image to form the watermarked image. The testing results confirm that the projected system facilitates authentication of images with a remarkable precision level. A discrete wavelet transform based digital image watermarking algorithm using probabilistic neural network was projected by AL-Nabhani et al. (2015) where robustness is considered as a top priority. In this approach a Haar filter is utilized with DWT to embed binary watermark in preferred coefficient regions of cover image. In the time of extraction of the watermark a probabilistic neural network is exploited. It is revealed from the experimental results that the method is useful to overcome the trade-off between imperceptibility and robustness.

A novel color image watermarking scheme is developed in spatial domain by Thongkor Kharittha et al. (2015). This is a blind method where regularized filters are utilized to insert watermark within the blue color component of the cover image. A hologram authentication scheme using reversible fragile watermarking was developed by Chan Hao-Tang et al. (2015). In this technique watermark is embedded into hologram image in transform domain, and then the image is laid up in spatial domain. The resolution of the image is restricted to provide transparency to the watermarked image. Zhou Wujie et al. (2016) proposed a fragile watermarking scheme for stereoscopic images that could be used for authentication through tamper detection. Here the embedding process is performed using just noticeable difference technique. The results show that the projected scheme provides better security with the hiding capacity and imperceptibility being justified. Sadreazami Hamidreza et al. (2016) introduced a new watermark decoder, designed in contourlet domain. This is basically a multiplicative decoder that utilizes the standard inverse Gaussian Probability Density Functions as a prior for the contourlet coefficients of images. Digital watermarking technique using Singular Value Decomposition and Discrete Wavelet Transform is also a new trend providing higher robustness, Shah P. et al. (2015). In this approach initially both of the cover image and watermark image are decomposed in the course of Discrete Wavelet Transform followed by Singular Value Decomposition in LL band. In next phase, through a scaling operation, the watermark values are injected by detecting and replacing the singular values in every sub-band. An HVS (human visual system) based adaptive image watermarking scheme was developed in spatial domain by Sur A. et al. (2009). In this technique watermark is embedded into the least salient regions of the cover image providing a better perceptual transparency for the watermark. A spectral residual based saliency map model was utilized in digital watermarking model was introduced by Basu A. et al. (2015). In this approach, first the cover image is segmented according the pixel saliency obtained from the saliency map. The watermark bits are adaptively embedded into the image in such a manner that the least salient regions contain maximum amount of information. The FPGA implementation of this algorithm was also developed for real time execution. In another approach by Basu A. et al. (2016) described a further saliency based algorithm where utmost data is implanted into most salient regions. The experimental results show that this technique provides a better data transparency than the previous method according to the human visual stimuli. Tsai C. et al. (2005) introduced reversible technique in data hiding process for binary images and a lossless reform of the image is done using pair-wise logical calculation. Another reversible data hiding scheme was developed by Gui X. et al. (2014) where an adaptive data embedding is performed based on generalized prediction-error expansion. This technique provides an increased payload capacity.

## WATERMARK EMBEDDING AND EXTRACTING FRAMEWORK

This proposed algorithm is developed based on LSB replacement process as it is a spatial domain approach and easy to implement in hardware. Moreover through this technique the watermark can be made robust against several signal processing attacks like cropping, lossy compression or addition of any undesired noise. The watermark, being injected through replacing the LSBs, does not make any visual distortion to the cover image pixels.

The authors have chosen a gray image of size A×B as cover image and a C×D binary image as watermark to implement the algorithm of watermark insertion and extraction.

Let the cover image ($I_c$) and watermark ($I_w$) is defined by equation (1) and (2) respectively.

$$I_c = \{ \, i(a,b): 0 \leq a < A, \, 0 \leq b < B \, ^\wedge i(a,b) \in [0, 1, 2, \ldots, 255] \} \tag{1}$$

$$I_w = \{ \, i(c,d): 0 \leq c < C, \, 0 \leq d < D \, ^\wedge i(c,d) \in [0, 1] \} \tag{2}$$

Where i(a,b) is any cover image pixel consists of 8 bits and i(c,d) represents any watermark bit.

### Watermark Insertion Procedure

The insertion or embedding process has been illustrated in Figure 2. Here first each of the cover image pixels is segmented into eight sub-blocks. Thus each block contains one bit at a time. For each cover image pixel an adaptive bit replacement is performed for the block consists of the second least significant bit. The bit is replaced with the watermark bit if the cover image pixel value satisfies a certain

*Figure 2. Block Diagram for watermark insertion*

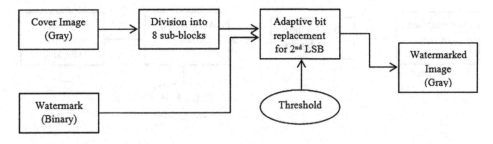

threshold value $i_t$. The value of $i_t$ can be varied suitably within the range of 0 to 255. Bits of all other sub-blocks together with the replaced watermark bit construct the watermarked image pixel. This process continued for all the pixels and multiple insertion process can be performed for a better robustness. It is obvious that the size of the original cover image and the watermarked image are same.

If the bits in the sub-blocks for any pixel i(a,b) of the cover image $I_C$ are noted as $x_0, x_1... x_7$ (from LSB to MSB), then the watermarked image $I_E$ can be defined as,

$$I_E = x_0 + 10.i(c,d) + \sum_{n=2}^{7} 10^n x_n \text{ for } I_C \geq i_t$$

$$= \sum_{n=0}^{7} 10^n x_n \text{ otherwise} \qquad (3)$$

Where i(c,d) is the watermark bit present in the queue at that time instant.

## Watermark Extraction Procedure

Similarity of a recovered watermark to the original one defines the authentication or originality of the cover object. Watermark extraction is performed through a method just reverse to the embedding algorithm. Here first the watermarked image pixels are segmented into 8 sub-blocks in a similar manner. Then the same threshold, used in during insertion process, is applied to obtain an adaptive extraction routine. Depending on the threshold value, 2nd LSBs from the image pixels are extracted. These retrieved bits together form the watermark that shows the novelty. The block diagram for watermark extraction is shown in Figure 3.

*Figure 3. Block Diagram for watermark extraction*

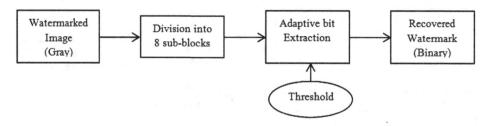

# HARDWARE IMPLEMENTATION OF WATERMARK EMBEDDING AND EXTRACTING ALGORITHMS

The proposed watermarking scheme is a simple copyright protection method. It is already discussed that copyright protection is a vital issue in digital communication and digital watermarking is the best solution to serve the purpose. So, this proposed methodology can be very useful to the owners willing to set copyright to their digital propoerties. For the software execution a system set-up is always required which may not be desirable for every time. Actually on-chip implementation is more effective than software as it leads to automation and distinct performance. Moreover running time is also justified in hardware or on-chip execution. Therefore, real-time implementation of this software based program is required for a fast execution with less power. Providing a better flexibility, easy execution and flawless performance, FPGA (field programmable gate arrays) techniques are mostly favored for hardware implementation. Similar to the software design, the hardware framework of any watermarking scheme also consists of two different algorithms: (i) Watermark Insertion and (ii) Watermark Extraction.

There are several units in both data embedding and extracting blocks and utilization of those units are discussed below. The FPGA architecture for watermark insertion is shown in Figure 4.

## Watermark Insertion Architecture

The embedding process starts with a cover image and a watermark being stored into a PIPO (Parallel-In-Parallel-Out) shift register and a 4×4 ROM respectively. Initially the cover image, resized into 8bits sub-blocks, is taken to the shift register. Then it passes through Flow Gate which consists of eight AND gate and its control the flow of data that if sub-blocks goes for watermarking or not. One input of each AND gate comes from output of PIPO and another input comes from 4bit counter which checks 2nd LSB bit of 16 sub-blocks are watermarked or not. The watermark embedding is performed by bit replacement process which depends on the decision of a combinational logic. If combinational logic value greater than or equal to the threshold value (which is "200" in decimal) then the 2nd bit of sub-block is replaced by data which is already stored in 4×4 ROM. ROM Outs preloaded 16bit data at a time and that will fed to Parallel-In-Serial-Out (PISO) register through which serially data replaces the 2nd bit of that 16 sub-blocks via 2:1 multiplexer whose select line comes from output of combinational circuit.

Data are out from encoder via Parallel-In-Parallel-Out (PIPO) shift register. All units of encoder are synchronized by one single clock.

*Figure 4. Block Diagram for FPGA design of watermark insertion*

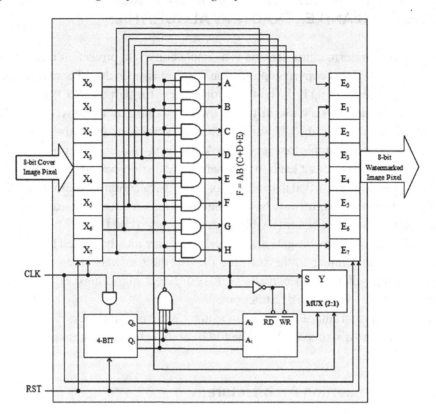

## Watermark Extraction Architecture

Extraction of the watermarked from a received image is essential to verify its novelty. Therefore designing a proper extraction algorithm for a corresponding embedding process is a vital issue. The watermark extraction framework also consists of numerous units like as watermark insertion block and some units have same function and utilization also. Here the received watermarked image, considered as the stego-image, is resized also into 1×8 sub-blocks and fed to Parallel-In-Parallel-Out (PIPO) and from there it is passes through Flow Gate (consist of AND gate) which control that al watermarked sub-blocks are passed through and watermark bits or logo are collected or not. The sub-blocks passes through then same combinational logic which is used in encoder and if decimal value of sub-block is equal or greater than threshold value(here this decimal value is "200") then 2nd LSB is send to a 16bit Serial-In-Parallel-Out (SIPO) and from SIPO we get the watermarked bits or logo. The FPGA block diagram of watermark extraction process is given in Figure 5.

*Figure 5. Block Diagram for FPGA design of watermark extraction*

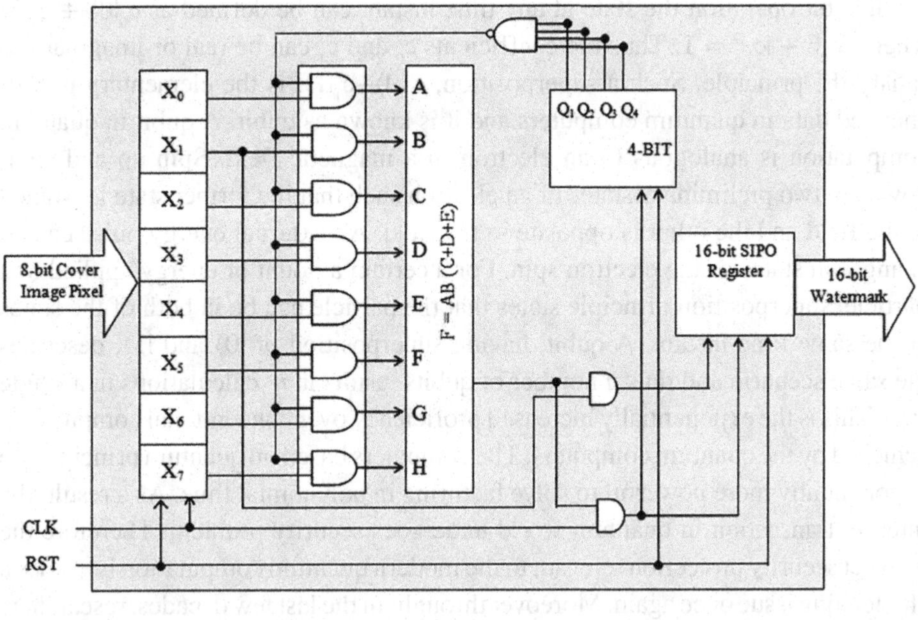

In the next section, the authors have projected how the reversible logic can be utilized in developing the real time circuit design for watermark embedding and extracting process. Here the combinational and sequential circuit units, involved in this process, are constructed through reversible logic gates. The operational behavior of those circuit blocks is also pointed out in this discussion.

## INTRODUCTION TO QUBIT AND REVERSIBLE LOGIC CIRCUITS:

Classical computing deals with the Boolean algebra where bits are physically represented by high and low voltages on wires or chip. The logic quantities process information in a sequence of '0' and '1' i.e. the digital data are quantized in two states i.e. '1' (as high) and '0' (as low). So, at a particular time instant it is considered to be in one state condition for the basic building blocks of the logic family like transistor, capacitor etc. But in practical the time taken for every transistor or capacitor to exchange states is quantifiable in billionths of a moment. Thus from the quantum-mechanics view point at any time instant the state of an information bit can be described in many different ways, Dasgupta S. et al., (2006). For an example, if the ground or OFF state is noted as |0⟩ and the excited or ON state is noted as $|1\rangle$, then according to the superposition principle of quantum theory, for a single bit operation the state at any time instant can be defined as $c_0|0\rangle + c_1|1\rangle$ where, $|c_0|^2 + |c_1|^2 = 1$. Thus the coefficients $c_0$ and $c_1$ can be real or imaginary to satisfy the principle. Such a superposition, $c_0|0\rangle+c_1|1\rangle$, is the elementary unit of encoded data in quantum computers and it is known as qubit. A qubit in quantum computation is analogous to an electron in a magnetic field. Spin-up and spin-down are two preliminary states of an electron such that the former state is aligned to the field and the other is opposite to the field. An external energy pulse causes changes in states of the electron spin. For a certain amount of energy applied to a particle, superposition principle states that the particle can be in both of the states at the same time instant. A qubit, having superposition of $|0\rangle$ and $|1\rangle$, describes the same scenario and thus $n$ number of qubits results in $n^2$ calculations in a single step. This is the exponentially increased proficiency over conventional computation achieved by the quantum computers. The computers based on quantum principle are exponentially more powerful to solve factoring in polynomial time. As a result, the internet transaction in quantum world undergoes security problem. Therefore the internet security protection relevant to the modern quantum computation becomes a challenging issue once again. Moreover throughout the last few decades, researchers successfully performed in quantum computation inspired network security and intelligence like Cryptography, Mayers D. (1998), image clustering, Pappas (1992), neural networks Rigatos, and Rzafestas (2006), Meng and Gong (2010) evolutionary algorithms, Vlachopiannts (2008), Zhang G. (2011), genetic algorithm, Han and Kim (2000) and others. Thus the quantum computation has acquired preferences in advanced digital signal processing.

The reversible logic was introduced by Feynman (1982, 1986) to link up the quantum principles with the classical computation. A system will be said reversible if it consists of $n$ number of outputs for $n$ number of inputs so that the input state of the system could be achieved from the output states at any time instant. This seems to have no information loss in reversible methodologies. Information loss results in energy dissipation in irreversible hardware computation. Landauer's research states that the quantity of energy dissipated for every irreversible bit action is at least KTln2 joules, where K is the Boltzmann's constant $=1.3806505\times10^{-23}$ $m^2kg^{-2}K^{-1}$ (Joule/Kelvin) and T is the temperature at which operation is carried out, Landauer R. (1961). The amount of heat generated for one bit information loss is negligible with respect to the room temperature. But the heat generation is significant for a high speed complex computational program where numerous information bits are lost. In this scenario the performance of the system gets affected by the excessive heat that results in a cutback of the life span of the components. In 1973, Bennett stated and proved that the energy dissipation can be reduced for the systems those permit to regenerate the inputs from received outputs, Bennett C.H. (1973). In addition reversible computation perks up energy efficiency that mostly boosts up the routine speed of the circuits. The portability of devices also enhanced through using reversible logic circuits as these logics reduce the size of the circuit elements to atomic size limits.

In establishment of any logic, reversibility means there should be no information concerned with the computational states that can be lost, so that the computation of any state from its previous or subsequently states through forward and backward computing process. This conditional function is acknowledged as logical reversibility. But the payback of logical reversibility is achieved only after making physically use of reversibility. For a device, physical reversibility fundamentally states that the analogous circuit operation does not dissipate any energy to heat. Therefore it is obvious that absolute physical reversibility is practically unfeasible. In a computing system, heat is generated with the changes of voltage levels from positive to negative or in other words, bits from zero to one. The largest part of the energy required to make that state modification is sent out in form of heat. Reversible circuit elements steadily shift charges from one node to the next in spite of altering voltages to new levels. In this fashion, a very diminutive amount of energy can be expected to lose on each alteration. Thus reversible computing sturdily influenced the practice of designing digital logics. In digital watermarking reversible logic can be utilized to recover the original watermark in terms state of inputs from the outputs i.e. the received watermarked image.

A circuit having **n** number of Boolean variables is reversible if it consists of exactly same number of inputs and outputs and there exists a unique pattern for inputs to map an inimitable output. Another essential criterion for a reversible logic circuit is that there should be no Fan-out. It is obvious that required input and outputs are not to be of same quantity. The constant inputs and garbage outputs are introduced to resolve this crisis. The constant inputs are to be retained constant (0/1) with the intention of synthesizing the given logical operation. Whereas the garbage outputs are the outputs, present in a reversible logic operation, which are unused but essential to attain reversibility. So, for a reversible logic circuit,

Actual Input + Constant Input = Actual Output + Garbage Output

The number of primitive reversible logic gates required to realize the circuit is known as the Quantum Cost.

A number of logic gates are available to achieve the reversible property. Few of them are discussed here.

## Feynman Gate

The Feynman Gate is a 2*2 reversible logic gate, also known as 'controlled-not' or 'quantum XOR' gate. Its quantum cost is measured as 1. For input vector I(A,B) and output vector O(X,Y) the truth table is shown in table 1. The logic operation is expressed in Figure 6(a).

From the truth table it is clear that the output Y acts as a NOT gate with respect to the input B when A is set as 1. That's why this is called controlled NOT. Again for B = 1, both outputs copy the value of A, i.e. acts as a copying gate.

## Double Feynman Gate

The 3*3 Double Feynman Gate has a quantum cost double to the Feynman Gate. If the input and output vectors are I(A,B.C) and O(X,Y,Z) then X=A, Y=A$\oplus$ B and

*Table 1. Truth table for Feynman Gate*

| A | B | X | Y |
|---|---|---|---|
| 0 | 0 | 0 | 0 |
| 0 | 1 | 0 | 1 |
| 1 | 0 | 1 | 1 |
| 1 | 1 | 1 | 0 |

*Figure 6. Block Diagram for (a) Feynman Gate (b) Double Feynman Gate (c) Toffoli Gate (d) Peres Gate (e) Fredkin Gate*

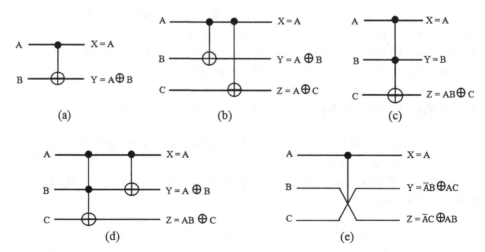

$Z=\oplus A$ C. The input output relationship is reflected from the truth table given in table 2 and operational diagram described in the Figure 6(b).

## Toffoli Gate

The logic operation of Toffoli gate or 3*3 Feynman gate or controlled-controlled-not gate, having quantum value 5, can be described as X=A; Y= B and Z= AB$\oplus$ C. As shown in Figure 6(c), here two inputs A and B act as control inputs to obtain the output Z as a complement of input C. the truth table of this gate is obtained from table 3.

*Table 2. Truth table for Double Feynman Gate*

| A | B | C | X | Y | Z |
|---|---|---|---|---|---|
| 0 | 0 | 0 | 0 | 0 | 0 |
| 0 | 0 | 1 | 0 | 0 | 1 |
| 0 | 1 | 0 | 0 | 1 | 0 |
| 0 | 1 | 1 | 0 | 1 | 1 |
| 1 | 0 | 0 | 1 | 1 | 1 |
| 1 | 0 | 1 | 1 | 1 | 0 |
| 1 | 1 | 0 | 1 | 0 | 1 |
| 1 | 1 | 1 | 1 | 0 | 0 |

*Table 3. Truth table for Toffoli Gate*

| A | B | C | X | Y | Z |
|---|---|---|---|---|---|
| 0 | 0 | 0 | 0 | 0 | 0 |
| 0 | 0 | 1 | 0 | 0 | 1 |
| 0 | 1 | 0 | 0 | 1 | 0 |
| 0 | 1 | 1 | 0 | 1 | 1 |
| 1 | 0 | 0 | 1 | 0 | 0 |
| 1 | 0 | 1 | 1 | 0 | 1 |
| 1 | 1 | 0 | 1 | 1 | 1 |
| 1 | 1 | 1 | 1 | 1 | 0 |

## Peres Gate

The logic operation of a 3*3 Peres gate with the input variables A, B, C and the output variables X, Y, Z is defined as X=A; Y= A⊕B and Z= AB⊕ C. The quantum cost of a Peres gate is measured as 4. The truth table and the logic operation of a 3*3 Peres gate are shown in table 4 and Figure 6(d) respectively.

## Fredkin Gate

In case of a 3*3 Peres gate consists of three input variables A, B, C and three output variables X, Y, Z, the reversible logic is built up as X=A; Y= $\overline{A}$ B⊕AC and Z= $\overline{A}$ C⊕AB. Its quantum cost is calculated as shown in table 5.

*Table 4. Truth table for Peres Gate*

| A | B | C | X | Y | Z |
|---|---|---|---|---|---|
| 0 | 0 | 0 | 0 | 0 | 0 |
| 0 | 0 | 1 | 0 | 0 | 1 |
| 0 | 1 | 0 | 0 | 1 | 0 |
| 0 | 1 | 1 | 0 | 1 | 1 |
| 1 | 0 | 0 | 1 | 1 | 0 |
| 1 | 0 | 1 | 1 | 1 | 1 |
| 1 | 1 | 0 | 1 | 0 | 1 |
| 1 | 1 | 1 | 1 | 0 | 0 |

*Table 5. Truth table for Fredkin Gate*

| A | B | C | X | Y | Z |
|---|---|---|---|---|---|
| 0 | 0 | 0 | 0 | 0 | 0 |
| 0 | 0 | 1 | 0 | 0 | 1 |
| 0 | 1 | 0 | 0 | 1 | 0 |
| 0 | 1 | 1 | 0 | 1 | 1 |
| 1 | 0 | 0 | 1 | 0 | 0 |
| 1 | 0 | 1 | 1 | 1 | 0 |
| 1 | 1 | 0 | 1 | 0 | 1 |
| 1 | 1 | 1 | 1 | 1 | 1 |

## LITERATURE SURVEY ON REVERSIBLE LOGIC INSPIRED DATA HIDING SCHEME

Besides surfacing on the various states of watermarking, this discussion also focused on the reversible logic synthesis methods which carry out a major role of this proposed work. Composition and decomposition are two well known multi level and very powerful tool used in synthesis procedures for reversible logic, Maslov D. et al. (2003). In composition methods, small and familiar reversible gates are composed to play the function of any complex reversible block, Dueck et al (2003), Miller et al. (2003). Then applying a conventional logic synthesis process, the network is synthesized. Decomposition methods operate like a top-down diminution of the function from the outputs to the inputs, Al-Rabadi A.N. (2004), Perkowski M. et al. (2001). Here a complex function is decomposed into several functions and these are individually implemented by distinct reversible circuits. The decomposition process is practiced based on several models like Ashenhurst-Curtis (AC) decomposition, Modified Reconstruct ability Analysis (MRA), Bi-decomposition (BD), etc. EXOR logic based methods are used mainly for heuristic synthesis Shende V.V. et al. (2002), Maslov D. et al. (2005). Combination of Toffoli gate, operating on EXOR logic, is utilized here to perform the reversible function. Genetic reversible algorithms introduce the evolutions concept proposed by Darwinian, Lamarckian and Baldwinian to minimize the logic functions Lukac M. et al. (2002), Lukac M. et al. (2003). The main drawback of these techniques is their poor scalability. Spectral techniques proposed by Miller (2002) are used to locate the finest gate to be composed in terms of NOT, CNOT or Toffoli gate. Then the gate is formed in a cascade-like manner. A set of the set of the actual outputs from each sub-block or their negations together describes the output function. To execute any Boolean function through reversible logic, binary decision diagram (BDD) methods can be applied Al-Rabadi A.N. (2004), Wille et al. (2008). In BDD based approaches all possible minimal networks are considered to find the most effective one in terms of quantum cost or circuit complexity. Thus it leads to a cheaper and faster realization. In the next section various watermarking techniques using these reversible logic has been discussed briefly.

As already discussed, digital watermarking embeds significant information (watermark) into multimedia for copyright protection. The insertion of watermark may cause distortion in the cover media. Furthermore, in some cases, the effects on the cover object may not be fully reversible after mining of the concealed insertion. Utilizing the perceptional imperfectness of human visual system the distortion can be optimized but the irreversibility cannot be tolerated for certain responsive applications like medical imaging or any legal issues. A loss less data hiding scheme obtained exigency in this purposes. Reversible watermarking, also called loss less data hiding allows us to implant a moderately large quantity of information into an image in such a manner that the inserted data can be rebuilt from the watermarked image. Thus the reversible logic serves the purpose to overcome the tradeoff between imperceptibility and payload capacity. Moreover, these reversible watermarking methods can provide robustness against most of the signal processing attacks. The watermark extraction process can also be made blind using reversible logic. So, these types of practices acquired fondness in copyright protection for multimedia objects like images and electronic documents. Numbers of reversible watermarking schemes are developed depending on several logics and methods like difference expansion, lossless data compression, bit planes modification, integer-to-integer wavelet transform, bijective transformation, histogram shifting and others. Some of existing reversible watermarking frameworks are discussed here.

Mintzer et al. (1997) first brought in the perception of a reversible watermark. They proposed a watermarking scheme where the original image could be formed from the watermarked image by taking off the watermark. This removal of the mark described the utilization of reversibility in watermarking. A hash function based method was proposed by Honsinger et al. (2001) where modulo-256 addition is used in implantation of hash value of the metadata. This algorithm enables reversibility and hampers the fact of watermark extraction under salt-and-pepper artifacts. Fridrich et al. (2001) introduced the practice of constriction of a set of chosen features from an image and insert the payload into the compressed region with a lossless computation scheme. Goljan et al (2001) developed a fragile data hiding scheme using called RS method. Here the watermark embedding is performed on the basis of the pixel group status which through a flipping operation using discrimination functions. This is also a lossless data approach. The exhaustive study of the RS method for JPEG images in DCT (Discrete Cosine Transfer) domain was made by Fridrich et al. (2002). Fridrich et al.'s methodology was improvised by the G-LSB (generalized-LSB) technique proposed by Celik et al. (2002). In their proposal a binary watermark is embedded into a gray level cover image through a simple LSB replacement method. The compression proficiency is enhanced by utilizing prediction based conditional entropy coder applied to the flat region of the input image. Celik et al. (2005) extended this version to obtain a generalized lossless data insertion. A semi-fragile lossless data hiding scheme is proposed by Vleeschouwer et al. (2003) which can sustain against high-quality JPEG compression. Here every information bit is associated to a pixel group formed by two equally distributed pseudo-random sets of pixels.

An IP (Inverted Pattern) based LSB substitution technique is developed by Yang (2008). The uniqueness of this approach is that the IP determines the hidden image regions to be inverted or not and this is utilized in the time of data extraction. Another prediction error based reversible data hiding approach is proposed by Thodi and

Rodriguez (2004) where histogram shifting also utilized to calculate the correlation between adjacent pixels. This technique offers a low distortion to the cover image. A circular interpretation is applied to the bijective transformations of cover image histograms to enrich the rustiness. A further improvement is done by producing a robust statistical reversible method, Ni et al (2008), which is not applicable only for an extremely lossy compression attack. A block based reversible information hiding scheme is developed by Ono et al. (2009) where the data is implanted into certain precise regions like image edges. No location map is required here to specify the hidden bit positions in the embedded image. To increase the payload capacity congruency based watermarking scheme is introduced by Chaumont and Puech (2009). According to their approach, each pixel of the cover image may lies on three states. These are the embedding state where an integer coefficient is to be implanted, to correct state where the pixels are modified without any type of embedding and original state where the pixels are corresponds to the original or unchanged one. The utilization of these three states enhances the embedding capacity.

Lossless compression of bit planes is another type of reversible data hiding framework which can be generated through manipulations of the bit planes and provides a transparent data analysis during embedding and extracting time. Generally the purpose of these methods is to find out the suitable region in the cover image with least redundancy to hold the endorsement data like hash. And assuming the media is not noisy, naturally the preferable regions to hide the hash are provided by the lower bit-planes. Fridrich et al. (2001a) developed a bit-plane compressing based reversible information hiding scheme. In this approach to compress the bit-planes, JBIG lossless compression algorithm, Sayood (2006), is utilized which starts with analyzing the fifth LSB plane.

Another image watermarking scheme was proposed by Song et al. (2009) for substance validation. This approach involves the bit-plane technique in an irreversible watermarking where the image feature obtained from least significant bit-plane is implanted into a preset bit-plane by regulating the analogous sub-band values. A relative or parallel method to the bit-plane compression is Bit Plane Complexity Segmentation (BPCS) which is applicable to the irreversible data embedding processes. It was first set up by Kawaguchi and Eason (1998). The purpose of this improvisation was to modify the deficiencies of simple LSB manipulation methods. Although there is no likeliness between the complexities of any two images, in this approach two different image complexities were deliberated. The work focused on determining the number of concerned pixel areas can be utilized to define the complex regions. Hirohisa (2002) and Ramani et al (2007) also developed some watermarking schemes based on this BPCS concept. Hirohisa (2002) introduced two new complexity events named as the run-length irregularity and the border noisiness to distinguish noisy regions accurately. Ramani et al (2007) proposed a replaceable inverse Wavelet transform (IWT) based methodology where the replaceable IWT coefficient regions were defined by a complex quantification. Thus being developed through irreversible aspects, these research works put some important contributions in the era of digital image watermarking.

The reversible watermarking schemes, discussed till now, are suitable to be performed in spatial domain. The main problem of spatial domain is reduced robustness which can be overcome in transfer domain. In case of classical transfer domain practices like discrete wavelet transform it is not assured that utilization of reversible logic can achieve reversibility properly. This crisis can be conquer through a reversible integer-to-integer wavelet transform based lifting scheme. This is principally a difference expansion oriented computation where flexible pixel pairs are used to embed data or watermark. A location map, generated to trace the positions of the pixels, is utilized to recover the hidden mark properly at the receiving end. The concept of difference expansion based reversible watermarking was pioneered by Tian (2002). In this proposal gray level cover image was taken and the expanded difference numbers between two neighboring pixels were computed to implant the watermark bits into the cover. The hiding capacity of Tian's framework is increased by allowing for triplets instead of the pair of the pixels to embed a pair of watermark bits, Alattar (2003). This is a color image watermarking algorithm where the triplets can be considered either in spatial domain or as cross-spectral pixels. A further extension of this algorithm is performed to obtain a enhanced payload capacity as well as generalization of the data insertion methodology, Alattar (2004), where three bitts are hidden in a quad of pixels having different values. It was verified that for required reversible integer transform, the perceptual image quality is affected with the increment of the number of inserting bits. Stach and Alattar (2004) utilize the generalized integer transform for vectors having any arbitrary length. The LSB prediction method proposed by Kamstra and Heijmans (2005) embeds the information enclosed in the most significant bit planes. This is a low payload capacitive scheme to improve image aesthetics. The insertion is performed based on the sorting process of the envisage LSBs, that depends on an estimation of the prediction feature, also improves the coding adeptness. One more improvement over Tian's (2002) method was made by Kallel et al. (2007). This is a spatial domain approach where the image is divided into several blocks and each block is considered as an array of numerous rows and column elements. These elementary pixels of each row and column generate corresponding authentication codes. These codes are treated as the watermark and embedded into the least significant bit planes of the expanded differences of preferred regions in each block. Kim et al. (2008) improvised the difference equation technique for low capacitive watermarking schemes by simplifying the generation of location map without reference of it at the extracting end. Another modification on difference expansion based execution in was done by Yaqub and Jaber (2006) terms of hiding capacity and computational cost. A set of expandable vectors are produced from the divergence between the median pixels and the other pixel values. Information is embedded into the differences of all probable expandable vectors. Gao and Gu (2007) utilizes both LSB replacement and difference expansion based reversible methodology. The image features, generated from image pixel blocks, are divided into two parts. One of them is embedded through LSB based technique and the other one is hidden into the differences. Thodi and Rodriguez (2007) developed another prediction-error based reversible information hiding scheme that utilizes the intrinsic correlation between neighboring pixels in place of difference expansion method. Lee et al. (2007) established a wavelet transform based reversible watermarking scheme where the wavelet transform of non-overlapping blocks of the cover image is computed and the watermark is embedded into the pixels having high frequency components in transform domain through LSB replacement process.

Information hiding through histogram shifting is another reversible watermarking scheme that was introduced by Ni et al. (2003). Image histogram modification is generally a human visual system based operation, Xuan et al. (2002). In the proposal of Ni et al. first a peak point or zero point is estimated in the image histogram to exploit the hiding capacity. Next by right shifting of the points next to it, vacant points are created at the zero point and another point near it. These vacant points are used to insert the watermark bit. A large number of watermark bits are embedded into the cover image by simply repeating the histogram shifting procedure in multiple times. Although the hiding capacity is limited according the cover image. Information hidden into the image can be recovered by a reverse process. Although this is a spatial domain approach, image histogram can also be formed from an integer-to-integer wavelet transform can also be utilized here instead of the spatial domain image. This algorithm was modified by increasing data capacity through gray-scale pixel adaptation and utilization of the zero points, Ni et al. (2006). Xuan et al. (2004) proposed a spread spectrum based watermarking scheme developed in wavelet transform domain. Later they utilized histogram modification with a threshold to the data insertion to put off overflow and underflow as well as to make this technique loss less and reversible, Xuan et al. (2005). Image histogram with integer wavelets was utilized by Xuan et al. (2006). The Laplacian distribution was engaged in creating more points to enhance payload capacity.

Fallahpur and Sedaaghi (2007) developed another histogram shifting based watermarking scheme. Here histogram is computed through a block based approach and data embedding is performed depending on the position of the zero points and peaks of the image histogram. Difference histogram in sub-sampled images is modified to generate a reversible data hiding scheme in the proposal of Kim et al (2009). Yang et al. (2009) utilize optimal several pairs of peaks and zeroes in the image histogram.

## HARDWARE IMPLEMENTATION OF WATERMARK EMBEDDING AND EXTRACTION USING REVERSIBLE LOGIC

Previously a number of reversible logic gates are initially briefed in this chapter. But the author developed their system designs basically using three logic gates – Feynman gate, Fredkin gate and Toffoli gate. The overtures of these three gates are already given. In this section, primarily the transistor implementation of the three logic gates are developed which is the designs of the other blocks using these logic gates.

As discussed earlier, one of the most well known (2*2) reversible gates is Feynman gate in which one of the input bits acts as a control signal. This gate is one-through gate which means that one input variable is also output. Feynman gate acts as a copying gate when the second input is zero by duplicating the first input at the output. The proposed transistor implementation of Feynman gate is given in Figure 7(a). Figure 7(b) shows the transistor implementation of the Fredkin Gate which requires only 4 transistors.

*Figure 7. Proposed Transistor Implementation for (a) Feynman Gate, (b) Fredkin Gate, (c) Toffoli Gate*

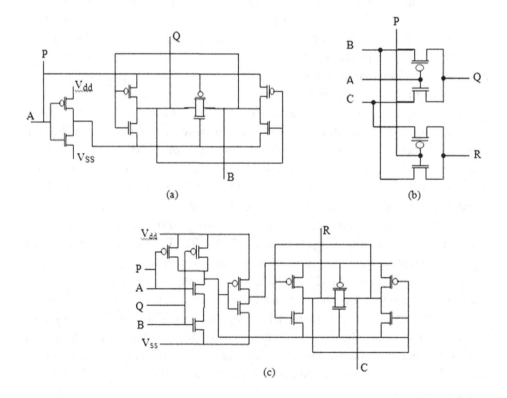

In the proposed implementation, the output P is directly taken from input A as it is simply hardwired. The existing implementation of the Fredkin gate in literature is with 10 transistors and 16 transistors respectively. Thus proposed design achieves 60% reduction in number of transistors compared to 10 transistors and 75% reduction compared to 16 transistors. It is to be noted that proposed transistor implementation is completely reversible suitable both for forward as well as backward computation. The transistor logic execution for Toffoli gate is shown in Figure 7(c). From this figure it is exposed that for the projected design 12 number of transistors are required to carry out the reversible operation through Toffoli gate. In Figure 8, the characteristic plots of these three gates are displayed taking V(A),V(B), V(C) as the input pulses and V(1), V(2), V(3) as the output pulses with a pulse width of 10ns and a time period of 20ns. The power dissipation for each state alternation in these gates for different operation frequency has been calculated for forward computation as well as backward computation also. The experimental results are shown through tabular form in table 6.

Along with these three gates, T Flip-flop and D flip-flop are also required to develop the operational blocks involved in watermark insertion and extraction process. Therefore obligatorily authors have designed a T flip-flop and a D flip-flop using reversible logic gates.

*Figure 8. Proposed Transistor Implementation for (a) Feynman Gate, (b) Fredkin Gate, (c) Toffoli Gate*

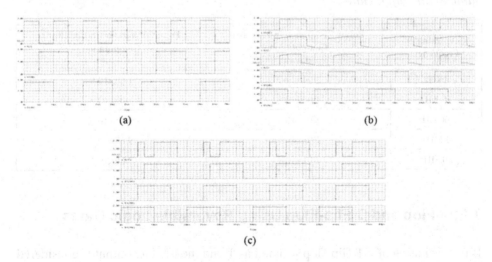

(a)        (b)

(c)

*Table 6. Power calculation for forward and backward computation in (a) Feynman Gate*

| Working Frequency | Power Dissipation in Forward Computation (in watt) | Power Dissipation in Backward Computation (in watt) |
|---|---|---|
| 1KHz | 1.06×10-9 | 1.60×10-9 |
| 10 KHz | 1.05×10-8 | 1.02×10-8 |
| 100 KHz | 1.02×10-7 | 9.65×10-8 |
| 1 MHz | 1.01×10-6 | 9.68×10-7 |
| 10 MHz | 1.01×10-5 | 9.66×10-6 |

*Table 7. (b) Fredkin Gate*

| Working Frequency | Power Dissipation in Forward Computation (in watt) | Power Dissipation in Backward Computation (in watt) |
|---|---|---|
| 1KHz | 4.53×10-12 | 4.50×10-12 |
| 10 KHz | 9.72×10-12 | 8.90×10-12 |
| 100 KHz | 3.37×10-11 | 2.27×10-11 |
| 1 MHz | 1.95×10-10 | 1.06×10-9 |
| 10 MHz | 1.07×10-9 | 4.98×10-9 |

*Table 8. (c) Toffoli Gate*

| Working Frequency | Power Dissipation in Forward Computation (in watt) | Power Dissipation in Backward Computation (in watt) |
|---|---|---|
| 1KHz | 1.04×10-9 | 1.60×10-9 |
| 10 KHz | 1.05×10-8 | 1.02×10-8 |
| 100 KHz | 1.02×10-7 | 9.65×10-8 |
| 1 MHz | 1.01×10-6 | 9.68×10-7 |
| 10 MHz | 1.01×10-5 | 9.66×10-6 |

## T Flip-Flop and D Flip-Flop Using Reversible Logic Gates

If the excitation of a T flip-flop is noted as T and the $n^{th}$ state output is considered as the present state and noted as $Q_n$, then with addition to the clock pulse Clk, the characteristic equation of the flip-flop can be written as $Q_{n+1} = \overline{\left( T.Q_n \right)} . \text{Clk} + ($

T.Q$_n$ $\overline{)}$.$\overline{\text{Clk}}$ . This equation can be directly mapped to Toffoli gate. The fan-out can be avoided and complementary output can be generated by using Toffoli gate with Fredkin Gate. The proposed design is shown in Figure 9(a). As shown in the figure, the first two inputs of the Toggle gate act as the clock input and the excitation T respectively and the other one is connected to the second output of the Fredkin gate. The first two out puts of it are made grounded and the other output, which is basically the output function of T flip-flop, is fed to the first input of the Fredkin gate. The other two inputs of the Fredkin gate are set to '1' and '0' respectively as default value. Therefore according to the logic, the first output of this gate provides its first input value and considered as output function of T flip-flop. The default values of the two inputs of this gate enable to copy the first output value to the second output value which is fed back to the last input of the Toffoli gate. A complement of the flip-flop output is obtained from the last one among the Fredkin gate outputs.

In case of D flip-flop, the characteristic equation with input excitation D is defined as, $Q_{n+1}$ = D. Clk $+ Q_n . \overline{\text{Clk}}$. This logic operation is executed through reversible logic using a Feynman gate sequentially connected to Fredkin gate as shown in Figure 9(b). Here the first two input of Fredkin gate act as the clock input and the input excitation D respectively and the other one is latched with the first out pt of the Feynman gate. The first two outputs of the Fredkin gate is grounded and the last output, producing the D function is fed to the first input of the Feynman gate. The other input of this gate is set to a default value of '0' and thus both of the outputs of the Feynman gate becomes its input value i.e. the D function. One of these output port is fed to the input of Fredkin gate and the other one is considered as the output of the flip-flop.

Now the discussion is lead to the implementation of the functional sub-blocks required in embedding and extracting block. According to the block diagrams shown in Figure 5 and 6, the functional circuits required to the process of watermarking

*Figure 9. Block diagram for implementation of Flip-flops using reversible gates: (a) T Flip-flop, (b) D Flip-flop*

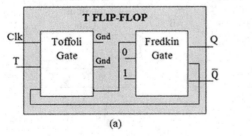

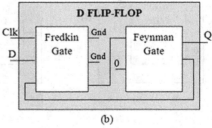

and recovery of the watermark are 2:1 MUX, 16-bit ROM, 4-bit synchronous up/down counter, AND gate, NAND gate and register (PISO, PIPO, SIPO). These logic circuits should be realized using reversible operation.

## AND Gate, NAND Gate and 2:1 MUX Using Reversible Logic

Each of the AND and NAND gate can easily implemented simply by using a single Toffoli gate only. In both of the cases the first two inputs of the Toffoli gate are considered as the inputs of AND or NAND gate. The third input value determines whether the Toffoli gate will act as an AND gate or a NAND gate. For the value is set to '0' or '1' then the gate behaves like an AND gate or NAND gate respectively. The first two outputs of the Toffoli gate is grounded and the last one operates like AND or NAND function as shown in the block diagrams given in Figure 10(a) and (b).

Fredkin gate itself operates like a 2:1 MUX when the first input is considered as the select line (S) and the other two as MUX inputs ($I_1$, $I_2$). The MUX output Y can be defined by the equation $Y = \overline{S} I_1 + S I_2$. In this design the functional behavior is also achieved from the last output port and the other outputs are made grounded. The operational diagram of 2:1 MUX using Fredkin gate is shown in Figure 10(c).

## SIPO and PISO Shift Register Using Reversible Logic

A SIPO (Serial-In-Parallel-Out) shift register takes serial input and it makes all the stored bits being available as outputs. Thus a parallel output is produced. Reversible implementation of SIPO shift register using clocked D flip-flops is shown in Figure 11(a). The serial data are entered to the $I_S$ input of the reversible left-most flip-flop while the outputs $O_1$, $O_2$, $O_3$, ... $O_n$ are available in parallel each output bit Q of the

*Figure 10. Block diagram for implementation using reversible logic: (a) AND Gate, (b) NAND Gate, (c) 2:1 MUX*

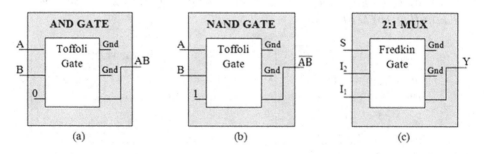

flip-flops. It requires n reversible clocked D flip-flops and n-1 Feynman gates. Thus, it requires a total of 3n-1 gates and produces n+1 garbage outputs with quantum cost 7n-1.

PISO shift register intakes the parallel data and shifts it to the next flip-flop when the register is clocked. Fig shows the reversible implementation of PISO shift register using clocked D flip flops. The operations are controlled by the enable signal E. When E is high, the inputs $I_1$, $I_2$, $I_3$ ... In are loaded in parallel into the register coincident with the next clock pulse. Again when E is low, the Q output of the flip-flop is shifted to the right by means of Fredkin gate. The desired register output is obtained serially from the $n^{th}$ D flip-flop output port. It allows accepting data n bits at a time on n lines and then sending them one bit after another on one line. It requires n reversible clocked D flip-flops and n Fredkin gates. Thus, it requires a total of 3n gates and produces 2n+2 garbage outputs with quantum cost 11n. The operational block diagram is shown in figure 11.

*Figure 11. Block diagram for implementation of Shift Register using reversible logic: (a) SIPO (b) PISO*

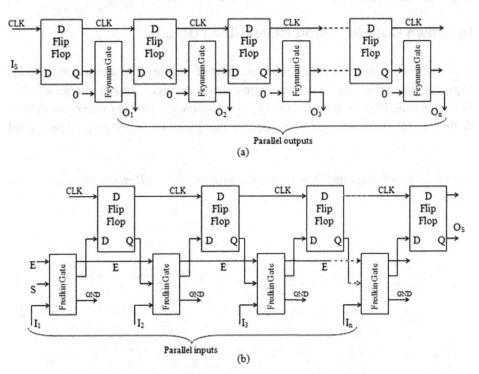

## PIPO Shift Register Using Reversible Logic

The purpose of the PIPO (parallel-in-parallel-out) shift register is to take in parallel data shift. Here a 4-bit PIPO shift register has been implemented. A higher order i.e. 8-bit or 16-bit register can be formed by connecting two or four registers in series. As shown in Figure 12, the four bit of input data is applied to a parallel-in/ parallel-out shift register at $D_1$, $D_2$, $D_3$ and $D_4$. A proper interconnected circuit, consists of D flip-flops, Feyman gates and Fredkin gates, operates to allow data being shifted one bit position for each clock pulse. The shifted data is available at the outputs $Q_1$, $Q_2$, $Q_3$ and $Q_4$. The "data in" and "data out" are provided for cascading of multiple stages.

## 4×4 ROM Using Reversible Logic

It can be developed using reversible D flip-flop and 16:1 MUX where the 16:1 MUX is being made using five 4:1 reversible MUX. A reversible 4:1 MUX is a combination of three Fredkin gates, each of which acts like a 2:1 MUX. Figure 13 shows the operational structure of a 4×4 ROM with addition to the 4:1 MUX block diagram using Fredkin gates and reversible D flip-flops.

## Up/Down Counter Using Reversible Logic

In an asynchronous counter, the output transition of one Flip-flop serves as a source for triggering other flip-flops. Two inputs are given to circuit i.e. enable and clock pulses in sequence and four outputs $Q_1$, $Q_2$, $Q_3$, $Q_4$ are obtained. Unlike to the conventional design, T flip-flops are used in this design along with Feynman gates. The control

*Figure 12. Block diagram for implementation of PIPO Shift Register using reversible logic*

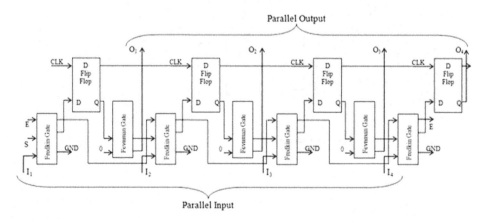

*Figure 13. Block diagram for implementation of (a) 4:1 MUX and (b) 4×4 ROM using reversible logic*

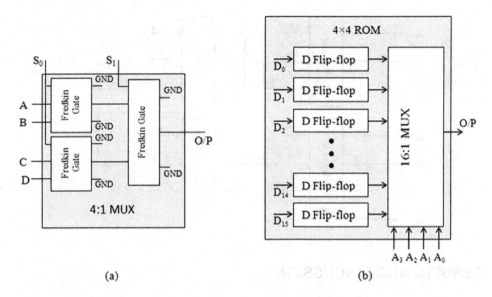

(a)             (b)

input value decides whether the counter will perform as an up or down counter. A '1' value of the control bit enables up operation whereas for '0' value causes down operation. Figure 14 defines the working blocks of an asynchronous up counter.

## Combinational Logic to Obtain Proposed Threshold Using Reversible Logic

A combinational logic is introduced to give a threshold in the watermarking process. This logic can also be developed using Reversible circuit. The threshold logic is defined by the function $F=AB(C+D+E)$ of which reversible logic implementation is shown in Figure 15.

*Figure 14. Block diagram for implementation of Up Counter*

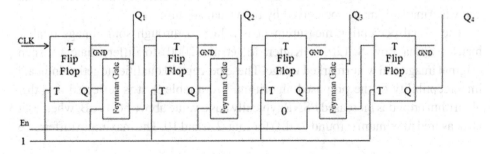

*Figure 15. Block diagram for implementation of the desired Combinational Logic to obtain threshold*

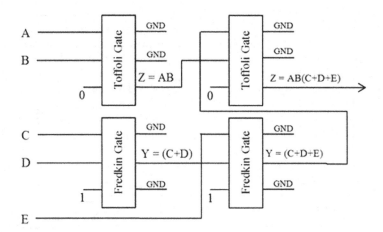

## RESULTS AND DISCUSSION

Experimental outcomes for this proposed watermarking algorithm have been achieved in terms of software computation and hardware execution. The acceptability of the logic of the method depends on three qualitative quantity i.e. imperceptibility, robustness and hiding capacity.

## Performance Estimation for Software Analysis

The author has chosen a database (USC-SIPI Image Database) of some images as cover images after adjusting each image to a 256×256 gray-scale image. Although all the images of the database are experienced the watermarking process for the same watermark, a few number of images have been shown in Figure 16(a). A binary image of size (16×16) shown in Figure 16(b) is built up to serve the purpose of watermark. The watermarked images obtained as the output of the embedding system for the corresponding original cover images are given in Figure 16(c). And as reflected from the figures, there are no perceptual differences between original and watermarked images perceived by the visual stimuli.

The visual perception measurement is achieved through some image quality metrics Sinha Roy, S. (2015) Kutter, M. et al. (2000) to differentiate between original image and watermarked image. These perceptual qualities together indicate imperceptibility of the proposed algorithm. From table 9, it is reflected that this algorithm provides increased PSNR typically has a value above 56.45 dB, whereas it is measured maximum (around 57 dB) for Img-2, 6 and 10. The maximum difference

*Figure 16. (a) Original cover images (b) Watermark Image (c) Watermarked Images*

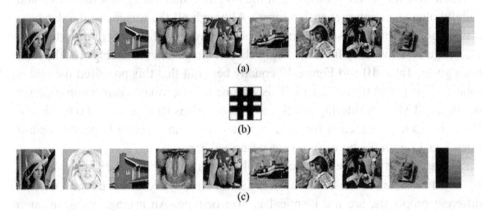

(a)

(b)

(c)

*Table 9. Imperceptibility measurement table*

| Parameter | Img-1 | Img-2 | Img-3 | Img-4 | Img-5 | Img-6 | Img-7 | Img-8 | Img-9 | Img-10 |
|---|---|---|---|---|---|---|---|---|---|---|
| MSE | 0.128540 | 0.127869 | 0.117920 | 0.123657 | 0.128296 | 0.121826 | 0.122314 | 0.125977 | 0.125183 | 0.122070 |
| LMSE | 0.001919 | 0.002362 | 0.001861 | 0.000492 | 0.001892 | 0.001137 | 0.003744 | 0.000819 | 0.003406 | 0.001352 |
| PSNR | 56.51 | 57.06 | 56.85 | 55.65 | 56.00 | 57.00 | 56.84 | 56.34 | 54.96 | 57.26 |
| SNR | 51.37 | 55.50 | 52.55 | 51.69 | 51.30 | 51.91 | 52.28 | 49.46 | 51.63 | 52.57 |
| MD | 2 | 2 | 2 | 2 | 2 | 2 | 2 | 2 | 2 | 2 |
| AD | 0.064270 | 0.063934 | 0.058960 | 0.061821 | 0.064148 | 0.060913 | 0.061157 | 0.062988 | 0.062592 | 0.061035 |
| NAD | 0.000518 | 0.000303 | 0.000427 | 0.000477 | 0.000533 | 0.000470 | 0.000448 | 0.000708 | 0.000473 | 0.000480 |
| NMSE | 0.000004 | 0.000001 | 0.000003 | 0.000003 | 0.000004 | 0.000003 | 0.000003 | 0.000006 | 0.000003 | 0.000003 |
| IF | 0.999993 | 0.999997 | 0.999994 | 0.999993 | 0.999993 | 0.999994 | 0.999994 | 0.999989 | 0.999993 | 0.999994 |
| SC | 0.999732 | 0.999809 | 0.999609 | 0.999638 | 0.999740 | 0.999645 | 0.999692 | 0.999725 | 0.999680 | 0.999849 |
| CQ | 142.209 | 214.966 | 153.545 | 140.852 | 143.940 | 145.822 | 151.658 | 125.006 | 137.625 | 173.532 |
| NQM | 36.990 | 39.269 | 38.105 | 37.474 | 36.812 | 37.477 | 37.626 | 35.619 | 37.843 | 34.198 |
| SSIM | 0.999671 | 0.999143 | 0.999212 | 0.999782 | 0.999626 | 0.999553 | 0.999422 | 0.999332 | 0.999637 | 0.998700 |
| HS | 4212 | 4190 | 3864 | 4052 | 4204 | 3992 | 4008 | 4128 | 4102 | 4000 |
| NCC | 0.999869 | 0.999906 | 0.999807 | 0.999822 | 0.999874 | 0.999825 | 0.999849 | 0.999868 | 0.999843 | 0.999927 |
| NAE | 0.000518 | 0.000303 | 0.000427 | 0.000477 | 0.000533 | 0.000470 | 0.000448 | 0.000708 | 0.000473 | 0.000480 |

is 1 for all the images as the number of maximum LSBs replaced in a pixel is 1. Image fidelity should be 1 for two identical images. Here it is found around 0.9999, which is very close to unity. Middling value of SSIM and SC for all the images are more or less than 0.999, which is also 1 for two indistinguishable images. So, this approach can be considered as a good imperceptible algorithm which also reflects from the values of the other parameters.

Table 10 exhibits the robustness of the proposed method against the above said spiteful attacks in comprehensive forms. Although all the images of the database is undergone through these robustness checking process, the effect of the attacks to the image is shown only for a randomly chosen image and the average results have been given. Table 10 and Figure 17 equally bear out that this proposed method is robust against most of the attacks. This scheme is least robust against non-uniform rotation and Median filtering attacks, as in these cases BER is around 6 to 8% and WDR is -15 to -19. Except from these, watermark can excellently persist against other attacks with 0% bit error rate as described here.

A relative study between the proposed algorithm and some other existing methods is shown in table 11. It is obvious that the watermark and cover images, used in different proposals, are not identical in size or type. An average value through watermark to document scale is approximated.

*Table 10. Performance results of robustness*

| Sl. No | Attacks | BER (%) | NC | PCC | WDR | SM | NHD |
|--------|---------|---------|-----|-----|-----|-----|-----|
| 1. | No attack | 0 | 1 | 1 | -∞ | 1 | 0 |
| 2. | 180° Rotation | 0 | 1 | 1 | -∞ | 1 | 0 |
| 3. | 90° Rotation | 0 | 1 | 1 | -∞ | 1 | 0 |
| 4. | 45° Rotation | 8.6 | 0.900 | 0.820 | -15.14 | 0.999 | 0.086 |
| 5. | Negative | 0 | 1 | 1 | -∞ | 1 | 0 |
| 6. | Cropping | 0 | 1 | 1 | -∞ | 1 | 0 |
| 7. | Median Filtering | 5.9 | 0.930 | 0.877 | -18.97 | 0.998 | 0.058 |
| 8. | Salt & Pepper | 0 | 1 | 1 | -∞ | 1 | 0 |
| 9. | Erode | 0 | 1 | 1 | -∞ | 1 | 0 |
| 10. | Dilate | 0 | 1 | 1 | -∞ | 1 | 0 |

*Figure 17. Recovered watermark after several attacks: (a) No attack; (b) 180° Rotation (c) 90° Rotation (d) 45° Rotation (e) Negative (f) Cropping (g) Median Filtering (h) Salt & Pepper (i) Erode (j) Dilate*

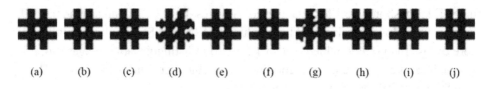

(a)    (b)    (c)    (d)    (e)    (f)    (g)    (h)    (i)    (j)

*Table 11. Proficiency comparison results*

| Sl. No | Method | PSNR (dB) |
|--------|--------|-----------|
| 1. | Proposed Method | 56.50 |
| 2. | Salient Region Watermarking, Wong et al. (2013) | 45.83 |
| 3. | IP LSB [Yang, 2008] | 35.07 |
| 4. | Pair wise LSB matching, Xu et al. (2010) | 35.05 |
| 5. | Optimal LSB pixel adjustment, Yang (2008) | 34.84 |
| 6. | Matrix Encoding based Watermarking, Verma et al. (2013) | 55.91 |
| 7. | LSB Replacement method, Goyal et al. (2014) | 54.8 |
| 8. | DWT and SVD based Watermarking, Majumdar et al. (2011) | 41.72 |
| 9. | Adaptive Pixel Pair Matching Scheme Hong, W. et al. (2012) | 40.97 |
| 10. | Reversible Data Hiding Scheme, Gui et al. (2014) | 34.26 |

Here it is observed that the projected watermarking scheme bids all other methods in terms of data transparency providing a high PSNR value. So, it can be concluded that this proposed watermarking algorithm is optimized in terms of both imperceptibility robustness.

## Performance Analysis for Hardware Accomplishment

In this section the simulation and synthesis results are exemplified. The top level RTL schematics of the watermark insertion and extraction systems substantiate that the VHDL codes are executable. Xilinx ISE 13.2 is employed to synthesis the high level execution and the obtained schematics are shown in Figure 18. To optimize the behavioral simulation results of the system, a test cover image of size 4×4 and a binary watermark of size 2×2 have been chosen. The simulation consequences are exposed in Figure 19. With 100ns time period, 1750ns time is required to execute each of insertion and extraction process for images having the said sizes. As the code is running properly the reversible logic could be applied for each operational sub-blocks of the embedding and extracting blocks as well as the size of cover and watermark images can also be varied.

## CONCLUSION

The hardware implementation of an adaptive LSB replacement based digital image watermarking scheme is developed here. Preliminary discussions on digital

*Figure 18. RTL schematic diagram for (a) Watermark Insertion (b) Watermark Extraction*

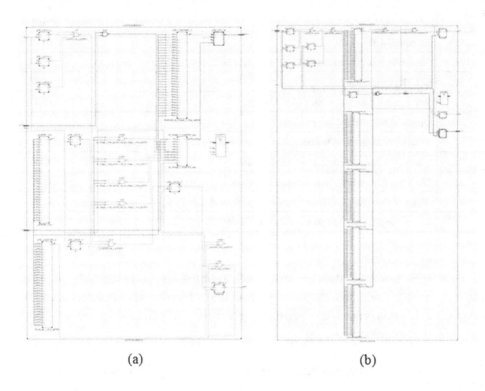

(a)　　　　　　　　　　　　　　　　　　(b)

*Figure 19. Behavioral simulation results for (a) Watermark Insertion (b) Watermark Extraction*

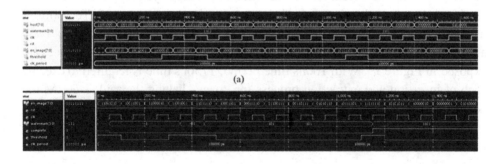

watermarking convey the importance and utilizations of it in new age digital communication as well as the significance for using reversible logic. The authors initially developed the watermark embedding and extracting system in spatial domain. Here the watermark bits are adaptively embedded into the cover image pixels by satisfying a particular threshold. After the successful software execution of the system, its real time implementation is established through reversible logic. The circuit diagrams for individual sub-blocks involved in data embedding and extracting system to obtain the desired output. Accuracy of the FPGA implementation is reflected from the behavioral simulation results of the watermark insertion and extraction systems and thus it is obvious that both of the circuits can be executed through the proposed reversible logics. Thus the power dissipation can be reduced in a large scale providing a higher operating speed. The experimental results show that the technique offers excellent quality of imperceptibility by means of high PSNR value. Moreover the robustness, offered by this method, is also defensible. So, it can be concluded that the proposed framework successfully achieved the objective of developing a low power effective digital watermarking scheme.

## REFERENCES

Al-Nabhani, Jalab, Wahid, & Noor. (2015). Robust watermarking algorithm for digital images using discrete wavelet and probabilistic neural network. *Journal of King Saud University – Computer and Information Sciences, 27*, 393-401.

Al-Rabadi, A. N. (2004). New classes of Kronecker-based reversible decision trees and their group-theoretic representation. *Proceedings of the International Workshop on Spectral Methods and Multirate Signal Processing (SMMSP)*, 233–243.

Alattar, A. M. (2003). Reversible Watermark Using Difference Expansion of Triplets. *Proc. of the International Conference on Image Processing, (ICIP 2003)*, 501-504. doi:10.1109/ICIP.2003.1247008

Alattar, A. M. (2004). Reversible Watermark Using Difference Expansion of Quads. *Proceedings of the IEEE International Conference on Acoustics, Speech, and Signal Processing, 3*, 377–380.

Basu, A., Sinha Roy, S., & Chattopadhayay, A. (2016). Implementation of a Spatial Domain Salient Region Based Digital Image Watermarking Scheme. *Int. Conf. Research in Computational Intelligence and Communication Networks*, 269-272. doi:10.1109/ICRCICN.2016.7813669

Basu, A., Sinha Roy, S., & Sarkar, S. (2015). FPGA Implementation of Saliency Based Watermarking Framework. *6th Int. Conf. on Computers and Devices for Communication.*

Bennett, C. H. (1973). Logical reversibility of Computation. *IBM Journal of Research and Development, 17*(6), 525–532. doi:10.1147/rd.176.0525

Celik, M. U., Sharma, G., Saber, E., & Tekalp, A. M. (2002). Hierarchical watermarking for secure image authentication with localization. *IEEE Transactions on Image Processing*, *11*(6), 585–595. doi:10.1109/TIP.2002.1014990 PMID:18244657

Celik, M. U., Sharma, G., Tekalp, A. M., & Saber, E. (2005). Lossless generalized-LSB data embedding. *IEEE Transactions on Image Processing*, *14*(2), 253–266. doi:10.1109/TIP.2004.840686 PMID:15700530

Chaumont, M., & Puech, W. (2009). A High Capacity Reversible Watermarking Scheme. *Visual Communications and Image Processing, Electronic Imaging.*

Dasgupta, S., Papadimitriou, C. H., & Vazirani, U. V. (2006). *Algorithms*. McGraw-Hill Education.

Dong, M. L., Dian, H. W., & Jie, L. (2012). A novel robust blind watermarking algorithm based on wavelet and Fractional Fourier Transform. *IEEE 14th International Conference on Communication Technology.*

Dueck, G. W., & Maslov, D. (2003). Reversible function synthesis with minimum garbage outputs. *Proceedings of the 6th International Symposium on Representations and Methodology of Future Computing Technologies (RM 2003)*, 154–161.

Emery, O. (1958). Des filigranes du papier. *Bulletin de l'Association technique de l'industrie papetiere, 6,* 185–188.

Fallahpur, M., & Sedaaghi, M. H. (2007). High capacity lossless data hiding based on histogram modification. *IEICE Electronics Express*, *4*(7), 205–210. doi:10.1587/elex.4.205

Feynman, R. (1982). Simulating physics with computers. *International Journal of Theoretical Physics*, *21*(6/7), 467–488. doi:10.1007/BF02650179

Feynman, R. (1986). Quantum mechanical computers. *Foundations of Physics*, *16*(6), 507–531. doi:10.1007/BF01886518

Fridrich, J. J., Goljan, M., & Du, R. (2001). Detecting LSB steganography in color, and gray-scale images. *IEEE MultiMedia*, *8*(4), 22–28. doi:10.1109/93.959097

Fridrich, J. J., Goljan, M., & Du, R. (2001a). Invertible authentication. *Security and Watermarking of Multimedia Contents III. Proceedings of the Society for Photo-Instrumentation Engineers*, (1): 197–208. doi:10.1117/12.435400

Fridrich, J. J., Goljan, M., & Du, R. (2002). Lossless data embedding: New paradigm in digital watermarking. *EURASIP Journal on Applied Signal Processing*, *2002*(2), 185–196. doi:10.1155/S1110865702000537

Gao, T., & Gu, Q. (2007). Reversible Image Authentication Based on Combination of Reversible and LSB Algorithm. *Proc. IEEE, Computational Intelligence and Security Workshops (CISW 07)*, 636-639. doi:10.1109/CISW.2007.4425576

Goljan, M., Fridrich, J. J., & Du, R. (2001). Distortion-free data embedding for images. LNCS, 2137, 27–41.

Goyal, R., & Kumar, N. (2014). LSB Based Digital Watermarking Technique. *International Journal of Application or Innovation in Engineering & Management*, *3*(9), 15–18.

Gui, X., Li, X., & Yang, B. (2014, May). A high capacity reversible data hiding scheme based on generalized prediction-error expansion and adaptive embedding. *Signal Processing*, *98*, 370–380. doi:10.1016/j.sigpro.2013.12.005

Hamidreza, Omair, & Swamy. (2016). Multiplicative Watermark Decoder in Contourlet Domain Using the Normal Inverse Gaussian Distribution. *IEEE Transactions on Multimedia*, *18*(2), 19 -207.

Han, K. H., & Kim, J. H. (2000). Genetic quantum algorithm and its application to combinatorial optimization problem. *Proc. of the 2000 Congress on evolutionary computation*, *2*, 1354–1360. doi:10.1109/CEC.2000.870809

Hao-Tang, C., Wen-Jyi, H., & Chau-Jern, C. (2015). Digital Hologram Authentication Using a Hadamard- Based Reversible Fragile Watermarking Algorithm. *Journal of Display Technology*, *11*(2), 193–203. doi:10.1109/JDT.2014.2367528

Hirohisa, H. (2002). A data embedding method using BPCS principle with new complexity measures. *Proc. of Pacific Rim Workshop on Digital Steganography*, 30-47.

Hong, L., Di, X., Rui, Z., Yushu, Z., & Sen, B. (2016). Robust and hierarchical watermarking of encrypted images based on Compressive Sensing. *Journal of Signal Processing: Image Communication*, *45*, 41–51.

Hong, W., & Chen, T. S. (2012). A Novel Data Embedding Method Using Adaptive Pixel Pair Matching. *IEEE Transactions on Information Forensics and Security*, *7*(1), 176–184. doi:10.1109/TIFS.2011.2155062

Honsinger, C. W., Jones, P., Rabbani, M., & Stoffel, J. C. (2001). *Lossless recovery of an original image containing embedded data*. US Patent Application, 6 278 791.

Hwai-Tsu, H., & Ling-Yuan, H. (2016). A mixed modulation scheme for blind image watermarking. *International Journal of Electronics and Communications*, *70*(2), 172–178. doi:10.1016/j.aeue.2015.11.003

Jaseena & John. (2011). Text Watermarking using Combined Image and Text for Authentication and Protection. *International Journal of Computer Applications, 20*(4).

Juergen, S. (2005). *Digital Watermarking for Digital Media*. IGI.

Kallel, M., Lapayre, J. C., & Bouhlel, M. S. (2007). A multiple watermarking scheme for medical image in the spatial domain. *Graphics. Vision and Image Processing Journal, 7*(1), 37–42.

Kamstra, L., & Heijmans, H. J. (2005). Reversible data embedding into images using wavelet techniques and sorting. *IEEE Transactions on Image Processing, 14*(12), 2082–2090. doi:10.1109/TIP.2005.859373 PMID:16370461

Kawaguchi, E., & Eason, R. O. (1998). Principle and Applications of BPCS Steganography. *Proc. of SPIE, Multimedia Systems and Applications, 3528*, 464–473.

Khandare, S., & Shrawankar, U. (2015). Image bit depth plane digital watermarking for secured classified image data transmission. *Procedia Computer Science, 78*, 698–705. doi:10.1016/j.procs.2016.02.119

Kharittha, T., Pipat, S., & Thumrongrat, A. (2015). Digital Image Watermarking based on Regularized Filter. *14th IAPR International Conference on Machine Vision Applications*.

Kim, H. J., Sachnev, V., Shi, Y. Q., Nam, J., & Choo, H. G. (2008). A Novel Difference Expansion Transform for Reversible Data Embedding. *IEEE Transactions on Information Forensics and Security, 3*(3), 456–465. doi:10.1109/TIFS.2008.924600

Kim, K. S., Lee, M. J., Lee, H. Y., & Lee, H. K. (2009). Reversible data hiding exploiting spatial correlation between sub-sampled images. *Pattern Recognition, 42*(11), 3083–3096. doi:10.1016/j.patcog.2009.04.004

Kutter, M. (1999). *Digital Watermarking: Hiding Information in Images* (PhD thesis). Swiss Federal Institute of Technology, Lausanne, Switzerland.

Kutter, M., & Petitcolas, F. A. P. (2000). A fair benchmark for image watermarking systems. *Journal of Electronic Imaging, 9*(4), 445–455. doi:10.1117/1.1287594

Lalitha, N. V., & Rao, S. (2013). DWT - Arnold Transform based audio watermarking. *IEEE Asia Pacific Conference on Postgraduate Research in Microelectronics and Electronics*. doi:.2013.6731204 doi:10.1109/PrimeAsia

Landauer, R. (1961). Irreversibility and heat generation in the computing process. *IBM Journal of Research and Development, 5*(3), 183–191. doi:10.1147/rd.53.0183

Lee, S., Yoo, C. D., & Kalker, T. (2007). Reversible Image Watermarking Based on Integer-to-Integer Wavelet Transform. *IEEE Transactions on Information Forensics and Security, 2*(3), 321–330. doi:10.1109/TIFS.2007.905146

Lin, P.-L. (2001). Oblivious Digital Watermarking Scheme with Blob-Oriented and Modular-Arithmetic- Based Spatial-Domain Mechanism. *Journal of Visual Communication and Image Representation, 12*(2), 136–151. doi:10.1006/jvci.2000.0454

Liu, N., Amin, P., Ambalavanan, A., & Subbalakshmi, K. P. (2006). An Overview of Digital Watermarking. In *Multimedia Security Technologies for Digital Rights Management*. Academic Press. doi:10.1016/B978-012369476-8/50009-9

Lukac, M., Perkowski, M., Goi, H., Pivtoraiko, M., Yu, C. H., Chung, K., ... Kim, Y.-D. (2003). Evolutionary approach to quantum and reversible circuits synthesis. *Artificial Intelligence Review, 20*(3–4), 361–417. doi:10.1023/B:AIRE.0000006605.86111.79

Lukac, M., Pivtoraiko, M., Mishchenko, A., & Perkowski, M. (2002). Automated synthesis of generalized reversible cascades using genetic algorithms. *5th International Workshop on Boolean Problems*, 33–45.

Maity, S. P., Kundu, M. K., & Seba, M. (2009). Dual Purpose FWT Domain Spread Spectrum Image Watermarking in Real-Time. *Computers & Electrical Engineering, 35*(2), 415–433. doi:.compeleceng.2008.06.00310.1016/j

Majumdar, S., Das, T. S., & Sarkar, S. K. (2011). DWT and SVD based Image Watermarking Scheme using Noise Visibility and Contrast Sensitivity. *Int. Conf. on Recent Trends in Information Technology*, 938-942. doi:10.1109/ICRTIT.2011.5972409

Maslov, D., & Dueck, G. W. (2003). Garbage in reversible designs of multiple output functions. *Proceedings of the 6th International Symposium on Representations and Methodology of Future Computing Technologies (RM 2003)*, 162–170.

Maslov, D., Dueck, G. W., & Miller, D. M. (2005). Synthesis of Fredkin-Toffoli reversible networks. *IEEE Transactions on Very Large Scale Integration (VLSI) Systems, 13*(6), 765–769. doi:10.1109/TVLSI.2005.844284

Mayers, D. (1998). *Unconditional Security in Quantum Cryptography*. quant-ph/9802025

Megalingam, R. K., Nair, M. M., Srikumar, R., Balasubramanian, V. K., & Sarma, V. S. V. (2010). Performance Comparison of Novel, Robust Spatial Domain Digital Image Watermarking with the Conventional Frequency Domain Watermarking Techniques. *International Conference on Signal Acquisition and Processing*. doi:10.1109/ICSAP.2010.79

Meng, Q., & Gong, C. (2010). Web information classifying and navigation based on neural network. *2nd Int. Conf. on signal processing systems*, *2*, V2-431-V2-433.

Miller, D. M. (2002). Spectral and two-place decomposition techniques in reversible logic. *Proceedings of the IEEE Midwest Symposium on Circuits and Systems (MWSCAS 02)*, II 493–II 496. doi:10.1109/MWSCAS.2002.1186906

Miller, D. M., Maslov, D., & Dueck, G. W. (2003). A transformation based algorithm for reversible logic synthesis. *Proceedings of the Design Automation Conference*, 318–323. doi:10.1145/775832.775915

Mintzer, F., Braudaway, G. W., & Yeung, M. M. (1997). Effective and ineffective digital watermarks. *Proceedings - International Conference on Image Processing*, *3*, 9–12.

Mislav, G., Kresimir, D., & Mohammed, G. (2009). *Recent Advances in Multimedia Signal Processing and Communications*. Springer Science & Business Media.

Mohanty, S. P. (1999). *Digital Watermarking: A Tutorial Review*. Retrieved from http://www.csee.usf.edu accessed

Mohanty, S. P., Parthasarathy, G., Elias, K., & Nishikanta, P. (2006). A Novel Invisible Color Image Watermarking Scheme using Image Adaptive Watermark Creation and Robust Insertion-Extraction. *Proceeding of the 8th IEEE International Symposium on Multimedia (ISM '06)*. doi:10.1109/ISM.2006.7

Mukherjee, D. P., Maitra, S., & Acton, S. T. (2004). Spatial domain digital watermarking of multimedia objects for buyer authentication. *IEEE Transactions on Multimedia*, *6*(1), 1–15. doi:10.1109/TMM.2003.819759

Ni, Z., Shi, W. Q., Ansari, N., Su, W., Sun, Q., & Lin, X. (2008). Robust Lossless Image Data Hiding Designed for Semi-Fragile Image Authentication. *IEEE Transactions on Circuits and Systems for Video Technology*, *18*(4), 497–509. doi:10.1109/TCSVT.2008.918761

Ni, Z., Shi, Y. Q., Ansari, N., & Su, W. (2003). Reversible data hiding. *Proc. of the 2003 Int. Symposium on Circuits and Systems (ISCAS 2003)*, 2, 912-915.

Ni, Z., Shi, Y. Q., Ansari, N., & Su, W. (2006). Reversible data hiding. *IEEE Transactions on Circuits and Systems for Video Technology*, *16*(3), 354–362. doi:10.1109/TCSVT.2006.869964

Ono, M., Han, S., Fujiyoshi, M., & Kiya, H. (2009). A location map-free reversible data hiding method for specific area embedding. *IEICE Electronics Express*, *6*(8), 483–489. doi:10.1587/elex.6.483

Pappas, T. E. (1992). An adaptive clustering algorithm for image segmentation. *INEE Trans. on Signal Processing*, *40*(4), 901–914. doi:10.1109/78.127962

Patra, J. C., Phua, J. E., & Rajan, D. (2010). DCT domain watermarking scheme using Chinese Remainder Theorem for image authentication. *IEEE International Conference on Multimedia and Expo*. doi:10.1109/ICME.2010.5583326

Perkowski, M., Jozwiak, L., & Kerntopf, P. (2001). A general decomposition for reversible logic. *Proceedings of the 5th International Workshop on Applications of Reed-Muller Expansion in Circuit Design (Reed-Muller'01)*, 119–138.

Ramani, K., Prasad, E. V., & Varadarajan, S. (2007). Steganography using BPCS to the Integer Wavelet Transformed image. *International Journal of Computer Science and Network Security*, *7*(7), 293–302.

Rigatos, G. G., & Rzafestas, S. G. (2006). Quantum learning for neural assicoative memories. *Fuzzy Sets and Systems*, *157*(13), 1797–1813. doi:10.1016/j.fss.2006.02.012

Sayood, K. (2006). Introduction to data compression. *Morgan Kaufmann Series in Multimedia Information and Systems, Elsevier*, *3E*, 183–217.

Shah, P. (2015). A DWT-SVD Based Digital Watermarking Technique for Copyright Protection. *International Conference on Electrical, Electronics, Signals, Communication and Optimization*. doi:10.1109/EESCO.2015.7253806

Shende, V. V., Prasad, A. K., Markov, I. L., & Hayes, J. P. (2002). Reversible logic circuit synthesis. *Proceedings of the International Conference on Computer Aided Design*, 125–132.

Sinha Roy, S., Saha, S., & Basu, A. (2015). Generic Testing Architecture for Digital Watermarking. *Proc. FRCCD-2015*, 50-58.

Song, W., Hou, J., & Li, Z. (2008). SVD and pseudorandom circular chain based watermarking for image authentication. *Journal of Beijing Jiaotong University*, *32*(2), 71–75.

Stach, J., & Alattar, A. M. (2004). A High Capacity Invertible Data Hiding Algorithm using a Generalized Reversible Integer Transform. *IS&T / SPIE's 16th International Symposium on Electronic Imaging*, *5306*, 386-396.

Sur, A., Sagar, S. S., Pal, R., Mitra, P., & Mukhopadhyay, J. (2009). A New Image Watermarking Scheme using Saliency Based Visual Attention Model. *Proceedings of IEEE Annual India Conference*. doi:10.1109/INDCON.2009.5409402

Tanaka, K., Nakamura, Y., & Matsui, K. (1990). Embedding secret information into a dithered multilevel image. *Proc. IEEE Military Communications Conference*. doi:10.1109/MILCOM.1990.117416

The USC-SIPI Image Database. (n.d.). Retrieved from http://sipi.usc.edu/database/database.php?volume=misc

Thodi, D. M., & Rodriguez, J. J. (2004). Reversible watermarking by prediction-error expansion. *Proceedings - IEEE Southwest Symposium on Image Analysis and Interpretation*, *6*, 21–25.

Thodi, D. M., & Rodriguez, J. J. (2007). Expansion Embedding Techniques for Reversible Watermarking. *IEEE Transactions on Image Processing*, *16*(3), 721–730. doi:10.1109/TIP.2006.891046 PMID:17357732

Tian, J. (2002). Reversible watermarking by difference expansion. *Proc. of Workshop on Multimedia and Security: Authentication, Secrecy, and Steganalysis*, 19-22.

Tirkel, A. Z., Rankin, G. A., Van Schyndel, R. M., Ho, W. J., Mee, N. R. A., & Osborne, C. F. (1993). *Electronic Water Mark. Digital Image Computing: Techniques and Applications 1993*. Macquarie University.

Tsai, C., Chiang, H., Fan, K., & Chung, C. (2005, November). Reversible data hiding and lossless reconstruction of binary images using pair-wise logical computation mechanism. *Pattern Recognition*, *38*(11), 1993–2006. doi:10.1016/j.patcog.2005.03.001

Verma, M., & Yadav, P. (2013). Capacity and Security analysis of watermark image truly imperceptible. *Int. Journal of Advanced Research in Computer and Communication Engineering*, *2*(7), 2913–2917.

Vlachopiannts, G., & Lee, K. Y. (2008). Quantum-inspired evolutionary algorithm for real and reactive power systems. *IEEE Transactions on Power Systems, 23*(4), 1627-1636.

Vleeschouwer, C. D., Delaigle, J. F., & Macq, B. (2003). Circular interpretation of bijective transformations in lossless watermarking for media asset management. *IEEE Transactions on Multimedia, 5*(1), 97–105. doi:10.1109/TMM.2003.809729

Weiner, J., & Mirkes, K. (1972). *Watermarking.* Appleton, WI: The Institute of Paper Chemistry.

Wille, R., Le, H. M., Dueck, G. W., & Grobe, D. (2008). Quantified synthesis of reversible logic. Design, Automation and Test in Europe (DATE 08), 1015–1020.

Wioletta, W., & Ogiela, M. R. (2016). Digital images authentication scheme based on bimodal biometric watermarking in an independent domain. *Journal of Visual Communication and Image Representation, 38*, 1–10. doi:10.1016/j.jvcir.2016.02.006

Wong, M. L. D., Lau, S. I. J., Chong, N. S., & Sim, K. Y. (2013). A Salient Region Watermarking Scheme for Digital Mammogram Authentication. *International Journal of Innovation, Management and Technology, 4*(2), 228–232.

Wujie, Z., Lu, Y., Zhongpeng, W., Mingwei, W., Ting, L., & Lihui, S. (2016). Binocular visual characteristicsbased fragile watermarking schemefor tamper detection in stereoscopic images. *InternationalJournal of Electronics and Communications, 70*(1), 77–84. doi:10.1016/j.aeue.2015.10.006

Xiang-yang, W., Yu-nan, L., Shuo, L., Hong-ying, Y., Pan-pan, N., & Yan, Z. (2015). A new robust digital watermarking using local polar harmonic transform. *Journal of Computers and Electrical Engineering, 46*, 403–418. doi:10.1016/j.compeleceng.2015.04.001

Xu, H., Wanga, J., & Kim, H. J. (2010). Near-Optimal Solution to Pair Wise LSB Matching Via an Immune Programming Strategy. *Information Sciences, 180*(8), 1201–1217. doi:10.1016/j.ins.2009.12.027

Xuan, G., Shi, Y. Q., Ni, Z. C., Chen, J., Yang, C., Zhen, Y., & Zheng, J. (2004). High capacity lossless data hiding based on integer wavelet transform. *Proceedings of IEEE 2004 International Symposium on Circuits and Systems, 2*, 29-32.

Xuan, G., Shi, Y. Q., Yang, C., Zheng, Y., Zou, D., & Chai, P. (2005). Lossless data hiding using integer wavelet transform and threshold embedding technique. *IEEE Int. Conf. on Multimedia and Expo (ICME05)*. doi:10.1109/ICME.2005.1521722

Xuan, G., Yao, Q., Yang, C., Gao, J., Chai, P., Shi, Y. Q., & Ni, Z. (2006). Lossless Data Hiding Using Histogram Shifting Method Based on Integer Wavelets. *5th Int. Workshop on Digital Watermarking (IWDW 2006), LNCS 4283*, p. 323-332. doi:10.1007/11922841_26

Xuan, G., Zhu, J., Chen, J., Shi, Y. Q., Ni, Z., & Su, W. (2002). Distortionless Data Hiding Based on Integer Wavelet Transform. *Electronics Letters, 38*(Dec), 1646–1648. doi:10.1049/el:20021131

Yang, C. H. (2008). Inverted pattern approach to improve image quality of information hiding by LSB substitution. *Pattern Recognition, 41*(8), 2674–2683. doi:10.1016/j.patcog.2008.01.019

Yang, Y., Sun, X., Yang, H., Li, C., & Xiao, R. (2009). A Contrast-Sensitive Reversible Visible Image Watermarking Technique. *IEEE Transactions on Circuits and Systems for Video Technology, 19*(5), 656–667. doi:10.1109/TCSVT.2009.2017401

Yaqub, M. K., & Jaber, A. (2006). Reversible watermarking using modified difference expansion. *Int. Journal of Computing and Information Sciences, 4*(3), 134–142.

Zhang, G. (2011). Quantum-inspired evolutionary algorithms: A survey and empirical study. *Journal of Heuristics, 17*(3), 303–351. doi:10.1007/s10732-010-9136-0

# Chapter 5
# Grayscale Image Segmentation With Quantum-Inspired Multilayer Self-Organizing Neural Network Architecture Endorsed by Context Sensitive Thresholding

**Pankaj Pal**
*RCC Institute of Information Technology, India*

**Siddhartha Bhattacharyya**
*RCC Institute of Information Technology, India*

**Nishtha Agrawal**
*RCC Institute of Information Technology, India*

## ABSTRACT

*A method for grayscale image segmentation is presented using a quantum-inspired self-organizing neural network architecture by proper selection of the threshold values of the multilevel sigmoidal activation function (MUSIG). The context-sensitive threshold values in the different positions of the image are measured based on the homogeneity of the image content and used to extract the object by means of effective thresholding of the multilevel sigmoidal activation function guided by the quantum superposition principle. The neural network architecture uses fuzzy theoretic concepts to assist in the segmentation process. The authors propose a grayscale image segmentation method endorsed by context-sensitive thresholding technique. This quantum-inspired multilayer neural network is adapted with self-organization. The architecture ensures the segmentation process for the real-life images as well as synthetic images by selecting intensity parameter as the threshold value.*

DOI: 10.4018/978-1-5225-5219-2.ch005

# INTRODUCTION

Image processing using image segmentation is a difficult task to recover the objects from multilevel images. So many research approaches have been taken out to reconstruct the object from the multilevel background, but it still remains a fallacy to recover the true objects ideally. The multilayer self organizing neural network (MLSONN) architecture is unable to extract the gray scale objects from the blurred and noisy atmosphere which is designed by Ghosh et al., 1993 (Ghosh et al., 1993) and is used to extract the binary objects efficiently. Here, interconnection weights of different layers viz. between input to hidden layer and hidden to output layer are updated by means of fuzzy measures. This architecture is limited only for the bi-level sigmoid activation function to segment the binary images. The authors (Pal et al., 1993) have described the color image segmentation technique using fuzzy and non-fuzzy methods considering segmentation of range images and neural network based approaches. The authors (Pantofaru et al., 2005) have presented the result of the mean shift segmentation and the efficient graph-based segmentation techniques for objective evaluation algorithm describing the three components viz. the Correctness, the Stability with respect to parameter choice and the Stability with respect to image choice. If these characteristics are fully satisfied by the segmentation technique, then it can be more useful by larger systems. The authors have considered the pixel location and color feature for each and every image for this segmentation algorithm using the Berkeley segmentation database. The authors (Bhattacharyya et al., 2007) have described on the true color image segmentation by self supervised PSONN architecture using multilevel sigmoidal activation function. Regarding this proposed architecture, it is the extension version of standard single self organizing neural network architecture (SONN) and comprises input or source layer, three middle layers for segmentation of three primary color components and the output layer or sink layer. To segment the color image for first object recovery in large image database, the probability of pixel distribution is implemented (Kang et al., 2008). After incorporating three channel images of R, G and B from the given image, and then applying pixel distribution is taken out using similarity measures using the well known defined distribution function Weibull, Exponential, Beta, Gamma, Normal, and Uniform. Using the measurement of sum least of square error, to fit the image to the distribution. Under consideration of minimum amount of error, image is quantized to gray levels for three channels of distribution using threshold value and then these three channel values are fused together to get the desired information. Few years' latter authors (Bhattacharyya et al., 2010) proposed multilevel image segmentation using a MUSIG activation function which is more efficient to extract the multilevel images by means of functionally modifying the network. The MUSIG activation function is characterized by ignoring heterogeneity of the image information content

142

for understanding equal and fixed class responses. The authors De S. et al. (De S. et al., 2010) described under consideration of the heterogeneity of the image information content in the segmented images by applying optimized MUSIG (OptiMUSIG) activation function. OptiMUSIG activation function is used in another way to segment the true color image segmentation (De S. et al, 2012) on optimized class responses on self organizing neural network architecture. The authors De S. et al. considered generic based optimized segmentation method. Gray scale image is segmented (De S. et al., 2012) on optimized class responses without considering the heterogeneity of image information content by optimization of MUSIG (OptiMUSIG) activation function. It may or may not generate good quality of segmented outputs. There are so many research works have been done to recover the object from the different images. Segmentation is one of the approaches where object is reconstructed from the image. The gray scale image is segmented to recover the object by means of context sensitive thresholding implementation technique. In this chapter, the authors propose a gray scale image segmentation method with a quantum inspired based neural network architecture having multilayer self organization nature with endorsed by context sensitive thresholding approaches, which is more efficient to extract the multilevel gray scale objects. The objective of this chapter is to extend the functional modification of QMLSONN architecture so as to segment the gray scale multilevel images by adapting the context sensitive thresholding using multilevel sigmoidal activation function (MUSIG) activation function as shown in Figure 1. Quantum computer has the ability to segment the gray scale images very efficiently as the extraction time is very less as compared to the classical computation technique. Quantum bit is able to do this job tactically using the quantum superposition principle. In this chapter, authors use the segmentation technique using a context sensitive thresholding concept to improve the image intensity information. In the process of image segmentation, image is subdivided i.e. segmented into different classes corresponding to correlate in different regions according to the required features of interest. Here the pixels of compactness of groups are taken together as a whole for the stipulated attributes of similar properties. Authors (Yogamangalam et al., 2013) have described the different image segmentation techniques, mentioning Markov Random Field (MRF) is the strongest and the simplest method for cancelling the noise to recover the object from the noisy atmospheric image. According to the authors' overview, the segmented parts are enclosed to cancel the noise more easily from the noisy image. Binary object is extracted from the noisy environment is efficiently done using quantum version of MLSONN architecture, proposed by Bhattacharyya et al. (Bhattacharyya et al., 2014).

Image segmentation using quantum computation plays an important role in the field of image processing to reconstruct and recollect the objects from the original background. In classical approaches, an image is segmented using the classical bits either zero ('0') or one ('1') in the thresholding technique. In this chapter authors propose the quantum version of MLSONN architecture that is known as QMLSONN architecture. It is used to segment the gray scale/ multilevel images efficiently using the multilevel sigmoidal activation function (MUSIG) activation function accompanied by context sensitive thresholding technique. In the QMLSONN architecture the inter connection weights are in the form of rotation gates and follow a second order neighborhood topology. The processing nodes of the different layers are simply qubits and are represented as

$$|\phi\rangle = \alpha|0\rangle + \beta|1\rangle$$

where, $\alpha$ and $\beta$ are the probability amplitudes corresponding to $|0\rangle$ and $|1\rangle$ respectively, provided that $\alpha^2 + \beta^2 = 1$. The qubits in the input layer, hidden layer and output layers look like as given:

$$\begin{pmatrix} \langle\beta_{11}| & \langle\beta_{12}| & \cdots & \cdots & \langle\beta_{1n}| \\ \cdots & \cdots & \cdots & \cdots & \cdots \\ \cdots & \cdots & \cdots & \cdots & \cdots \\ \cdots & \cdots & \cdots & \cdots & \cdots \\ \langle\beta_{m1}| & \langle\beta_{m2}| & \cdots & \cdots & \langle\beta_{mn}| \end{pmatrix} \begin{pmatrix} \langle\lambda_{11}| & \langle\lambda_{12}| & \cdots & \cdots & \langle\lambda_{1n}| \\ \cdots & \cdots & \cdots & \cdots & \cdots \\ \cdots & \cdots & \cdots & \cdots & \cdots \\ \cdots & \cdots & \cdots & \cdots & \cdots \\ \langle\lambda_{m1}| & \langle\lambda_{m2}| & \cdots & \cdots & \langle\lambda_{mn}| \end{pmatrix}$$

*Qubits of input layer*      *Qubits of hidden layer*

$$\begin{pmatrix} \langle\delta_{11}| & \langle\delta_{12}| & \cdots & \cdots & \langle\delta_{1n}| \\ \cdots & \cdots & \cdots & \cdots & \cdots \\ \cdots & \cdots & \cdots & \cdots & \cdots \\ \cdots & \cdots & \cdots & \cdots & \cdots \\ \langle\delta_{m1}| & \langle\delta_{m2}| & \cdots & \cdots & \langle\delta_{mn}| \end{pmatrix}$$

*Qubits of output layer*

The organization of this chapter is as follows. Firstly introduction section illustrates the use of MUSIG activation function on MLSONN and QMLSONN architectures along with the concepts of qubits in the input, hidden and output layers. After that the concept of fuzzy logic behind the image pixels intensity using the fuzzy hostility, fuzzy cardinality, etc are described and measured. Covering these discussions the architectures of MLSONN and QMLSONN are explained one by one for gray scale image segmentation. In the next phase of this chapter, the various segmentation techniques are explained. Here gray scale image segmentation using quantum computation by means of superposition principle is discussed. After that, the various thresholding techniques in existence are discussed. In this phase it is illustrated as to how the segmentation efficiency is measured and the skewness measurement in thresholding is done using various threshold strategies. Last but not least, there is a result, discussion and comparison between the MLSONN and QMLSONN architectures. The final section of this chapter ends with a conclusion and few references are given for further study.

## QUBITS AND RELATED THINGS

The basic unit of quantum computation is known as quantum bits or simply qubits. In classical computation system, the bit is represented either '0' or '1' but in quantum computation qubit is the superposition of '0' and '1'. At any moment qubit represents '0' and '1' simultaneously. The qubit can be represented as

*Figure 1. Three types of MUSIG functions*

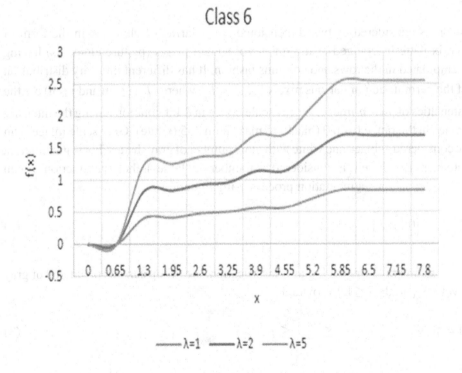

$$|\phi\rangle = \alpha|0\rangle + \beta|1\rangle \tag{1}$$

Here, $\alpha$ and $\beta$ represent the probability amplitudes of $|\phi\rangle$ for finding $|0\rangle$ and $|1\rangle$ respectively provided $\alpha^2 + \beta^2 = 1$

The notation $|\ \rangle$ is represented as ket notation. In quantum gates, qubit acts as unitary operator in Hillbert space (Aytekin et al., 2013).

The qubit is represented in matrix notation as $\begin{bmatrix} \cos\varphi \\ \sin\varphi \end{bmatrix}$

To process the information on qubit, the rotation gate is used and is used as

$$R(\theta) = \begin{bmatrix} \cos\theta & -\sin\theta \\ \sin\theta & \cos\theta \end{bmatrix}$$

In quantum mechanics, the qubits have distinct properties such as superposition, entanglement, coherence, de-coherence, etc., which is more useful to design quantum gates to process the information (Bhattacharyya et al., 2013).

## CONCEPT OF IMAGE

Image is considered as two dimensional $m \times n$ array of elements in the form of matrix pattern arranged as a numbers of square pixels (picture elements) having manipulated in the rows and columns fashion. It has different intensity distribution of the permutation of various pixels $I_{ij}$. $I = I_{ij}$, where, $I_{ij}$ ($i \leq$ m and j $\leq$ n) are the intensities of $m \times n$ image. A gray scale image in 8-bit notation having the intensity values in the range from 0 (black) to maximum 255 (white). Gray scale images can be considered as black and white with more number of gray shades. For segmentation, into class L (where L is considered as number of classes), then the function 'f' can be written as for segmentation process using Equation 2.

$$f : I \rightarrow \begin{bmatrix} 0......L \end{bmatrix} \tag{2}$$

For 256 gray levels of L class classification, the group can be considered of gray levels as {pl: 0≤ l ≤ L} provided

$$0 = p_0 \leq p_1 \leq p_2 \cdots\cdots \leq p_{L-1} \leq p_L \tag{3}$$

all the pixels having the gray levels $s_L$ belong to $\left[p_{L-1}, p_L\right]$ of L class contribution. For a particular class in the L class classification the following conditions must be satisfied $s_L \cap s_R = 0$, for $L \neq R, 1 \leq l, R \leq L$ and $\cup_{l=1}^{L} s_L = \left[0 \cdots 255\right]$

## FUZZY SET BASICS

Image is considered as a matrix of different fuzzy intensity levels of pixels. So, a fuzzy set can be characterized as a membership function of $\mu_A\left(x_i\right)$ of different pixels of fuzzy set (Ross et al., 1995) $A = \left\{x_1, x_2, x_3, \cdots \cdots x_n\right\}$, where $0 \leq \mu_A\left(x_i\right) \leq 1$ .The degree of containment of the fuzzy set is defined by the member ship (Bhattacharyya et al., 2010) function. More is the degree of containment the membership value of the fuzzy set is close to 1 and less is the degree of containment, lower is the membership value. To understand the fuzziness for two kinds of fuzzy sets A and B having the membership functions $f_A\left(x\right)$ and $f_B\left(x\right)$, the truth values must lie within the range $\begin{bmatrix} 0 & 1 \end{bmatrix}$. Two fuzzy sets A and B should be equal provided $f_A\left(x\right) = f_B\left(x\right)$, $\forall$ x∈X. The complement of the fuzzy set A can be written as $A' = 1 - A$. If $C$ be a union of two fuzzy sets A and B having membership functions $f_A\left(x\right)$ and $f_B\left(x\right)$, then $C = A \cup B$, provided the membership functions are related by the equation $f_C(x) = Max\left[f_A(x), f_B(x)\right], \forall x \in X$, where, $f_C\left(x\right)$ is the membership function of the fuzzy set C. If $C$ generates a fuzzy set having the membership function $f_C\left(x\right)$ after insertion of two kinds of fuzzy sets A and B, having the membership functions $f_A\left(x\right)$ and $f_B\left(x\right)$, then C is given by $C = A \cap B, \forall x \in X$ and the membership function $f_C\left(x\right)$ is given by $f_C(x) = Min\left[f_A(x), f_B(x)\right], \forall x \in X$ ; the truth values lie within the range $\begin{bmatrix} 0 & 1 \end{bmatrix}$.

## Fuzzy Cardinality

Considering finite number of elements, the fuzzy cardinality is defined as the sum of the membership values present within the fuzzy set (Bhattacharyya et al., 2010) and is defined as in the Equation 4 as

$$\xi_A = \sum_{i=1}^{n} \mu_A\left(x_i\right) \tag{4}$$

The fuzzy cardinality will be more if higher is the degree in containment of the elements within the fuzzy set and when the degree of contentment of the element in the fuzzy set is less, and then fuzzy cardinality will be less.

## Fuzzy Hostility Index

Any image can be considered as the fuzzy set intensity function. Image is formed by the subsets of neighbors of candidate pixel having different fuzzy set intensity values. The homogeneity of the neighborhood pixels is determined by the closer membership values. Closer are the membership values, higher is the homogeneity and the candidate key is less hostile to its neighbors. The heterogeneity on the other hand determines the rear membership values having the dissimilar intensity values. The neighbors having the homogeneity or heterogeneity are determined by the parameter called hostility index ($\zeta$). The degree of the hostility index for the case of homogeneity or heterogeneity pixels of neighbors for the $n^{th}$ order neighborhood can be determined by equation (Bhattacharyya et al., 2010)

$$\zeta = \frac{3}{2^{n+1}} \sum_{i=1}^{2^{n+1}} \frac{|\mu_p - \mu_{qi}|}{|\mu_p + 1| + |\mu_{qi} + 1|} \tag{5}$$

Where, $\mu_p$ = membership values of the candidate pixels and $\mu_{qi}$ = membership values of the $i^{th}$ neighbors of the corresponding pixels. Hostility index ($\zeta$) lies in the range of 0 and 1 $[0 \leq \zeta \leq 1]$. It indicates that the lesser the hostility index ($\zeta$), higher is the homogeneity and higher the hostility index ($\zeta$) higher the heterogeneity.

## MLSONN ARCHITECTURE

The classical version of the Multilayer Self Organizing Neural Network Architecture (MLSONN) is shown in Figure 2. It (Ghosh et al., 1993) has the ability to extract objects from noisy blurred images. This self supervised self organizing multilayer neural network architecture is more useful for removal of noise from the real life noisy images for extraction of the objects. It comprises three layers viz. input layer, hidden layer and the output layer. There are two types of connection weights, one is input to hidden layer and another is hidden to output layer. The sigmoidal activation function as shown in equation 6 is applied to initiate the process of noise removing from the

*Figure 2. MLSONN Architecture*

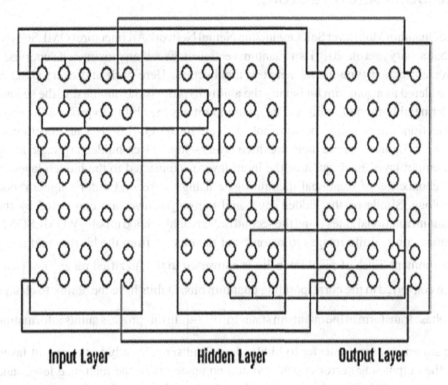

**Input Layer**          **Hidden Layer**          **Output Layer**

noise state of images. Each pixel is connected of the input layer by the connection weight to the pixels of the hidden layer. Similarly, connection weight connects the output layer with the hidden layer. At the output stage the error is calculated and for unrecognized output the process is backpropagated from the output layer to the input layer. This process is continued until a stable output is achieved. The bipolar sigmoidal activation function is illustrated by

$$f(x) = \frac{1}{1 + e^{-\lambda(x-\theta)}} \tag{6}$$

Here, $\lambda$ parameter decides how the function is stiffer and the parameter $\theta$ determines the bias or the threshold value of this function. This bi-level sigmoidal activation function lies in the range 0 to 1 and generates two types of responses, one is bright (1) and another is black (0).

## QMLSONN ARCHITECTURE

The Quantum Multilayer Self Organizing Neural Network Architecture (QMLSONN) (Bhattacharyya et al., 2014) is a quantum version of the self organizing self supervised error correction type neural network architecture. Here each and every pixel is considered as a quantum bit having the ability to process the qubit using the second order neighborhood topology. The quantum bit has the ability to process the error correction ability using the threshold values. In the QMLSONN architecture as shown in figure 3, where there are three layers – input layer, hidden layer and lastly the output layer. Each qubit of the input layer is connected to the hidden layer by the connection of rotational quantum gate using the second order neighborhood topology. Similarly, the hidden layer and the output layer are connected by the quantum rotational gates using the second order neighborhood topology. QMLSONN operates on real life images to reconstruct the objects from the blurred and noisy environment. Each of pixel intensity is converted to the fuzzified range $\begin{bmatrix} 0 & 1 \end{bmatrix}$ and then converted to the corresponding quantum bits. Qubits have the ability to change its phase transform in the quantum states to $\begin{bmatrix} 0 & \dfrac{\pi}{2} \end{bmatrix}$. In this process qubits information are summed up and transfer to hidden layer and subsequently to the output layer. At the output stage error is detected and compared with the reference levels and then processed information is fed back to the input layer for further processing by the quantum backpropagation principle. When the error is considered as minimum and the stabilization is achieved then we get the desire output. The single qubit rotational gate (as shown in Equation 7) (Bhattacharyya et al., 2014) is applied to the quantum bits, rotational gate is transformed to the required format to generate the output (as shown below in Equation 8) (Bhattacharyya et al., 2014).

$$R\left(\theta\right) = \begin{bmatrix} \cos\theta & -\sin\theta \\ \sin\theta & \cos\theta \end{bmatrix} \tag{7}$$

$$R'\left(\theta\right) = \begin{bmatrix} \cos\theta & -\sin\theta \\ \sin\theta & \cos\theta \end{bmatrix}\begin{bmatrix} \cos\varphi_0 \\ \sin\varphi_0 \end{bmatrix} = \begin{bmatrix} \cos\left(\theta + \varphi_0\right) \\ \sin\left(\theta + \varphi_0\right) \end{bmatrix} \tag{8}$$

*Figure 3. Schematic of QMLSONN*

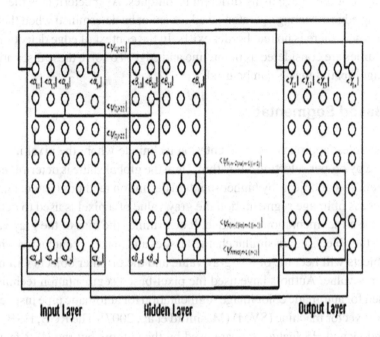

**Input Layer**        **Hidden Layer**        **Output Layer**

## IMAGE SEGMENTATION CLASSIFICATION FUNDAMENTAL AND THE RELATED DIFFERENT METHODS

Image segmentation plays an important role to retrieve the feature measurement for an object belonging to a particular category. Various types of segmentation techniques are adapted for image segmentation viz. Edge-Based Segmentation, Pixel-Based Segmentation, Region-based Segmentation, Model-Based Segmentation, Clustering Based Segmentation, Watershed Based Segmentation, PDE based Segmentation, ANN Based Segmentation, etc. Authors describe these topics one by one in this chapter.

### Edge-Based Segmentation

In this method the information is collected from the edges of the image. Categorically all the edge detection operators are two types. One belongs to 1st order derivatives and other belongs to the 2nd derivatives. Prewitt operator, Sobel operator, Canny operator, Test operator are of 1st order derivatives types where as Laplacian operator, Zero-crossings are of the 2nd derivatives types (Saini et al., 2014). Within this edge it can be determined either by the zero crossing for 2nd order derivatives or by the extremity of the 1st order derivatives. If segmentation of image is not accepted for the segmented outcome, then it can be grouped into chains and are added to recover the whole border of the image using different techniques. As it determines the edge by considering edge detecting operator, so edge cannot be determined when there is no border or where there is no real border exists. In the context of edge detection, three discontinuities are considered as point, line and edge. To solve these discontinuities of an image, spatial masks can be used.

## Pixel-Based Segmentation

It is the simplest approach for segmentation technique where the pixel intensity is considered by proper selection algorithm. Here the global value is determined using the different sets of objects by higher standard definition methods (Das et al., 2015). In the process of image segmentation the gray value of a pixel is used to determine the pixel based segmentation technique. It determines the bias of the gray value on the size of the objects for dissimilar characteristics and makes a conclusion where the darker objects will become of low gray value and the brighter objects will become of high gray value. Authors have used the pixel-based segmentation technique for pixel based for automatic color image segmentation for automatic pipe inspection by the support vector machine (SVM) (Mashford et al., 2007). The RGB, HSB, Gabor, local window and HS feature sets are used by the authors but the HSB feature set gives better performance.

## Region-Based Segmentation

Here image is segmented into different sub regions based on continuity method considering similar gray values of one kind of region and different gray values of other kind of regions. To determine the object information, the region based segmentation process may be considered where the candidate pixels and with its neighbors (Saini et al., 2014) have the same gray values. It is very much useful where the noise immunity is high. It is simpler than that of edge based segmentation. In the edge based partition the intensity is changed rapidly from the nearer to the edges and in the region based method partition is based on a predetermined method. Region growing is based on the accumulation of the pixels to make a larger region. To determine the region-based segmentation the algorithm can be described is as follows: (a) selecting the candidate pixel from the original image as considered as seed pixel. (b) Using the selection of the similarities measures according to the intensity value, color, noise, etc. (c) arrange the group of pixels according to predetermined characteristics having similar type of characteristics. (d) stop the region growing procedure when no more pixels can be accommodated with this criterion (Saini et al., 2014).

## Model-Based Segmentation

Using this approach, labels are collected by means of pixels having priory known objectives of the image data. Ambiguity or uncertainty may be introduced to generate the labels to (Suetens 1991) pixels. The low level image features may be considered such as homogeneity, discontinuity, etc for pixels generations from the labels in a deterministic approach. Another author has presented the model based segmentation approach where the method is explained in two parts. The first part is the localization process and the second part optimizes the procedure.

## Clustering Based Segmentation

It is an unsupervised approach to segment the image to get better information and betterment of the object information (Bora et al., 2014). When partition is being done using clustering based segmentation we consider two properties viz. High Cohesion and Low Coupling. In this clustering technique, the data items having the high similarities may be considered belonging to the High Cohesion property and for Low Coupling prosperity each and every cluster should have different data items. In the clustering principles the cluster is divided in two categories- one is Hard Clustering and another is Soft Clustering. In the hard clustering technique the data items are tightly bound from the other clustering but in case of Soft Clustering the membership values of the data items include their presence in the different clusters. Due to low computational complexity K-Means algorithm is best way for hard clustering technique (Bora et al., 2014).

## Watershed Based Segmentation

Before going to watershed based segmentation technique, the segmentation of image is done using the different intensity levels of each pixels and the clusters are generated having the minimum distance. In (Salman, 2006) have combined between K-means, watershed segmentation method, and Difference In Strength (DIS) have been combining for segmentation. At first it is used to determine the watershed segmentation by means of average intensity value of segmented images. In the second part an edge strength method is designed to measure the accurate edge map without the help of watershed algorithm considering the raw data images. Using the different gray values, the image is segmented in different regions (Salman., 2006).

## PDE Based Segmentation

An image is segmented by means of Partial Differential Equation (PDE) based mathematical (Sharma et al., 2015) segmentation technique where the boundary is not easily determined or defined. In this numerical approach of PDE based image segmentation technique, the image is segmented in different sections/parts to retrieve the meaningful information and extract the object from the inaccurate background. In this methodology the contour is determined and boundary is selected for the partitioning of the image to analyze the object information. The authors envisage the contour depending on the level set function considering the two criterions viz. one is outside the boundary and other is inside the boundary for the stipulated segmented region provided the zero level is set at the boundary.

## ANN Based Segmentation

Artificial Neural Network (ANN) segmentation technique is very much useful for segmenting images for determination of the object from different noisy perspectives. Authors have used Optical Character Recognition (OCR) (Blumenstein et al., 1998) to retrieve the hand writing using the conventional algorithm along with the ANN based algorithm. Authors have segmented the scanned hand writing character in the height and width accordingly. After segregating the checking is done according to the column of pixels.

## MULTILEVEL IMAGE THRESHOLDING

Gray scale image is generally considered as multilevel image. Image is segmented into the different regions depending on the intensity levels. For color image segmentation the intensity value is calculated from the color and for gray scale image segmentation, the intensity value is used from gray levels. (Mishra et al., 2014) design the thresholding technique using particle Swarm Optimization technique for multilevel image segmentation. Considering, the Kapur's entropy criterion method as fitness function to segment an image. In this method they think about the result as better when the swarm size small. Choice of threshold values of the image segmentation process is decided in different ways. Here authors discuss the two kinds of thresholding processes, one is Global Thresholding and another is Multilevel Thresholding.

## Global Thresholding

In this segmentation process one threshold value is taken into account. There are two partitions one whose gray value is more than threshold (Mishra et al., 2014) and another is whose gray value is less corresponding to that threshold point. Two segmentation procedures are discussed in this section.

$$I^T(x;y) = 1 \qquad (9)$$

for $I(x;y) \geq T$ and

$$I^T(x;y) = 0 \qquad (10)$$

for $I(x;y) \langle 0$

Here, $I^T(x;y)$ and $I(x;y)$ are the segmented image and the pixel of the original image at the pixel point (x, y). It is very easy to implement this type of design. But one problem arises when the intensity value of color image is same as that of gray scale intensity. Then the sharp pixel intensities are lost. Semi- thresholding is one kind (Mishra et al., 2014) of Global Thresholding technique where the procedure is same but the new intensity value is changed. The intensity value is more than that of original image pixel intensity. Lower intensity value of the pixels below the threshold limit generates a '0' value. As in this case two types of partitions are segregated, so this process is known as bi-level thresolding.

$$I^T(x;y) = I(x,y) \qquad (11)$$

for $I(x;y) \geq T$ and

$$I^T(x;y) = 0 \qquad (12)$$

for $I(x;y)\langle 0$

## Multilevel Thresholding

To overcome the difficulty in the Global Thresholding process that is in the absence of sharp pixels, the Multilevel Thresholding process is adapted. More thresholding values are used to segment (Mishra et al., 2014) an image. For n number of threshold values, there will be (n+1) partitions. From the mathematical relation one can implement the Multilevel Thresholding having two intensity values $T_1$ and $T_2$ for three portions of the segmented image as given below:

$$I^T(x,y) = \begin{cases} V_1 \ if & I(x,y) \geq T_2 \\ V_2 \ if \ I(x,y) \leq I(x,y) < T_2 \\ V_3 \ if & I(x,y) \leq T_1 \end{cases} \tag{13}$$

## MULTILAVEL SIGMOIDAL ACTIVATION FUNCTION (MUSIG)

For binary image extraction the MLSONN is competent and is able to extract the objects from a noisy environment using a bi-level sigmoidal activation function. It is extended to incorporate the segmentation of gray scale images using the multilevel sigmoidal activation function which is robust in structure and is easier to segment the gray scale images using the QMLSONN architecture. The MUSIG function generates multiple outputs at multiple gray levels to segment multilevel images. In this chapter authors describe the modification of the QMLSONN architecture which is used to gray scale object extraction by means of segmentation technique. The compact form of sigmoidal activation function (as shown in Figure 1) is defined as

$$y = f_M(x) = \frac{1}{\alpha_\gamma + e^{-\lambda(x-\theta)}} \tag{14}$$

where $\lambda$ represents and decides the steepness of the function; $\alpha_\gamma$ controls the multilevel class responses (Bhattacharyya et al., 2010) and is defined as $\alpha_\gamma = \dfrac{C_N}{c_\gamma - c_{\gamma-1}}$ Here, $\gamma$ is called the gray scale object index and its range is $(1 \leq \gamma < K)$. Here, K= Number of gray scale object index or classes; $c_\gamma = \gamma^{th}$ gray scale contribution class and $c_{\gamma-1} = (\gamma-1)^{th}$ gray scale contribution class. $C_N$ = Neighborhood gray scale contribution class. If we consider $\alpha_\gamma = 1$ then the function behaves as the standard bi-level sigmoidal activation function and is given by

$$y = f_{sig}(x) = \frac{1}{1 + e^{-\lambda(x-\theta)}} \tag{15}$$

$\theta$ = fixed threshold or bias value and is depend on the activation function behavior. From equation (14) one can determine the responses ($y_{s_{\alpha\gamma}}$) of different subnormal function, where, $(0 \leq y_{s_{\alpha\gamma}} \leq 1)$ by fixing the suitable parameter $\alpha_\gamma$. To determine the ultimate multilevel activation function, we superimpose different subnormal responses, which is more useful for multi- polar responses. The generalized version of the MUSIG function is given below (Bhattacharyya et al., 2010):

$$f(x; \alpha_\gamma, c_\gamma) \leftarrow f(x; \alpha_\gamma, c_\gamma) + (\gamma - 1)f(\gamma c_\gamma), c_{\gamma-1} \leq x < \gamma c_\gamma; \text{ Where,}$$

$$f(x; \alpha_\gamma, c_\gamma) = \frac{1}{\alpha_\gamma + e^{-\lambda(x-(\gamma-1)c_{\gamma-1}-\theta)}} \tag{16}$$

The MUSIG function is in closer form is given by

$$f_{MUSIG}(x) = \sum_{\lambda=1}^{K} x + (\lambda - 1)c_{\gamma-1}, c_{\gamma-1} \leq x < \gamma c_\gamma \tag{17}$$

Using equation (16), we get MUSIG function as

$$f_{MUSIG}(x; \alpha_\gamma, c_\gamma) = \frac{1}{\alpha_\gamma + e^{-\lambda(x-(\gamma-1)c_{\gamma-1}-\theta)}} \tag{18}$$

For the overall gray scale range, if $c_\gamma$ is of equal values, then it generates the similar subnormal responses $(y_{s_{\alpha\gamma}})$. The ultimate MUSIG activation function constitutes many identical subnormal responses. However, for different $c_\gamma$, it generates different subnormal lobes with different ranges and different shapes. Using the different values of $\alpha_\gamma$, the different values of subnormal lobes are combined together to generate the continuity of the resultant multilevel sigmoidal activation f unction (MUSIG). MUSIG function also generates the bi-level sigmiodal function considering $\alpha_\gamma = 1$. For the input image, the subnormal responses $(y_{s_{\alpha\gamma}})$, can be obtained from the subnormal lobes generates the multilevel response. To generate the number of transition lobes, it requires more number of class responses and can be obtained by using the gray scale contribution $c_\gamma$ . The multilevel sigmoidal activation depends on the thresholding parameter $\theta$. The thresholding aspect is discussed in the next article.

## THRESHOLDING CONCEPTS OF MULTILEVEL SIGMOIDAL ACTIVATION FUNCTION (MUSIG)

As the threshold parameter $\theta$ is considered as a bias value, so, it depends on the design of the multilevel sigmoidal activation function. For better responses, here it is considered as a single fixed point thresholding parameter $\theta$. It ensures that the images are homogeneous in nature. But in the real life situation, real life images are considered as a heterogeneous mixture. So, the thresholding strategy should to adapt to the heterogeneity by tuning the thresholding parameter $\theta$ so as to incorporate image information content. In the next subsection, these are elaborated.

Threshold Parameters: $\theta_{\chi_1}$ and $\theta_{\chi_2}$ realization of image intensity information based on Skewness

Variation of the intensity of the image pixels depends on the skewness. It is a similarity measurement of pixels having the same intensity or the different intensity levels for a particular image corresponding to a certain limit. Skewness equals to zero means equal distribution of pixels. That means there is a normal distribution. The threshold value of the MUSIG function depends upon the cumulative intensity contribution on the neighbor pixels as the pixel geometry is taken into account. The skewness distribution of relative contributive to each pixel furnishes the overall cumulative contribution. Two types of intensities are considered regarding the brightness controls, one is the brighter side another is the darker side. The scope of the skewness distribution to the brighter end specifies more number of brighter pixels than lesser number of darker pixels. That means more number of brighter pixel populations in the brighter side than the darker one. Another way to scope the skewness distribution on the darker side specifies more number of darker pixels than lesser number of brighter pixels. Therefore the threshold values of the brighter and the darker pixels are different. For candidate pixels, the neighbors are arranged as having nearly equal types of skewness factor on the threshold. Bhattacharyya et al., 2010 defined the skewness factor $\chi_1$ and $\chi_2$ for the rearranged or sorted neighbor pixels intensity distribution as

$$\chi_1 = \tau_r - \tau_l \tag{19}$$

Here, $\tau_r$ and $\tau_l$ are the two cumulative skew numbers but having different relations regarding the pixels intensity levels. If we consider the average intensity level for the pixels to be $\Omega$ and any arbitrary pixel intensity levels is p, so we can write $\tau_r$ exists for $p < \Omega$ and $\tau_l$ exists for $p \geq \Omega$. For the second skewness factor $\chi_2$ depends on the medium intensity levels ($\nu$) as well as average intensity levels ($\Omega$) and is given by the relation as

$$\chi_2 = \Omega - \nu . \tag{20}$$

After recognizing the skewness factor $\chi_1$ and $\chi_2$, if $\chi_{12}$ be the resultant skewness factor, so the resultant threshold parameter $\theta_{\chi_{12}}$ can be written as

$$\theta_{\chi_{12}} = \theta \left[ \frac{1 - \Omega \chi_{12}}{2\Omega} \right] \tag{21}$$

where, $\theta$ is the single fixed point uniform threshold parameter of the MUSIG activation function. Therefore the MUSIG activation function can be written as

$$f_{MUSIG}(x; \alpha_\gamma, c_\gamma) = \sum_{\gamma=1}^{K-1} \frac{1}{\alpha_\gamma + e^{-\lambda(x - (\gamma-1)c_\gamma - \theta_{\phi_{12}})}} \tag{22}$$

Threshold Parameters: $\theta_\zeta$ realization of pixel neighborhood fuzzy subsets based on the fuzzy cardinality

According to the concept of fuzzy cardinality $\xi$, the degree of the containment is high when degree of cardinality is high. That means the elements are tightly bound in the fuzzy set. The determination of the pixels having high intensity levels in the fuzzy set of containment to determine the $\theta_\zeta$ threshold parameters. The determination of the threshold parameters $\theta_\zeta$ depends on the darker pixels and the brighter pixels having the cardinality values are $\zeta_d$ and $\zeta_b$ and is defined as under considering the single fixed point uniform threshold parameter $\theta$ as

$$\theta_\xi = \theta\left[1 - \frac{(\theta_b - \theta_d)}{(\theta_b + \theta_d)}\right] \tag{23}$$

Therefore the MUSIG activation function is determined according to the threshold parameter $\theta_\zeta$ is specified as given below

$$f_{MUSIG}(x; \alpha_\gamma, c_\gamma) = \sum_{\gamma=1}^{K-1} \frac{1}{\alpha_\gamma + e^{-\lambda(x-(\gamma-1)c_\gamma - \theta_\xi)}} \tag{24}$$

## SEGMENTATION PERFORMANCE OF SEGMENTED GRAY SCALE IMAGES

Determination of the different types of the quality of segmentation is proposed by authors (Liu et al., 1994) using unsupervised manner is discussed here. Evaluation performance functions are designed in three different ways viz. $F(I)$, $F'(I)$, $Q(I)$.

### Segmented Efficiency Measurement $\left(F(I)\right)$

$$F(I) = \sqrt{K} \sum_{n=1}^{K} \frac{e_n^2}{\sqrt{S_n}} \tag{25}$$

where, $F(I)$ = Evaluation performance function; $K$ = no. of regions to be segmented; $S_n = |R_n|$ is the $n^{th}$ region; $e_n$ = error of the $n^{th}$ gray scale region. The error of the gray scale region is defined as

$$e_n^2 = \sum_{x\varepsilon r=g=b} \sum_{p\varepsilon R_n} (C_x(p) - \bar{C}_x(R_n)^2) \tag{26}$$

where, $\bar{C}_x(R_n)$ is defined as the mean value of the gray scale feature x of region n of $p^{th}$ pixel and $\bar{C}_x(R_n)$ is defined as

$$\bar{C}_x(R_n) = \frac{\sum\limits_{p \varepsilon R_n} C_x(p)}{S_n} \tag{27}$$

$C_x(p)$ is known as the gray scale feature x of pixel p.

## Segmented Efficiency Measurement $\left(F'\left(I\right)\right)$

The authors (Borsotti et al.,1998) have proposed the modified version of the segmentation efficiency, which is more useful to represent the gray scale segmented image and is defined as hereunder

$$F'(I) = \frac{1}{1000S_I} \sqrt{\sum_{a=1}^{Max_{Area}} (N(a))^{1+\frac{1}{a}} \times \sum_{k=1}^{N} \frac{e_n^{\,2}}{\sqrt{S_n}}} \tag{28}$$

Here, N (a) =segmented number of the area a; $Max_{Area}$ =Maximum area of the estimated segmented region; $S_I$ = Area of the gray scale segmented region of interest under consideration.

## Segmented Efficiency Measurement $\left(Q\left(I\right)\right)$

Improvement of the gray scale image segmentation efficiency as disused in Equation 28, the performance is improved as indicated by Borsotti et al. (Borsotti et al., 1998) and also given by equation below:

$$Q(I) = \frac{1}{1000S_I} \sqrt{N} \sum_{n=1}^{N} \left[ \frac{e_n^{\,2}}{1 + \log S_I} + \left( \frac{N\left(S_I\right)}{S_I} \right)^2 \right] \tag{29}$$

Here, $N\left(S_I\right)$ = no. of regions corresponding the area $S_I$ .

# EXPERIMENTAL RESULT AND ANALYSIS

Three types of segmented efficiency measurements are discussed on the basis of two types of gray scale images. One is Baboon image as shown in Figure 4 and another is Lena image as shown in Figure 5 respectively using three classes, viz. class 4, class 6 and class 8. Selected measurement values are shown in boldface type on the table. The values of the segmented efficiency ($\nu$) $F$, $F'$ and $Q$ using QMLSONN architecture on gray scale Lena image of class 4 are 0.5770, 0.6811 and 0.7432 corresponding to extraction time 25.35s with respect to threshold parameter $\theta_\chi$, where as using MLSONN architecture, these values are 0.8558, 0.9007 and 0.9500 and corresponding to extraction time is 28.49s but when considering threshold parameter $\theta_\zeta$, the values of the segmented efficiency using the QMLSONN architecture are 0.5770, 0.6814 and 0.7432 with extraction time is 24.5s, and when using the MLSONN architecture these values are 0.8551, 0.9007 and 0.95 with corresponding time is 28.2s. All the outputs are collected and recorded as shown in the Table 1 for Lena image and in the Table 2 for Baboon image respectively. The segmented object outputs for class 4 corresponding to threshold parameter $\theta_\chi$ on Baboon image and Lena image as shown in Figure 6. Here, Figure 6 (a, c, e, g, i, k, m, o) shows segmented Baboon images and Figure 6 (b, d, f, h, j, l, n, p) shows

*Figure 4. Gray scale Baboon image*

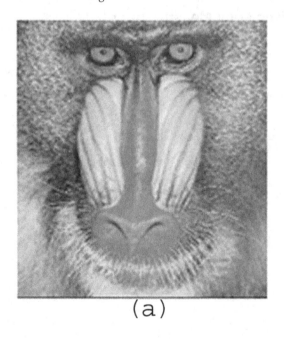

(a)

*Figure 5. Gray scale Lena image*

(b)

*Table 1. Quality of segmentation (υ) on MLSONN and QMLSONN architectures for Lena image*

| Quality of Segmentation (υ) | | | MLSONN Architecture for Lena Image | | | | QMLSONN Architecture for Lena Image | | | |
|---|---|---|---|---|---|---|---|---|---|---|
| Class | υ | Set | $\theta_\chi$ | Time (s) | $\theta_\xi$ | Time (s) | $\theta_\chi$ | Time (s) | $\theta_\xi$ | Time (s) |
| 4 | F | $s_1$ | 0.9002 | 28.3 | 0.9002 | 28.1 | 0.6297 | 27.23 | 0.6291 | 25.61 |
| | | $s_2$ | 0.8917 | 28.01 | 0.8919 | 28.3 | 0.6108 | 27.11 | 0.6109 | 27.15 |
| | | $s_3$ | 0.8763 | 28.54 | 0.8768 | 28.11 | 0.5852 | 26.19 | 0.5852 | 25.22 |
| | | $s_4$ | **0.8558** | 28.49 | **0.8551** | 28.2 | **0.5770** | 25.35 | **0.5770** | 24.5 |
| | F' | $s_1$ | 0.9518 | 28.3 | 0.952 | 28.1 | 0.7083 | 27.23 | 0.7085 | 25.61 |
| | | $s_2$ | 0.9400 | 28.01 | 0.9400 | 28.3 | 0.7117 | 27.11 | 0.7115 | 27.15 |
| | | $s_3$ | 0.9274 | 28.54 | 0.927 | 28.11 | 0.6900 | 26.19 | 0.69 | 25.22 |
| | | $s_4$ | **0.9007** | 28.49 | **0.9007** | 28.2 | **0.6811** | 25.35 | **0.6814** | 24.5 |
| | Q | $s_1$ | 0.9879 | 28.3 | 0.9879 | 28.1 | 0.7904 | 27.23 | 0.7904 | 25.61 |
| | | $s_2$ | 0.9700 | 28.01 | 0.97 | 28.3 | 0.7750 | 27.11 | 0.7750 | 27.15 |
| | | $s_3$ | 0.9598 | 28.54 | 0.95 | 28.11 | 0.7578 | 26.19 | 0.7578 | 25.22 |
| | | $s_4$ | **0.9500** | 28.49 | **0.95** | 28.2 | **0.7432** | 25.35 | **0.7432** | 24.5 |

*Table 2. Quality of segmentation (ν) on MLSONN and QMLSONN architectures for Baboon image*

| Quality of Segmentation (ν) | | | MLSONN Architecture for Baboon Image | | | | QMLSONN Architecture for Baboon Image | | | |
|---|---|---|---|---|---|---|---|---|---|---|
| **Class** | **ν** | **Set** | $\theta_\chi$ | **Time (s)** | $\theta_\xi$ | **Time (s)** | $\theta_\chi$ | **Time (s)** | $\theta_\xi$ | **Time (s)** |
| 4 | F | $s_1$ | 0.9013 | 28.01 | 0.9013 | 27.91 | 0.6593 | 25.10 | 0.6591 | 25.00 |
| | | $s_2$ | 0.8916 | 28.2 | 0.8918 | 27.9 | 0.6470 | 27.13 | 0.6470 | 27.1 |
| | | $s_3$ | 0.8796 | 28.1 | 0.8796 | 28.3 | 0.6220 | 24.11 | 0.6217 | 23.03 |
| | | $s_4$ | **0.8660** | 27.89 | **0.8660** | 28.1 | **0.6183** | 22.75 | **0.6185** | 22.58 |
| | F' | $s_1$ | 0.9300 | 28.01 | 0.9301 | 27.91 | 0.7193 | 25.10 | 0.7195 | 25.00 |
| | | $s_2$ | 0.9310 | 28.2 | 0.9311 | 27.9 | 0.7008 | 27.13 | 0.7008 | 27.1 |
| | | $s_3$ | 0.9115 | 28.1 | 0.9114 | 28.3 | 0.6861 | 24.11 | 0.6861 | 23.03 |
| | | $s_4$ | **0.9100** | 27.89 | **0.91** | 28.1 | **0.6658** | 22.75 | **0.6658** | 22.58 |
| | Q | $s_1$ | 0.9550 | 28.01 | 0.9550 | 27.91 | 0.7803 | 25.10 | 0.78 | 25.00 |
| | | $s_2$ | 0.9489 | 28.2 | 0.9489 | 27.9 | 0.7794 | 27.13 | 0.7794 | 27.1 |
| | | $s_3$ | 0.9489 | 28.1 | 0.9329 | 28.3 | 0.7500 | 24.11 | 0.75 | 23.03 |
| | | $s_4$ | **0.9223** | 27.89 | **0.9223** | 28.1 | **0.7413** | 22.75 | **0.7413** | 22.58 |

Lena images respectively. In Figure 6 (a, b, c, d, e, f, g, h), the extracted object outputs are shown using the MLSONN architecture and Figure 6 (i, j, k, l, m, n, o, p), the extracted object outputs are shown using the QMLSONN architecture.

The extracted object output as shown in Figure 7 for Baboon and Lena images using threshold parameter $\theta_\zeta$. Here, Figure 7 (a, b, c, d, e, f, g, h) shows the extracted object outputs using MLSONN architecture and Figure 7 (i, j, k, l, m, n, o, p) shows the extracted object outputs using QMLSONN architecture respectively. In Baboon image for class 4, the values of the segmented efficiency F, F' and Q are 0.6183, 0.6658 and 0.7413 respectively, using QMLSONN architecture with extraction time 22.75s for threshold parameter $\theta_\chi$ and using MLSONN architecture the values of the segmented efficiency are 0.8660, 0.9100 and 0.9223 with extraction time 27.89s. When the threshold parameter $\theta_\zeta$ is considered, the value of the gray scale image segmented efficiency (ν) F, F' and Q using QMLSONN architecture, the values of are 0.6185, 0.6658 and 0.7413 with time 22.58s and in case of MLSONN architecture 0.8660, 0.91 and 0.9223 with time 28.1s.

Authors have determined the values of segmented efficiency (ν) F, F' and Q are 0.4781, 0.4005 and 0.3486 corresponding to the extraction time 25.2s for gray scale

*Figure 6. Class 4 segmented output using threshold parameter $\theta_\chi$*

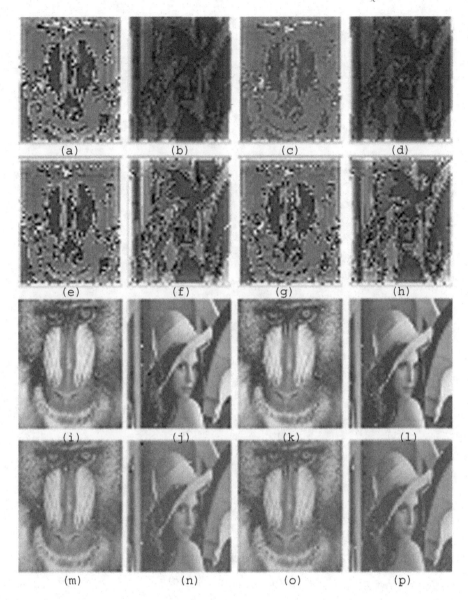

Lena image for class 6 using QMLSONN architecture for threshold parameter $\theta_\chi$ where as using MLSONN architecture the values of the efficiency are 0.8773, 0.7411 and 0.9221 with time 28.89s. Using the QMLSONN architecture, based on threshold parameter $\theta_\zeta$ and experiment is performed on Lena image, the values of the segmented

*Figure 7. Class 4 segmented output using threshold parameter* $\theta_\zeta$

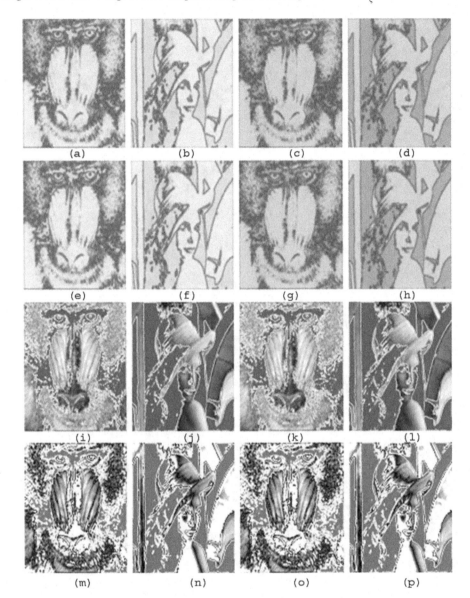

efficiency $(\nu)$ $F$, $F'$ and $Q$ are 0.4776, 0.4005 and 0.3487 with extraction time 27.72s but when it is performed using MLSONN architecture for threshold parameter $\theta_\zeta$, the values of the segmented efficiency $(\nu)$ $F$, $F'$ and $Q$ are 0.8772, 0.7419 and 0.9221 with time 33.94s. It is experimented using QMLSONN architecture on the gray scale Baboon image, for the threshold parameter $\theta_\chi$, the values of the segmented efficiency ($\nu$) $F$, $F'$ and $Q$ for class 6 are 0.4500, 0.4899 and 0.5338 respectively with extraction time 27.13s and another values of the segmented efficiency 0.8596, 0.7710 and 0.9463 with time 29.05s, when using the threshold parameter $\theta_\zeta$. The values of the segmented efficiency are 0.4500, 0.4899 and 0.5338 with extraction time 26.58s for QMLSONN architecture and using the MLSONN architecture these values are 0.8596, 0.771 and 0.9462 with time 35.15s.

All the outputs are collected and presented for class 6 as shown in the Table 3 for Lena image and in the Table 4 for Baboon image respectively for both using the threshold parameters $\theta_\chi$ and $\theta_\zeta$. The segmented output for class 6 corresponding to threshold parameter $\theta_\chi$ on gray scale Baboon image and Lena image as shown in Figure 8. Segmented gray scale object outputs are for Baboon images and Lena images (Figure 8 (a, c, e, g, i, k, m, o) and Figure 8 (b, d, f, h, j, l, n, p)) respectively. Figure 8 (a, b, c, d, e, f, g, h) shows extracted segmented object outputs using MLSONN architecture and Figure 8 (i, j, k, l, m, n, o, p) shows the extracted object outputs using QMLSONN architecture. The extracted gray scale object output as shown in Figure 9 for Baboon and Lena images using threshold parameter $\theta_\zeta$ for

*Table 3. Quality of segmentation ($\nu$) on MLSONN and QMLSONN architectures for Lena image*

| Quality of Segmentation ($\nu$) | | | MLSONN Architecture for Lena Image | | | | QMLSONN Architecture for Lena Image | | | |
|---|---|---|---|---|---|---|---|---|---|---|
| Class | $\nu$ | Set | $\theta_\chi$ | Time (s) | $\theta_\xi$ | Time (s) | $\theta_\chi$ | Time (s) | $\theta_\xi$ | Time (s) |
| 6 | F | $s_1$ | 0.8856 | 28.9 | 0.8861 | 33.15 | 0.5611 | 25.21 | 0.5611 | 27.69 |
| | | $s_2$ | 0.9059 | 29.01 | 0.8973 | 43.15 | 0.5300 | 25.12 | 0.5301 | 27.54 |
| | | $s_3$ | 0.8806 | 28.84 | 0.8806 | 34.34 | 0.4800 | 25.14 | 0.4801 | 27.87 |
| | | $s_4$ | **0.8773** | 28.89 | **0.8772** | 33.94 | **0.4781** | 25.2 | **0.4776** | 27.72 |
| | F' | $s_1$ | 0.7973 | 28.9 | 0.7978 | 33.15 | 0.4718 | 25.21 | 0.4718 | 27.69 |
| | | $s_2$ | 0.7891 | 29.01 | 0.7892 | 43.15 | 0.4511 | 25.12 | 0.4512 | 27.54 |
| | | $s_3$ | 0.7624 | 28.84 | 0.762 | 34.34 | 0.4297 | 25.14 | 0.429 | 27.87 |
| | | $s_4$ | **0.7411** | 28.89 | **0.7419** | 33.94 | **0.4005** | 25.2 | **0.4005** | 27.72 |
| | Q | $s_1$ | 0.9621 | 28.9 | 0.963 | 33.15 | 0.3996 | 25.21 | 0.3996 | 27.69 |
| | | $s_2$ | 0.9590 | 29.01 | 0.959 | 43.15 | 0.3817 | 25.12 | 0.3822 | 27.54 |
| | | $s_3$ | 0.9341 | 28.84 | 0.9341 | 34.34 | **0.3486** | 25.14 | **0.3487** | 27.87 |
| | | $s_4$ | **0.9221** | 28.89 | **0.9221** | 33.94 | 0.3571 | 25.2 | 0.3571 | 27.72 |

*Table 4. Quality of segmentation (ʋ) on MLSONN and QMLSONN architectures for Baboon image*

| Quality of Segmentation (ʋ) | | | MLSONN Architecture for Baboon Image | | | | QMLSONN Architecture for Baboon Image | | | |
|---|---|---|---|---|---|---|---|---|---|---|
| Class | ʋ | Set | $\theta_\chi$ | Time (s) | $\theta_\xi$ | Time (s) | $\theta_\chi$ | Time (s) | $\theta_\xi$ | Time (s) |
| 6 | F | $s_1$ | 0.8997 | 29.13 | 0.8999 | 35.14 | 0.5598 | 27.2 | 0.561 | 26.51 |
| | | $s_2$ | 0.8895 | 29.11 | 0.8895 | 35.20 | 0.5218 | 27.15 | 0.522 | 26.55 |
| | | $s_3$ | 0.8659 | 29.07 | 0.8658 | 35.15 | 0.4595 | 27.12 | 0.4595 | 26.56 |
| | | $s_4$ | **0.8596** | 29.05 | **0.8596** | 35.15 | **0.4500** | 27.13 | **0.4500** | 26.58 |
| | F' | $s_1$ | 0.7812 | 29.13 | 0.792 | 35.14 | 0.5794 | 27.2 | 0.5794 | 26.51 |
| | | $s_2$ | 0.7899 | 29.11 | 0.7889 | 35.20 | 0.5423 | 27.15 | 0.5423 | 26.55 |
| | | $s_3$ | 0.7798 | 29.07 | 0.7797 | 35.15 | 0.4978 | 27.12 | 0.4976 | 26.56 |
| | | $s_4$ | **0.7710** | 29.05 | **0.771** | 35.15 | **0.4899** | 27.13 | **0.4899** | 26.58 |
| | Q | $s_1$ | 0.9811 | 29.13 | 0.9816 | 35.14 | 0.5998 | 27.2 | 0.5998 | 26.51 |
| | | $s_2$ | 0.9695 | 29.11 | 0.969 | 35.20 | 0.5724 | 27.15 | 0.5724 | 26.55 |
| | | $s_3$ | 0.9518 | 29.07 | 0.9519 | 35.15 | 0.5477 | 27.12 | 0.5476 | 26.56 |
| | | $s_4$ | **0.9463** | 29.05 | **0.9462** | 35.15 | **0.5338** | 27.13 | **0.5338** | 26.58 |

class 6. Figure 9 (a, b, c, d, e, f, g, h) shows extracted gray scale object outputs using MLSONN architecture and Figure 9 (i, j, k, l, m, n, o, p) shows extracted gray scale object outputs using QMLSONN architecture.

For class 8 using QMLSONN architecture on gray scale Lena image, the segmented efficiency (ʋ) F, F' and Q are 0.2797, 0.3270 and 0.4143 for threshold parameter $\theta_\chi$ when the extracted time is 22.49s where as in MLSONN architecture, these are 0.6373, 0.5763 and 0.9534 with corresponding time is 31.38s but in case of threshold parameter $\theta_\zeta$, the values of the segmented efficiency for QMLSONN are 0.2810, 0.3272 and 0.4149 when the extracted time is 25.25s and in case of MLSONN architecture, these are 0.6236, 0.5785 and 0.9749 for corresponding time is 31.88s. All the outputs are collected placed as shown in the Table 5 for Lena image and in the Table 6 for Baboon image respectively using the threshold parameters $\theta_\chi$ and $\theta_\zeta$. The segmented gray scale object output for class 8 corresponding to threshold parameter $\theta_\chi$ for Baboon image and Lena images as shown in Figure 10. The Figure 10 (a, c, e, g, i, k, m, o) shows for Baboon images segmented output and Figure 10

*Figure 8. Class 6 segmented output using threshold parameter* $\theta_\chi$

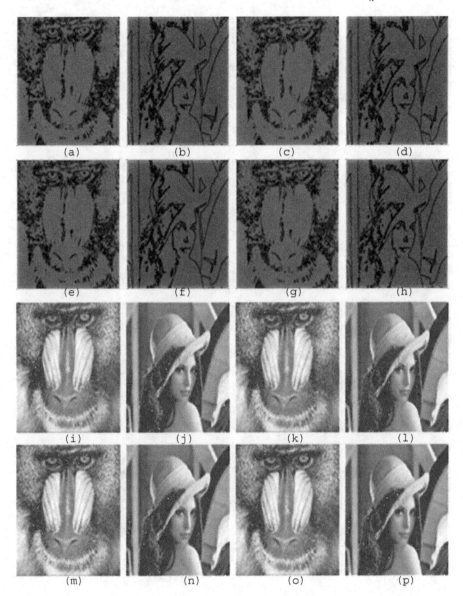

(b, d, f, h, j, l, n, p) shows for Lena images segmented output respectively. Figure 10 (a, b, c, d, e, f, g, h) shows the extracted gray scale object outputs using MLSONN architecture and Figure 10 (i, j, k, l, m, n, o, p) shows the gray scale object outputs using QMLSONN architecture. The gray scale object output as shown in Figure 11

*Figure 9. Class 6 segmented output using threshold parameter* $\theta_\zeta$

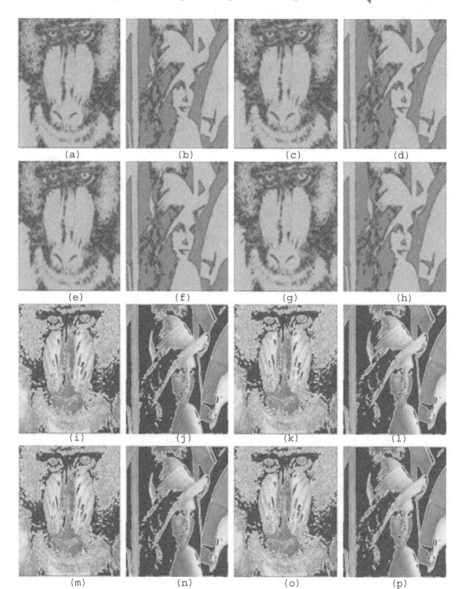

(a) (b) (c) (d)

(e) (f) (g) (h)

(i) (j) (k) (l)

(m) (n) (o) (p)

for Baboon and Lena images using threshold parameter $\theta_\zeta$. Figure 11 (a, b, c, d, e, f, g, h) represents the gray scale object outputs using MLSONN architecture and Figure 11 (i, j, k, l, m, n, o, p) represents the gray scale object outputs using QMLSONN architecture for threshold parameter $\theta_\zeta$. The values of the segmented

*Table 5. Quality of segmentation (ν) on MLSONN and QMLSONN architectures for Lena image*

| Quality of Segmentation (ν) | | | MLSONN Architecture for Lena Image | | | | QMLSONN Architecture for Lena Image | | | |
|---|---|---|---|---|---|---|---|---|---|---|
| Class | ν | Set | $\theta_\chi$ | Time (s) | $\theta_\xi$ | Time (s) | $\theta_\chi$ | Time (s) | $\theta_\xi$ | Time (s) |
| 8 | F | $s_1$ | 0.7214 | 31.28 | 0.7276 | 31.21 | 0.3233 | 23.10 | 0.3317 | 24.19 |
| | | $s_2$ | 0.6891 | 30.58 | 0.6871 | 31.10 | 0.3073 | 23.52 | 0.3067 | 24.20 |
| | | $s_3$ | 0.6685 | 30.37 | 0.6598 | 31.70 | 0.2957 | 24.01 | 0.2961 | 25.18 |
| | | $s_4$ | **0.6373** | 31.38 | **0.6236** | 31.88 | **0.2797** | 22.49 | **0.2810** | 25.25 |
| | F' | $s_1$ | 0.7279 | 31.28 | 0.7276 | 31.21 | 0.3891 | 23.10 | 0.3874 | 24.19 |
| | | $s_2$ | 0.5954 | 30.58 | 0.5789 | 31.10 | 0.3711 | 23.52 | 0.3699 | 24.20 |
| | | $s_3$ | **0.5763** | 30.37 | 0.587 | 31.70 | 0.3533 | 24.01 | 0.3521 | 25.18 |
| | | $s_4$ | 0.5806 | 31.38 | **0.5785** | 31.88 | **0.3270** | 22.49 | **0.3272** | 25.25 |
| | Q | $s_1$ | **0.9534** | 31.28 | 0.9762 | 31.21 | 0.4695 | 23.10 | 0.4598 | 24.19 |
| | | $s_2$ | 0.9609 | 30.58 | **0.9749** | 31.10 | 0.4518 | 23.52 | 0.4635 | 24.20 |
| | | $s_3$ | 0.9582 | 30.37 | 0.9771 | 31.70 | 0.4394 | 24.01 | 0.4518 | 25.18 |
| | | $s_4$ | 0.9594 | 31.38 | 0.9768 | 31.88 | **0.4143** | 22.49 | **0.4149** | 25.25 |

*Table 6. Quality of segmentation (ν) on MLSONN and QMLSONN architectures for Baboon image*

| Quality of Segmentation (ν) | | | MLSONN Architecture for Baboon Image | | | | QMLSONN Architecture for Baboon Image | | | |
|---|---|---|---|---|---|---|---|---|---|---|
| Class | ν | Set | $\theta_\chi$ | Time (s) | $\theta_\xi$ | Time (s) | $\theta_\chi$ | Time (s) | $\theta_\xi$ | Time (s) |
| 8 | F | $s_1$ | 0.7351 | 30.21 | 0.7356 | 30.95 | 0.3308 | 24.11 | 0.3425 | 24.25 |
| | | $s_2$ | 0.6956 | 30.31 | 0.6943 | 31.02 | 0.3191 | 24.56 | 0.3188 | 24.56 |
| | | $s_3$ | 0.6804 | 30.22 | 0.6812 | 31.16 | 0.3039 | 25.42 | 0.3035 | 25.50 |
| | | $s_4$ | **0.6748** | 30.58 | **0.6749** | 31.22 | **0.288** | 24.93 | **0.2873** | 25.00 |
| | F' | $s_1$ | 0.7197 | 30.21 | 0.7197 | 30.95 | 0.4742 | 24.11 | 0.4753 | 24.25 |
| | | $s_2$ | 0.6388 | 30.31 | 0.6387 | 31.02 | 0.4593 | 24.56 | 0.4598 | 24.56 |
| | | $s_3$ | 0.6297 | 30.22 | 0.6295 | 31.16 | 0.4435 | 25.42 | 0.4439 | 25.50 |
| | | $s_4$ | **0.6034** | 30.58 | **0.6041** | 31.22 | **0.3942** | 24.93 | **0.3953** | 25.00 |
| | Q | $s_1$ | 0.9910 | 30.21 | 0.9911 | 30.95 | 0.4995 | 24.11 | 0.4987 | 24.25 |
| | | $s_2$ | 0.9858 | 30.31 | 0.9848 | 31.02 | 0.4892 | 24.56 | 0.4891 | 24.56 |
| | | $s_3$ | 0.9795 | 30.22 | 0.9794 | 31.16 | 0.4760 | 25.42 | 0.4761 | 25.50 |
| | | $s_4$ | **0.9731** | 30.58 | **0.9732** | 31.22 | **0.4477** | 24.93 | **0.4489** | 25.00 |

*Figure 10. Class 8 segmented output using threshold parameter $\theta_\chi$*

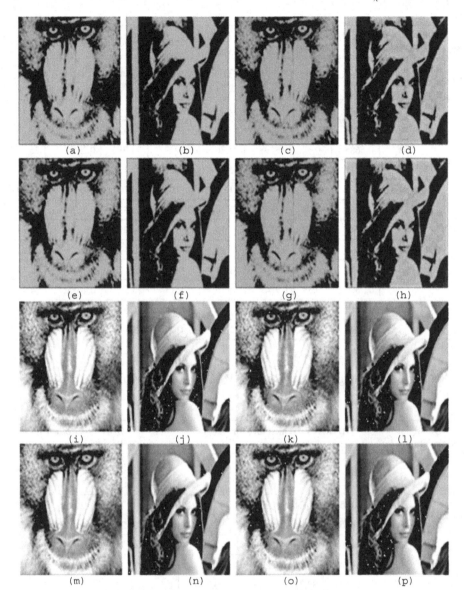

efficiency $F$, $F'$ and $Q$ on gray scale Baboon image for class 8 using QMLSONN architecture are 0.288, 0.3942 and 0.4477 with extraction time 24.93s considering the threshold parameter $\theta_\chi$ and using the MLSONN architecture the values of the segmented efficiency are 0.6748, 0.6034 and 0.9731 with extracted time 30.58s.

*Figure 11. Class 8 segmented output using threshold parameter $\theta_\zeta$*

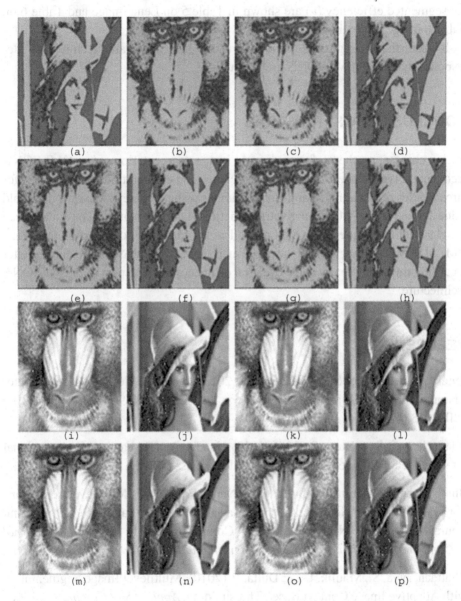

When the threshold parameter $\theta_\zeta$ is considered the gray scale segmented efficiency ($\nu$) $F$, $F'$ and $Q$ using QMLSONN architecture are 0.2873, 0.3953 and 0.4489 with extraction time 25.00s and in case of MLSONN architecture the corresponding values are 0.6749, 0.6041 and 0.9732 with time 31.22s.

The output corresponding class 8 gray scale Lena and Baboon images using the segmented efficiency ($\nu$) are shown in Table 5 on Lena image and Table 6 on Baboon image respectively.

It is seen that the segmented efficiency using QMLSONN architecture has better response than that of MLSONN architecture.

## CONCLUSION AND REMARKS

In this chapter, a scheme for gray scale image segmentation using QMLSONN architecture is presented. Segmented efficiency and elapsed time are measured for three classes of Lena image and Baboon image using a context sensitive threshold value applied on the MUSIG activation function. A comparison is taken out between the classical technique MLSONN as well as the quantum computation technique QMLSONN. It is observed that the performance of QMLSONN architecture is better regarding time complexity and extraction efficiency with respect to the MLSONN architecture.

## REFERENCES

Aytekin, C., Kiranyaz, S., & Gabbouj, M. (2013). Quantum Mechanics in Computer Vision: Automatic Object Extraction. *Proc. ICIP 2013*, 2489–2493. doi:10.1109/ICIP.2013.6738513

Bhattacharyya, S., & Dutta, P. (Eds.). (2013). Handbook of Research on Computational Intelligence for Engineering, Science, and Business (vol. 1). IGI Global.

Bhattacharyya, S., Dutta, P., Maulik, U., & Nandi, P. K. (2007). Multilevel Activations For True Color Image Segmentation Using a Self Supervised Parallel Self Organizing Neural Network (PSONN) Architecture: A Comparative Study. *International Journal of Computer, Electrical, Automation, Control and Information Engineering*, *1*(8).

Bhattacharyya, S., Maulik, U., & Dutta, P. (2010). Multilevel Image Segmentation with Adaptive Image Context Based Thresholding. *Applied Soft Computing*, *11*(1), 946–962. doi:10.1016/j.asoc.2010.01.015

Bhattacharyya, S., Pal, P., & Bhowmick, S. (2014). Binary Image Denoising Using a Quantum Multilayer Self Organizing Neural Network. *Applied Soft Computing*, *24*, 717–729. doi:10.1016/j.asoc.2014.08.027

Blumenstein, M., & Verma, B. (1998). An artificial neural network based segmentation algorithm for off-line handwriting recognition. *Proceedings of the Second International Conference on Computational Intelligence and Multimedia Applications.*

Bora, D. J., & Gupta, A. K. (2014). A Novel Approach Towards Clustering Based Image Segmentation. *International Journal of Emerging Science and Engineering, 2*(11).

Bora, D. J., & Gupta, A.K. (2014). A Comparative study Between Fuzzy Clustering Algorithm and Hard Clustering Algorithm. *International Journal of Computer Trends and Technology, 10*(2), 108-113.

Borsotti, M., Campadelli, P., & Schettini, R. (1998). Quantitative evaluation of color image segmentation results. *Pattern Recognition Letters, 19*(8), 741–747. doi:10.1016/S0167-8655(98)00052-X

Das, D., & Mukhopadhyay, S. (2015). *A Pixel Based Segmentation Scheme for Fingerprint Images; Information Systems Design and Intelligent Applications. In Advances in Intelligent Systems and Computing* (Vol. 340, pp. 439–448). New Delhi: Springer; doi:10.1007/978-81-322-2247-7_45

De, S., & Bhattacharyya, S. (2015). Color Magnetic Resonance Brain Image Segmentation by ParaOptiMUSIG Activation Function: An Application. *Hybrid Soft Computing Approaches, 611*, 185-214.

De, S., Bhattacharyya, S., & Chakraborty, S. (2012). Color image segmentation using parallel OptiMUSIG activation function. *Applied Soft Computing, 12*(10), 3228–3236. doi:10.1016/j.asoc.2012.05.011

De, S., Bhattacharyya, S., Chakraborty, S., Sarkar, B. N., Prabhakar, P. K., & Bose, S. (2012). Gray Scale Image Segmentation by NSGA-II Based OptiMUSIG Activation Function. *CSNT '12 Proceedings of the 2012 International Conference on Communication Systems and Network Technologies*, 104-108.

De, S., Bhattacharyya, S., & Dutta, P. (2010). Efficient grey-level image segmentation using an optimized MUSIG (OptiMUSIG) activation function. *International Journal of Parallel, Emergent and Distributed Systems, 26*(1), 1–39.

Ghosh, A., Pal, N. R., & Pal, S. K. (1993). Self organization for object extraction using a multilayer neural network and fuzziness measures. *IEEE Transactions on Fuzzy Systems, 1*(1), 54–68.

Kang, S.D., Park, S.S., Shin, Y.G., Yoo, H.W., & Jang, D.S. (2008). Image Segmentation using Statistical approach via Perception-based Color Information. *International Journal of Computer Science and Network Security, 8*(4).

Kapur, J. N., Sahoo, P., & Wong, A. K. C. (1980). A new method for gray-level picture thresholding using the entropy of the histogram. *Computer Vision Graphics and Image Processing, 29*(3), 273–285.

Liu, J., & Yang, Y. H. (1994). Multi-resolution color image segmentation. *IEEE Transactions on Pattern Analysis and Machine Intelligence, 16*(7), 689–700. doi:10.1109/34.297949

Mashford, J., Davis, P., & Rahilly, M. (2007). Pixel-Based Color Image Segmentation Using Support Vector Machine for Automatic Pipe Inspection. *Australasian Joint Conference on Artificial Intelligence: AI 2007: Advances in Artificial Intelligence*, 739-743.

Mishra, D., Bose, I., De, U. C., & Pradhan, B. (2014). A Multilevel Image Thresholding Using Particle Swarm Optimization. *International Journal of Engineering and Technology, 6*(2), 1204-1211.

Pal, N. R., & Pal, S. K. (1993). A Review on Image Segmentation Techniques. *Pattern Recognition, 26*(9), 1277–1294. doi:10.1016/0031-3203(93)90135-J

Pantofaru, C., & Hebert, M. (2005). *A Comparison of Image Segmentation Algorithms, CMU-RI-TR-05-40, September 1, 2005*. Pittsburgh, PA: The Robotics Institute, Carnegie Mellon University.

Ross, T.J., & Ross, T. (1995). *Fuzzy Logic with Engineering Applications*. McGraw Hill College Div.

Saini, S., & Arora, K. (2014). A Study Analysis on the Different Image Segmentation Techniques. *International Journal of Information & Computation Technology, 4*(14), 1445-1452.

Salman, N. (2006, April). Image Segmentation Based on Watershed and Edge Detection Techniques. *The International Arab Journal of Information Technology, 3*(2).

Sharma, V. C. (2015). A Review: PDE based Segmentation Method and Color Models. *SSRG International Journal of Computer Science and Engineering*. Retrieved from www.internationaljournalssrg.org

Suetens P., Verbeeck R., Delaere D., Nuyts J., & Bijnens B. (1991). Model-Based Image Segmentation: Methods and Applications. *AIME, 91,* 3-24. DOI: .10.1007/978-3-642-48650-0_1

Yogamangalam, R., & Karthikeyan, B. (2013). Segmentation Techniques Comparison in Image Processing. *International Journal of Engineering and Technology, 5.*

Zadeh, L. A. (1965). Fuzzy sets. *Information and Control, 8*(3), 338–353. doi:10.1016/S0019-9958(65)90241-X

Chapter 6

# Landcover Change Detection Using PSO-Evaluated Quantum CA Approach on Multi-Temporal Remote-Sensing Watershed Images

**Kalyan Mahata**
*Government College of Engineering and Leather Technology, India*

**Rajib Das**
*Jadavpur University, India*

**Subhasish Das**
*Jadavpur University, India*

**Anasua Sarkar**
*Jadavpur University, India*

## ABSTRACT

*Computer science plays a major role in image segmentation and image processing applications. Despite the computational cost, PSO evaluated QCA approaches perform comparable to or better than their crisp counterparts. This novel approach, proposed in this chapter, has been found to enhance the functionality of the CA rule base and thus enhance the established potentiality of the fuzzy-based segmentation domain with the help of quantum cellular automata. This new unsupervised method is able to detect clusters using 2-dimensional quantum cellular automata model based on PSO evaluation. As a discrete, dynamical system, cellular automaton explores uniformly interconnected cells with states. In the second phase, it utilizes a 2-dimensional cellular automata to prioritize allocations of mixed pixels among overlapping land cover areas. The authors experiment on Tilaya Reservoir Catchment on Barakar River. The clustered regions are compared with well-known PSO, FCM, and k-means methods and also with the ground truth knowledge. The results show the superiority of the new method.*

DOI: 10.4018/978-1-5225-5219-2.ch006

# INTRODUCTION

There is no universal approach on image segmentation as yet that performs uniformly well on all types of images. This is primarily because image segmentation is subjective and suffers from uncertainty. They are strongly application-dependent, in other words, there are no general algorithms vis-à-vis color spaces that are uniformly good for all color images. Pixel classification of watershed satellite image is a challenging task in remote sensing. Uses of Particle swarm Optimisation and Cellular Automata are significant methods in watershed image segmentation. This paper proposes a method of pixel classification using a new hybrid Particle Swarm Optimization- Quantum Cellular automata approach. The proposed unsupervised method identifies clusters using 2-Dimensional Cellular Automata model over particle swarm optimization. PSO is an optimization stochastic method based on populations, following the social behaviour like bird flocks. This new method identifies vague clusters utilizing initial fuzzy membership values. Cellular Automata is a dynamic and discrete model comprises of inter-connected cells uniform with states. We utilize 2D cellular automata method on Barakar river catchment area. The segmented regions are compared with existing methods, which shows superiority of our new method. Quantum CA theory provides us with a suitable tool that can represent the uncertainties arising in image segmentation and can model water image analysis of Tilaya catchment of Barakar river by quantum CA approach.

Introducing Remote sensing by Cogalton and Green in 1999 to be a method for obtaining knowledge of any object with no direct physical contact on it. For grouping pixels among predefined classes, a vast set of approaches exists (like turbid water or an urban area) in satellite images.

Remote sensing to interpret features for considering geospatial data, objects and classes on Earth's surface is a method without actual contact with it. There exists canopy of methods for segmenting pixels (for example, turbid water or an urban area) in remote sensing images.

Clustering, the unsupervised classification method, is based on maximum intra-class similarity and minimum inter-class similarity. Particle swarm optimisation method is used to experiment the state-of-the-art clustering methods for pixel classification in remote sensing images. To explore the best position in the search space, PSO, a population-based optimization algorithm is explored. In PSO, a particle which is called individual moves in direction of its own best previous position stochastically and the whole swarm's best previous position. A Rastrigrin function based PSO, initial decision rule generation, is proposed by us to predict pixel classification of remote sensing imagery

Cellular automaton, a uniformly interconnected cell, are a discrete, dynamical system composed of very simple well-known method to detect states in cellular spaces.

A 2-dimensional cellular automaton to K-Means based initial allocation is proposed by us to predict pixel classification of remote sensing imagery, The integration of K-Means optimal clustering with cellular automata based neighbourhood priority correction for pixel classification in remote sensing imagery is the focus of this present study. Association of clusters with initial K-Means classes containing different land cover regions that occur in remote sensing images. The most widely used clustering algorithms for pixel classification analysis are Hierarchical clustering (Lior, 2005), K-Means clustering (Hughes, 2001), (Hoon, 2004) and SOM (Spang, 2003).

We experiment the performance our proposed PSO based approach to classify pixels in chosen LANDSAT image on catchment of river Barakar. Quantitive evaluation using external validity measures, is used to compare our experimental results with solutions obtained from K-Means, FCM, PSO and our implementation of PSOQCA algorithms over the Barakar catchment area including Tilaya Dam. The quantitative evaluation of efficiency of our new PSO based Quantum Cellular Automata (CA) corrected algorithm (PSOQCA) to detect land cover clusters is indicated by the two existing internal validity indices. We verify our obtained solutions with the ground truth knowledge. The statistical evaluation over both datasets also denote the significance of the proposed PSOQCA approach over K-Means, FCM and PSO methods to detect imprecise clusters.

## Existing Works

Recently finding out significant solutions from the canopy of existing works on remote sensing image analysis, exploiting hybrid intelligences, has become a trend in challenging tasks. Jacobsen [Jacobsen, 1998] identifies hybrid intelligent systems of four categories, based on the systems' overall architecture:

1.  Single component systems,
2.  Fusion–based systems,
3.  Hierarchical systems, and
4.  Hybrid systems.

programming can be remodelled as a fuzzy problem with infinite number of fuzzy constraints [Fakharzadeh J., 2015]. It is a hybrid cutting-plane algorithm, solving sub problems using ZImmerman methods.

Hybrid intelligent systems have been experimented over incomplete information system recently. Xiao et al. (Xin, 2016) develops three different kind of approaches for incomplete knowledge engineering. They combine the variable precision rough set method and hybrid multi-granulation rough set methods in one approach. In the other approaches, they experiment with variable precision with the hybrid multigranulation rough sets based on similarity relation and limited relation of tolerance. Several other hybrid intelligent approaches in theoretical analysis in Computer Science fields are also enhancing new dimensions for applicable computational approaches recently (Shah, 2016),(Nehi, 2016), (Zia, 2015), (Scarlat, 2015).

Raouzaiou et al. (Kollias, 2002) exploits the facial expression recognition problem from the view of the appropriateness of a hybrid intelligence architecture for sub symbolic to symbolic mapping. Furkan et al. (Furkan, 2015) implements a Hybrid Fuzzy Support Vector Regression (HF-SVR) model for the linear and non-linear fuzzy regression modelling. They utilize combined SVM and least squares principle for parameter estimates. Varying different kernel functions, different learning machines for nonlinear fuzzy regression can be constructed. Multi-disciplinary approaches to utilize artificial intelligence in real-life applications have been explored earlier in several works. Goel (Goel, 2010) proposes a Land Cover Feature Extraction method using hybrid Swarm intelligence methods, which is a combination of ACO2/BBO classification, over a training set of the 7-Band Alwar image. In this hybrid approach, he utilizes the rough set theory toolkit in Rosetta software for discretizing each of 20 clusters using the semi-native algorithm.

Similarly, Singh et al. (Singh, 2012) experiment to estimate the Agricultural land in India using a new hybrid intelligence approach of Neuro-Fuzzy method. As widely termed Neuro-fuzzy hybridization is Fuzzy Neural Network (FNN) or Neuro-Fuzzy System (NFS) in the literature. A neuro-fuzzy system is based on a fuzzy system which is trained by a learning algorithm derived from neural network theory.

Application of hybrid intelligence for pattern recognition is a wide area of exploration. Recently, Teh et al. (Lim, 2006) proposes a hybrid system to combine SOM (Self-Organizing Map), kMER (kernel-based maximum entropy learning rule) algorithm and PNN (Probabilistic Neural network) methods for fault detection and analysis. According to Teh, SOM never achieves optimum usage for its resources. To overcome this problem, they use a topographic map formation algorithm, namely kMER, to generate equi-probablistic map with maximum entropy learning rule. However, kMER algorithm lacks for its computational efficiency. This drawback is covered by SOM method without using RF (receptive field) region. Therefore, in this hybrid intelligent system, they overcome the limitations the drawbacks of individual methods in a combined manner. This is the benefit of hybrid intelligent techniques in real-world applications.

Biomedical applications of hybrid intelligence systems also provide several improvements in clinical diagnosis treatment methodologies in recent years. (Fontela-Romero, 2002) also works with hybrid intelligent methods in cardio to cographic signals using a tightly coupled hybrid system. They propose CAFE (Computer Aided Foetal Evaluator) (Fontela-Romero, 2002) as an intelligent tightly coupled hybrid system to overcome the difficulties inherent in CTG (cardio to graph) analysis.

Villar et al. (Trejo, 2015) experiments with a hybrid implementation of the intelligent recognition models and algorithms for the early detection of strokes.

Their approach combines two wearable devices to monitor movement data in phases: Human Activity Recognition (HAR) and alarm generation. Hybridization of two HAR methods: one using genetic fuzzy finite-state machines, and the other using Time Series (TS) analysis has been done with Symbolic Aggregate approXimation (SAX) TS representation for alarm generation. They valuate their intelligent system over data gathered from healthy individuals.

Park et al (Lee, 2015) develop a method for filtering Quantum Noise from low dose medical X-ray CT images. They propose a neural network (NN) based hybrid filter combining bilateral filters (BFs), a single or multiple neural edge enhancer(s) (NEE), and a neural filter (NF). This hybrid filter can be applied to various images with different modalities, without considering the filter selection for fusion.

In other work, to develop a decision support systems of hybrid intelligent for risk analysis and discovery of evolving economic clusters in Europe, (Beber, 2017), propose based on evolving agents in a dynamic environment. Rule-based agents and neural networks are evolved from incoming data and expert knowledge. From the neural network module, the predictive value is combined with expert rules on the current political and economic situation in a fuzzy inference module. Kumar et al. (Singh, 2016) implement a novel hybrid approach based on Bacterial Foraging Optimization (BFO) and Particle swarm optimization (PSO) methods for the selection of feature vectors of best facial. This selection enhances the identification accuracy of the individual recognition. This hybrid approach reduces facial features irrelevantly in the feature space, and thus enhances accuracy.

Kasabov et al. in (Denfis, 2001), define another dynamic evolving neural-fuzzy inference system, on-line and on line learning adaptively, and their application of dynamic time series prediction. It uses a fuzzy inference system based on m-most activated fuzzy rules which are dynamically chosen from a fuzzy rule set.

Negnevitsky (Santoso) propose an approach for short term wind power forecasting using a hybrid intelligent system. Abraham et al. (Abraham, 2001) proposes a soft computing techniques hybridized for automated stock market forecasting and trend analysis. Using principal component analysis Input data were pre-processed and fed to an artificial neural network for stock forecasting. Values of the predicted stock are further fed to analyze the trend of the market to neuro-fuzzy system.

In similar research domain, Araujo et al. [Araujo, 2012] solves problem in the financial time series forecasting analysis using a new concept of time phase adjustment by random walk dilemma (RWD). They develop a mo del, namely the increasing decreasing linear neuron (IDLN) in stock market forecasting with high frequency. Hybridization is implemented using another descending gradient-based in their model method with automatic time phase adjustment. They demonstrated and tested their work over a set of different market with high-frequency financial time series, as for example such as the Brazilian stock market.

In their other work, Araujo et al. (A. Araujo, 2012) develops a morphological-linear model, which is called the dilation-erosion-linear perceptron (DELP), used for financial forecasting. This is a hybrid model based on morphological operators under context of lattice theory and a linear operator. They incorporate a gradient-based method with another automatic phase fix procedure to adjust time phase distortions observed in financial phenomena. They analyse the S&P 500 Index, with five well-known performance metrics to assess the forecasting performance.

Palauch et al. (Paluch, 2014) develops a new method of combining Artificial Neural Networks (ANN), with technical analysis and fractal analysis for predicting share prices on the Warsaw Stock Exchange. The hybrid model combining ANN with association of technical and fractal analysis is to provide the closing values of the asset for the next day.

Some recent developments in this field has been proposed by Khemaja (Khemaja, 2016) in his hybrid intelligent tutoring system. He develops a knapsack based model and solution in order to implement it's intelligent decision making in the context of fast changing Information and Communication Technology (ICT) about best combination and delivery of e-training activities and resources especially in ICT domain and its required skills.

Dennis et al (Denis, 2016) proposes a blended strategy for a plug-in hybrid electric vehicle (PHEV). It uses a driving pattern recognition scheme in real-time regarding current driving conditions that allows control adaptation. They use the k-nearest neighbour (KNN) algorithm based on a driving pattern recognition module. PHEV is such an associate speed pattern recognition of the trip length with knowledge to form an original strategy in full blended form.

Bagher (Bagher, 2016) proposes a method which describe hybridizing artificial hormones controller with type-two fuzzy controller. He explores three feasible scenarios for full hybridizing two controllers. Several performance for controlling indicators, like settling time, steady state error, overshoot, integral absolute error [IAE], integral squared error [ISE], integral time-weighted absolute error [ITAE] and integral of time multiplied by the squared error [ITSE] are estimated for his work. He also demonstrates that the energy consumption for the hybrid controller is 20 to 30% less than the allowable base controller.

Masoud et al. (Masoud, 2016) proposes three Meta-heuristic algorithms using genetic algorithm method by heterogeneous for waste collection problem of vehicles with multiple separated compartments. In their approach, they combine the multi-depot carriers vehicle routing problem and the mixed close-open system vehicle routing problems. They propose a new mathematical MIP model for minimizing the cost of servicing with respect to customer's available constraints.

To develop hybrid intelligent transportation system, Lopez-Garcia (Lopez-Garcia, 2016) develop a system of a hybridization of a genetic algorithm (GA) with their full application with the cross-entropy (CE) method. He refers to this method as GACE. This method optimize the elements of a hierarchy of a system called of fuzzy-rule-based systems (FRBSs) by passing through different weights for both GA and CE combined techniques. This methods can predict short-term congestion.

Hybrid intelligence has also been applied to the vision-based navigation methods recently. Lima et al. (Lima, 2016) develops a hybrid control approach for autonomous robotic automobiles in urban environments. This is a combined approach of the line-following visual surveying (VS) controller for road lane as per the following (as deliberative control) and this is an image-based dynamic window approach (IDWA) which is used for obstacle avoidance (as reactive control). This guarantee the safe movement of the car in urban environments considering the car kinematics.

Hybrid intelligent systems can be utilized to improve Energy management system (EMS). Qi et al. (Qi, 2016) proposes a method of contemporary evolutionary algorithm (EA)-which is based EMS with a self-adaptive state-of-charge (SOC) control strategy basically used for and applied for plug-in hybrid electric vehicles (PHEVs). This system is less sensitive to the common errors which are very frequently proclaiming in predicting propulsion power demand in real-time, appropriate for on-line easy to handle implementation.

Ming et al. (Ming, 2015) develop a hybrid system of a tracked bulldozer using fuzzy control with an application to wavelet transform-based energy management strategy is proposed. EMS is verified using HILS (hardware in loop simulation) to increase the fuel efficiency of the effectiveness of the engine with how to prolong the working life of the used battery pack.

Singla et al (Singla, 2015) applied hybrid swarm intelligence techniques to analyse the land cover regions in Alwar in India. They applied hybrid ACO (Ant Colony Optimization)/BBO (Biogeography Based Optimization), hybrid CS (Cuckoo Search)/PSO(Particle Swarm Optimization), hybrid CS(Cuckoo Search)/ACO(Ant Colony Optimization) and hybrid ABC(Artificial Bee Colony Optimization)/ BBO(Biogeography Based Optimization) methods in their experiments.

Ayerdi et al. (Ayerdi, 2016) proposes Spectral Spatial Processing with spectral image and Anticipative Hybrid Extreme Rotation operation on Hyperspectral Image analysis using Forest Classification. Developing a spectral classifier, namely anticipative hybrid extreme rotation forest (AHERF) with a spatial-spectral semi supervised approach for their analysis.

Travelling Tournament Problem (TTP) is a NP-hard problem, which minimizes the total distance measured by travelling by all the teams in a sports league during the tournament. Gupta et al. [Gupta, 2013] proposes a novel hybrid approach of

Biogeography Based optimization (BBO) which uses Simulated Annealing (SA) based heuristics to calculate and generate schedules for mirrored version of TTP.

The problem of batch scheduling (Miho, 2011) independently minimize the make span and flow time. They use two hybridizations, namely GA(TS) and GA TS, to solve this problem, where GA refers to Genetic Algorithms and TS refers to Tabu Search method. These two methods implemented in main control and cooperation among both methods. The hierarchic and simultaneous optimization modes both are experimented for this bi-objective scheduling problem.

## Particle Swarm Optimization

PSO is one of the swarm intelligence methods used for solving the optimization problems. It is a population based search algorithm where each individual is referred to as particle and represents a candidate solution. Each single candidate solution is assumed to be "an individual bird of the flock", i.e, a particle in the search space. Each particle makes use of its individual memory and knowledge to find the best solution. All the particles are given its own fitness values, which are evaluated by fitness function and have velocities which direct the movement of the particles. The particles move through the problem space by following a current of optimum particles.

The initial swarm is generally created in such a way that the population of the particles is distributed randomly over the search space. At every iteration, each particle is updated by following two "best" values, called *pbest* and *gbest*. Each particle keeps track of its coordinates in the problem space, which are associated with the best solution (fitness value). This fitness value is called *pbest*. When a particle takes the whole population as its Topological neighbor, the best value is a global best value and is called $g_{best}$. The detailed algorithm is given below:

**Step 1:** The constants $q_{max}, c_1, c_2, r_1, r_2, w$ are fixed during the process.

The particle positions $x_0(i)$ for $i = 1, 2 \ldots \ldots p$ are randomly initialized.
The particle velocities $v_0(i)$ for $i = 1, 2 \ldots \ldots p$ are randomly initialized.

**Step 2:** The process is initiated with $q = 1$.
**Step 3:** The function value $f_q$ is evaluated using design space coordinates $x_q(i)$.

$$f_q \geq f_{p_{best}}, then \ p_{best}(i) = x_q(i) \tag{1.1}$$

If $f_q \geq f_{g_{best}}$, then $g_{best} = x_q(i)$ (1.2)

**Step 4:** The particle velocity is adjusted using the following equation

$$v_{q+1}(i) = w * \left(v_q(i)\right) + c_1 r_1 * \left(P_{best_q}(i) - x_q(i)\right) + c_2 r_2 \left(g_{best_q} - x_q(i)\right)$$ (1.3)

The particle position vector is adjusted using the following equation

$$x_{q+1}(i) = x_q(i) + v_{q+1}(i)$$ (1.4)

**Step 5:** The value of '$i$' is incremented by $1$. If $i > p$, then increment $q$ and set $i = 1$.

**Step 6:** The steps 3 to 5 is repeated until $q_{max}$ is reached, where

$q_{max} = maximum\ iteration\ number$

$w = inertia\ weight\ factor$

$c_1, c_2 = cognitive\ and\ social\ acceleration\ factors$

$r_1, r_2 = random\ numbers\ in\ the\ range(0,1).$

   In this work, each of the candidate solution is represented by a particle (string of bits) with 16 bits corresponding to the number of features. An initial random population of 100 particles is formed to initiate the optimization. The initial coding for each particle is randomly generated. A suitable fitness function is estimated for each individual. This process continues for a particular number of iterations and finally the fittest chromosome is calculated based on the fitness function. The features with a bit value "**1**" are accepted and the features with the bit value of "**0**" are rejected. The fitness function used in this work is given by:

$$\textbf{\textit{Fitness}} = \left(\tau * \gamma\right) + \frac{\psi * (c - r)}{c}$$

where,

$\gamma$ classification accuracy

$c$ total number of features

$r$ length of the chromosome (number of '1's)

$\tau \varepsilon [0,1] \, and \, \psi = 1 - \tau$.

The goodness of each position is evaluated by this fitness function. The criteria are to maximize the fitness values. An optimal solution is obtained at the end of the maximum iteration. This value is binary coded with fourteen bits. The bit value of "1" represents a selected feature whereas the bit value of "0" represents a rejected feature. Thus an optimal set of features are selected from the PSO technique. Though the size of the input feature vector is not too high, feature selection is still necessary because the presence of even a single insignificant feature may reduce the classification accuracy. Also, for retinal image applications, the time period factor is extremely important and hence it is advisable to use a feature set which is as small as possible. Feature selection removes the insignificant features besides reducing the training time period of the classifiers irrespective of the size of the input feature set. These set of optimal features are further given as input to the BPN network for the classification process. The number of input neurons used in this architecture is different from the number of neurons used for the conventional BPN and the GA optimized BPN. The other details such as the training algorithm and the parameter fixation remain the same as that of conventional BPN and GA optimized BPN.

1. The various parameters are initialized and the population is formed using the same procedure followed by the GA technique.
2. The particle position and the particle velocity are the two important parameters of PSO algorithm. The candidate solution is represented by the particle position.
3. The particle positions and particle velocities are updated in an iterative manner and values of 'pbest' and 'gbest' are noted for each iterations based on the fitness function.
4. The binary representation of the population is converted to decimal form and then used in this work. Finally, the decimal values of the particle positions are converted into binary values.
5. The optimal particle position ('gbest') is finally determined at the end of the maximum number of iterations.
6. The optimal features are further estimated based on the bit values (one or zero) in the 'gbest' particle position.

7.    These features are then used to train the three AI classifiers and the performance measures are estimated.

The size of the initial population used in this work is 100 and each member of the population is represented by 16 bits. The average number of iterations used in this work is 520 which is very much lesser than the number of iterations required for GA. The convergence of the particle position is achieved with less number of iterations when compared with the GA.

The values of the parameters used for the classifiers are same as that of the values used in the implementation of the GA. The only difference is that the number of optimal features yielded by GA is different from PSO which ultimately results in the change of input layer neurons for the neural classifiers.

## PSO Algorithm

In Computer Science, particle swarm optimization (PSO) is a computational method that optimizes a problem by iteratively trying to improve a candidate solution with regard to a given measure of quality. PSO is a population-based algorithm that uses a population of individuals to probe the best position in the search space. In PSO, the individual is called a particle, which moves stochastically in the direction of its own best previous position and the whole swarm's best previous position. Suppose that the size of the swarm is $N$ and the search space is $M$ dimensional, then the position of the $i$th particle is presented as $X_i = \{x_{i1}, x_{i2}, \ldots, x_{iM}\}$. The velocity of this particle is presented as $V_i = \{v_{i1}, v_{i2}, \ldots, v_{iM}\}$. The best previous position of this particle is denoted as $P_i = \{p_{i1}, p_{i2}, \ldots, p_{iM}\}$. Consequently, the best previous position discovered by the whole swarm is denoted as $P_S = \{p_{S1}, p_{S2}, \ldots, p_{SM}\}$. Let the maximum number of iteration be $T$ and $t$ be the present iteration. The unit time is denoted by $\Delta\tau$. Then the position of a particle and its velocity are changed following the constraints shown below (Gonzalez, 1992), (Lukashin, 1999)(Xu, 1999),

$$v_{im}^{t+1} = \omega^t * v_{im}^t + \frac{rand(\ ) * c_1 * \left(p_{im} - x_{im}^t\right)}{\Delta\tau} + \frac{rand(\ ) * c_2 * \left(p_{Sm} - x_{im}^t\right)}{\Delta\tau} \tag{2}$$

$$x_{im}^{t+1} = x_{im}^t + v_{im}^t * \Delta\tau \tag{3}$$

$$\omega^t = \omega_{max} - \frac{t*\left(\omega_{max} - \omega_{min}\right)}{T} \tag{4}$$

where $1 \leq t \leq T$ , $1 \leq m \leq M$ , and *rand()* generates the random number with uniform distribution $U(0,1)$. $c_1$ and $c_2$ are acceleration coefficients. $\omega$ is the inertia weight, with $\omega_{max}$ and $\omega_{min}$ as the maximum and minimum values respectively.

For the initial matrix, $X = \begin{bmatrix} x_{11} & x_{12} & x_{1M} \\ x_{21} & x_{22} & x_{2M} \\ x_{n1} & x_{n2} & x_{NM} \end{bmatrix}$ , the equation to generate particle value is,

$$x_{initial} = x_{im} = x_{min} + \left(x_{max} - x_{min}\right)*rand\left(\ \right), \forall m = \left\{1,...,M\right\}, n = \left\{1,...,N\right\}. \tag{5}$$

Then the boundary constraints for $x_{im}^{t+1}$ and $v_{im}^{t+1}$ are as follows,

$$x_{im}^{t+1} = \begin{cases} x_{im}^{t+1} \ , & x_{min} \leq x_{im}^{t+1} \leq x_{max} \\ x_{initial} \ , & x_{im}^{t+1} > x_{max} \\ x_{initial} \ , & x_{im}^{t+1} < x_{min} \end{cases} \tag{6}$$

$$v_{im}^{t+1} = \begin{cases} v_{im}^{t+1} \ , & -v_{max} \leq v_{im}^{t+1} \leq v_{max} \\ v_{max} \ , & v_{im}^{t+1} > v_{max} \\ -v_{max} \ , & v_{im}^{t+1} < -v_{max} \end{cases} \tag{7}$$

where $\left\{v_{max}, v_{min}\right\}$ and $\left\{x_{max}, x_{min}\right\}$ are respectively maximum and minimum values for $v$ and $x$, respectively.

## Cellular Automata Method

A classical CA is a transition system in Q defined by a global transition function $F$: $Q^n \rightarrow Q^n$ where $F(q)i = f(qi-1, qi, qi+1)$ and $f: Q*Q*Q \rightarrow Q$ is a local transition function. When $Q = \{0, 1\}$, a local transition function is defined by the eight values $f(0,0,0) = r0, f(0,0,1) = r1, f(0,1,0) = r2, f(0,1,1) = r3, f(1,0,0) = r4, f(1,0,1) =$

*Table 1. Local transition rules for rule no 204, 240 and 170.*

| 204 | 1 1 1<br>1 | 1 1 0<br>1 | 1 0 1<br>0 | 1 0 0<br>0 | 0 1 1<br>1 | 0 1 0<br>1 | 0 0 1<br>0 | 0 0 0<br>0 |
|-----|------------|------------|------------|------------|------------|------------|------------|------------|
| 240 | 1 1 1<br>1 | 1 1 0<br>1 | 1 0 1<br>1 | 1 0 0<br>1 | 0 1 1<br>0 | 0 1 0<br>0 | 0 0 1<br>0 | 0 0 0<br>0 |
| 170 | 1 1 1<br>1 | 1 1 0<br>0 | 1 0 1<br>1 | 1 0 0<br>0 | 0 1 1<br>1 | 0 1 0<br>0 | 0 0 1<br>1 | 0 0 0<br>0 |

$r5, f(1,1,0) = r6$ and $f(1,1,1) = r7$ $(ri = 0,1)$. The rule number $R$ of a local transition function $f$ is defined by $R = 2^7 r + 2^6 r + 2^5 r + 2^4 r + 2^3 r + 2^2 r + 2^1 r + r$.

The local transition function of rule number $R$ is denoted by $fR$. The local transition rules with rule number 204, 240 and 170 are illustrated in Table 1 as $f204$, $f240$ and $f170$ are identity, shift-right and shift-left functions respectively. Table 2 shows some standard Boolean functions synthesized with different quantum gates.

*Table 2. Standard Boolean Functions Synthesized with Different Quantum Gates*

| Standard Functions with Serial No. | Realization of Standard Functions using different Logic gates and finally synthesized without complemented (NOT) variable or gate. |
|---|---|
| 1) F1 = AB'C | (i) F1 = MV(MV(0, A, B'), C, 0)<br>F1 = MV(NNI(1, A, B), C, 0)<br>F1 = NNI(NNI(A, B, 0), C, 1)<br>(ii) F1 = MV(MV(B', C, 0), MV(A, B', C'), MV(A', B, 0))<br>F1 = NNI(NNI(C, B, 0), NNI(B, A, C), NNI(B, A, 0)) |
| 2) F2 = AB | (i) F2 = MV(A, 0, B)<br>(ii) F2 = MV(MV(A', 0, 1), MV(A, B, 0), MV(A, 1, 0))<br>F2 = MV(NNI(A, 0, 0), MV(A, B, 0), MV(A, 1, 0))<br>F2 = NNI(NNI(A, 1, B), NNI(A, 0, 0), NNI(A, 0, 0)) |
| 3) F3 = A'BC<br>+ A'B'C' | (i) F3 = MV(MV(A', 1, 0), MV(B', C', 0), MV(B, C, 0))<br>F3 = MV(NNI(A, 1, 1), NNI(B, 0, C), MV(B, C, 0))<br>F3 = NNI(NNI(0, A, 1), NNI(B, 0, C), NNI(B, 1, C))<br>(ii) F3 = MV(MV(A', B', C), 0, MV(A', B, C'))<br>F3 = MV(NNI(A, C, B), 0, NNI(A, B, C)) |
| 4) F4 = A'BC<br>+ AB'C' | F4 = MV(MV(A, B, 1), MV(B', C', 0), MV(A', C, 0))<br>F4 = MV(NNI (B, 0, C), MV(A, B, 1), NNI(A, C, 1))<br>F4 = NNI(MV(B, C, 1), MV(A, B, 1), NNI(C, A, 1))<br>F4 = NNI(NNI(A, 0, B), NNI(B, 0, C), NNI(C, A, 0)) |
| 5) F5 = A'B +<br>BC' | (i) F5 = MV(0, MV(1, A', C'), B)<br>F5 = MV(0, NNI(A, 1, C), B)<br>(ii) F5 = MV(MV(A', B, C'), MV(B, 1, 0), MV(A, B', 0))<br>F5 = NNI(NNI(B, 0, 0), NNI(A, B, C), NNI(A, B, 0)) |
| 6)) F6 = AB' +<br>A'BC | F6 = MV(MV(A, B, C), MV(A, B', 0), MV(A', B', 1))<br>F6 = MV(MV(A, B, C), NNI(B, A, 1), NNI(A, 1, B))<br>F6 = NNI(NNI(A, B, 0), MV(A, B, C), MV(A, B, 0))<br>F6 = NNI(NNI(A, 0, B), NNI(B, A, 1), NNI(C, A, 0)) |

*continued on following page*

*Table 2. Continued*

| Standard Functions with Serial No. | Realization of Standard Functions using different Logic gates and finally synthesized without complemented (NOT) variable or gate. |
|---|---|
| 7) F7 = A'BC + ABC' + A'B'C' | (i) F7 = MV(MV(A', C, 0), MV(A', B, C'), MV(A, B', C'))<br>F7 = MV(NNI(A, C, 1), NNI(A, B, C), NNI(B, A, C))<br>(ii) F7 = MV(MV(A', B, C'), MV(A, B, C), MV(B', 0, C'))<br>F7 = MV(NNI(A, B, C), MV(A, B, C), NNI(B, 0, C))<br>(iii) F7 = MV(MV(A', B, C'), MV(A, B', 1), MV(A', BC, 0))<br>F7 = NNI(NNI(A, B, 1), NNI(A, B, C), NNI(BC, A, 0)) |
| 8) F8=A | F8 = MV(A, 0, 1)<br>F8 = NNI(0, A, 1) |
| 9) F9 = AB + BC + CA | (i) F9 = MV(A, B, C)<br>(ii) F9 = MV(MV(A, B, 1), MV(A, B, C), MV(A', B', 0))<br>F9 = MV(MV(A, B, 1), MV(A, B, C), NNI(A, 0, B))<br>F9 = NNI(MV(A, B, 1), MV(A, B, C), NNI(A, 0, B))<br>(iii) F9 = MV(MV(A, B, 1), MV(C, 1, 0), MV(A, B, 0))<br>F9 = NNI(NNI(A, 0, B), NNI(1, C, 0), NNI(A, 1, B)) |
| 10)F10=A'B+B'C | (i) F10 = MV(MV(A', B, 0), 1, MV(B', C, 0))<br>F10 = MV(NNI(A, B, 1), 1, NNI(B, C, 1))<br>F10 = NNI(NNI(B, A, 0), 1, NNI(C, B, 0))<br>(ii) F10 = MV(MV(A', B, C), MV(A', B', 1), MV(B', C, 0))<br>F10 = NNI(NNI(B, A, C), NNI(A, 1, B), NNI(C, B, 0)) |
| 11) F11= A'B + BC + AB'C' | F11 = MV(MV(A, B, 1), MV(A', B, C), MV(B', C', 0))<br>F11 = NNI(NNI(B, A, C), MV(A, B, 1), MV(B, C, 1))<br>F11 = NNI(NNI(A, 0, B), NNI(B, 0, C), NNI(B, A, C)) |
| 12) F12 = AB + A' B' | (i) F12 = MV(MV(A, B, 0), MV(A', B', 0), 1)<br>F12 = MV(MV(A, B, 0), NNI(A, 0, B), 1)<br>F12 = NNI(MV(A, B, 1), MV(A, B, 0), 0)<br>(ii) F12 = MV(MV(A', B, 1), MV(A', B', 0), MV(A, B, 0))<br>F12 = NNI(NNI(B, A, 1), NNI(A, 0, B), NNI(A, 1, B)) |
| 13) F13 = ABC'+AB'C+ A'BC+A'B'C' | (i) F13 = MV(MV(A', B, C'), MV(A, B, C), MV (B', 0, 1))<br>F13 = MV(MV(A', B, C'), MV(A, B, C), B')<br>F13 = MV(NNI(A, B, C), MV(A, B, C), NNI(B, 0, 0))<br>(ii) F13 = MV(MV(A', B, C'), MV(A, B', 1), MV(A'BC, AB'C, 1))<br>F13 = MV(NNI(A', B', 0), NNI(A, B, C), MV(MV(A', BC, 0), 1, MV(B', AC, 0)))<br>F13 = NNI(NNI(A, B, 1), NNI(A, B, C), NNI(NNI(A, BC, 1), 0, NNI(B, AC, 1))) |
| **Table – II** | Different Realization of Standard Functions |
| 1) F1=ABC | (i) F1 = MV(MV(A, B, C'), MV(B, C, 0), MV(A', B', 0))<br>F1 = NNI(NNI(A, C, B), MV(B, C, 0), MV(A, B, 1))<br>F1 = NNI(NNI(A, C, B), NNI(A, 0, B), NNI(B, 1, C))<br>(ii) F1 = MV(MV(0, A, B), C, 0)<br>F1 = NNI(NNI(A, 1, B), C, 1) |
| 2) F2=AB | (i) F2 = MV(A, 0, B)<br>(ii) F2 = MV(MV(A', 0, 1), MV(A, B, 0), MV(A, 1, 0))<br>F2 = MV(NNI(A, 0, 0), MV(A, B, 0), MV(A, 1, 0))<br>F2 = NNI(NNI(A, 1, B), NNI(A, 0, 0), NNI(A, 0, 0)) |

*continued on following page*

191

*Table 2. Continued*

| Standard Functions with Serial No. | Realization of Standard Functions using different Logic gates and finally synthesized without complemented (NOT) variable or gate. |
|---|---|
| 3) F3 = ABC + AB'C' | F3 = MV(MV(A, 0, 1), MV(A', B, C), MV(B', C', 0))<br>F3 = NNI(NNI(B, A, C), MV(A, 0, 1), MV(B, C, 1))<br>F3 = NNI(NNI(B, A, C), NNI(B, 0, C), NNI(A, 1, 1)) |
| 4) F4 = ABC + A'B'C' | F4 = MV(MV(A', B, 1), MV(B', C', 0), MV(A, C, 0))<br>F4 = MV(NNI(A, B, 0), MV(A, C, 0), NNI(B, 0, C))<br>F4 = NNI(MV(B, C, 1), MV(A, C, 0), NNI(B, A, 1))<br>F4 = NNI(NNI(B, A, 1), NNI(B, 0, C), NNI(A, 1, C)) |
| 5) F5 = AB + BC | (i) F5 = MV(MV(A, B, C), MV(A, B, 0), MV(A', C, 0))<br>F5 = MV(MV(A, B, C), MV(A, B, 0), NNI(A, C, 1))<br>F5 = NNI(NNI (A, 1, B), MV(A, B, C), NNI(C, A, 0))<br>(ii) F5 = MV(MV(1, A, C), B, 0)<br>F5 = NNI(NNI(A, 0, C), B, 1) |
| 6) F6 = AB + A'B'C | F6 = MV(MV (A', B, 1), MV(A, B, 0), MV(B', C, 0))<br>F6 = MV(NNI(A, B, 0), MV(A, B, 0), NNI(B, C, 1))<br>F6 = NNI(NNI (B, A, 1), NNI(B, C, 1), NNI(A, 1, B)) |
| 7) F7 = ABC + A'BC' + AB'C' | F7 = MV(MV(A, B, C'), MV(A', B, C), MV(A, B', 0))<br>F7 = NNI(NNI (A, C, B), NNI(B, A, 1), NNI(B, A, C)) |
| 8) F8=A | (i) F8 = MV(A, 0, 1)<br>F8 = NNI(0, A, 1)<br>(ii) F8 = MV(MV (A, B, 0), 1, MV (A, B', 0))<br>F8 = MV(MV(A, B, 0), 1, NNI (B, A, 1)) |
| 9) F9 = AB + BC + CA | (i) F9 = MV(A, B, C)<br>(ii) F9 = MV(MV(A, B, 1), MV(A, B, C), MV(A', B', 0))<br>F9 = MV(MV(A, B, 1), MV(A, B, C), NNI(A, 0, B))<br>F9 = NNI(MV(A, B, 1), MV(A, B, C), NNI(A, 0, B))<br>(iii) F9 = MV(MV(A, B, 1), MV(C, 1, 0), MV(A, B, 0))<br>F9 = NNI(NNI(A, 0, B), NNI(1, C, 0), NNI(A, 1, B)) |
| 10) F10 = AB + B'C | (i) F10 = MV(MV(A, B, C), MV(A, B', 1), MV(B', C, 0))<br>F10 = MV(NNI(B, A, 0), MV(A, B, C), NNI(B, C, 1))<br>F10 = NNI(NNI(A, B, 1), MV(A, B, C), NNI(C, B, 0))<br>(ii) F10 = MV(MV(A, B, 0), 1, MV(B', C, 0))<br>F10 = NNI(NNI(A, 1, B), 1, NNI(0, B, C)) |
| 11) F11 = AB + BC + A'B'C' | (i) F11 = MV(MV(A', B, 1), MV(A, B, C), MV(B', C', 0))<br>F11 = MV(NNI(A, B, 0), MV(A, B, C), NNI(B, 0, C))<br>F11 = NNI(NNI(B, A, 1), MV(A, B, C), MV(B, C, 1))<br>(ii) F11 = MV(MV(A', B, C'), MV(A, B', 1), MV(B, C, 0))<br>F11 = NNI(NNI(A, B, 1), NNI(A, B, C), NNI(B, 1, C)) |
| 12) F12 = AB + A' B' | (i) F12 = MV(MV(A, B, 0), MV(A', B', 0), 1)<br>F12 = MV(MV(A, B, 0), NNI(A, 0, B), 1)<br>F12 = NNI(MV(A, B, 1), MV(A, B, 0), 0)<br>(ii) F12 = MV(MV(A', B, 1), MV(A', B', 0), MV(A, B, 0))<br>F12 = NNI(NNI(B, A, 1), NNI(A, 0, B), NNI(A, 1, B)) |
| 13) F13 = ABC + A'B'C + AB'C' + A'BC' | F13 = MV(MV(A, B, C'), MV(A', B, C), MV(B', 0, 1))<br>F13 = NNI(NNI (A, C, B), NNI(B, 0, 0), NNI(B, A, |

# PARTITIONED QUANTUM CELLULAR AUTOMATA

## Application to Pixel Classification

MATLAB 7.0 on HP 2 quad processor with 2.40 GHz is used to implement the new PSO evaluated QCA algorithm. Dunn (Dunn, 1973), Davies-Bouldin (DB) (Davies & Bouldin, 1979) and Silhouette (Rousseeuw, 1987) validity indices evaluate the effectiveness of PSO QCA over K-Means and FCM quantitatively. The clustered

*Figure 1. The flowchart of PSOQCA algorithm for remote sensing classification*

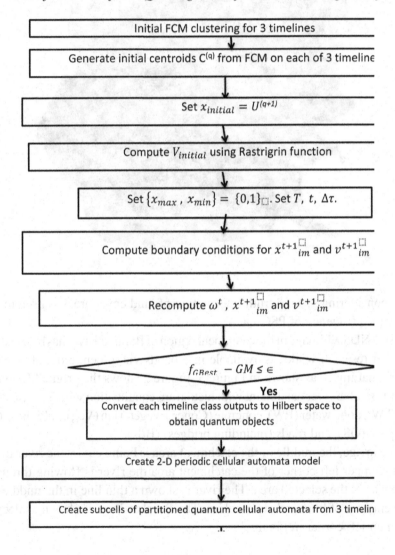

*Figure 2. Original image of the catchment area of Barakar river in 2005*

images considering ground truth information of land cover areas is used to verify visually the efficiency of PSO QCA.

The LANDSAT image of the catchment region of Barakar River has been extracted for further research works, is available in 3 bands viz. green, red and blue bands with original image as shown in Figure 3. Figure 3 shows the original LANDAST image of Barakar river catchment with histogram equalization with 7 classes: turbid water (TW), pond water (PW), concrete (Concr.), vegetarian (Veg), habitation (Hab), open space (OS), and roads (including bridges) (B/R).

In the image, the middle of the catchment area is being cut by the river Barakar. From the upper left corner of the catchment area the river is flowing through the middle part of the selected area. The river is shown a thin line in the middle of the catchment area of blue and river colors. The Barakar Dam is shown as deep gray color in up-left corner in Figure 3.

*Figure 3. Pixel classification of Barakar river catchment area in 2005 obtained by K-Means algorithm (with K=7)*

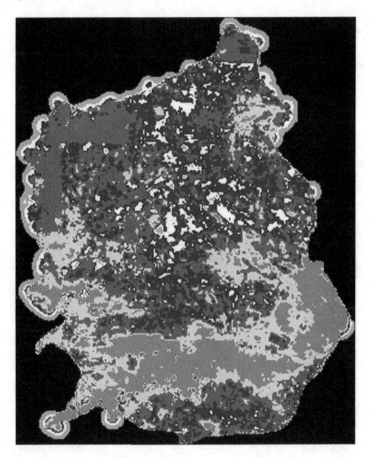

The segmented catchment area of Barakar river images obtained by K-Means and FCM algorithms respectively are shown in Figures 4 and 5 for (K = 7). In Figure 3, K-Means algorithm fails to classify the catchment area from the background. FCM clustering solutions in Figure 5 also fails to detect the catchment area properly from the background in the middle part. Some waterbodies part and the background are mixed in both K-Means and FCM clustering solutions in Figure 4 and 5 respectively. However, our new PSOQCA algorithm in Figure 6 is able to separate all catchment areas from the background. These indicate that PSOQCA algorithm detects the overlapping arbitrary shaped regions significantly with better efficiency than K-Means and FCM algorithms.

*Figure 4. Pixel classification of Barakar river catchment area in 2005 obtained FCM algorithm (with K=7)*

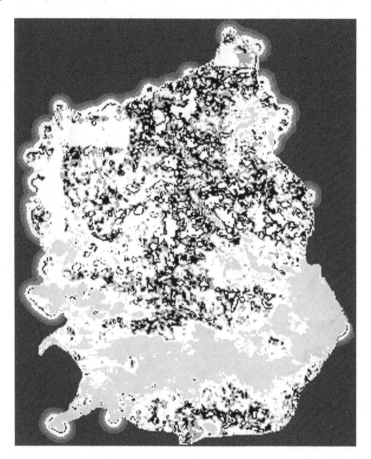

## QUANTITATIVE ANALYSIS

Measuring validity measures Davies-Bouldin (DB) and Dunn index, as defined in (Dunn, 1973) and (Davies & Bouldin, 1979) respectively, for K-Means, FCM and PSOQCA algorithms on the Barakar river catchment remote sensing image in Table 3 is used to objectively evaluate the results of cluster. PSOQCA produces best final value for minimized DB index as 0.5135, while K-Means obtains a DB value of 0.7342 and FCM obtains 0.5780. Similarly, the Dunn index produced by PSOQCA algorithm (maximizing Dunn) is 1.3845, but K-Means algorithm provides smaller Dunn value.

*Figure 5. Pixel classification of Barakar river catchment area in 2005 obtained PSO algorithm (with K=7)*

*Table 3. Validity indices values of the classified remote sensing image provided by k-means, Fcm, Pso and PSOQCA algorithms*

| Index | Barakar Catchment | | | | |
|-------|------|---------|-----|-----|--------|
| | Year | K-Means | FCM | PSO | PSOQCA |
| Davies-Bouldin index | 2005 | 0.5134 | 0.5058 | 0.5250 | 0.5346 |
| | 2010 | 0.5076 | 0.5048 | 0.5165 | |
| | 2015 | 0.5138 | 0.5124 | 0.5284 | |
| Dunn index | 2005 | 0.7500 | 0.7046 | 0.7894 | 0.8658 |
| | 2010 | 0.7533 | 0.7924 | 0.7613 | |
| | 2015 | 0.8673 | 0.8398 | 0.7997 | |

*Figure 6. Original image of the catchment area of Barakar river in 2010*

That PSOQCA optimizes DB and Dunn indices more than both K-Means and FCM is established by these results. Thus we can easily convey that PSOQCA, comparable in goodness of solutions to K-Means and FCM algorithms sometimes outperform to obtain superior clustering results.

## STATISTICAL ANALYSIS

A statistical non-parametric significance test for independent samples has been conducted at 5% significance level (Hollander & Wolfe, 1999). The performance scores, DB index values produced by 10 consecutive runs of K-Means, FCM and PSOQCA algorithms on the chosen remote sensing Image. It is observed from

*Figure 7. Pixel classification of Barakar river catchment area in 2010 obtained by K-Means algorithm With k=7*

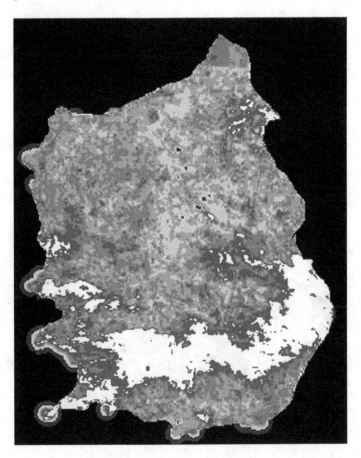

the medians of each group on the dataset in Table 4 that PSOQCA provides better median values than K-Means and FCM algorithms.

It has been shown in Table 5 that P-values and H-values produced by Wilcoxon's rank sum test for comparison of two groups, PSOQCA-K-Means and PSOQCA-FCM. All the P-values reported in the Table 5 are less than 0.005 (5% significance level). For the chosen remote sensing Image on the catchment area of Barakar, comparative P-value of rank sum test between PSOQCA and K-Means is very small 2.00E-003, indicating the performance metrics produced by PSOQCA to be statistically significant and not occurred by chance. Similar results are obtained for another group with FCM algorithm also. Hence, all results establish the significant superiority of PSOQCA over K-Means and FCM algorithms.

*Figure 8. Pixel classification of Barakar river catchment area in 2010 obtained FCM algorithm (with K=7)*

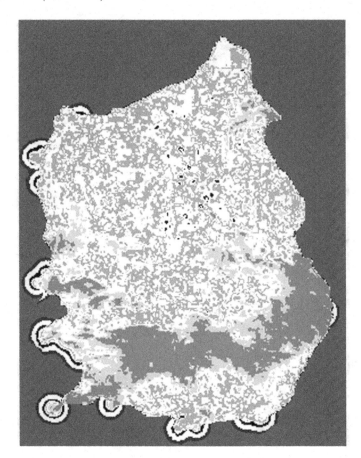

*Table 4. Median values of performance parameter DB index over 10 consecutive runs on different alogthrims*

| Data | Algorithms | | | |
|---|---|---|---|---|
| | **K-Means** | **FCM** | **PSO** | **PSOQCA** |
| Catchment Area of Barakar river Image | 0.5027 | 0.4861 | 0.5249 | 0.5346 |

*Figure 9. Pixel classification of Barakar river catchment area in 2010 obtained PSO algorithm (with K=7)*

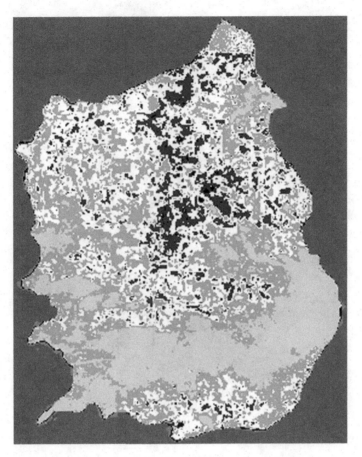

*Table 5. P-Values produced by rank sum while comparing PSOQCA with k-means and PSOQCA with FCM respectively*

| Algorithm | Comparison with PSOQCA | |
|---|---|---|
| | H | P-value |
| K-Means | 1 | 0.0195 |
| FCM | 1 | 0.0020 |
| PSO | 1 | 0.0273 |

*Figure 10. Original image of the catchment area of Barakar river in 2015*

## FUTURE RESEARCH DIRECTIONS

Considering the states of the cells in each CA, in our CA model with two dimension for neighbourhood based method of priority correction, as per cluster algorithm allocation from PSO based automatic initial classification. A CA consists of a spatial lattice of cells, each of which stores a discrete variable at a time t that refers to the present state of cell according to the PSO based initial clustering phase allocations. The cells in CA denote the pixels in their positions in the chosen satellite image. The cells state number in the model initially denote the assigned clusters from the first phase of our algorithm. State 0 denotes that the pixel has been assigned to cluster 0 in first phase. If the left most and right most cells are neighbours of each other,

*Figure 11. Pixel classification of Barakar river catchment area in 2015 obtained by K-Means algorithm (with K=7)*

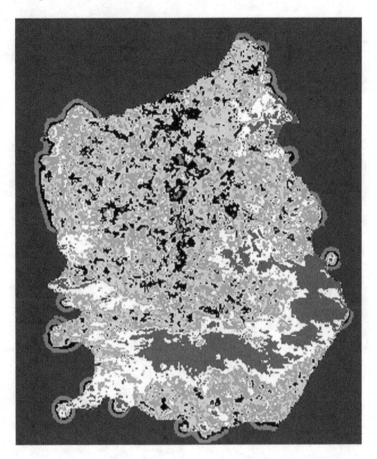

the CA is periodic boundary, otherwise it is null boundary CA. In our implemented model, we adopt the CA with null boundary condition. We have used deterministic CA for our experiments. Our 2-dimensional CA model has been depicted according to the clustering allocations from the rough set based automatic initial classification phase. The cells in CA denote the pixels in their positions in the chosen remote sensing image. The state numbers of the cells in the model initially denote the assigned clusters from the first phase of our algorithm. State 0 denotes that the pixel has been assigned to cluster 0 in first phase. In our model as proposed, we adopt the CA with null boundary condition. We have used deterministic CA for our experiments. The CA model has been depicted in the Flowchart in Figure 2.1. The following problems are left for further study.

*Figure 12. Pixel classification of Barakar river catchment area in 2015 obtained FCM algorithm (with K=7)*

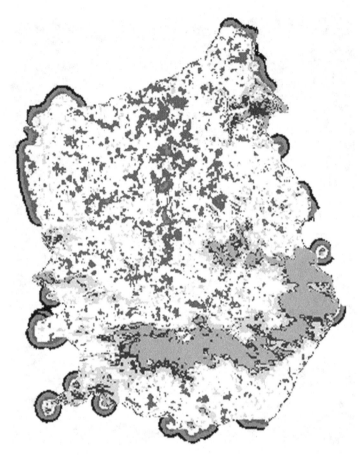

1.  To design a simpler 2D-CA (i.e. to reduce the number of states) that supports self-reproduction for spectral image analysis.
2.  To design a 2D CA that supports both computation and construction universality of remote sensing satellite image.

Based on the cluster allocations outputs, the first stage CA is developed from the initial rough set based automatic classification on remote sensing image as chosen. If among 4 neighbours (left, right, top, bottom), if at least two neighbours show lower cluster values, the priority of current cell decreases to be of lower cluster value. In this case, the present state of current cell, therefore, decreases by 1 towards 0 priority. If more than 2 neighbours have higher cluster values than current cell, similarly, the next state of current cell increases by 1, to make it belongs to higher

*Figure 13. Pixel classification of Barakar river catchment area in 2015 obtained PSO algorithm (with K=7)*

clusters depending on neighbourhood pixels. Iterating through the CA matrices we obtain proper neighbourhood corrections for pixels in the chosen remote sensing image. Further work is to be done to synthesize the proposed theoretical framework and to implement the model in a widespread remote sensing image.

## CONCLUSION

Image segmentation algorithms are most challenging methods used in remote sensing to help to interpret the land use land cover models in the satellite imagery. Cellular automata model provides the changes in cell states depending on their neighbourhood, which occur in discrete time form. Therefore, the cellular automata model can be

*Figure 14. Combined Pixel classification of Barakar river catchment areas in 2005, 2010 and 2015 as obtained by PSOQCA algorithm*

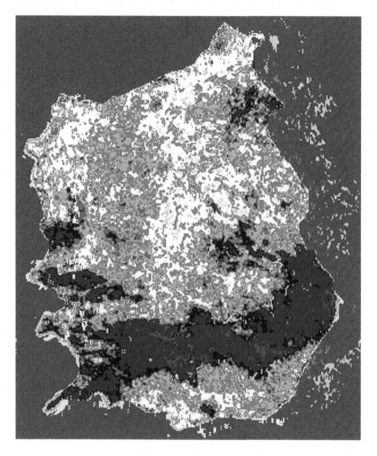

used to analyze land cover segments in remote sensing images, considering the neighbourhood pixel classes. This article contribution lies in significant improvement over detection of mixed land cover regions in the satellite image than existing partitioning algorithm. This new approach introduces a hybrid soft set based pixel segmentation with cellular automata based neighbourhood upgradation in our proposed PSOQCA algorithm for clustering. The contributions primarily of this work are to utilize one new soft PSO based initial clustering in satellite images with Cellular Automata based neighbourhood corrections. The neighbourhood correction helps phase to correct the outlier allocations to overlapping clusters significantly. It verifies allocations overall with respect to the neighbourhood, to obtain improved land cover regions. The performance of proposed PSOQCA approach is demonstrated on chosen satellite image of over the catchment area of Barakar river in 2015 including Tilaya dam. Significant efficiency of proposed PSOQCA segmentation method in comparison with well-known K-Means and FCM methods is established both quantitatively and statistically. For quantitative evaluation, two internal external validity indices are analysed over the catchment image. The ground truth knowledge verification also exhibits significant superiority of new PSOQCA algorithm over other two well-known algorithms. Statistical tests are also performed to establish the statistical significance of PSOQCA solutions when comparing with K-Means and FCM algorithms on remote sensing chosen image. This scheme is highly adaptive in concurrent topological changes and is, therefore, well suited for use in any remote sensing satellite image.

# REFERENCES

Abraham, Nath, & Mahanti. (2011). Hybrid intelligent systems for stock market analysis. In *Computational science*. Springer-Verlag.

Alves de Lima, D., & Correa Victorino, A. (2016). A hybrid controller for vision-based navigation of autonomous vehicles in urban environments. *IEEE Transactions on Intelligent Transportation Systems, 17*(8), 2310–2323. doi:10.1109/TITS.2016.2519329

Araujo, Oliveira, & Meira. (2012). *A Hybrid Model for S&P500 Index Forecasting*. Springer Berlin Heidelberg.

Ayerdi, B., & Grana Romay, M. (2016). Hyperspectral image analysis by spectral-spatial processing and anticipative hybrid extreme rotation forest classification. *IEEE Transactions on Geoscience and Remote Sensing, 54*(5), 2627–2639. doi:10.1109/TGRS.2015.2503886

Bandyopadhyay, S. (2005). Satellite image classification using genetically guided fuzzy clustering with spatial information. *International Journal of Remote Sensing, 26*(3), 579–593. doi:10.1080/01431160512331316432

Baser, F., & Apaydin, A. (2015). Hybrid fuzzy support vector regression analysis. *Journal of Intelligent & Fuzzy Systems, 28*(5), 2037–2045. doi:10.3233/IFS-141482

Chakraborty, D., Sarkar, A., & Maulik, U. (2016). A New isotropic locality improved kernel for pattern classifications in remote sensing imagery. *Spatial Statistics, 17*, 71–82. doi:10.1016/j.spasta.2016.04.003

Church, G. M., Tavazoie, S., Hughes, J. D., Campbell, M. J., & Cho, R. J. (1999). Analysis of temporal gene expression pro?les, clustering by simulated annealing and determining optimal number of clusters. *Nature Genetics, 22*(3), 281–285. doi:10.1038/10343 PMID:10391217

*Congalton & Green. (1999). Assessing the accuracy of classifications of remotely sensed data: Principles and practices.* Boca Raton, FL: Lewis Publications.

Davies & Bouldin. (1979). A Cluster Separation Measure. *IEEE Transactions on Pattern Analysis and Machine Intelligence, 1*(2), 224–227.

Dembele, D., & Kastner, P. (2003). Fuzzy c-means method for clustering microarray data. *Bioinformatics (Oxford, England), 19*(8), 973–980. doi:10.1093/bioinformatics/btg119 PMID:12761060

Denis, Dubois, Dub'e, & Desrochers. (2016). Blended power management strategy using pattern recognition for a plugin hybrid electric vehicle. *Int. J. Intelligent Transportation Systems Research, 14*(2), 101–114. doi:10.1007/s13177-014-0106-z

Dunn, J. C. (1973). A Fuzzy Relative of the ISODATA Process and Its Use in Detecting Compact Well-Separated Clusters. *Journal of Cybernetics, 3*(3), 32–57. doi:10.1080/01969727308546046

Fakharzadeh & Khosravi. (2015). A hybrid method for solving fuzzy semi-infinite linear programming problems. *Journal of Intelligent & Fuzzy Systems, 28*(2), 879–884.

Fakhrzad, M. B., & Rahdar, M. A. (2016). Optimization of hybrid robot control system using artificial hormones and fuzzy logic. *Journal of Intelligent & Fuzzy Systems, 30*(3), 1403–1410. doi:10.3233/IFS-152053

T. Friedrich, F. Neumann, & A. M. Sutton (Eds.). (2016). Intelligent on-line energy management system for plug-in hybrid electric vehicles based on evolutionary algorithm. In *Genetic and Evolutionary Computation Conference, GECCO 2016* (pp. 167–168). ACM.

Ganzha, L. M. (Ed.). (2014). The influence of using fractal analysis in hybrid mlp model for short-term forecast of closing prices on warsaw stock exchange. In Proceedings of the 2014 Federated Conference on Computer Science and Information Systems *(vol. 2, pp. 111–118). IEEE.

Goel. (2010). Land Cover Feature Extraction using Hybrid Swarm Intelligence Techniques - A Remote Sensing Perspective. *ACEEE Int. J. on Signal and Image Processing*, 14–16.

Gonzalez & Woods. (1992). *Digital image processing*. Addison Wesley.

Guijarro-Berdiñas, B., Alonso-Betanzos, A., & Fontenla-Romero, O. (2002). Intelligent analysis and pattern recognition in cardiotocographic signals using a tightly coupled hybrid system. *Artificial Intelligence, 136*(1), 1–27. doi:10.1016/S0004-3702(01)00163-1

Gupta, Goel, & Aggarwal. (2013). A hybrid biogeography based heuristic for the mirrored traveling tournament problem. In *Sixth International Conference on Contemporary Computing* (pp. 325–330). IEEE.

*Hollander & Wolfe. (1999). Nonparametric statistical methods* (2nd ed.). Wiley.

Hoon, de Imoto, Nolan, & Miyano. (2004). Open source clustering software. *Bioinformatics (Oxford, England), 20*(9), 1453–1454. PMID:14871861

Jacobsen. (1998). A generic architecture for hybrid intelligent systems. *Proceedings of the IEEE Fuzzy Systems*.

Kasabov & Song. (2001). *Denfis: Dynamic evolving neural-fuzzy inference system and its application for time-series prediction*. Academic Press.

Khemaja. (2016). Using a knapsack mo del to optimize continuous building of a hybrid intelligent tutoring system: Application information technology professionals. *International Journal of Human Capital and Information Technology Professionals, 7*(2), 1–18. doi:10.4018/IJHCITP.2016040101

Kumar, S., & Singh, S. K. (2016). Hybrid BFO and PSO swarm intelligence approach for biometric feature optimization. *International Journal of Swarm Intelligence Research, 7*(2), 36–62. doi:10.4018/IJSIR.2016040103

Lin, Wang, Liu, Han, & Lu. (2016). Hybrid multigranulation rough sets of variable precision based on tolerance. *Journal of Intelligent & Fuzzy Systems, 31*(2), 717–725.

Lior & Maimon. (2005). *Clustering methods. Data mining and knowledge discovery handbook*. Springer US.

L´opez-Garc´ia, Onieva, Osaba, Masegosa, & Perallos. (2016). A hybrid metho d for short-term tra c congestion forecasting using genetic algorithms and cross entropy. *IEEE Transactions on Intelligent Transportation Systems, 17*(2), 557–569. doi:10.1109/TITS.2015.2491365

Masulli, F., & Palm, G¨. (Eds.). (2012). A hybrid model for s&p500 index forecasting. In *Lecture Notes in Computer Science: Vol. 7553. Artificial Neural Networks and Machine Learning* (pp. 573–581). Springer.

Maulik & Sarkar. (2012). E cient parallel algorithm for pixel classification in remote sensing imagery. *GeoInformatica, 16*(2), 391–407. doi:10.1007/s10707-011-0136-5

Maulik, Mukhopadhyay, & Bandyopadhyay. (2009). Combining Pareto-Optimal Clusters using Supervised Learning for Identifying Coexpressed Genes. *BMC Bioinformatics, 10*, 27. doi:10.1186/1471-2105-10-27 PMID:19154590

Nehi, H. M., & Keikha, A. (2016). TOPSIS and choquet integral hybrid technique for solving MAGDM problems with interval type-2 fuzzy numbers. *Journal of Intelligent & Fuzzy Systems, 30*(3), 1301–1310. doi:10.3233/IFS-152044

Pan, M., Yan, J., Tu, Q., & Jiang, C. (2015). Fuzzy control and wavelet transform-based energy management strategy design of a hybrid tracked bulldozer. *Journal of Intelligent & Fuzzy Systems, 29*(6), 2565–2574. doi:10.3233/IFS-151959

Park, Lee, & Lee. (2015). Hybrid filter based on neural networks for removing quantum noise in low-dose medical x-ray CT images. *Int. J. Fuzzy Logic and Intelligent Systems, 15*(2).

Rabbani, Farrokhi-asl, & Rafiei. (2016). A hybrid genetic algorithm for waste collection problem by heterogeneous eet of vehicles with multiple separated compartments. *Journal of Intelligent & Fuzzy Systems, 30*(3), 1817–1830. doi:10.3233/IFS-151893

Raouzaiou, Tsapatsoulis, Tzouvaras, Stamou, & Kollias. (2002). A hybrid intelligent system for facial expression recognition. *Proceedings of the European Symposium on Intelligent Technologies, Hybrid Systems and their implementation on Smart Adaptive Systems.*

Sarkar & Das. (2015). *Remote sensing image classification using Fuzzy PSO hybrid approach*. IGI-Global.

Scarlat & Maracine. (2015). The hybrid intelligent systems design using grey systems theory. *Grey Systems: T&A, 5*(2), 194–205.

Shah & Adhyaru. (2016). Hjb solution-based optimal control of hybrid dynamical systems using multiple linearized model. *Control and Intelligent Systems, 44*(2).

Singh, Maurya, Singh, & Singh. (2012). Analysis of remote sensed data using hybrid intelligence system: a case study of Bhopal region. *Proceedings of National Conference on Future Aspects of Artificial intelligence in Industrial Automation (NCFAAIIA 2012)*, 26–31.

Singla, Jarial, & Mittal. (2015). An analytical study of the remote sensing image classification using swarm intelligence techniques. *International Journal for Research in Applied Science and Engineering Technology, 3*(6), 492–497.

Smith III. (1971). Two-dimensional formal languages and pattern recogni-tion by cellular automata. *Proceedings of IEEE Conference Record of 12th Annual Symposium on Switching and Automata Theory.*

Spang, R. (2003). Diagnostic signatures from microarrays, a bioinformatics concept for personalized medicine. *BIOSILICO, 1*(2), 64–68. doi:10.1016/S1478-5382(03)02329-1

Tavakkoli-Moghaddam, R., Sadri, S., Pourmohammad-Zia, N., & Mohammadi, M. (2015). A hybrid fuzzy approach for the closed-loop supply chain network design under uncertainty. *Journal of Intelligent & Fuzzy Systems, 28*(6), 2811–2826. doi:10.3233/IFS-151561

Tavazoie, Hughes, Campbell, Cho, & Church. (2001). Systematic determination of genetic network architecture. *Bioinformatics (Oxford, England), 17*, 405–414. PMID:11331234

Teh & Lim. (2006). *A Hybrid Intelligent System and Its Application to Fault Detection and Diagnosis.* Springer.

Villar, Chira, Sedano, Gonz´alez, & Trejo. (2015). A hybrid intelligent recognition system for the early detection of strokes. *Integrated Computer-Aided Engineering, 22*(3), 215–227.

Wolfram, S. (1983). Statistical mechanics of cellular automata. *Reviews of Modern Physics, 55*(3), 601–644. doi:10.1103/RevModPhys.55.601

Wolfram, S. (1986). Cryptography with cellular automata. *Lecture Notes in Computer Science, 218*, 429–432. doi:10.1007/3-540-39799-X_32

Xhafa, Kolodziej, Barolli, Kolici, Miho, & Takizawa. (2011). Evaluation of hybridization of GA and TS algorithms for independent batch scheduling in computational grids. In *2011 International Conference on P2P, Parallel, Grid, Cloud and Internet Computing* (pp. 148–155). IEEE Computer Society.

Xu, Olman, & Xu. (1999). Clustering gene expression data using a graph theoretic approach, an application of minimum spanning trees. *Bioinformatics (Oxford, England), 17*, 309–318.

## KEY TERMS AND DEFINITIONS

**Cellular Automata:** A discrete, dynamical system composed of very simple, uniformly interconnected cells.

**Clustering:** Assigning similar elements to one group, which increases intra-cluster similarity and decreases inter-cluster similarity.

**K-Means Algorithm:** Clustering algorithm to classify n elements in k clusters, which iteratively computes the cluster centroids as the means of all elements in one cluster.

**QCA (Quantum Cellular Automata):** A quantum cellular automaton (QCA) is an abstract model of quantum computation, devised in analogy to conventional models of cellular automata introduced by von Neumann.

Chapter 7

# True Color Image Segmentation by MUSIG Activation Function Using Self–Supervised QMLSONN Architecture With Context–Sensitive Thresholding

**Pankaj Pal**
*RCC Institute of Information Technology, India*

**Siddhartha Bhattacharyya**
*RCC Institute of Information Technology, India*

## ABSTRACT

*In this chapter, the authors propose the true color image segmentation in real-life images as well as synthetic images by means of thresholded MUSIG function, which is learnt by quantum-formulated self-supervised neural network according to change of phase. In the initial phase, the true color image is segregated in the source module to fragment three different components—red, green, and blue colors—for three parallel layers of QMLSONN architecture. This information is fused in the sink module of QPSONN to get the preferred output. Each pixel of the input image is converted to the corresponding qubit neurons according to the phase manner. The interconnection weights between the layers are represented by qubit rotation gates. The quantum measurement at the output layer destroys the quantum states and gets the output for the processed information by means of quantum backpropagation algorithm using fuzziness measure.*

DOI: 10.4018/978-1-5225-5219-2.ch007

## INTRODUCTION

To recover the object from the noisy environment is a difficult task and the research is continuing up to the knowledge of extent to collect more information regarding image processing. Though image processing starts from early 1990, at that time the object extraction from the blured and noisy environment has been evolved by the MLSONN architecture and is designed by few scientists (Ghosh et al., 1993) for extraction the object. Sigmoid response for the graded neuron is used in case of the neural model (Hopfield, 1984). In this regards the neuron characteristics is very similar to that of McCulloch - Pitt's neurons model for this deterministic characterization. Here, neurons collectively act together to operate just like biological neurons. The basic neural network architecture is shown in Figure 1 reckoning with different nodes comprising input layer, hidden layer and output layer. Extraction of the binary objects from the noisy environmental images is an intricate work in the computer vision research fields. After few times have been elapsed the binary object is extracted by means of QMLSONN architecture (Bhattacharyya at al., 2014). It is used significantly to train the qubit neurons with the noisy atmosphere, constituting three layered architecture by applying the sigmoidal activation function. At that juncture authors have designed to recover the object from the noisy perspective for pure noisy color images (Bhattacharyya et al., 2015) using quantum version parallel neural network architecture by applying the quantum back propagation algorithm and guided by the sigmoidal activation function. Authors use three parallel QMLSONN networks each having three layers input, hidden and output for red, green and blue color components segmentation accordingly.

The image segmentation is another application to reconstruct the object from the noisy perspective. It is a nice approach to segment the image in various portions / class depending on the application of the thresholding strategy. Here the segmentation of the image to detect the boundary or object (Singh et al., September 2010) to maintain the visualization characteristics of the pixels. Each pixel is grouped with similar types of characteristics like intensity, color, texture, etc. to maintain the grouping of the class. For the binary image segmentation Model-Based Segmentation is very much useful where local information processing can be taken place. When the local visualization is not sufficient to collect the local information for collecting the pixels to make a similar class then the geometric shape of the object may be considered and compared with the characteristics of the local information.

Another kind of learning principle such as autoencoders (Baldi P., 2012) can be used to solve the segmentation process by the neural network architecture, but it is applicable for unsupervised principle and also in deep architecture for transferring the learning information. The linear autoencoders can solve the numerical problem on real numbers and Boolean autoencoders is used to solve the learning clustering algorithm problem in polynomial time provided the cluster sizes are small. QMLSONN performs better computation time complexity and object extraction time is low over SONN by converting the classical bit to quantum bit on quantum states using quantum superposition principle.

The chapter is organized as follows. In the next part it illustrates the fundamental scenario of the image processing concepts on the basis of fuzzy set theoretic strategies, definition and different types of parameters related to this chapter. In the next phase an elaborate discussion is made on the principle of quantum computation with the relation to the image processing. The segmentation principle is discussed in the next following section with different strategies. The next phase is pointing to the characteristics of the MUSIG activation function with neat diagram. The MLSONN architecture is illustrated in the next section. The next three parts discuss PSONN, QMLSONN and QPSONN principles respectively. Thresholding strategies are discussed in the next part of the QPSONN principle, algorithm and mathematical detail. The color image segmentation principle is applied for the next section of the thresholding strategies. Efficiency measurement is discussed in the following section. Before the last stage of the conclusion, result and discussion with Tables and Figures are presented. The last but not least stage is illustrated with conclusion and remarks for this chapter and lastly few references are given for further study and understanding this chapter.

*Figure 1. Shows the basic neural network architecture*

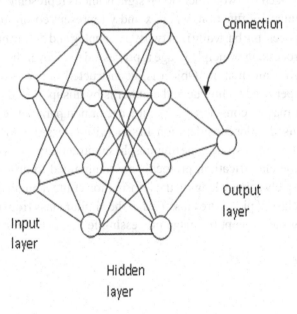

In this neural network architecture one input layer, two hidden layers and one output layer with corresponding interconnection weights between layers are shown. This neural network is used to implement the character recognition system (Mamedov et al.). Character matrix creation and suitable network structure are the combination of the key element for this implementation. Feed forward algorithm is imposed to transmit the information from input layer to output layer through hidden layer to generate the output. Here, inter connection weights are updated between the consecutive layers after imposing backpropagation algorithm when error is appreciable more corresponding to the threshold limit at the output layer. The output is achieved after error is calculated minimum and the network is stabilized.

Neural network also be applicable for optimizing simulations (Laguna et al., 2002), prediction and classification technique. In optimizing simulations, genetic algorithm, simulated annealing, tabu search are used as a global search method for optimizing simulations. In order to merit of the new proposal to this kind of system the training developer's motto is more important on accuracy than the training speed. Laguna et al. emphasized on the training procedure to achieve the accuracy within the stipulated period of time.

## BASIC CONCEPT OF IMAGE PROCESSING

Image is the basically two dimensional array of pixels of same or different intensity values characterized by two dimensional signals and is represented mathematically as $f(x, y)$ of intensity function, where x and y represent co-ordinates of intensity value. Image processing basically is of two types, analog and digital image processing. In the image processing principle image is processed to recover the object for getting more meaningful information. Object is reconstructed in two ways, one is by the principle of supervised technique and another is by unsupervised technique (Kalra et al., 2013) or may be considered as parametric or non parametric, etc., depending on the method used under consideration. In supervised classification principle object is processed in two phases, one is the training phase and another one is the classification phase. Using the classification, protocols are maintained to differentiate between the classes uniquely acknowledging the information content but in the classification phase trained classed pixels are classified in the similar class from the training data file. Regarding the concept of image processing few relevant points are discussed as under:

## Fuzzy Set Theoretic Concepts

Uncertainty realization in the mathematical design for a problem can be described using the fuzzy set theory. Fuzzy logic is described where the mathematical model is difficult to design or has some uncertainty to explain the concrete structure.

## Definitions of Fuzzy Set

Definitions of the fuzzy set can be demonstrated as under (L.A. Zadeh, 1965):

The fuzzy set $F = \{x_1, x_2, x_3, \ldots, x_n\}$, where $x_i \in X$ and i= 1 to n, having a membership function $\mu_F$, where $\mu_F \to [0,1]$

It is hypothesized that the membership value $\mu_F : F \to P$, where $P$ is poset.

$\mu_F(x_i)$ is called the grade of membership function of x in $\mu_F$

F is an ordinary set if and only if $\mu_F \to [0,1]$

## Characteristics of Fuzzy Set

There are few characteristics of fuzzy logic which can be stated as (a) each approximate reason can be modeled to its limiting one. (b) Each and every matter can be viewed as a fuzzy set. (c) Fuzzy logic is demonstrated or implemented far beyond any logical concepts. (d) Collection of instance, information, etc. of knowledge on a variable can be described be means of fuzzy logic. (e) Propagation of elastic constraints is described by the process of inference (L.A. Zadeh, 1965).

## Fuzzy Cardinality

Cardinality $(\xi_X)$ of a fuzzy set X is the algebraic sum of the membership value $(\mu_F)$ of the elements of the set (Bhattacharyya et al., 2007). It is described as

$$(\xi_X) = \sum_{i=1}^{n} \mu_X(x_i).$$

It is a measure of the degree of containment of the elements present in the fuzzy set. Higher value of the cardinality means higher degree of containment and vice versa. It indicates that the numbers of elements present in the fuzzy set have the same kind of membership values (Dhar M., 2013). The cardinality of the fuzzy set for the natural numbers in the universe is also a fuzzy set. It is applied in many applications where the functional output cannot be found out. Fuzzy theoretic approach is applied in medical imaging, biochemical engineering, forensic department for investigation of imperial articles, motion sensing devices, etc. where general set theoretic approaches do not stand.

## Hostility Index

The image is considered as the number of pixels having different intensity values. So, the pixels have different characteristics with their neighbors of subsets of the pixels. The variation of pixel intensity can be considered as a fuzzy set. Considering the fuzzy set $F = \{x_1, x_2, x_3, \ldots, x_n\}$, where $x_i \in X$ and i= 1 to n, having a membership function $\mu_A(x_i)$, $\mu_A(x_i)$ belongs to the boundary conditions between '0' and '1'. Membership value stands for the degree of containment of an object for a particular class. A membership value of the object close to 1 indicates greater probability of the object to be present within the set and membership value of the object close to 0 indicates lesser probability to stay within the set (Bhattacharyya et al., 2007). It is a measure of homogeneity of intensity characteristics of the pixels. More is the homogeneity of the pixels to its neighbor more closely they are related to each other and the candidate pixels are less hostile and vice versa. Using the fuzzy hostility index $(\zeta)$, the degree of homogeneity or heterogeneity of the neighborhood pixels can be determined. Assuming the neighborhood pixels of having the $n^{th}$ order alignment, the fuzzy hostility index is defined as $\zeta = \dfrac{3}{2^{n+1}} \sum_{i=1}^{2^{n+1}} \left( \dfrac{\left|\mu_a - \mu_{b_i}\right|}{\left|\mu_a + 1\right| + \left|\mu_{b_i} + 1\right|} \right)$

; where, $\mu_a$ = membership value of the candidate pixel element, $\mu_{b_i}$ = membership value of the $i^{th}$ element of the neighborhood element of the candidate pixel (Bhattacharyya et al., 2007). The cardinality value $\zeta$ lies between 0 and 1. Effectiveness of the value of $\zeta$ determines the concept of the degree of homogeneity, if the value of $\zeta$ is more, the more homogeneity is achieved and vice versa.

## FUNDAMENTALS OF QUANTUM COMPUTATION

Quantum computational plays a vital role in the image processing application based on quantum mechanics principle. Quantum bit known as qubit corresponding to the pixel has the ability to recover the object from the blurred and noisy environment in a very efficient way within a little amount of time. Quantum mechanics plays a drastic role on qubits to maintain on the principle of the quantum entanglement, quantum superposition principle, etc. Large number of factorization can be done within a stipulated time but it may take large amount of time or cannot be solvable by using the classical computational approach. In classical approach, bits are considered as '0' or '1' but in quantum computational approach it will be either '0' or '1' or combinational of both.

## Concept of Qubit

Any qubit can be represented as

$$|\psi\rangle = \alpha|0\rangle + \beta|1\rangle \tag{1}$$

Where, $\alpha$ and $\beta$ are the probability amplitudes for finding $|\psi\rangle$ on $|0\rangle$ and $|1\rangle$ respectively, provided

$$|\alpha|^2 + |\beta|^2 = 1 \tag{2}$$

and the notation $|\ \rangle$ is known as ket (Bhattacharyya et al., 2014). Here qubit operates as unitary operator in the Hilbart space (Aytekin et al., 2013).

## Qubit Rotation Gate

When the transformation is taken place on qubit to process the information, the rotation gate is used and it is represented as

$$R(\theta) = \begin{bmatrix} \cos\theta & -\sin\theta \\ \sin\theta & \cos\theta \end{bmatrix} \tag{3}$$

The single qubit is represented as $\begin{bmatrix} \cos\varphi \\ \sin\varphi \end{bmatrix}$

When rotational gate is operated on a qubit the angular transformation is modified and the processed qubit looks like as

$$R'(\theta) = \begin{bmatrix} \cos\theta & -\sin\theta \\ \sin\theta & \cos\theta \end{bmatrix} \begin{bmatrix} \cos\varphi \\ \sin\varphi \end{bmatrix} = \begin{bmatrix} \cos(\theta+\varphi) \\ \sin(\theta+\varphi) \end{bmatrix} \tag{4}$$

## FUNDAMENTALS OF IMAGE SEGMENTATION

Image is segmented to reconstruct the object by means of different approaches for meaningful analysis of information. Two outcomes are generally achieved, one is to segment the image to collect the different features from different parts of the segmented image and other part is to collect the insignificant information from the pixels of the segmented image. Segmentation means to segment the different regions having meaningful correlated regions with features such as texture, intensity, etc. of interest in the image region (Dubey et al., 2016). Preprocessing is done before segmentation which incorporates enhancement, smoothening, filtering, restoration and pixel representation for enhancing the process of image segmentation and filtering. Researchers have developed many approaches to segment images for various degree of accuracy and various angles by recognizing the different aspects such as intensity, size of the pixels, texture, etc. There are different types of segmentation approaches in the literature but few of them are discussed here for understanding of the image segmentation principle. Different types of segmentation techniques are discussed hereunder. Image comprises the permutation of pixels intensity levels depending on the intensity distribution. The image is segmented in different regions to retrieve and collects more information from the image by the appropriate selection of the feature such as intensity, texture, special coordinate, etc. Considering the image intensity $p_{ij}$ be the intensity values of the segmented image corresponding to the intensity distribution, then total intensity values of the whole image $P = \sum_{i=1}^{m}\sum_{j=1}^{n} p_{ij}$ for an $m \times n$ image (Bhattacharyya et al., 2007). To describe the segmentation process, if $K$ = number the segmented class, then the function f can be defined as in Equation 5:

$$f : P \rightarrow [0. \quad . \quad . \quad K]$$ (5)

Image segmentation is done using adaptive thresholding is used by V. Boskovitz and H. Guterman (Boskovitz et al., 2002) using levels. The segmentation is basically followed for edge detection technique and is known as auto adaptive neuro-fuzzy segmentation. This network architecture follows the feed forward technique using multilayer perceptron where the levels are automatically preselected by fuzzy clustering principle. Digital image segmentation is also categorized into two categories. One is discontinuity measured and another is similarity measured. Discontinuity is connected to edge-based analysis and similarity measure is related to the region-based approach (Dubey et al., 2016). The image segmentation depends on the feature of interest are categorized as under:

Segmentation Categorized:

- Pixel based
    - Thresholding
        - Otsu
        - Global
        - Adaptive
    - Clustering
        - K-means
        - Fuzzy C-Means
- Edge based
    - Edge detection
    - Gradient mode
    - Active contours
    - Level sets
- Region based
    - Region growing
    - Split or merge
    - Graph cut

## Pixel Based Segmentation

Pixel based segmentation is considered as a supervised technique where thresholding or clustering technique is considered. The authors use the Fingerprint image segmentation using pixel based classification (Das et al., 2015 January]. Here, an automatic fingerprint identification system is used having low time requirement for segmentation. To differentiate the pixel intensity, the mathematical moment is also a counterpart for pixel based segmentation process. Authors use the local threshold value to determine the pixels belonging to the foreground side or background side.

- **Thresholding:** It is the process of retrieving the gray scale image to corresponding binary image by means of sigmoldal activation function (Devi, 2006). In this process the intensity value of each pixel is mapped to recover the object from the noisy images. In the context of thresholding, two kinds of thresholding strategies are used, one is called Global thresholding algorithm and another is Local or adaptive thresholding algorithm. For Global thresholding algorithm, only one threshold value is used under consideration to retrieve the gray scale object and for Local or adaptive thresholding algorithm, the dynamic range of threshold values is used depending on the local area. Otsu, Global and Adaptive types of algorithms are well known algorithms for thresholding.

- **Clustering:** Clustering process is used to segment the image in an unsupervised way. It can be classified in two different ways; K-means clustering and Fuzzy C- means clustering (Naik et al., 2014). Clustering is done by means of feature selection in the feature space of the pixels. In K-means clustering approach, $k$ number of clusters is made from n number of observations, where $n\rangle k$ having the nearest mean. For low level of composition high quality of the clusters is designed using K-means clustering technique. Unsupervised Fuzzy C- means clustering approach is used where feature analysis, clustering and classifier design are required. It is useful in the image processing, medical image analysis, etc.

## Edge Based Segmentation

Image segmentation basically depends on discontinuity or similarity. Here the authors (Sain et al., 2014 November) discuss the comparison between edge based segmentation, region-based segmentation, region growing, region splitting and merging and watershed transformation. In the edge based segmentation technique edge or boundary is selected where the pixels have abrupt change of intensity levels. Generally it is applicable on the gray scale images and the process is sometimes called the edge or boundary based segmentation. It is important to identify the meaningful discontinuity boundary between regions and hence it is called boundary based segmentation. Discontinuity generally is of three types, point, line and edge. Edge detection is very much important for image recognition in computer vision research field. It is applicable on medical imaging, biometric, etc. Different types of operators are used to detect the edges of an object in an image. The operators can be grouped together in two ways, one is 1st order derivative and another is 2nd order derivative. Prewitt operator, Sobel operator, Canny operator and Test operator belong to the 1st order Derivative and within the 2nd order derivative, Laplacian operator and Zero-crossings operators are used.

## Segmentation Using Level Set Method

The authors have used the Level Set segmentation method (Akshay et al., 2016) to segment the biomedical images in different sections of human body. Level Set method is very much applied on liver tumor from CT images, liver images, etc. Authors use the liver image and segment the different regions depending on the selection using Fuzzy a C-means algorithm. It is a numerical approach for generating shape and tracking interface (Barman et al., 2011). Here a contour is generated by means of zero level set using the implicit function of higher dimensional formula known as level set function and is implemented with partial differential equation (PDE).

## Region Based Segmentation

It is one of the simplest segmentation methods. It is classified as pixel based segmentation where the selection is based on the seed points (Manish et al., 2015). Here the seed points are collected from the different regions of the image. Depending on the seed, it is to be segmented from the segmented image. Regions are accumulated and grow increasingly by collecting pixels from all of the unallocated neighbor pixels. Segmentation depends on the properties of the pixels i.e. intensity value, texture, color, etc. In region growing segmentation, all the pixels are connected according to their data set to a given condition of the locality of the pixels. Region based segmentation is basically named as document based segmentation. But document based segmentation does not always impart good results because some regions are removed or extra regions are added when an image is segmented. It is generally used for gray scale image segmentation.

## CHARACTERISTICS OF MULTILEVEL SIGMOIDAL ACTIVATION FUNCTION (MUSIG)

The sigmoidal activation function is used to extract binary objects from a noisy perspective in MLSONN architecture proposed by the author in 1993 (Ghosh et al., 1993). It has the good functional ability to extract the object within the range [0 1] from the noisy environment. The output is 0 when object is black and 1 when the object is white. Using the sigmoidal activation function, the qubit is processed with the help of quantum superposition principle by the QMLSONN architecture (Bhattacharyya et al., 2016) to extract binary objects efficiently from a noisy condition in a subsequent manner. The multilevel sigmoidal activation function can be adapted for the gray scale image segmentation to extract the gray scale objects for the multilevel responses in a better way (Bhattacharyya et al., 2007). The pure color object extraction is implemented by means of multilevel sigmoidal activation function in an efficient way using supervised neural network architecture QPSONN using quantum superposition principle considering the processing bit as qubit neurons corresponding to the pixels and using the second order neighborhood characteristics (Bhattacharyya et al., 2015).

The general form of the MUSIG activation function is shown in equation 6.

$$y_M = f_M(x) = \frac{1}{\alpha_\gamma + e^{-\lambda(x-\theta)}} \tag{6}$$

Where $y_M$ define the multilevel output response which is equal to the functional output $f_M(x)$, here $\alpha_\gamma = \dfrac{C_N}{c_\gamma - c_{\gamma-1}}$ is the controlling parameter of the multilevel class responses (Bhattacharyya et al., 2007), which determines the slope of the characteristic curves, $\theta$ gives the information regarding the threshold parameter and $x$ is the input variable in the horizontal axis. If we consider $\alpha_\gamma = 1$, then the characteristic is known as bi-level sigmoidal activation function where, $\gamma$ is called gray scale object index lies in the range $(1 \leq \gamma < K)$. Where, $C_N$, $c_\gamma$ and $c_{\gamma-1}$ are defined as gray

*Figure 2. Shows the characteristics of MUSIG function for class 6 at λ=1, λ=2 and λ=5.*

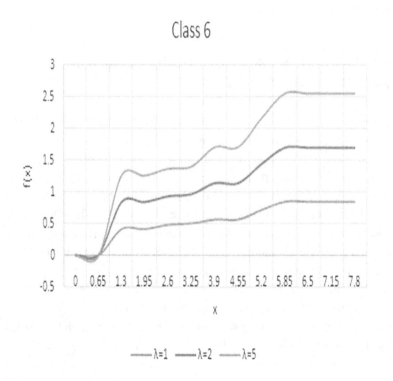

scale contributions of the neighborhood, for $\gamma^{th}$ and $\gamma^{(t-1)th}$ class respectively. The value of the maximum fuzzy intensity level ($T_i$) is equal to 1 and $C_N = \sum_{i=1}^{9} T_i = 9$, if candidate pixel and its eight surrounding neighbors are maintained in a second order neighborhood geometrical structure.

## MULTILAYER SELF ORGANIZING NEURAL NETWORK ARCHITECTURE (MLSONN)

This architecture is efficient to extract binary objects from a noisy and blurred background (Ghosh et al., 1993). It is designed in a supervised manner and contains input layer, number of hidden layers and the output layer and the corresponding MLSONN network as shown in Figure 3. In this classical approach each neuron of input layer is connected to the hidden layer by means of the connection weights as well as the neurons of the hidden layer are connected to the output layer by the connection weights. Each neuron of the different layers is constituted by the second order topology. The information is processed by the neurons using the sigmoidal

*Figure 3. Shows the MLSONN network with different interconnection weights*

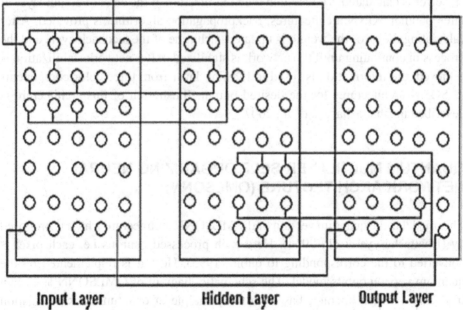

**Input Layer**     **Hidden Layer**     **Output Layer**

activation function to propagate to the next layer in the forward direction i.e. input layer to the hidden layer as well as to the output layer and error is generated at the output layer by means of the thresholding concepts. It is consider that if the process output belongs to the lower bound of the threshold level the output generates '0' and if it is above the threshold limit it is '1'. At the output stage of the layer the error is generated by means of fuzziness and the connection weight is updated by the principle of the backpropagation algorithm. The process continued until the error is below appreciable amount and the system is stabilized. Details regarding the principle of operation of the architecture are available in Ghosh et al., 1993.

## PSONN ARCHITECTURE

It is self supervised self organizing neural network architecture is used to segment the true color image in very efficient way (Bhattacharyya et al., 2007). This architecture comprises one sink layer for gathering the information, three parallel self organizing neural architectures (SONN) processing information for three primary colors red, green and blue components and one sink layer for extraction of output. At the sink layer the input information is processed corresponding from true color image and it segregates into three primary components and fed to three parallel SONN architectures. Here, sigmoidal activation function segments true color image to extract objects for three primary color components using fuzyness measure in the component levels and error is calculated. To maintain the minimization of the error at output layer of three parallel SONN architectures, backpropagation algorithm is provided. After calculating the error the weight is updated each time of the feedback cycle and the process in continuing until the network is stabilized. After network stabilization is achieved, the information is fused to the sink layer from three color components of SONN architectures for the desired output. Illustration of this architecture is described in Bhattacharyya et al., 2007.

## QUANTUM MULTILAYER SELF ORGANIZING NEURAL NETWORK ARCHITECTURE (QMLSONN)

This model is the quantum version of the MLSONN architecture which is proposed by (Bhattacharyya et al., 2014). Here each processed neurons i.e. each pixel is converted to the corresponding to qubit., 1993). Here it is implemented by the quantum version qubits model. The schematic diagram of QMLSONN as shown in Figure 4 which operates based on the principle of quantum backpropagation

*Figure 4. Shows the schematic of PSONN with different interconnection weights*

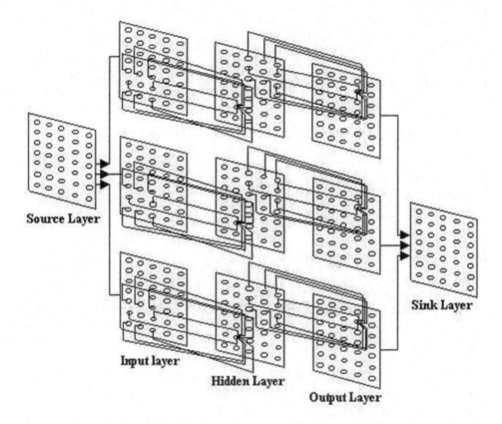

algorithm (Bhattacharyya et al., 2016). Here each processed neurons i.e. each pixel is converted to the corresponding qubit. In QPSONN architecture qubit neurons of different layers i.e. source layer, input layer, hidden layer, output layers and sink layer looks like.

$$\begin{pmatrix} \langle \alpha_{11} | & \langle \alpha_{12} | & \cdots & \cdots & \langle \alpha_{1n} | \\ \cdots & \cdots & \cdots & \cdots & \cdots \\ \cdots & \cdots & \cdots & \cdots & \cdots \\ \cdots & \cdots & \cdots & \cdots & \cdots \\ \langle \alpha_{m1} | & \langle \alpha_{m2} | & \cdots & \cdots & \langle \alpha_{mn} | \end{pmatrix}$$

Qubits neurons of the source layer of QPSONN architecture

$$\begin{pmatrix} \langle\beta_{11}| & \langle\beta_{12}| & \cdots & \cdots & \langle\beta_{1n}| \\ \cdots & \cdots & \cdots & \cdots & \cdots \\ \cdots & \cdots & \cdots & \cdots & \cdots \\ \cdots & \cdots & \cdots & \cdots & \cdots \\ \langle\beta_{m1}| & \langle\beta_{m2}| & \cdots & \cdots & \langle\beta_{mn}| \end{pmatrix}$$

Qubits neurons of the input layer of QMLSONN architecture

$$\begin{pmatrix} \langle\gamma_{11}| & \langle\gamma_{12}| & \cdots & \cdots & \langle\gamma_{1n}| \\ \cdots & \cdots & \cdots & \cdots & \cdots \\ \cdots & \cdots & \cdots & \cdots & \cdots \\ \cdots & \cdots & \cdots & \cdots & \cdots \\ \langle\gamma_{m1}| & \langle\gamma_{m2}| & \cdots & \cdots & \langle\gamma_{mn}| \end{pmatrix}$$

Qubits neurons of the hidden layer of QMLSONN architecture

$$\begin{pmatrix} \langle\delta_{11}| & \langle\delta_{12}| & \cdots & \cdots & \langle\delta_{1n}| \\ \cdots & \cdots & \cdots & \cdots & \cdots \\ \cdots & \cdots & \cdots & \cdots & \cdots \\ \cdots & \cdots & \cdots & \cdots & \cdots \\ \langle\delta_{m1}| & \langle\delta_{m2}| & \cdots & \cdots & \langle\delta_{mn}| \end{pmatrix}$$

Qubits neurons of the output layer of QMLSONN architecture

$$\begin{pmatrix} \langle\lambda_{11}| & \langle\lambda_{12}| & \cdots & \cdots & \langle\lambda_{1n}| \\ \cdots & \cdots & \cdots & \cdots & \cdots \\ \cdots & \cdots & \cdots & \cdots & \cdots \\ \cdots & \cdots & \cdots & \cdots & \cdots \\ \langle\lambda_{m1}| & \langle\lambda_{m2}| & \cdots & \cdots & \langle\lambda_{mn}| \end{pmatrix}$$

Qubits neurons of the sink layer of QPSONN architecture

The processed information of each pixel is converted to the fuzzified range [0 1] of the input image and then converted to the corresponding qubits in the quantum states. Interconnection weights are connected between input layers to the hidden layer as well as between hidden layers to the output layer. These inter connection weights are represented by the quantum rotation gates. As qubits are arranged and maintain the second order topology in every layer, so each qubit processed information are summed up and propagated to the hidden layer and from hidden layer to the output layer as well. As the qubits performs in the quantum states so, there is a phase transform between the ranges $\begin{bmatrix} 0 & \pi/2 \end{bmatrix}$. The schematic diagram of QMLSONN as shown in Figure 5 having the interconnection weights between the different qubit layers are maintained second order topology. Detailed functional principle and explanation is given in (Bhattacharyya et al., 2016).

## QUANTUM PARALLEL SELF ORGANIZING NEURAL NETWORK (QPSONN) ARCHITECTURE

It is a self supervised technique for which objects can be reconstructed from a noisy image. The quantum Parallel Self Organizing Neural Network (QPSONN) architecture (Bhattacharyya et al., 2015) has the ability to find out the true color objects from a blurry atmospheric image using quantum superposition principle applying quantum backpropagation algorithm to maintain minimization of the error at the output stage after a quantum measurement. This architecture comprises three sections, one is

*Figure 5. Shows the schematic QMLSONN with different interconnection weights*

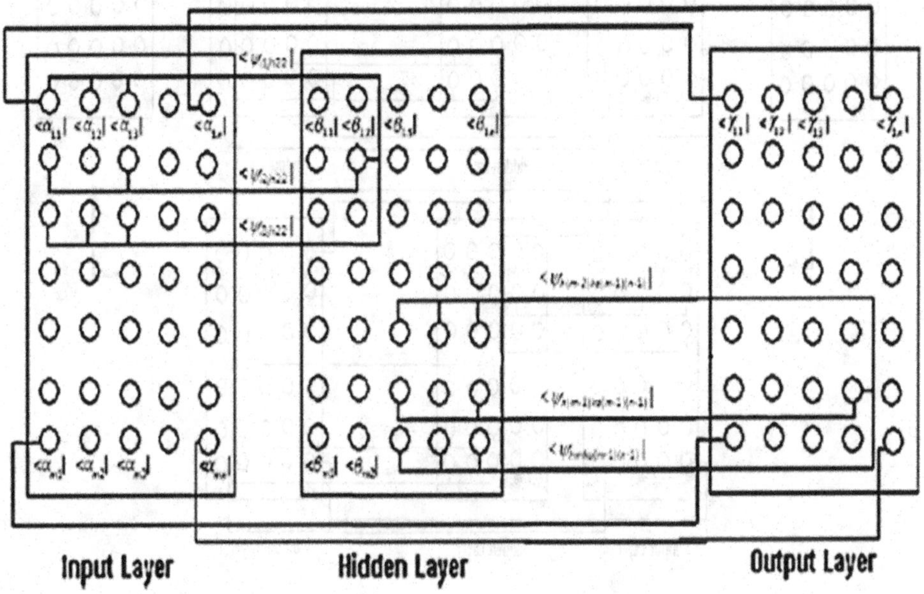

Input Layer          Hidden Layer                    Output Layer

source layer, middle one has three parallel QMLSONN architectures and the last section is known as sink layer. At the initial stage, each pixel intensity is converted to the fuzzified range [0 1] and this pixel is converted to the qubit model using quantum superposition principle. Each and every qubit follow the second order topology. The schematic of QPSONN is shown in Figure 6. The information propagates through

*Figure 6. Shows the schematic of QPSONN with different interconnection weights*

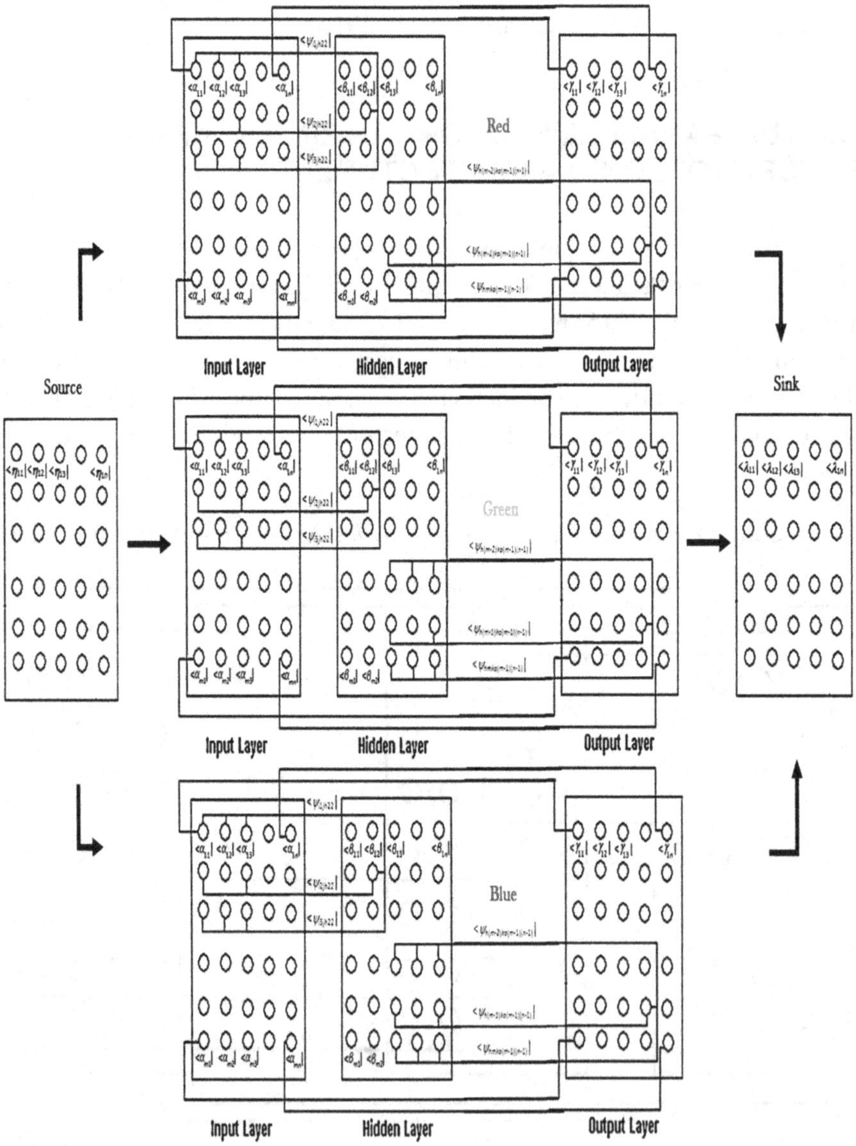

the quantum rotation gate (Bhattacharyya et al., 2014) (connection weight) between the layers. The three QMLSONN architectures are used here for the processing of three color components in parallel. At the sink layer of the output stage, red, green and blue information are fused together to get the true color object.

## Algorithm and Mathematical Details of QPSONN Architecture

The algorithm for the proposed QPSONN architecture for true color image segmentation to recover the objects is carried out in six phases and the corresponding flow diagram is shown in Figure 7.

*Figure 7. Shows the flow diagram of true color image segmentation using QPSONN architecture*

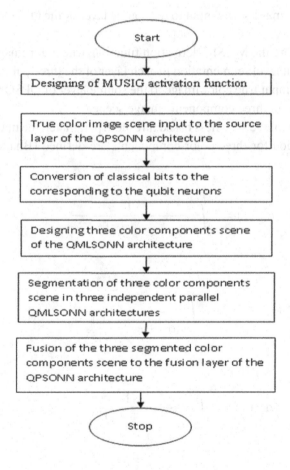

The six different phases are discussed in details in this section.

1.   Designing the MUSIG activation function

It is the vital stage to design the MUSIG activation function having equal class responses to segment the true color image for three parallel multilevel QMLSONN architectures of classes 4, 6, 8 of three different multilevel responses. Transition lobes of the MUSIG activation function is designed on depending upon the number of the target classes and is used to segment true color image. Three multilevel functions (equation 6) of three classes are used for processing units of each layer of three parallel (red, green and blue) quantum multilevel self organizing neural network (QMLSONN) architectures of the input true color scene.

The general form of the MUSIG activation function is shown in Equation 6.

2.   True color image scene input to the source layer of the QPSONN architecture

After designing the MUSIG activation function, true color image is segmented in the component level segmentation in each layer of the three parallel QMLSONN architectures of input true color image to the source layer of QPSONN architecture after segregation in three components image scene.

Incorporation of the skewness based threshold parameter, the multilevel MUSIG activation function for three color components are defined (Bhattacharyya et al., 2007) as

$$y_{\theta_\chi}(\mathrm{Re}\,d) = f_{\theta_\chi}(x,\alpha_\gamma,c_\gamma) = \int_{\gamma=1}^{\gamma=K-1} \frac{1}{\alpha_\gamma + e^{-\lambda[x-(\gamma-1)]c_\gamma - \theta_{\chi R}}} \tag{7}$$

$$y_{\theta_\chi}(Green) = f_{\theta_\chi}(x,\alpha_\gamma,c_\gamma) = \int_{\gamma=1}^{\gamma=K-1} \frac{1}{\alpha_\gamma + e^{-\lambda[x-(\gamma-1)]c_\gamma - \theta_{\chi G}}} \tag{8}$$

$$y_{\theta_\chi}(Blue) = f_{\theta_\chi}(x,\alpha_\gamma,c_\gamma) = \int_{\gamma=1}^{\gamma=K-1} \frac{1}{\alpha_\gamma + e^{-\lambda[x-(\gamma-1)]c_\gamma - \theta_{\chi B}}} \tag{9}$$

232

Where, $\theta_{\chi R}$, $\theta_{\chi G}$ and $v\theta_{\chi B}$ are the threshold parameters based on skewness factors corresponding to the red, green and blue counterpart of pixels intensity information respectively.

3.    Conversion of classical bits to the corresponding to the qubit neurons

After segregation each pixel corresponding to the neurons of the segregated output of true color image in the input layer of three parallel the QMLSONN architectures is converted to the equivalent qubit neurons using equations 1 to 3. Qubit has the ability to extract image information from the segmented image using quantum superposition principle in quantum states.

In the input layer of the QMLSONN architectures, information is first converted to equivalent fuzzified value in the range $\begin{bmatrix} 0 & 1 \end{bmatrix}$, then converts to the corresponding to quantum input after phase conversion within $\begin{bmatrix} 0 & \pi/2 \end{bmatrix}$ in quantum states.

$y_i^I = \dfrac{\pi}{2}\left(input_i\right)$. Here, $y_i^I$ is quantum input qubits and $input_i$ is general input for classical bits, $i=1$ to $l$ for input neurons, $I=$ red, green and blue respectively. Detail regarding the principle of QMLSONN architectures is discussed in Bhattacharyya et al., 2015.

4.    Designing three color components scene of the QMLSONN architecture

Three multilevel QMLSONN architectures are designed from multicolor image to three color components viz. red, green and blue image scene for processing the qubit neurons from segmented image scene. One of the QMLSONN architecture receives red component and processes the red information, second MLSONN architecture receives green component and processes the green information and third QMLSONN architecture receives blue component and processes the blue information through input layer to hidden layer to output layer with their interconnection weights of the corresponding QMLSONN architecture.

$y_i^{Red}$, $y_i^{Green}$ and $y_i^{Blue}$ are the quantum outputs from the input layer and fed to the hidden layer through the connection weight. The input to the hidden layer is determined (Bhattacharyya et al., 2015) by the equation below for red scene:

$$u_j^{Red} = \sum_{i=1}^{l} f\left(\psi_{ipjhll}\right) f\left(y_i^{Red}\right) - f\left(\lambda_j^{Red}\right) \tag{10}$$

$$= \sum_{i=1}^{l} e^{i\left(\psi_{ipjhll} + y_i^{Red}\right)} - e^{i\left(\lambda_i^{Red}\right)} \tag{11}$$

$$= \cos\left(\psi_{ipjhll} + y_i^{Red}\right) + i\sin\left(\psi_{ipjhll} + y_i^{Red}\right) - \cos\left(\lambda_j^{Red}\right) - i\sin\left(\lambda_j^{Red}\right) \tag{12}$$

The input to the hidden layer is determined by the equation below for green scene:

$$u_j^{Green} = \sum_{i=1}^{l} f\left(\psi_{ipjhll}\right) f\left(y_i^{Green}\right) - f\left(\lambda_j^{Green}\right) \tag{13}$$

$$= \sum_{i=1}^{l} e^{i\left(\psi_{ipjhll} + y_i^{Green}\right)} - e^{i\left(\lambda_i^{Green}\right)} \tag{14}$$

$$= \cos\left(\psi_{ipjhll} + y_i^{Green}\right) + i\sin\left(\psi_{ipjhll} + y_i^{Green}\right) - \cos\left(\lambda_j^{Green}\right) - i\sin\left(\lambda_j^{Green}\right) \tag{15}$$

The input to the hidden layer is determined by the equation below for blue scene:

$$u_j^{Blue} = \sum_{i=1}^{l} f\left(\psi_{ipjhll}\right) f\left(y_i^{Blue}\right) - f\left(\lambda_j^{Blue}\right) \tag{16}$$

$$= \sum_{i=1}^{l} e^{i\left(\psi_{ipjhll} + y_i^{Blue}\right)} - e^{i\left(\lambda_i^{Blue}\right)} \tag{17}$$

Where, $\psi_{ipjhll}$ are the connections weights between input layers to hidden layers $\lambda_j^{Red}$, $\lambda_j^{Green}$ and $\lambda_j^{Blue}$ are the threshold values corresponding to the $j^{th}$ hidden neuron respectively.

Therefore, the respective outputs from the hidden layer of corresponding component ere given by

$$y_j^{Red} = \frac{\pi}{2} g\left(\delta_j^{Red}\right) - \arg\left(u_j^{Red}\right) \tag{18}$$

$$= \frac{\pi}{2} g\left(\delta_j^{\mathrm{Red}}\right) - \tan^{-1}\left(\frac{\sum\left(\sin\left(\psi_{ipjhll} + y_i^{\mathrm{Red}}\right) - \sin\left(\lambda_j^{\mathrm{Red}}\right)\right)}{\sum\left(\cos\left(\psi_{ipjhll} + y_i^{\mathrm{Red}}\right) - \cos\left(\lambda_j^{\mathrm{Red}}\right)\right)}\right) \qquad (19)$$

$$= \frac{\pi}{2} g\left(\delta_j^{\mathrm{Red}}\right) - \tan^{-1} z_{\mathrm{Red}} \qquad (20)$$

Similarly, for green counterpart is given by

$$y_j^{Green} = \frac{\pi}{2} g\left(\delta_j^{Green}\right) - \tan^{-1} z_{Green}, \qquad (21)$$

and for blue counterpart is

$$y_j^{Blue} = \frac{\pi}{2} g\left(\delta_j^{Blue}\right) - \tan^{-1} z_{Blue} \qquad (22)$$

Where, $z_h = \left(\dfrac{\sum\left(\sin\left(\psi_{ipjhll} + y_i^I\right) - \sin\left(\lambda_j^I\right)\right)}{\sum\left(\cos\left(\psi_{ipjhll} + y_i^I\right) - \cos\left(\lambda_j^I\right)\right)}\right)$; h={Red, Green, Blue}; I= {Red, Green, Blue}.

$\arg\left(u_j^h\right)$ is the phase extracted from complex number $u$ for particular value of h={Red, Green, Blue} and $\delta_j^h$ is the reversible parameter of $j^{th}$ hidden neuron.

Similarly, from hidden layer to output layer in QMLSONN architecture same procedure is done and following results are achieved as below:

$y_j^{\mathrm{Red}}$, $y_j^{Green}$ and $y_j^{Blue}$ are the quantum outputs from the hidden layer and fed to the output layer through the connection weight. The hidden to the output layer is determined (Bhattacharyya et al., 2015) by the equation for red scene as under:

$$u_k^{\mathrm{Red}} = \sum_{j=1}^{m} f\left(\psi_{hqkoll}\right) f\left(y_j^{\mathrm{Red}}\right) - f\left(\lambda_k^{\mathrm{Red}}\right) \qquad (23)$$

235

$$= \sum_{j=1}^{m} e^{i\left(\psi_{hqkoll} + y_j^{\text{Red}}\right)} - e^{i\left(\lambda_j^{\text{Red}}\right)} \tag{24}$$

$$= \cos\left(\psi_{hqkoll} + y_k^{\text{Red}}\right) + i\sin\left(\psi_{hqkoll} + y_k^{\text{Red}}\right) - \cos\left(\lambda_k^{\text{Red}}\right) - i\sin\left(\lambda_k^{\text{Red}}\right) \tag{25}$$

The input to the hidden layer is determined by the equation below for green scene:

$$u_k^{Green} = \sum_{j=1}^{m} f\left(\psi_{hqkoll}\right) f\left(y_j^{Green}\right) - f\left(\lambda_k^{Green}\right) \tag{26}$$

$$= \sum_{j=1}^{m} e^{i\left(\psi_{hqkoll} + y_j^{Green}\right)} - e^{i\left(\lambda_j^{Green}\right)} \tag{27}$$

$$= \cos\left(\psi_{hqkoll} + y_j^{Green}\right) + i\sin\left(\psi_{hqkoll} + y_j^{Green}\right) - \cos\left(\lambda_k^{Green}\right) - i\sin\left(\lambda_k^{Green}\right) \tag{28}$$

The input to the hidden layer is determined by the equation below for blue scene:

$$u_k^{Blue} = \sum_{j=1}^{m} f\left(\psi_{hqkoll}\right) f\left(y_j^{Blue}\right) - f\left(\lambda_k^{Blue}\right) \tag{29}$$

$$= \sum_{j=1}^{m} e^{i\left(\psi_{hqkoll} + y_j^{Blue}\right)} - e^{i\left(\lambda_j^{Blue}\right)} \tag{30}$$

Where, $\psi_{hqkoll}$ are the connections weights between hidden layers to output layers $\lambda_k^{\text{Red}}$, $\lambda_k^{Green}$ and $\lambda_k^{Blue}$ are the threshold values corresponding to the $k^{th}$ output neuron respectively.

Therefore, the respective outputs from the output layer of corresponding component are given by

$$y_k^{\text{Re}d} = \frac{\pi}{2} g\left(\delta_k^{\text{Re}d}\right) - \arg\left(u_k^{\text{Re}d}\right) \tag{31}$$

$$= \frac{\pi}{2} g\left(\delta_k^{\text{Re}d}\right) - \tan^{-1}\left|\frac{\sum\left(\sin\left(\psi_{hqkoll} + y_j^{\text{Re}d}\right) - \sin\left(\lambda_k^{\text{Re}d}\right)\right)}{\sum\left(\cos\left(\psi_{hqkoll} + y_j^{\text{Re}d}\right) - \cos\left(\lambda_k^{\text{Re}d}\right)\right)}\right| \tag{32}$$

$$= \frac{\pi}{2} g\left(\delta_k^{\text{Re}d}\right) - \tan^{-1} z_{\text{Re}d} \tag{33}$$

Similarly, for green counterpart is given by

$$y_k^{Green} = \frac{\pi}{2} g\left(\delta_k^{Green}\right) - \tan^{-1} z_{Green}, \tag{34}$$

and for blue counterpart is

$$y_k^{Blue} = \frac{\pi}{2} g\left(\delta_k^{Blue}\right) - \tan^{-1} z_{Blue} \tag{35}$$

Where, $z_k = \left|\dfrac{\sum\left(\sin\left(\psi_{hqkoll} + y_j^I\right) - \sin\left(\lambda_k^I\right)\right)}{\sum\left(\cos\left(\psi_{hqkoll} + y_j^I\right) - \cos\left(\lambda_k^I\right)\right)}\right|$; k={Red, Green, Blue}; I= {Red, Green, Blue}.

$\arg\left(u_k^h\right)$ is the phase extracted from complex number $u$ for particular value of k={Red, Green, Blue} and $\delta_k^k$ is the reversible parameter of $k^{th}$ output neuron.

5. Segmentation of three color components scene in three independent parallel QMLSONN architectures

Segmentation of three color components are designed for processing of three colors, red, green and blue image scene of true color image segmentation for extracted three different color components information to fuse in the sink layer of QPSONN architecture. Each component of QMLSONN architecture generates the system error at the output layer by means of multilevel sigmoidal activation function depending

237

on the transition lobes to the significant target classes. Backpropagation algorithm is used to minimize the system error and the process is continued until the system is stabilized in three different QMLSONN architectures.

The segmented performance is measured by the three equations 36, 37 and 38 respectively below after the output generated of each component level of QMLSONN architectures.

$$F(I) = \sqrt{N_R} \sum_{i=1}^{N_R} \frac{e_i^2}{\sqrt{A_i}} \tag{36}$$

$$F'(I) = \frac{1}{1000 \times S_l} \sqrt{\sum_{a=1}^{max(area)} [N(a)]^{(1+\frac{1}{a})} \sum_{i=1}^{N} \frac{e_i^2}{A_i}} \tag{37}$$

$$Q(I) = \frac{1}{1000 \times S_l} \sqrt{N} \sum_{i=1}^{N} \left[ \frac{e_i^2}{1 + \log S_i} + \left( \frac{N(S_i)}{S_i} \right)^2 \right] \tag{38}$$

Where $N_R$ = number of the region of interest for random shaped, $e_i = i^{th}$ region color error, $A_i = |S_i|$, is the area of $i^{th}$ region of interest. Here, $e_i$ is determine by the equation

$$e_i = \sqrt{\sum_{x \in r,g,b} \sum_{p \in S_i} (C_x(p) - \bar{C}_x(S_i))^2} \tag{39}$$

where, $\bar{C}_x(S_i)$ = average value of the feature characteristics value of red, green and blue respectively for pigments corresponding to the pixel p and $\bar{C}_x(S_i)$ is related to the value of feature x (red, green and blue) and $A_i = |S_i|$, the relation is given below (Liu et al., 1994):

$$\bar{C}_x(S_i) = \frac{\sum_{p \in S_i} C_x(p)}{A_i} \tag{40}$$

The segmented outputs components of QMLSONN architectures are transfer to the sink layers of the QPSONN architecture.

6. Fusion of the three segmented color components scene to the fusion layer of the QPSONN architecture

Three segmented outputs are obtained after being the system stabilized from three parallel QMLSONN architectures and are fused to the sink layer to get the segmented true color image scene of the QPSONN architecture.

## THRESHOLDING STRATEGIES FOR INTENSITY INFORMATION

Image is segmented using any kind of activation function, which has the ability to reconstruct the object from the noisy environment with some thresholding parameter value $\theta$. Depending on the thresholding constraint, the activation function undergoes to segment the noisy image from the blurred environment to reproduce the object depending on the homogeneity of the pixel intensity information. A bi-level sigmoidal activation function using only one thresholding parameter $\theta$ segments the noisy image in different segmented regions to redefine the objects in two categories, i.e. black and white components. In the true color image segmentation principle, the multilevel activation function has the ability to segment the images in different shaded regions to acquire the object for getting some meaningful information. In this chapter, the authors use two kinds of thresholding parameters: one is threshold parameter $\theta_\chi$ based on skewness of intensity distribution of the neighboring image pixels and another is threshold parameter $\theta_\xi$ based on the cardinality measures of intensity distribution of the neighboring image pixels. These are elaborated in the following subsections.

Threshold parameter $\theta_\chi$ based on skewness of intensity distribution of the neighboring image pixels

As each candidate pixel with its neighbors in a second order geometry constitutes the cumulative intensity distribution, it is recommended to obtain the corresponding threshold value for its neighborhood pixel intensity levels. In the process of true color image segmentation for red, green and blue counterparts, the pixel intensity values are more for brighter pixels than that of darker pixels. The brightness of the red pixel regions defines more number of brighter pixels as compared to the darker pixels which indicates the skewness to the brighter direction. It is similarly used for green and blue components also. Skewness in the direction of lighter side defines more number of lighter pixels present as compared to the brighter pixels. So the pixel intensity largely varies from one region to the region depending on the skewness factor (Bhattacharyya et al., 2007) of the intensity information of the pixel neighborhood. This dissimilar behavior of the skew factor $\chi$ changes the skewness threshold parameter $\theta_\chi$. There are two kinds of skew factors present in the intensity distribution of the pixels of the fragmented image.

One skew factor is defined as $\chi_1 = \tau_l - \tau_g$, depending on the cumulative value of skewness intensity information of the sorted neighborhood pixels of the candidate pixel element and another is defined as $\chi_2$, depending on the median intensity level that is how much the pixel intensity value changes from its average level, where, $\tau_l$ is the lower skew value of cumulative pixel intensity level below the average intensity level and $\tau_g$ is the upper skew value of cumulative pixel intensity level above the average intensity level.

Another skew factor is defined as $\chi_2 = \tau_a - \tau_m$, depending on the median value of skewness intensity information of the neighborhood pixels of the candidate pixel element which is the difference between skew factors of average intensity value and the median intensity value of the neighborhood pixel elements. When these two skew factors $\chi_1$ and $\chi_2$ are taken together, the resultant threshold parameter $\theta_\chi$ is formed and is defined as $\theta_\chi = \theta \left[ \dfrac{1 - \tau_a \chi}{2\tau_a} \right]$, (Bhattacharyya et al., 2007); where $\chi$ is the resultant skew factor of the combination of $\chi_1$ and $\chi_2$; $\theta$ is the thresholding parameter corresponding to the uniform of single fixed point value. After incorporation of the skewness based threshold parameter, the MUSIG activation function is defined (Bhattacharyya et al., 2007) in Equations 6, 7, 8 and 9.

Threshold parameter $\theta_\xi$ based on fuzzy cardinality realization of fuzzy subset of the neighboring image pixels

Fuzzy cardinality factor $(\xi)$ determines the overall containment of the pixel intensity value of the neighborhood of the fuzzy subset. For true color image segmentation process, three fuzzy cardinality factors $(\xi_R)$, $(\xi_G)$ and $(\xi_B)$ are determined. These cardinality factors determine the relative distribution of the brighter and lighter pixels of the neighbor pixels intensity information (Bhattacharyya et al., 2007). The threshold parameter $\theta_\xi$ based on fuzzy cardinality of fuzzy subset for the MUSIG activation function is determined under consideration of the brighter pixel intensity $(p_b)$ and lighter pixel intensity $(p_l)$ and is given by

$$\theta_\xi = \theta \left[ 1 - \frac{\left( \xi_b - \xi_l \right)}{\xi_b + \xi_l} \right]; \tag{41}$$

where, $\theta$ is the single fixed point uniform thresholding parameter for MUSIG activation function, $\left( \xi_b \right)$ and $\left( \xi_l \right)$ are the fuzzy cardinality estimation for brighter and lighter pixel intensity information. The MUSIG functions corresponding to the red, green and blue counterparts incorporating the threshold parameter $\theta_\xi$ based on fuzzy cardinality are given by

$$y_{\theta_x} (\mathrm{Re}\,d) = f_{\theta_x} (x, \alpha_\gamma, c_\gamma) = \int_{\gamma=1}^{\gamma=K-1} \frac{1}{\alpha_\gamma + e^{-\lambda \left[ x - (\gamma-1) \right] c_\gamma - \theta_{\xi_R}}} \tag{42}$$

$$y_{\theta_x} (Green) = f_{\theta_x} (x, \alpha_\gamma, c_\gamma) = \int_{\gamma=1}^{\gamma=K-1} \frac{1}{\alpha_\gamma + e^{-\lambda \left[ x - (\gamma-1) \right] c_\gamma - \theta_{\xi_G}}} \tag{43}$$

$$y_{\theta_x} (Blue) = f_{\theta_x} (x, \alpha_\gamma, c_\gamma) = \int_{\gamma=1}^{\gamma=K-1} \frac{1}{\alpha_\gamma + e^{-\lambda \left[ x - (\gamma-1) \right] c_\gamma - \theta_{\xi_B}}} \tag{44}$$

Where, $\theta_{\xi R}$, $\theta_{\xi G}$ and $\theta_{\xi B}$ are the threshold parameters based on cardinality measure of fuzzy subset corresponding to the red, green and blue counterpart of pixel intensity information, respectively.

## TRUE COLOR IMAGE SEGMENTATION

The True color image segmentation is designed in self-supervised approach (Bhattacharyya et al., 2007) for classical implementation approach is used. In this chapter authors use the quantum approach for true color image segmentation by quantum superposition principle using Self Supervised Neural Network as shown in Figure 5. The multilevel sigmoidal activation function has the ability to segment the true color images for extracting the true color object from noisy and blurred environment in different classes. Here authors use 4, 6, 8 classes to segment the images for extracting more meaningful information from the segmented images to recover the object. Quantum computation has the superposition principle on the qubit to extract the object by means of processing the information from the true color images. After few eras have been elapsed the authors (Bhattacharyya et al., 2015) have proposed the pure color object extraction from the noisy environment. At that time (Pal et al., 2016) have devised the architecture for pure color object extraction from a noisy state using Quantum Version Parallel Self Organizing Neural Network (QVPSONN). It is robust in design and is used for extracting the object from real life as well as synthetic pure color images. In this chapter authors use the architecture where three kinds of layers are used, one is the source layer, three parallels (QMLSONN) architecture define as input layer, hidden layer and output layer and one sink layer. At the source layer the information is subdivided into three parallel state components red, green and blue which are to be processed by means of MUSIG activation function. The information is sum up at the sink layer using parallel processing for three-color components and is fuse together to get the desired information as output after the measurement has been done. At the output stage if error is generated that should be minimized and stabilized by the quantum back propagation algorithm. Authors use two types of thresholding strategies ($\theta_\chi$ and $\theta_\xi$) for segmenting the true color images.

## THRESHOLDING IMPLEMENTATION FOR EFFICIENCY MEASUREMENT

Segmentation technique is one of the approaches to segment the true color images, here considering Baboon and Lena images as shown in Figure 8 to extract satisfactory information for determining of the quality of the segmented efficiency. In the literature there are so many unsupervised approaches but in supervised way it can be determine the segmented efficiency and is developed by Liu and Yang on 1994 (Liu et al., 1994). According to this technique for segmentation the evaluation functions in Equation 36 as

$$F(I) = \sqrt{N_R} \sum_{i=1}^{N_R} \frac{e_i^2}{\sqrt{A_i}} \tag{45}$$

Where $N_R$ = number of the region of interest for random shaped, $e_i = i^{th}$ region color error, $A_i = |S_i|$, is the area of $i^{th}$ region of interest. The $i^{th}$ region color error is defined as

$$e_i = \sqrt{\sum_{x \in r,g,b} \sum_{p \in S_i} (C_x(p) - \bar{C}_x(S_i))^2} \tag{46}$$

where, $\bar{C}_x(S_i)$ = average value of the feature characteristics value of red, green and blue respectively for pigments corresponding to the pixel p and $\bar{C}_x(S_i)$ is related to the value of feature x (red, green and blue) and $A_i = |S_i|$, the relation is given below (Liu et al., 1994):

$$\bar{C}_x(S_i) = \frac{\sum_{p \in S_i} C_x(p)}{A_i} \tag{47}$$

Another Figure of merit is described by (Borsotti et al., 1998) which is the modified version of $F(I)$ (Liu et al., 1994) and is defined as

$$F'(I) = \frac{1}{1000 \times S_l} \sqrt{\sum_{a=1}^{\max(area)} [N(a)]^{(1+\frac{1}{a})} \sum_{i=1}^{N} \frac{e_i^2}{A_i}} \tag{48}$$

Here, $S_l$ = area of selected image which is to be segmented and $N(a)$ = segmented number of the image of the area 'a' and max (area) is defined as the maximum area of the region of the segmented image.

To determine the segmentation efficiency Borsotti et al. (Borsotti et al., 1998) proposed a well known function known as evaluation function $Q(I)$ and is defined below:

$$Q(I) = \frac{1}{1000 \times S_I} \sqrt{N} \sum_{i=1}^{N} \left[ \frac{e_i^2}{1 + \log S_i} + \left( \frac{N(S_i)}{S_i} \right)^2 \right] \tag{49}$$

Here, $S_i$ defined as the image $(I)$ area to be segmented in $N(S_i)$ number of regions.

Another mathematical formula is used for an evaluation function for entropy measurement is explained by (Zhang et al., 2004) for the $i^{th}$ region and is defined as

$$H\left(R_i\right) = -\sum_{m \in V_i} \frac{L_i\left(m\right)}{S_i} \times \log_2 \left(\frac{L_i\left(m\right)}{S_i}\right) \tag{50}$$

Here, $V_i$ = luminance value for the set of all possible combination of the target region i and $L_i\left(m\right)$ is the corresponding pixel numbers for the luminance value f of the original image $I$. According to the Zhang et al. (Zhang et al., 2004) the evaluation function $E$ is the combination of the layout entropy $H_l\left(I\right)$ and expected region entropy $E_r\left(I\right)$, i.e.

$$E = H_l\left(I\right) + E_r\left(I\right) \tag{51}$$

Where,

$$H_l\left(I\right) = \sum_{i=1}^{N} \frac{S_i}{S_I} \log \frac{S_i}{S_I} \quad bits \, / \, pixel \tag{52}$$

Here, $\dfrac{S_i}{S_I} = p_i$, is the probability of the region I and under consideration each pixel under probabilistic assumption is independently selected. For Hartley's theoretic concepts base of the logarithm is assumed as 10. $N$ is the arbitrary shaped region.

## EXPERIMENTAL RESULTS

True color image segmentation using MUSIG activation function is being carried out on two kinds of images. Baboon image and Lena image as shown in Figure 8 of dimensions of 512×512 in pixel values with adapted context sensitive thresholding strategies for 4, 6 and 8 classes each of having 4 sets of values for different values of multilevel class responses $\alpha_\gamma$. Three goodness measurements of the quality of image segmentations $F$, $F'$ and $Q$ are achieved using two kinds of self supervised architectures PSONN and QPSONN for true color images for object extraction and result shows in Tables 1 and 2 for class 4, Tables 3 and 4 for class 6 and Tables 5 and 6 for class 8 respectively for comparison purposes. In this experiment the outputs of QPSONN architecture shows the better performance as shown in boldface for easily understand in the given Tables 1, 2, 3, 4, 5 and 6 for two kinds of thresholding

*Figure 8. Shows the true color Baboon and Lena images*

(a)                                        (b)

*Table 1. Shows the comparison of quality of true color image segmentation ($\nu$) on PSONN and QPSONN architectures for Baboon image for class 4*

| Quality of segmentation ($\nu$) | | | PSONN architecture for Baboon image | | | | QPSONN architecture for Baboon image | | | |
|---|---|---|---|---|---|---|---|---|---|---|
| Class | $\nu$ | Set | $\theta_\chi$ | Time (s) | $\theta_\xi$ | Time (s) | $\theta_\chi$ | time(s) | $\theta_\xi$ | Time (s) |
| 4 | F | $s_1$ | **0.6994** | 73.04 | **0.6903** | 73.19 | **0.2399** | 47 | **0.2201** | 49 |
| | | $s_2$ | 0.7017 | 74.2 | 0.7023 | 74.9 | 0.2561 | 48 | 0.252 | 48 |
| | | $s_3$ | 0.7286 | 72.88 | 0.7300 | 72 | 0.2605 | 47 | 0.2439 | 48 |
| | | $s_4$ | 0.7300 | 75.01 | 0.7314 | 74.8 | 0.2947 | 47 | 0.257 | 47 |
| | F' | $s_1$ | **0.7291** | 73.04 | **0.7299** | 73.19 | **0.3318** | 47 | **0.3319** | 49 |
| | | $s_2$ | 0.7362 | 74.2 | 0.7401 | 74.9 | 0.3406 | 48 | 0.3406 | 48 |
| | | $s_3$ | 0.7481 | 72.88 | 0.7498 | 72 | 0.3519 | 47 | 0.3371 | 48 |
| | | $s_4$ | 0.7507 | 75.01 | 0.75115 | 74.8 | 0.36003 | 47 | 0.3503 | 47 |
| | Q | $s_1$ | **0.9271** | 73.04 | **0.92** | 73.19 | **0.3800** | 47 | **0.3848** | 49 |
| | | $s_2$ | 0.9383 | 74.2 | 0.9406 | 74.9 | 0.3897 | 48 | 0.3907 | 48 |
| | | $s_3$ | 0.9500 | 72.88 | 0.9502 | 72 | 0.3972 | 47 | 0.4077 | 48 |
| | | $s_4$ | 0.9608 | 75.01 | 0.961 | 74.8 | 0.4284 | 47 | 0.4392 | 47 |

*Table 2. Shows the comparison of quality of true color image segmentation (v) between on PSONN and on QPSONN architectures for Lena image for class 4*

| Quality of segmentation ($v$) | | | PSONN architecture for Lena image | | | | QPSONN architecture for Lena image | | | |
|---|---|---|---|---|---|---|---|---|---|---|
| Class | $v$ | Set | $\theta_\chi$ | Time (s) | $\theta_\xi$ | Time (s) | $\theta_\chi$ | Time (s) | $\theta_\xi$ | Time (s) |
| 4 | F | $s_1$ | **0.6933** | 73.5 | 0.6981 | 72 | **0.2371** | 46 | **0.2388** | 47 |
| | | $s_2$ | 0.6950 | 73.3 | **0.6949** | 74.3 | 0.2548 | 48 | 0.2539 | 48 |
| | | $s_3$ | 0.7097 | 72.98 | 0.711 | 72.22 | 0.2696 | 47 | 0.2732 | 47 |
| | | $s_4$ | 0.7119 | 74.1 | 0.7161 | 74.5 | 0.3284 | 48 | 0.2994 | 49 |
| | F' | $s_1$ | 0.7220 | 73.5 | 0.726 | 72 | **0.3284** | 47 | **0.3295** | 47 |
| | | $s_2$ | **0.7193** | 73.3 | **0.7203** | 74.3 | 0.3366 | 48 | 0.3407 | 48 |
| | | $s_3$ | 0.7330 | 72.98 | 0.7341 | 72.22 | 0.3478 | 47 | 0.3499 | 47 |
| | | $s_4$ | 0.7451 | 74.1 | 0.7499 | 74.5 | 0.3594 | 48 | 0.3600 | 49 |
| | Q | $s_1$ | **0.9101** | 73.5 | **0.9112** | 72 | **0.3779** | 47 | **0.3793** | 47 |
| | | $s_2$ | 0.9138 | 73.3 | 0.9147 | 74.3 | 0.3858 | 48 | 0.3882 | 48 |
| | | $s_3$ | 0.9281 | 72.98 | 0.9301 | 72.22 | 0.3909 | 47 | 0.401 | 47 |
| | | $s_4$ | 0.9338 | 74.1 | 0.9350 | 74.5 | 0.4005 | 48 | 0.4039 | 49 |

parameters $\theta_\chi$ and $\theta_\xi$ in different stiffness parameter of $\lambda$ values are chosen for measurement purposes with adapted context sensitive thresholding strategies. The true color extracted object outputs are shown in Figures 9, 10 and 11 respectively for PSONN architecture and Figures 12, 13 and 14 respectively are for QPSONN outputs after performing the segmentation processes for three classes 4, 6 and 8 using MUSIG activation function for Lena and Baboon images of having four sets of values of $s_1$, $s_2$, $s_3$, and $s_4$ respectively.

It is evident from Table 1 that boldface numbers are the best result for PSONN and QPSONN on Baboon image. Lower the values more is the efficient. For this comparison Table it is understood that quality of segmentation ($v$) $F$ is 0.2371 and 0.2388 using QPSONN architecture where as using PSONN architecture these are 0.6933 and 0.69497 for class 4 segmentation using MUSIG activation function. For the measurement of the quality of segmentation in case of $F'$ for PSONN architecture is 0.71934 and 0.7203 but in case of QPSONN architecture it is 0.3284 and 0.3295 for same class and another quality of segmentation $Q$ for PSONN architecture is 0.9101 and 0.9112 but in case of QPSONN architecture it is 0.3779 and 0.3793 for same class.

From the comparison of the quality of true color image segmentation ($\nu$) between the PSONN architecture and QPSONN architecture on Lena image on the basis of experimental result, the outcome based on QPSONN architecture shows better as shown in the Table2 for class 4 in segmentation principle. The quality of segmentation ($\nu$) $F$ for MLSONN principle is 0.6933 and 0.69497 but in using the QPSONN principle it is 0.2371 and 0.2388, i.e. very low and the quality of segmentation is achieved in better way. Another quality of segmentation ($\nu$) $F'$ is find out which is also the better in QPSONN is 0.3284 and 0.3295 as compared to the PSONN architecture which is 0.71934 and 0.7203 for class classification. Betterment of the quality of true color image segmentation ($\nu$) $Q$ is outcome using QPSONN architecture is 0.3779 and 0.3793 but in case of PSONN architecture is 0.9101 and 0.9112. Here it is also seen that the quality of true color image segmentation using QPSONN architecture is better as shown in Table 2 in boldface values.

In class 6 using MUSIG activation function on Baboon image as shown in Figure 8 and the result is shown in Table 3 and the comparison is carried out after the experimental results on QPSONN and on PSONN architectures using the different values of the threshold parameters $\theta_\chi$ and $\theta_\xi$. It is in reality shows that in QPSONN and PSONN techniques the three different kinds of quality of true color image

*Table 3. Shows the comparison of the quality of true color image segmentation ($\nu$) on PSONN and QPSONN architectures for Baboon image for class 6*

| Quality of segmentation($\nu$) | | | PSONN architecture for Baboon image | | | | QPSONN architecture for Baboon image | | | |
|---|---|---|---|---|---|---|---|---|---|---|
| Class | $\nu$ | Set | $\theta_\chi$ | time(s) | $\theta_\xi$ | Time (s) | $\theta_\chi$ | Time (s) | $\theta_\xi$ | Time (s) |
| 6 | F | $s_1$ | **0.6594** | 74.02 | **0.6607** | 75.1 | **0.2121** | 48 | **0.239** | 46 |
| | | $s_2$ | 0.7190 | 76.55 | 0.7200 | 76.51 | 0.2503 | 47 | 0.2573 | 47 |
| | | $s_3$ | 0.6960 | 74.98 | 0.7085 | 74.13 | 0.2400 | 43 | 0.2496 | 48 |
| | | $s_4$ | 0.6993 | 76.77 | 0.7099 | 77.43 | 0.2303 | 43 | 0.2500 | 46 |
| | F' | $s_1$ | **0.6697** | 74.02 | **0.6721** | 75.1 | 0.3298 | 48 | 0.3305 | 46 |
| | | $s_2$ | 0.7281 | 76.55 | 0.7330 | 76.51 | 0.3375 | 47 | 0.3408 | 47 |
| | | $s_3$ | 0.6991 | 74.98 | 0.7041 | 74.13 | **0.3189** | 43 | **0.3209** | 48 |
| | | $s_4$ | 0.7098 | 76.77 | 0.7182 | 77.43 | 0.3399 | 43 | 0.3487 | 46 |
| | Q | $s_1$ | **0.9019** | 74.02 | **0.9184** | 75.1 | **0.4017** | 48 | **0.4124** | 46 |
| | | $s_2$ | 0.9399 | 76.55 | 0.9420 | 76.51 | 0.4223 | 47 | 0.4284 | 47 |
| | | $s_3$ | 0.9410 | 74.98 | 0.9487 | 74.13 | 0.4270 | 43 | 0.4299 | 48 |
| | | $s_4$ | 0.9486 | 76.77 | 0.9550 | 77.43 | 0.4385 | 43 | 0.447 | 46 |

segmentation performances $F$, $F'$ and $Q$ are determined and lower values of segmented performance in QPSONN architecture than PSONN architecture. So, the performance in QPSONN is better. For the measurement of $F$, $F'$ and $Q$ in QPSONN principle are 0.2121, 0.2391, 0.3189, 0.3209, 0.40176 and 0.41243, where as in PSONN principle these are 0.659410.6607, 0.6697, 0.6721, .9019 and 0.9184.

In class 6 on Lena image as shown in Figure 8, the experiments are carried out and the result as shown in Table 4 and the results show the quality of true color image segmentation in QPSONN output is better than PSONN. In QPSONN for class 6 on Lena image the $F$ values are 0.2057, 0.2113, $F'$ values are 0.30086, 0.3036 and $Q$ values are 0.3515 and 0.35201 where as in PSONN output the performance for the $F$ values are 0.65142, 0.6497, $F'$ values are 0.67931, 0.6862 and corresponding $Q$ values are 0.8836 and 0.8908. Here it is seen the QPSONN output is better than PSONN.

For class 8 using MUSIG activation function on Baboon image the experiments are carried out to determine the segmented performance of true color image segmentation using PSONN and QPSONN architectures. The experimental results show the quality of segmentation in true color image QPSONN outputs are better than that of PSONN outputs and the result is shown in the Table 5 and 6. Experimental

*Table 4. Shows the comparison of the quality of True color image segmentation ($\nu$) on PSONN and QPSONN architectures for Lena image using class 6*

| Quality of segmentation ($\nu$) | | | PSONN architecture for Lena image | | | | QPSONN architecture for Lena image | | | |
|---|---|---|---|---|---|---|---|---|---|---|
| Class | $\nu$ | Set | $\theta_\chi$ | Time (s) | $\theta_\xi$ | Time (s) | $\theta_\chi$ | Time (s) | $\theta_\xi$ | Time (s) |
| 6 | F | $s_1$ | 0.6563 | 75.109 | **0.6497** | 76.01 | **0.2057** | 47 | **0.2113** | 42 |
| | | $s_2$ | 0.6692 | 76.93 | 0.6730 | 76.54 | 0.2199 | 45 | 0.2307 | 47 |
| | | $s_3$ | 0.6803 | 74.44 | 0.6877 | 75.66 | 0.2441 | 43 | 0.2514 | 44 |
| | | $s_4$ | **0.6514** | 76.08 | 0.6604 | 76.95 | 0.2901 | 43 | 0.2876 | 43 |
| | F' | $s_1$ | **0.6793** | 75.109 | **0.6862** | 76.01 | **0.3008** | 47 | **0.3036** | 42 |
| | | $s_2$ | 0.6880 | 76.93 | 0.6947 | 76.54 | 0.3103 | 45 | 0.3273 | 47 |
| | | $s_3$ | 0.6975 | 74.44 | 0.7008 | 75.66 | 0.3215 | 43 | 0.3369 | 44 |
| | | $s_4$ | 0.7031 | 76.08 | 0.7097 | 76.95 | 0.3239 | 43 | 0.3359 | 43 |
| | Q | $s_1$ | **0.8836** | 75.109 | **0.8908** | 76.01 | **0.3515** | 47 | **0.3520** | 42 |
| | | $s_2$ | 0.9005 | 76.93 | 0.9195 | 76.54 | 0.3602 | 45 | 0.3676 | 47 |
| | | $s_3$ | 0.9098 | 74.44 | 0.9281 | 75.66 | 0.3780 | 43 | 0.3800 | 44 |
| | | $s_4$ | 0.9220 | 76.08 | 0.9337 | 76.95 | 0.3800 | 43 | 0.3858 | 43 |

*Table 5. Shows the comparison of the quality of true color image segmentation ($\nu$) on PSONN and QPSONN architectures for Baboon image for class 8*

| Quality of segmentation ($\nu$) | | | PSONN architecture for Baboon image | | | | QPSONN architecture for Baboon image | | | |
|---|---|---|---|---|---|---|---|---|---|---|
| Class | $\nu$ | Set | $\theta_\chi$ | time(s) | $\theta_\xi$ | Time (s) | $\theta_\chi$ | Time (s) | $\theta_\xi$ | Time (s) |
| 8 | F | $s_1$ | **0.6539** | 78.426 | **0.6518** | 80.004 | **0.2098** | 46 | **0.2198** | 46 |
| | | $s_2$ | 0.7381 | 89.255 | 0.7593 | 79.104 | 0.2499 | 43 | 0.2561 | 46 |
| | | $s_3$ | 0.6871 | 79.806 | 0.7019 | 82.579 | 0.2301 | 44 | 0.2291 | 48 |
| | | $s_4$ | 0.6815 | 85.118 | 0.7152 | 81.397 | 0.2286 | 45 | 0.2302 | 46 |
| | F' | $s_1$ | **0.6486** | 78.426 | **0.6595** | 80.004 | **0.331** | 46 | 0.3407 | 46 |
| | | $s_2$ | 0.7227 | 89.255 | 0.7381 | 79.104 | 0.3240 | 43 | 0.3392 | 46 |
| | | $s_3$ | 0.6801 | 79.806 | 0.7085 | 82.579 | 0.3098 | 44 | **0.3207** | 48 |
| | | $s_4$ | 0.6900 | 85.118 | 0.7117 | 81.397 | 0.3337 | 45 | 0.3486 | 46 |
| | Q | $s_1$ | **0.8963** | 78.426 | **0.9228** | 80.004 | **0.4003** | 46 | **0.4209** | 46 |
| | | $s_2$ | 0.9391 | 89.255 | 0.9519 | 79.104 | 0.4102 | 43 | 0.4305 | 46 |
| | | $s_3$ | 0.929 | 79.806 | 0.9300 | 82.579 | 0.4186 | 44 | 0.4276 | 48 |
| | | $s_4$ | 0.9308 | 85.118 | 0.9447 | 81.397 | 0.4229 | 45 | 0.4406 | 46 |

*Table 6. Shows the results for comparison of the quality of image segmentation ($\nu$) on PSONN and QPSONN architectures for Lena image for class 8*

| Quality of segmentation ($\nu$) | | | PSONN architecture for Lena image | | | | QPSONN architecture for Lena image | | | |
|---|---|---|---|---|---|---|---|---|---|---|
| Class | $\nu$ | Set | $\theta_\chi$ | Time (s) | $\theta_\xi$ | Time (s) | $\theta_\chi$ | Time (s) | $\theta_\xi$ | Time (s) |
| 8 | F | $s_1$ | **0.6207** | 84.855 | **0.6397** | 85.384 | **0.1997** | 40 | **0.2036** | 38 |
| | | $s_2$ | 0.6400 | 79.116 | 0.6410 | 86.994 | 0.2185 | 43 | 0.2115 | 44 |
| | | $s_3$ | 0.6573 | 80.887 | 0.6646 | 83.713 | 0.2261 | 43 | 0.2313 | 45 |
| | | $s_4$ | 0.6599 | 82.102 | 0.6691 | 84.529 | 0.288 | 45 | 0.2943 | 45 |
| | F' | $s_1$ | **0.6598** | 84.855 | **0.6683** | 85.384 | **0.2814** | 40 | **0.2841** | 38 |
| | | $s_2$ | 0.6709 | 79.116 | 0.6896 | 86.994 | 0.3007 | 43 | 0.3110 | 44 |
| | | $s_3$ | 0.6873 | 80.887 | 0.6990 | 83.713 | 0.3194 | 43 | 0.3207 | 45 |
| | | $s_4$ | 0.6991 | 82.102 | 0.7096 | 84.529 | 0.3263 | 45 | 0.3384 | 45 |
| | Q | $s_1$ | **0.8675** | 84.855 | **0.8771** | 85.384 | **0.3485** | 40 | **0.3593** | 38 |
| | | $s_2$ | 0.8910 | 79.116 | 0.9103 | 86.994 | 0.3610 | 43 | 0.3687 | 44 |
| | | $s_3$ | 0.9093 | 80.887 | 0.9286 | 83.713 | 0.3771 | 43 | 0.3810 | 45 |
| | | $s_4$ | 0.9187 | 82.102 | 0.9338 | 84.529 | 0.3810 | 45 | 0.4009 | 45 |

results are shown on Table 5 for Baboon image and Table 6 for Lena image. The segmentation performance parameters $F$ are 0.2098 and 0.2198, $F'$ values are 0.331 and 0.32071 and for $Q$ are 0.40031 and 0.4209 using QPSONN architecture and for PSONN architecture $F$ values are 0.6539 and 0.6518, $F'$ values are 0.6486 and 0.65957 and $Q$ values are 0.8963 and 0.92281.

The experimental results reveals as shown in Table 6, the comparison for class 8 true colors Lena image segmentation for the quality of segmentation is better in QPSONN architecture over PSONN architecture. The different types of the quality of the segmentations $F$, $F'$ and $Q$ are achieved after getting the experimental results for more information regarding the different types of threshold values. The $F$ values are in case of QPSONN architecture 0.1997 and 0.2036 and in PSONN architecture it is 0.6207 and 0.6397. The $F'$ values are QPSONN and PSONN are (0.2814, 0.2841) and (0.65987, 0.6683) respectively and $Q$ value for QPSONN and PSONN are (0.3485, 0.3593) and (0.8675, 0.87716) respectively for class 8 segmentation using MUSIG activation function for different values of thresholding parameters. From the experimental results it is observed that quality of true color image segmentation for Lena image is better in QPSONN over PSONN architecture for different values of the thresholding parameters $\theta_\chi$ and $\theta_\xi$ using MUSIG activation function as the quality of the segmentation values are less as shown in boldface in Table 6.

Tables 7, 8 and 9 are shown the results for the selection of four sets of values of $s_1$, $s_2$, $s_3$, and $s_4$ for the segmented classes of class 4, class 6 and class 8 respectively. In Table 7 of class 4 three color components red, green and blue having three different segmented levels are shown. For class 6 shown in Table 8 represents the three color components of red, green and blue of having five different arbitrary levels. In Table 9 using the class 8 having seven different levels is shown for three color components red, green and blue for segmentation purposes of MUSIG activation function.

In Figure 9 {(a), (c), (e), (g), (i), (k), (m) and (o)} corresponding to segmented object outputs of Baboon image and 9 {(b), (d), (f), (h), (j), (l), (n) and (p)} corresponding to segmented object outputs of Lena image for class 4 using MUSIG activation function corresponding to the PSONN architecture.

For class 6 as shown in Figure 10 {(a), (c), (e), (g), (i), (k), (m) and (o)} corresponding to segmented object outputs of Baboon image and 10 {(b), (d), (f), (h), (j), (l), (n) and (p)} corresponding to segmented object outputs of Lena image using MUSIG activation function corresponding to the PSONN architecture.

In Figure 11 {(a), (c), (e), (g), (i), (k), (m) and (o)} represents the segmented object outputs of Baboon image and 11 {(b), (d), (f), (h), (j), (l), (n) and (p)} represents the segmented object outputs of Lena image for class 8 using MUSIG activation function corresponding to the PSONN architecture.

*Table 7. Shows the four sets of segmented range of values of three levels corresponding to three color components red, green and blue of the class 4 for Baboon and Lena images*

| Class 4 | | | | |
|---|---|---|---|---|
| Set 1 | Red | 0-65 | 65-175 | 175-255 |
| | Green | 0-50 | 50-140 | 140-255 |
| | Blue | 0-30 | 30-123 | 123-255 |
| Set 2 | Red | 0-70 | 70-138 | 138-255 |
| | Green | 0-60 | 60-150 | 150-255 |
| | Blue | 0-45 | 45-100 | 100-255 |
| Set 3 | Red | 0-45 | 45-160 | 160-255 |
| | Green | 0-40 | 40-135 | 135-255 |
| | Blue | 0-60 | 60-115 | 115-255 |
| Set 4 | Red | 0-50 | 50-169 | 169-255 |
| | Green | 0-30 | 30-180 | 180-255 |
| | Blue | 0-40 | 40-148 | 148-255 |

*Table 8. Shows the four sets of segmented range of values of five levels corresponding to three color components red, green and blue of the class 6 for Baboon and Lena images*

| Class 6 | | | | | |
|---|---|---|---|---|---|
| Set 1 | Red | 0-60 | 60-100 | 100-170 | 170-210 | 210-255 |
| | Green | 0-40 | 40-80 | 80-130 | 130-200 | 200-255 |
| | Blue | 0-20 | 20-60 | 60-120 | 120-195 | 195-255 |
| Set 2 | Red | 0-80 | 80-100 | 100-140 | 140-198 | 198-255 |
| | Green | 0-50 | 50-75 | 75-156 | 156-210 | 210-255 |
| | Blue | 0-20 | 20-55 | 55-91 | 91-163 | 163-255 |
| Set 3 | Red | 0-50 | 50-100 | 100-153 | 153-210 | 210-255 |
| | Green | 0-30 | 30-65 | 65-121 | 121-195 | 195-255 |
| | Blue | 0-55 | 55-90 | 90-110 | 110-175 | 175-255 |
| Set 4 | Red | 0-40 | 40-95 | 95-169 | 169-221 | 221-255 |
| | Green | 0-30 | 30-125 | 125-180 | 180-235 | 235-255 |
| | Blue | 0-50 | 50-105 | 105-148 | 148-210 | 210-255 |

*Table 9. Shows the four sets of segmented range of values of seven levels corresponding to three color components red, green and blue of the class 8 for Baboon and Lena images*

| | | | | | | | | |
|---|---|---|---|---|---|---|---|---|
| **Class 8** | | | | | | | | |
| | Red | 0-57 | 57-69 | 69-145 | 145-152 | 152-182 | 182-234 | 234-555 |
| Set 1 | Green | 0-42 | 42-68 | 68-101 | 101-108 | 108-161 | 161-229 | 229-255 |
| | Blue | 0-18 | 18-44 | 44-74 | 74-110 | 110-`139 | 139-191 | 191-255 |
| | Red | 0-88 | 88-139 | 139-142 | 142-154 | 154-222 | 222-227 | 227-255 |
| Set 2 | Green | 0-55 | 55-66 | 66-102 | 102-189 | 189-197 | 197-213 | 213-255 |
| | Blue | 0-15 | 15-33 | 33-82 | 82-117 | 117-159 | 159-222 | 222-255 |
| | Red | 0-45 | 45-70 | 70-100 | 100-120 | 120-150 | 150-180 | 180-255 |
| Set 3 | Green | 0-30 | 30-50 | 50-90 | 90-110 | 110-180 | 180-200 | 200-255 |
| | Blue | 0-43 | 43-65 | 65-86 | 86-106 | 106-140 | 140-175 | 175-255 |
| | Red | 0-50 | 50-70 | 70-145 | 145-186 | 186-199 | 199-220 | 220-255 |
| Set 4 | Green | 0-28 | 28-74 | 74-130 | 130-155 | 155-175 | 175-200 | 200-255 |
| | Blue | 0-20 | 20-50 | 50-100 | 100-150 | 150-175 | 175-215 | 215-255 |

In Figure 12 {(a), (c), (e), (g), (i), (k), (m) and (o)} represents the segmented object outputs of Baboon image and 12 {(b), (d), (f), (h), (j), (l), (n) and (p)} represents the segmented object outputs of Lena image for class 4 using MUSIG activation function corresponding to the QPSONN architecture.

For class 6 as shown in Figure 13 {(a), (c), (e), (g), (i), (k), (m) and (o)} represents the segmented object outputs of Baboon image and 13 {(b), (d), (f), (h), (j), (l), (n) and (p)} represents the segmented object outputs of Lena image using MUSIG activation function for the QPSONN architecture.

In Figure 14 {(a), (c), (e), (g), (i), (k), (m) and (o)} represents the segmented object outputs of Baboon image and 14 {(b), (d), (f), (h), (j), (l), (n) and (p)} represents the segmented object outputs of Lena image for class 8 using MUSIG activation function corresponding to the QPSONN architecture.

## CONCLUSION AND REMARKS

The proposed fundamental principle is applied to segment true color images to determine the quality of the segmentation evaluation measurement for class 4, 6 and 8. The multilevel sigmoidal activation function (MUSIG) is used for input output transfer characteristics for two different thresholding parameters. The measurement

*Figure 9. { (a), (c), (e), (g), (i), (k), (m), (o) and (b), (d), (f), (h), (j), (l), (n), (p)} shows the segmented object outputs for Baboon and Lena images using PSONN architecture for class 4*

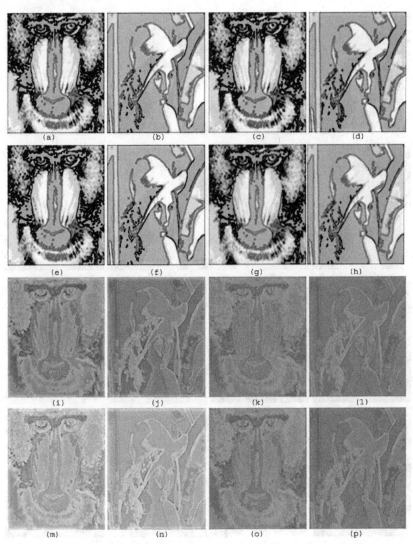

*\*For a more accurate representation see the electronic version.*

of the efficacy and the efficiency of the quality of the segmentation evaluation on the two true color images viz. Baboon and Lena images are demonstrated by applying two kinds of self supervised neural networks PSONN and QPSONN architectures adaptive context sensitive fuzzy thresholding strategies.

*Figure 10. {(a), (c), (e), (g), (i), (k), (m), (o) and (b), (d), (f), (h), (j), (l), (n),(p)} shows the segmented object outputs for Baboon and Lena images using PSONN architecture for class 6*

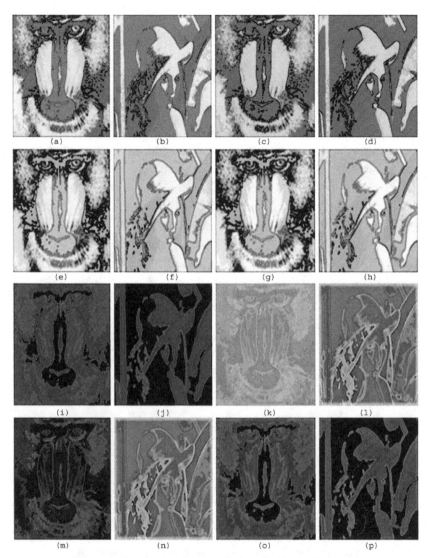

*\*For a more accurate representation see the electronic version.*

The performance of the PSONN and QPSONN architectures on the basis of three kinds of segmentation evaluation measures using two types of thresholding strategies are presented. The comparison Tables for illustration of the self supervised classical neural network PSONN architecture and quantum superposition principle endorsed self supervised neural network QPSONN architectures are provided.

*Figure 11. {(a), (c), (e), (g), (i), (k), (m),(o) and (b), (d), (f), (h), (j), (l), (n),(p)} shows the object outputs for Baboon and Lena images using PSONN architecture for class 8*

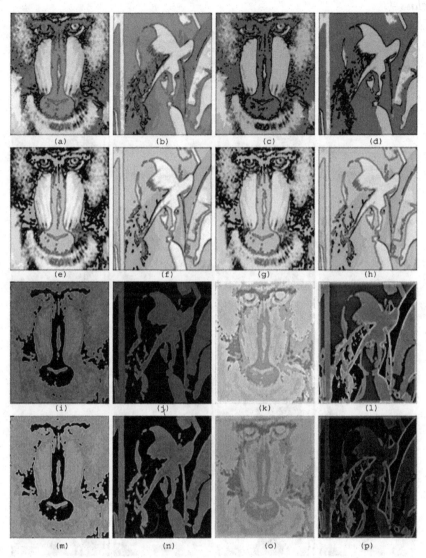

*\*For a more accurate representation see the electronic version.*

The segmented objects for three classes 4, 6 and 8 are presented for different multilevel characteristics of MUSIG activation functions along with original true color Baboon and Lena images.

It is found that the proposed QPSONN architecture outperforms the classical PSONN architecture both with respect to segmented outputs and time efficiency.

*Figure 12. {(a), (c), (e), (g), (i), (k), (m),(o) and (b), (d), (f), (h), (j), (l), (n) and (p)} shows the object outputs for Baboon and Lena images using QPSONN architecture for class 4*

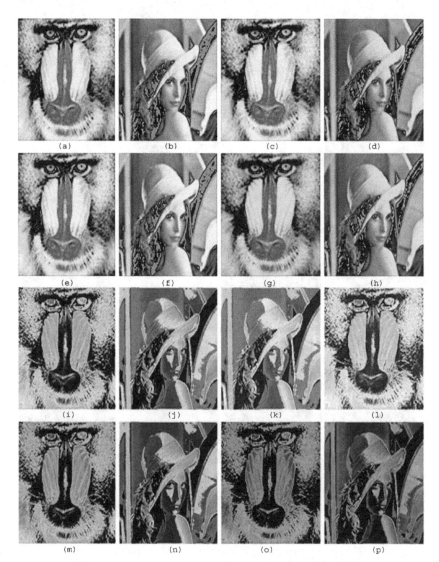

*\*For a more accurate representation see the electronic version.*

*Figure 13. {(a), (c), (e), (g), (i), (k), (m), (o) and (b), (d), (f), (h), (j), (l), (n), (p)} shows the object outputs for Baboon and Lena images using QPSONN architecture for class 6*

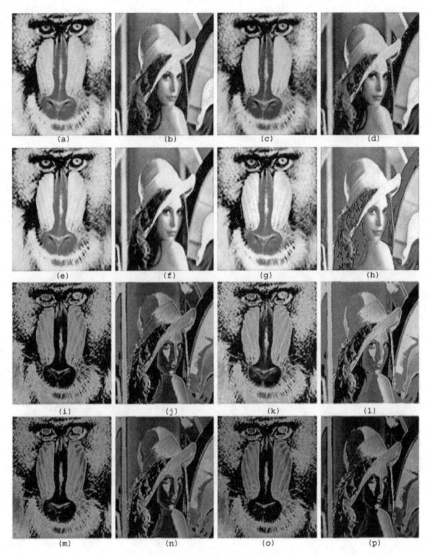

*For a more accurate representation see the electronic version.*

*Figure 14. {(a), (c), (e), (g), (i), (k), (m),(o) and (b), (d), (f), (h), (j), (l), (n),(p)}
shows the object outputs for Baboon and Lena images using QPSONN architecture
for class 8*

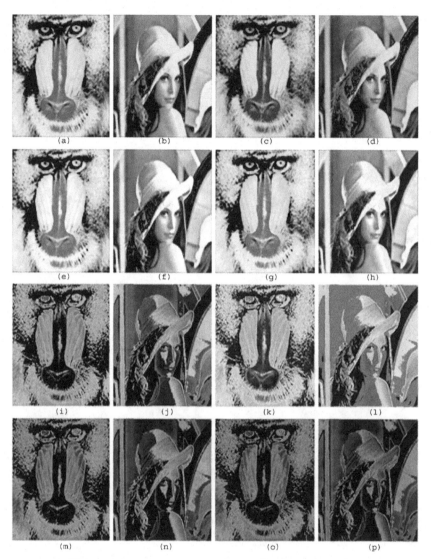

*For a more accurate representation see the electronic version.*

This technique is applied to the real life application such as medical imaging as well as to synthetic images.

Computational overhead depends upon the number of lobes in the MUSIG activation function present and the number of class is considered in segmentation involved.

The authors are betrothed in this direction for more investigation regarding the different types of thresholding strategies with nonlinear transfer function characteristics for further improvement.

# REFERENCES

Aytekin, C., Kiranyaz, S., & Gabbouj, M. (2013). Quantum Mechanics in Computer Vision: Automatic Object Extraction. *Proc. ICIP 2013*, 2489–2493. doi:10.1109/ICIP.2013.6738513

Baldi, P. (2012). Autoencoders, Unsupervised Learning, and Deep Architectures. *JMLR Workshop and Conference Proceedings*, 27, 37–50.

Barman, P. C., & Miah, S. (2011, December). MRI Image Segmentation Using Level Set Method and Implement An Medical Diagnosis System. *Computer Science & Engineering International Journal (Toronto, Ont.)*, 1(5).

Bhattacharyya, S., Dutta, P., Maulik, U., & Nandi, P. K. (2007). Multilevel Activation Functions For True Color Image Segmentation Using a Self Supervised Parallel Self Organizing Neural Network (PSONN) Architecture: A Comparative Study; World Academy of Science, Engineering and Technology International Journal of Computer, Electrical, Automation. *Control and Information Engineering Vol*, 1(:8), 2007.

Bhattacharyya, S., Pal, P., & Bhowmick, S. (2014). Binary Image Denoising Using a Quantum Multilayer Self Organizing Neural Network. *Applied Soft Computing*, 24, 717-729. doi:.2014.08.02710.1016/j.asoc

Bhattacharyya, S., Pal, P., & Bhowmick, S. (2014). A Quantum Multilayer Self Organizing Neural Network For Object Extraction From A Noisy Background. *Proceedings of 4th IEEE International Conference On Communication System and Network Technologies (CSNT-2014)*, 512-517. doi:10.1109/CSNT.2014.108

Bhattacharyya, S., Pal, P., & Bhowmick, S. (2015). A Quantum Parallel Self Organizing Neural Network (QPSONN) For Pure Color Object Extraction From A Noisy Background. *Proceedings of 5th IEEE International Conference On Communication System and Network Technologies (CSNT-2015)*, 1129-1135. DOI: doi:10.1109/CSNT.2015.55

Borsotti, M., Campadelli, P., & Schettini, R. (1998). Quantitative evaluation of color image segmentation results. *Pattern Recognition Letters*, 19(8), 741–747. doi:10.1016/S0167-8655(98)00052-X

Boskovitz, V., & Guterman, H. (2002). An adaptive neuro-fuzzy system for automatic image segmentation and edge detection. *IEEE Transactions on Fuzzy Systems, 10*(2), 247-262. doi:10.1109/91.995125

Das D. & Mukhopadhyay S. (2015). A Pixel Based Segmentation Scheme for Fingerprint Images. *Information Systems Design and Intelligent Applications*, 439-448. DOI: 10.1007/978-81-322-2247-7_45

Devi, H. K. A. (2006). Thresholding: A Pixel-Level Image Processing Methodology Preprocessing Technique for an OCR System for the Brahmi Script. *Ancient Asia.*, *1*, 161–165. doi:10.5334/aa.06113

Dhar, M. (1994). Cardinality of Fuzzy Sets: An Overview. *International Journal of Energy, Information and Communications, 4*(1).

Dubey, S., Gupta, Y. K., & Soni, D. (2016). Comparative Study of Various Segmentation Techniques with their Effective Parameters. *International Journal of Innovative Research in Computer and Communication Engineering, 4*(10).

Ghosh, A., Pal, N. R., & Pal, S. K. (1993). Self organization for object extraction using a multilayer neural network and fuzziness measures. *IEEE Transactions on Fuzzy Systems, 1*(1), 54–68. doi:10.1109/TFUZZ.1993.390285

Hopfield, J. J. (1984, May). Neurons with graded response have collective computational properties like those of two-state neurons. *Proceedings of the National Academy of Sciences of the United States of America, 81*(10), 3088–3092. doi:10.1073/pnas.81.10.3088 PMID:6587342

Kalra, K., Goswami, A. K., & Gupta, R. (2013). A comparative study of supervised image classification algorithms for satellite images. *International Journal of Electrical, Electronics and Data Communication, 1*(10).

Laguna, M., & Marti, R. (2002). Neural network prediction in a system for optimizing simulations. *IIE Transactions, 34*(3), 273–282. doi:10.1080/07408170208928869

Liu, J., & Yang, Y. (1994). Multiresolution color image segmentation. *IEEE Transactions on Pattern Analysis and Machine Intelligence, 16*(7), 689–700. doi:10.1109/34.297949

Manish, T. W., Keshao, D. K., & Mahendra, P. D. (2015). Document Image Segmentation using Region Based Methods. *International Journal of Computing Science and Information Technology, 3*(3). Retrieved from http://ijcsit.org

Naik, D., & Shahet, P. (2014). A Review on Image Segmentation Clustering Algorithms. *International Journal of Computer Science and Information Technologies, 5*(3).

Pal, P., Bhattacharyya, S., & Mani, A. (2016). Pure Color Object Extraction from a Noisy State using Quantum Version Parallel Self Organizing Neural Network. *International Journal of Computers and Applications,* 164-186. 10.1080/1206212X.2016.1237164

Saini, S., & Arora, K. (2014). A Study Analysis on the Different Image Segmentation Techniques. *International Journal of Information & Computation Technology,* 4(14), 1445-1452.

Singh, K. K., & Singh, A. (2010). A Study of Image Segmentation Algorithms For Different Types Of Images. *International Journal of Computer Science Issues, 7*(5).

Zadeh, L. A. (1965). Fuzzy sets. *Information and Control, 8*(3), 338–353. doi:10.1016/S0019-9958(65)90241-X

Zhang, H., Fritts, J., & Goldman, S. (2004). An entropy-based objective evaluation method for image segmentation. *Proceedings of SPIE Storage and Retrieval Methods and Applications for Multimedia.*

# Chapter 8

# An Efficient Handwritten Character Recognition Using Quantum Multilayer Neural Network (QMLNN) Architecture:

## Quantum Multilayer Neural Network

**Debanjan Konar**
*Sikkim Manipal Institute of Technology, India*

**Suman Kalyan Kar**
*Sikkim Manipal Institute of Technology, India*

## ABSTRACT

*This chapter proposes a quantum multi-layer neural network (QMLNN) architecture suitable for handwritten character recognition in real time, assisted by quantum backpropagation of errors calculated from the quantum-inspired fuzziness measure of network output states. It is composed of three second-order neighborhood-topology-based inter-connected layers of neurons represented by qubits known as input, hidden, and output layers. The QMLNN architecture is a feed forward network with standard quantum backpropagation algorithm for the adjustment of its weighted interconnection. QMLNN self-organizes the quantum fuzzy input image information by means of the quantum backpropagating errors at the intermediate and output layers of the architecture. The interconnection weights are described using rotation gates. After the network is stabilized, a quantum observation at the output layer destroys the superposition of quantum states in order to obtain true binary outputs.*

DOI: 10.4018/978-1-5225-5219-2.ch008

# INTRODUCTION

Owing to wide variations in writing styles, variations in sizes and orientation of the handwritten characters, recognition of characters remains an uphill task in computer vision and pattern recognition community. Numerous image processing applications are relying on the techniques of identification and recognition of characters from real-life applications of text documents and images. The primary objective of handwritten character recognition lies in the conversion of characters present in an image into character codes pertaining to text and image processing. Artificial Neural Networks (ANN) often offers to solve unorganized machine learning problems like associative pattern recognition tasks, image processing tasks in parallel processing mode. Basic feed forward ANN is employed by many computer vision researchers to solve pattern recognition problems with high time complexity. The character recognition problem can be solved using various feature selection techniques and neural network classifiers. The significant contributions of feed forward ANNs assisted by back-propagation algorithms in character recognition problems deserves special mention (Devireddy, 2005). The Bayesian Network classifiers (Bouchain, 2007; Bonci et al, 2006) are one of the most suitable probabilistic approach for recognition of characters. In handwritten character recognition, high recognition accuracy can be obtained using back-propagation learning algorithm in multilayer neural network architectures.

A Hidden Markov Model (HMM) based approach is proposed by Kundu and Chen (2002) achieved 88% recognition accuracy working with 100 postal words. Tomoyuki *et al.* (2002) also achieved 80% recognition accuracy in experiment while considering 1646 city names of Europe as data sets. A K-NN classifier has been employed by Gatos et al. (2006) to recognize 3799 words from IAM database which yields 81% accuracy. A plethora of supervised artificial neural networks (Samadiani et al, 2005; Chi et al, 1995) have been suggested to obtain real time results. In addition, numerous neighborhoods based supervised neural network architectures have been entrusted upon for pattern recognition and it has been found efficient in recognizing handwritten characters. However, owing to interconnection weight adjustments using standard back-propagation algorithms in these supervised network architectures, the time complexity increases manifold. Efforts have been made to combine quantum computing with the standard back-propagation algorithm resulting in time efficient network architectures.

Micro-quantum level effects offer to perform computational tasks using time effect procedures in Quantum computing and also outperform the classical computing approaches in terms of computational time (Mcmohan, 2008). The popularity of artificial neural network combined with quantum computing is growing in leaps and bounds due to implied parallelism offered by quantum computing. An array of quantum dots -assisted Quantum Neural Network (QNN) architecture is proposed by Behrman *et al.* (1994). Matsui *et al.* *(2000)* also projected a quantum multilayer feed forward neural network model referred as QNN using quantum learning technique. Quantum associative memory (Ventura et al, 2000; Perus, 1998) and neural network quantum dots (Behramam 1994) are the basic components of QNN research. An automated pattern recognition algorithm is proposed by Aytekin *et al.* (2013) guided by the principle of quantum mechanics. A novel model of QNN is also suggested by Ezhov (2001) to solve classification problems. Moreover, quantum back-propagation based neural network architecture is introduced in (2013) to encounter the pattern recognition tasks.

In this chapter, a time efficient novel quantum inspired neural network architecture referred to as Quantum Multilayer Neural Network architecture (QMLNN) for handwritten character recognition has been proposed. The novelty of the proposed QMLNN lies in the fact that learning and classification can be performed simultaneously. The QMLNN architecture comprises of *qubits* and rotation gates. This architecture is composed of an input, an intermediate and an output layer of neurons in quantum environment. The input information as *qubits* are feed forwarded from input layer to intermediate layer and output layer. It also counter propagates its network states from output to intermediate layer. The interconnected weights are adjusted using quantum back-propagation algorithm illustrated below. The standard sigmoid activation function is employed to characteristic activation through the quantum cardinality estimates of 8-connected neighborhoods pixels. The performance of the proposed QMLNN architecture is focused on the time efficiency and recognition accuracy from noisy handwritten characters, as compared to the classical MLNN (Devireddy et al, 2005; Matan et al, 1990; Patil et al, 2011).

## LITERATURE SURVEY

In the field of pattern recognition and machine learning, the problem of recognition of handwritten characters has gained much attention. With growing popularity and requirement for office automation, it has become to provide effective and real time solutions (Rahman et al, 2005; Dineshkumar et al, 2005; Samadiani et al, 2015). However, owing to wide variations in structural, topological and statistical information do not assist in handwritten character recognition (Shelke et al, 2011). Self Organizing Feature Map (SOM) neural network based method suggested by Najmeh Samadiani *et al.* for recognition of printed English characters (Samadiani et al, 2015) received much attention. The contribution of integrated neural network for feature extraction task of alpha alphanumeric characters has been projected by using Junchuan Yang *et al.* (2012). Several pattern recognition approaches have been reported in this paper with improved accuracy. The contribution of pattern transformations and additive input noise annealing approach for handwritten character recognition proposed by J.M. Alonso-Weber *et al.* (2014) is also notable. In this paper, the proposed combined approach achieved less than 0.43% test error while compared with Convolution Neural Network and Deep Learning Neural Networks. Handwritten character recognition in Marathi language has been proposed by Amitkumar Shinde *et al.* (2015) incorporating forty-six Marathi sign language alphabets and 500 words of sign language. The some work based on fuzzy model based handwritten number recognition proposed by O.V. Ramana Murthy *et al.* (2007) contributed fuzzy model based handwritten character recognition which deals with number detection of both Hindi and English numerals. In this fuzzy logic based model, fuzzy exponential membership functions, suitable for deriving character features, are modified.

In the field of online handwritten character recognition, the combination of Hidden Markov Model (HMM) and dynamic programming has contributed significantly for cursive handwritten character recognition (Sin et al, 1999).

In the last decade, Artificial Neural Network (ANN) has gained huge popularity in research areas such as pattern recognition and machine learning. The simplified ANN could not match with the rising demands of volume of data and complexity of information. The large scale of data and complexity, therefore lead to the construction of more complex hybridized ANN with more biological and physical features and mathematical basics (Cheng et al, 2006). One of the notable examples in this direction is Quantum Neural Networks (QNN), a hybridization of quantum computation and neural networks. Perus proposed a QNN which draws much attention in international research community. In addition, multi-universe theory of quantum mechanics has been introduced by Menneer and Narayanan, which deals with neural network training and the superposition of the networks to construct the complete network. An array of quantum dots -assisted Quantum Neural Network (QNN) architecture is proposed by Behrman *et al.* (1994). According to quantum mechanics, the suggested system is evolved in real-time by incorporating single quantum dot molecule for every input neuron. The hidden layer neurons are presented as different time interval. Therefore, the number of hidden neurons is directly proportional to measures applied to the time pieces. In recent times, there are wide applications of QNN, which includes the Quantum Associative Memory (QAM) (Ventura et al, 200; Perus 1998). the quantum competition learning (Pyllkkanen et al, 1995), quantum dots associated neural network (Behrman 1996), quantum Hopfield networks and quantum transform function. Neural networks, which are constituted by quantum gated nodes, facilitate features of biological systems more efficiently than their classical counterparts (Shafee, 2007). Recently, a quantum back-propagation algorithm based neural model (Li et al, 2008) has been proposed and the quantum back-propagation learning algorithm is completely relying on single-*qubit* rotation gate and two-*qubit* controlled-NOT gates.

## Quantum Computing Concepts

Quantum mechanics and quantum algorithms are two basic components exploited in the field of soft computing research. Quantum mechanical operations like superposition, entanglement (Shor, 1994) are applied on them. The efficacy of quantum computing over classical computation has thrown open new horizons in current developments. Quantum factoring problem is one of the notable examples in this direction using a polynomial type RSA-129 algorithm over classical factoring problem and it has been found that quantum factoring problem can be solved in few seconds (Grover, 1996). A quantum algorithm for data base search is developed by Grover (1996) whose time complexity was reduced to $O(\sqrt{n})$. Both proposed quantum algorithms are guided by inherent parallelism offered by quantum computing. In order to gain maximum parallelism in quantum computing, a superposition procedure is followed on all inputs to obtain suitable possible outputs. The primary disadvantage with this superposition approach is that parallelism fails due to the unavailability of all possible outputs once quantum observation is performed.

Deutsch first developed true Quantum Turing Machine (QTM) (Nielson et al, 2000), draws significant features in quantum computing. This novel feature has turned out to be the key to most successful quantum algorithms. The following subsections merely review the basic concepts of quantum computation.

## Concept of Qubits

In quantum computing basic building block is a quantum bit or *qubit* (Mcmohan, 2008) for processing of information. The linear superposition of dual eigenstates I0 > and I1 > constitutes a qubit in quantum computer. It is defined as

$$|\text{Á}>= a|0> +b|1\rangle \tag{1}$$

The probabilities for occurrence of I0> and I1> are I $a$ I² and I $b$ I² respectively where, $a$ and $b$ are complex numbers and subjected to normalization constraint

$$|a|^2 + |b|^2 \tag{2}$$

266

The quantum logic gates are implemented on Hilbert space using various linear and unitary operations (Aytekin et al, 2013).

## Single Qubit Rotation Gate

Updation of single *qubit* is done using a rotation gate is as follows

$$\begin{bmatrix} a' \\ b' \end{bmatrix} = \begin{bmatrix} \cos\alpha & -\sin\alpha \\ \sin\alpha & \cos\alpha \end{bmatrix} \begin{bmatrix} a \\ b \end{bmatrix} \tag{3}$$

A *qubit* $(a,b)$ is modified to $(a',b')$ using single qubit rotation gate with a rotation angle $\alpha$.

## Quantum Observation

A postulate of quantum mechanics (Feynman et al, 1965; Mu et al, 2013) states that "if a coherent or linearly superposed system interacts with its environment, then on measurement, the superposition is destroyed". A quantum system, $\mu$ containing quantum states, $|\rho_i>$, exists in a Hilbert space and is defined as

$$|\mu\rangle = \sum_{j=1}^{p} d_j |\rho_j > \tag{4}$$

The coherence of basic states $|j>$ forms $|\mu\rangle$. The quantum system $|\mu\rangle$ is observed in the state $|\rho_i>$ and the occurrence of $|\mu\rangle$ measured using probability with amplitude $|d_j|^2$ where $d_j$ is the complex coefficient.

## Quantum Multilayer Neural Network (QMLNN) Architecture

The information processing neurons in QMLNN architecture are composed of *qubits*. There are three layers of neurons namely the input, intermediate and output layers which are described by *qubit* representation. The following matrices are used to illustrate all three layers.

$$\text{Input layer} \begin{bmatrix} \mid x_{11} > & \dots & \mid x_{1n} > \\ \mid x_{21} > & \dots & \mid x_{2n} > \\ \dots & \dots & \dots \\ \dots & \dots & \dots \\ \mid x_{m1} > & \dots & \mid x_{mn} > \end{bmatrix}$$

$$\text{Intermediate layer} \begin{bmatrix} \mid y_{11} > & \dots & \mid y_{1n} > \\ \mid y_{21} > & \dots & \mid y_{2n} > \\ \dots & \dots & \dots \\ \dots & \dots & \dots \\ \mid y_{m1} > & \dots & \mid y_{mn} > \end{bmatrix}$$

$$\text{Output layer} \begin{bmatrix} \mid z_{11} > & \dots & \mid z_{1n} > \\ \mid z_{21} > & \dots & \mid z_{2n} > \\ \dots & \dots & \dots \\ \dots & \dots & \dots \\ \mid z_{m1} > & \dots & \mid z_{mn} > \end{bmatrix}$$

The network inputs in terms of quantum bits are fed into the input layer of QMLNN architecture which is acts like a switching layer. The input layer of QMLNN architecture accepts image information as *qubits* and propagated to the hidden layer for further processing.

The 8-connected neighborhood based neurons of all three layers are accumulated at the seed neuron of next subsequent layer and stored as quantum information through interconnected strengths.

There are twofold techniques for inter-layer connections introduced in this presented QMLNN architecture. The rotation gates have been employed to set inter-connection weights between the adjacent layers of corresponding neurons. The relative measure of quantum bits at the constituent neurons of each layer of QMLNN architecture determines the angle of rotation for rotation gates. Figure 1 illustrates the architecture of QMLNN. The sigmoid function governs the activations of the constituent neurons of the intermediate and the output layer, is one of the salient features of the network. The counter propagation of intermediate states in terms of *qubits* are transformed in to outputs at back propagation layer of the QMLNN architecture.

*Figure 1. Quantum Multilayer Neural Network (QMLNN) architecture (Intra –layer connections are not shown for clarity. (Konar et. al, 2016)*

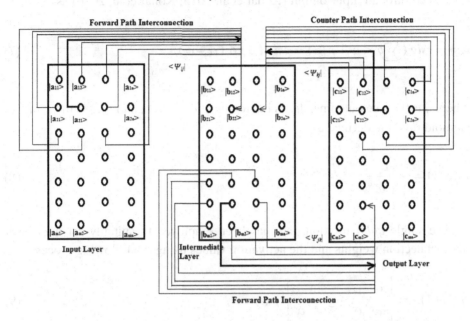

## Network Operation Using Quantum Back-Propagation Algorithm

The novelty of the proposed algorithm lies in the fact that learning and classification can be performed simultaneously. The input handwritten image pixel informations are received at the switching or input layer of QMLNN architecture and input binary values [0, 1] are converted into the quantum phase [0, Å/ 2] .

$$q_j = \frac{\pi}{2} b_j \qquad (5)$$

where, $q_i$ is quantum bits and $b_i$ is the binary information.

*Qubits* have been employed to present the interconnected weights and activation values are presented in QMLNN architecture. The angle of rotation and activation are expressed as $\alpha$ and $\rho$ respectively where

$$< A| = \begin{bmatrix} \cos \phi \\ \sin \phi \end{bmatrix} \qquad (6)$$

269

The constituent neurons of each adjacent layer of QMLNN architecture are associated through input-output (Konar et al, 2015; Konar et al, 2016) as

$$<q| = gsig \left( \sum_{j=1}^{p} b_j <\mu_j | \rho_k> \right) = gsig \left( b_j \cos(\alpha_j - \phi) \right) \tag{7}$$

where $q$ is the true outcome, $\mu_j$ is interconnection weight and *gsig* is the standard sigmoid function defined as

$$gsig (y) = \frac{1}{1 + e^{-y}} \tag{8}$$

The single *qubit* rotation gate has been employed to suitably set inter-layer interconnection weights and the activation values using the following process.

$$|\mu (i+1)> = \begin{bmatrix} \cos' \alpha & -\sin' \alpha \\ \sin' \alpha & \cos' \alpha \end{bmatrix} |\mu (i)> \tag{9}$$

$$|\eta (i+1)> = \begin{bmatrix} \cos' \beta & -\sin' \beta \\ \sin' \beta & \cos' \beta \end{bmatrix} |\eta (i)> \tag{10}$$

where $\alpha (i+1) = \alpha (i) + {}'\alpha_i$ (11)

$$\beta (i+1) = \beta (i) + {}'\beta_i \tag{12}$$

If $\bar{q}$ and $q$ are target normalized output and real output respectively then, the network error function is defined as follows:

$$Err = \overline{(q - q)}^2 \frac{1}{2} \tag{13}$$

The real outputs are obtained after quantum measurement of each quantum states and the network is stabilized once the error *Err* is achieved tolerable limit.

## EXPERIMENTAL RESULTS AND DISCUSSIONS

The proposed QMLNN and its classical counterpart Classical Multilayer Neural Network (CMLNN) have been trained and classified with exactly 50 samples of each character image of size 32 x 32. During learning and classification procedure, the characters with lowest error value at the output layer with the input handwritten image have been considered for classification. The overall average classification accuracy found to be very promising and it is above 88%.

In the proposed handwritten character recognition experiment, the QMLNN network has been tested by each of the 26 characters 50 times i.e. 1300 (50×26=1300) character image samples from the database has been involved in the learning process. Input handwritten characters and target output images are provided in Figure 2.

The efficacy of the proposed QMLNN over classical MLNN has been reported in Table 1 and Table 2. The comparative result reflects the superiority of the QMLNN with its classical counterpart in terms of recognition accuracy and time complexity. In order to match the true output with the target normalized image, the percentage of correct classification pixels (pcc) is evaluated as:

*Figure 2. Original Input and Target Images*

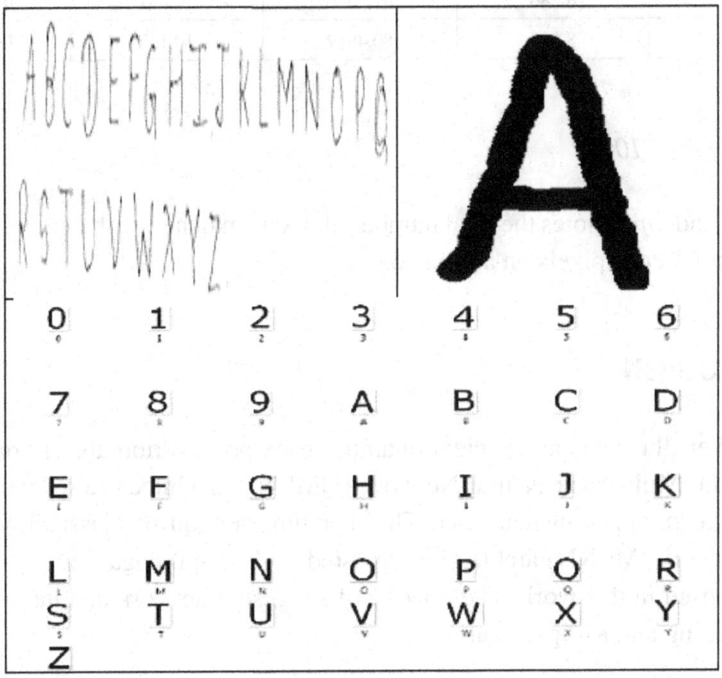

*Table 1. Comparative performance results of QMLNN and CMLNN*

| English Characters | QMLNN | | CMLNN | |
|---|---|---|---|---|
| | *t (secs)* | *% of Accuracy* | *t (secs)* | *% of Accuracy* |
| C | 8.666 | 89.0328 | 10.533 | 88.0017 |
| A | 8.026 | 89.4966 | 10.501 | 79.3338 |
| E | 8.060 | 69.2785 | 10.102 | 63.8994 |
| 1 | 8.406 | 94.0380 | 10.323 | 84.5355 |
| 2 | 8.647 | 93.5917 | 10.302 | 89.0240 |
| 3 | 8.127 | 92.7813 | 10.312 | 88.9866 |

*Table 2. Comparative performance results of QMLNN and CMLNN*

| English Characters | QMLNN | | CMLNN | |
|---|---|---|---|---|
| | *t (secs)* | *% of Accuracy* | *t (secs)* | *% of Accuracy* |
| X | 8.216 | 91.8043 | 10.372 | 88.8154 |
| Y | 8.526 | 87.7326 | 10.249 | 84.8165 |
| Z | 8.316 | 88.4941 | 10.934 | 85.1285 |
| 8 | 8.607 | 84.9063 | 10.372 | 84.5345 |
| 7 | 8.286 | 82.3846 | 10.891 | 79.9292 |
| 9 | 8.086 | 80.4917 | 10.133 | 78.7587 |

$$pcc = tcc / tnp *100 \tag{14}$$

where *tcc* and *tnp* denotes the total number of pixels matched with target output and the total number of pixels on an image.

## CONCLUSION

This chapter illustrates an efficient quantum back propagation algorithm refereed as Quantum Multi-layer Neural Network (QMLNN) architecture for handwritten character recognition in real-time. The quantum version of classical Multilayer neural network (MLNN) architecture assisted by back-propagation algorithm has been proposed in this work. The novelty of suggested network architecture lies in its functioning and its operations.

The basic components used in the suggested QMLNN architecture are designated by qubits for each constituent processing node and in order to reduce computation time of the back-propagation algorithm rotation gates have been employed. The weighted interconnections between different layers are also represented using *qubits* and quantum thresholding have been incorporated to propagate quantum fuzzified information. At the output layer of the proposed network QMLNN, a quantum measurement is performed to obtain the true output (Recognized Characters) by changing the quantum bits or states into 0's and 1's according to the probability.

The effectiveness of the suggested network architecture is established using comparative analysis of the results as far as the quality of extracted output images are concerned and recognition time over the classical MLNN. In addition, the future direction of research of suggested QMLNN is aiming for recognition of handwritten characters using self-supervised neural network architecture. Currently, the authors are engaged in this new paradigm of research.

# REFERENCES

Alonso-Weber, J. M., Sesmero, M. P., & Sanchis, A. (2014). Combining additive input noise annealing and pattern transformations for improved handwritten character recognition. Elsevier.

Aytekin, C., Kiranyaz, S., & Gabbouj, M. (2013). Quantum Mechanics in Computer Vision: Automatic Object Extraction. *Proc. ICIP 2013*, 2489–2493. doi:10.1109/ICIP.2013.6738513

Behraman, E. (1994). A quantum dot neural network. *Proc. Workshop onPhysics of Computation*, 22–24.

Bhattacharyya, S., Pal, P., & Bhowmick, S. (2014). Binary Image Denoising Using a Quantum Multilayer Self Organizing Neural Network. *Applied Soft Computing*, *24*, 717–729. doi:10.1016/j.asoc.2014.08.027

Bonci, A., Leo, T., & Longhi, S. (2005). A Bayesian approach to the Hough transform for line detection. *IEEE Trans. Systems Man Cybernet., Part A. Syst. Humans*, *35*(6), 945–955. doi:10.1109/TSMCA.2005.853481

Bouchain, D. (2007). *Character Recognition Using Convolutional Neural Networks*. Seminar Statistical Learning Theory University of Ulm,Germany Institute for Neural Information Processing.

Cheng, J. L., Feng, D. H., & Liu, F. (2006). *Immune Optimization Computation, Learn and Recognition*. Beijing: Science Press.

Chi, Z., Wu, J., & Yan, H. (1995). Handwritten numeral recognition using self-organizing maps and fuzzy rules. *Pattern Recognition, 28*(1), 59–66. doi:10.1016/0031-3203(94)00085-Z

Deutsch, D. (1985). Quantum Theory, the Church-Turing Principle and the Universal Quantum Computer. *Proceedings of the Royal Society of London, A400*(1818), 97–117. doi:10.1098/rspa.1985.0070

Devireddy, S., & AppaRao, S. (2005). Hand Written Character Recognition Using Back Propagation Network. *Journal of Theoretical and Applied Information Technology*, 257-269.

Dineshkumar, R., & Suganthi, J. (2015). Sanskrit Character Recognition System using Neural Network. *Indian Journal of Science and Technology, 8*(1), 65–69. doi:10.17485/ijst/2015/v8i1/52878

Ezhov, A. A. (2001). Pattern Recognition with Quantum Neural Networks. Proc. Advances in Pattern Recognition ICAPR:2001, 60–71.

Feynman, R. P., Leighton, R. B., & Sands, M. (1965). *The Feynman Lectures on Physics* (Vol. 3). Addison-Wesley Publishing Company.

Gatos, B., Pratikakis, I., & Perantonis, S. J. (2006). Hybrid off-line cursive handwriting word recognition. *Proceedings of 18th international conference on pattern recognition (ICPR'06)*, 2, 998–1002. doi:10.1109/ICPR.2006.644

Grover, L. (1996). A Fast Quantum Mechanical Algorithm for Database Search. *Proc. 28th Annual ACM Symposium on the Theory of Computing*, 212–221. doi:10.1145/237814.237866

Hanmandlu, M., & Ramana Murthy, O. V. (2007). Fuzzy model based recognition of handwritten numerals. Pattern Recognition, 40, 1840 – 1854.

Konar, D., Bhattachrayya, S., Das, S., & Panigrahi, B. K. (2015). A quantum bi-directional self-organizing neural network (QBDSONN) for binary image denoising. *Proc. ICACCI*, 54-68. doi:10.1109/ICACCI.2015.7275780

Konar, D., Bhattachrayya, S., Panigrahi, B. K., & Nakamatsu, K. (2016). Quantum bidirectional self-organizing neural network (QBDSONN) architecture for binary object extraction from a noisy perspective. *Applied Soft Computing, 46*, 731–752. doi:10.1016/j.asoc.2015.12.040

Kundu, Y. H., & Chen, M. (2002). Alternatives to variable duration HMM in handwriting recognition. *IEEE Transactions on Pattern Analysis and Machine Intelligence, 20*(11), 1275–1280. doi:10.1109/34.730561

Li, C. P., & Li, S. Y. (2008). Learning algorithm and application of quantum BP neural networks based on universal quantum gates. *Journal of Systems Engineering and Electronics, 19*(1), 167–174. doi:10.1016/S1004-4132(08)60063-8

Matan, O. (1990). Handwritten Character Recognition Using Neural Network Architecture. *Proceedings of the 4th USPS Advanced Technology Conference*, 1003-1011.

Matsui, N., Takai, M., & Nishimura, H. (2000). A network model based onqubit-like neuroncorresponding to quantum circuit. *Inst. Electr. Inform. Commun. Jpn. (Part III: Fundam. Electr. Sci), 83*(10), 67–73.

Mcmohan, D. (2008). *Quantum Computing Explained*. Hoboken, NJ: John Wiley & Sons, Inc.

Mu, D., Guan, Z., & Zhang, H. (2013). Learning Algorithm and Application of Quantum Neural Networks with Quantum Weights. *IJCTE, 5*, 788–792. doi:10.7763/IJCTE.2013.V5.797

Mu, D., Guan, Z., & Zhang, H. (2013). *Learning Algorithm and Application of Quantum Neural Networks with Quantum Weights* (Vol. 5). IJCTE.

Nielson, M. A., & Chung, I. L. (2000). *Quantum computation and quantum information*. Cambridge University Press.

Perus, M., & Ecimovic, P. (1998). Memory and pattern recognition in associative neural networks. *International Journal of Applied Science and Computation, 4*, 283–310.

Perus, M., & Ecimovic, P. (1998). Memory and pattern recognition in associative neural networks. *International Journal of Applied Science and Computation, 4*, 283–310.

Pyllkkanen, P., & Pylkko, P. (1995). New directions in cognitive science. *Proc. the International Symposium*, 77-89.

Rahman, M., Akhand, M. A. H., Islam, S., & Shill, P. S. (2005). *Bangla Handwritten Character Recognition using Convolutional Neural Network*. I.J. Image, Graphics and Signal Processing.

Samadiani, N., & Hassanpour, H. (2005). *A neural network based approach for recognizing Multi-font printed English characters*. Academic Press.

Samadiani, N., & Hassanpour, H. (2015). *A neural network based approach for recognizing Multi font printed English characters*. Academic Press.

Shafee, F. (2007). Neural networks with quantum gated nodes. *Engineering Applications of Artificial Intelligence*, *20*(4), 429–437. doi:10.1016/j.engappai.2006.09.004

Shelke, S., & Shaila, A. (2011). A Multistage Handwritten Marathi Compound character recognition scheme using Neural Networks and Wavelet Features. *International Journal of Signal Processing, Image Processing and Pattern Recognition, 4*.

Shinde, A., & Kagalkar, R. (2015). Sign Language to Text and Vice Versa Recognition using Computer Vision in Marathi. *International Journal of Computers and Applications*, 23–28.

Shor, P. W. (1994). Algorithms for Quantum Computation: Discrete Logarithms and Factoring. *Proc. 35th Annual Symposium on the Foundation of Computer Science*, 20-22. doi:10.1109/SFCS.1994.365700

Sin, B.-K., & Ha, J.-Y. (1999). Network-Based Approach to Online Cursive Script Recognition. *IEEE Transactions on Systems, Man, and Cybernetics. Part B, Cybernetics*, *29*(2), 321–328. doi:10.1109/3477.752808 PMID:18252307

Tomoyuki, H., Takuma, A., & Bunpei, I. (2007). An analytic word recognition algorithm using a posteriori probability. *Proceedings of the 9th international conference on document analysis and recognition*, 2, 669–673.

Ventura, D., & Martinez, T. R. (2000). Quantum associative memory. *Information Science*, *124*(1-4), 237–296. doi:10.1016/S0020-0255(99)00101-2

Vijay Patil, V., & Shimpi, S. (2011). Handwritten English Character Recognition using Neural Network. *Journal of Elixir Comp. Sci. &Engg*, *41*, 5587–5591.

Yang, J., Yan, X., & Yao, B. (2012). Character Feature Extraction Method based on Integrated Neural Network. *AASRI Procedia*, *3*, 197–202. doi:10.1016/j.aasri.2012.11.033

# Chapter 9

# A Quantum NeuroIS Data Analytics Architecture for the Usability Evaluation of Learning Management Systems

**Raul Valverde**
*Concordia University, Canada*

**Beatriz Torres**
*University of Quebec in Outaouais, Canada*

**Hamed Motaghi**
*University of Quebec in Outaouais, Canada*

## ABSTRACT

*NeuroIS uses tools such as electroencephalogram (EEG) that can be used to measure high brainwave frequencies that can be linked to human anxiety. Past research showed that computer anxiety influences how users perceive ease of use of a learning management system (LMS). Although computer anxiety has been used successfully to evaluate the usability of LMS, the main data collection mechanisms proposed for its evaluation have been questionnaires. Questionnaires suffer from possible problems such as being inadequate to understand some forms of information such as emotions and honesty in the responses. Quantum-based approaches to consciousness have been very popular in the last years including the quantum model reduction in microtubules of Penrose and Hameroff (1995). The objective of the chapter is to propose an architecture based on a NeuroIS that collects data by using EEG from users and then use the collected data to perform analytics by using a quantum consciousness model proposed for computer anxiety measurements for the usability testing of a LMS.*

DOI: 10.4018/978-1-5225-5219-2.ch009

## INTRODUCTION

NeuroIS uses neurotechnology tools such as galvanic skin response (GSR) and Electroencephalogram (EEG) for research in Information Systems (IS) (Dimoka et al 2010). High brainwave frequencies can be linked to human anxiety and neurotechnology can be used to measure these frequencies (Valverde 2015). Past research showed that computer anxiety influences how users perceive ease of use of a learning management system (Saade & Kira 2009). Although computer anxiety has been used successfully to evaluate the usability of learning management systems, the main data collection mechanisms proposed for its evaluation has been questionnaires. Questionnaires suffer from possible problems such inadequate to understand some forms of information such as emotions, lacks validity, possible lack of thought and honesty in the responses (Ackroyd & Hughes 1981).

Learning management systems (LMS) are designed to facilitate the learning process and have been used in recent years extensively in Business Schools (Condon & Valverde 2014). However, it has been reported that as many as fifty percent of adults, including first-year University students, have some sort of computer-related phobia and previous studies have shown that computer anxiety influences how users perceive ease of use and computer self-efficacy an information system (Saade & Kira 2009). Much effort has been devoted to creating user friendly interfaces in resent years (Venkatesh & Morris, 2000) in particular with the use of NeuroIS (Dimoka et al 2010). Motivated by previous computer-anxiety studies and the lack of studies that incorporate data collection and analytical techniques using neuroscience that can better capture the perception of computer users for the purpose of usability evaluations, the objective of this study is to provide an understanding on how to use neuroscience techniques for data collection of the use of a LMS and provide the analytical tools that can process computer anxiety measurements for usability testing.

Quantum based approaches to consciousness have been very popular in the last years. Some of the approaches include the Quantum emission probabilities (Eccles, 1986), where the two-way mental-neural interaction (with the electric/magnetic fields as a link) is supposed to be realized in a manner analogous to probability fields in quantum Mechanics, the Photon-corticon interaction (Jibu & Yasue, 1995), where consciousness was reduced to the creation and annihilation dynamics of photons (as quanta of an electromagnetic field) and corticons (as quanta of a rotational field of water dipoles) and the quantum model reduction in microtubules (Hameroff, 1998;Penrose & Hameroff, 1995), where quantum coherence occurs by exciting quasicrystalline water molecules as dipoles buried in microtubules.

The objective of the chapter is to propose an architecture based on a NeuroIS that collects data by using neurotechnology from users and then use the collected data to perform analytics by using the quantum consciousness model proposed by Pop-

Jordanov & Pop-Jordanova (2010) for computer anxiety measurements that can be used for the usability testing of a learning management system. This model proposes a theoretical approach to explain the characteristic empirical interdependence between the states of arousal (representing the level of consciousness) and EEG activity.

As a NeuroIS does not use surveys for data collection and instead uses direct brain wave measurements from the user's brain, the proposed approach contributes to the literature by incorporating data collection techniques based on neuroscience that can better capture the perception of computer users and also propose a set of analytical tools by using a quantum based approach that can be used for the purpose of usability evaluations of LMS.

# LITERATURE REVIEW

## Quantum Neural Network

Quantum Neural Networks (QNNs) are models, systems or devices that combine features of quantum theory with the properties of neural networks. Neural networks (NNs) are models of interconnected units based on biological neurons feeding signals into one another. A large class of NNs uses binary McCulloch-Pitts neurons, thus reducing the complex process of signal transmission in neural cells to the two states 'active/resting'. The analogy with the two-level qubit serving as the basic unit in quantum computing gives an immediate connection between NN models and quantum theory. The majority of proposals for QNN models are consequently based on the idea of a qubit neuron (or 'quron' as we suggest to name it), and theoretically construct neurons as two-level quantum systems. Although close to discussions about the potential 'quantumness of the brain, QNNs do not intend to explain our brain functions in terms of quantum mechanics. Neurons are macroscopic objects with dynamics on the timescale of microseconds, and a quron's theoretically introduced two quantum states refer to a process involving millions of ions in a confined space, leading to estimated decoherence times in the order of $10-13$ sec and less, thus making quantum effects unlikely to play a role in neural information processing. However, QNNs promise to be very powerful computing devices. Their potential lies in the fact that they exploit the advantages of superposition-based quantum computing and parallel-processed neural computing at the same time. QNN research can furthermore be seen as a part of a growing interest of scientist and IT companies to develop quantum machine learning algorithms for efficient big data processing. Artificial neural networks thereby play an important role as intelligent computational methods for pattern recognition and learning (Schuld & Petruccione 2014).

Brain-computer interface (BCI) has been identified to function as an extra channel between brain and external environment to transmit information bypassing the spinal and peripheral neuromuscular systems and has also found applications in rehabilitation, neuroscience and cognitive psychology. Existing research in applications of BCI is composed of two main areas. For assistive technology, BCI makes it possible for people with motor disabilities to regain the interactions with external environment in order to improve the quality of their lives. The second area aims at training the subject to emit a specific brain activity. In this application, BCI is called as Neurofeedback (NFB), it becomes a therapy tool which helps subjects recover their cognitive function by consciously altering some features of their electroencephalographic (EEG) signals in order to stay in certain brain state. These features can be used to activate a certain action, including visual/ auditory representations. By continuous neurofeedback training humans can learn how to change their brain electrical activity in a desired direction. It can assist individuals with a variety of conditions and disabilities in which the brain is not working as well as it might be (Wang et al. 2007).

## Memory for Learning

Replication of the outstanding functions of the human brain in a computer, based on analysis and modeling of the essential functions of a biological neuron and its complicated networks has recently become an active research field. Several studies in this field have revealed successful developments of learning and memory which inspired by neural architectures in the brain. In general, from the engineering view, quantum mechanics (QM) has been developed as a theory to explain the fundamental principles of substance. QM provides several mathematical concepts, such as duality of waves and particles, complementarity, and nonlocality, to improve the comprehension of the microworld. From the biological perspective, on the other hand, it is hypothesized that QM is based on mesoscopic features in the physical and biological or physiological processes of the brain, and it has the potential to illustrate the dynamics of neurons in the human brain by the quantum information. In fact, in the internal structure of neuron in the brain, the presence of the two quantum states in tubulin, which are proteins of the size 4 nm×8 nm and having a 20-nm gap between the synapse, suggest that artificial neural networks would be handled as a descriptive subject from QM perspective. In other words, the QIC is expected to be possible to bring a new standpoint for cognitive process of brain from a biological viewpoint.

Memory Capacity is a significant factor for performance in associative memory. The memory capacity, in general, is responsive to the number of neurons, e.g., the memory capacity of model is directly affected by the magnitude of number of neurons. Moreover, the differences in number of neurons between layers is another significant factor for the performance of memory capacity. Therefore, in regards to memory capacity, the two types of conditions are considered; the constant

number of neurons being set in layers, and different number of neurons applied to layers. From the above-mentioned two conditions, it can be evaluated that the sensitivity of the memory capacity from the viewpoint number of neurons. Here, the layer 1 is assigned with desired information while others are assigned the random bipolar patterns as the initial conditions (Masuyama et. al 2017).

## The Early Quantum Model of Brain

In the quantum model, the brain elementary constituents are not the neurons and the other cells (which cannot be considered as quantum objects), but, in analogy with the QFT approach to living matter, they have been identified with the vibrational electric dipole field of the water molecules and other biomolecules present in the brain, and with the NG bosons (called the dipole wave quanta (dwq)) generated in the breakdown of the rotational symmetry of the electrical dipoles.

Memory printing is achieved under the action of external stimuli producing the breakdown of the continuous phase symmetry. In the quantum model of brain it is thus imported all the machinery of the spontaneous breakdown of symmetry introduced in the previous Section. The information storage function is thus represented by the coding of the ground state (the lowest energy state, or vacuum) through the coherent condensation of dwq collective modes. The memory capacity can be enormously enlarged by considering the intrinsic dissipative character of the brain dynamics: the brain is an open system continuously coupled to the environment. The dissipative quantum model seems to imply that the conscious identity emerges at any instant of time, in the present, as the minimum energy brain state which separates the past from the future, that point on the mirror of time where the conjugate images A and Ã join together. In the absence of such a mirroring there is neither consciousness of the past, nor its projection in the future: the suggestion is that consciousness does not arises solely from the subject (first person) inner activity,

without opening to the external world. In the dissipative quantum model the intrinsic dissipative character of the brain dynamics strongly points to consciousness as dialogue with the inseparable own Double (Vitiello 2003).

## Stochastic Neurodynamics

Stochastic dynamics of relative membrane potential in the neural network is investigated. It is called stochastic neurodynamics. The least action principle for stochastic neurodynamics is assumed, and used to derive the fundamental equation.

It is called a neural wave equation. A solution of the neural wave equation is called a neural wave function and describes stochastic neurodynamics completely. As a simple application of stochastic neurodynamics, a mathematical representation of static neurodynamics in terms of equilibrium statistical mechanics of spin system is derived (Yasue et. al. 1988).

## Quantum Neural Computing

A quantum neural computer is a single machine that reorganizes itself, in response to a stimulus, to perform a useful computation. Selectivity offered by such a reorganization appears to be at the basis of the gestal style of biological information processing. Clearly, a quantum neural computer is more versatile than the conventional computing machine.

Paradigm of science and technology draw on each other. Thus Newton's conception of the universe was based on the clockworks of the day; thermodynamics followed the heat engines of the 19th century; and computer followed the development of telegraph and telephone. From another point of view, modern computers are based on classical physics. Since classical physics has been superseded by quantum mechanics in the microworld and animal behavior of being seen in terms of information processing by neural networks, one might ask the question if a new paradigm of computing based on quantum mechanics and neural networks can be constructed. (Kak 1995)

We define a quantum neural computer as a strongly connectionist system that is nevertheless characterized by a wavefunction. In contrast to a quantum computer, which consists of quantum processes are supported. The neural network is a self-organizing type that becomes a different measuring system based on association triggered by an external or an internally generated stimulus. We consider some characteristics of a quantum neural computer and shoe that information is not a locally additive variable in such a computer (Kak 1995).

## Virtual Learning Environment

Virtual learning environments and quantum mechanics efforts have made possible the virtual learning environment StudentResearcher proposed by Pedersen et al. (2016) for the learning of Quantum mechanics. Learning management systems (LMS) are designed to facilitate the learning process and have been used during many years in the academic environment (Condon & Valverde 2014). It has been reported that as many as fifty percent of adults have some sort of computer-related phobia (Saade & Kira 2009). Past research shows that computer anxiety influences how users perceive ease of use of an information system. Saade & Kira (2009) identified several variables of computer self-efficacy and computer anxieties. Self-efficacy is determined by levels of anxiety such that reduced anxiety and increased experience improves performance indirectly by increasing levels of self-efficacy (Saade & Kira 2009). Saade & Kira (2009) investigated the influence of computer anxiety on perceived ease of use and the mediating effect of computer self-efficacy on this relationship, within an e-learning context.

Although Saade & Kira (2009) contributed with computer anxiety effect in computer systems usability, the studied relied mainly in a survey methodology approach. Ackroyd and Hughes (1981) acknowledge some of the main disadvantages of surveys as:

- Is argued to be inadequate to understand some forms of information - i.e. changes of emotions, behaviour, feelings etc.
- Lacks validity.
- There is no way to tell how truthful a respondent is being.
- There is no way of telling how much thought a respondent has put in.
- The respondent may be forgetful or not thinking within the full context of the situation.
- People may read differently into each question and therefore reply based on their own interpretation of the question - i.e. what is 'good' to someone may be 'poor' to someone else, therefore there is a level of subjectivity that is not acknowledged.
- There is a level of researcher imposition, meaning that when developing the questionnaire, the researcher is making their own decisions and assumptions as to what is and is not important...therefore they may be missing something that is of importance.

Given the arguments of Ackroyd and Hughes (1981), surveys might not be the best way to measure levels of anxiety among computer users. Although computer anxiety has been proven as effective in the measurement of computer usability, biofeedback and neuro biofeedback might have better solutions to measure computer anxiety. Demoka et al (2010) highlighted the potential of cognitive neuroscience for IS research in particular for the domain of human-computer interaction (HCI).

Biofeedback and neuro biofeedback instruments measure muscle activity, skin temperature, electro-dermal activity (sweat gland activity), respiration, heart rate, heart rate variability, blood pressure, brain electrical activity and blood flow. These technologies are able to capture analog electrical signals from the body and translate those signals into meaningful information through complex algorithmic software that a technician can then decipher. Biofeedback is also used by computer scientists in order to build human computer interactions (Valverde, 2011).

Bioofeedback has been applied in the field of psychology for the measurement of anxiety. (Valverde 2015). Biofeedback uses sensors to monitor physiological relaxation indicators, like skin temperature and muscle tension. It expands classical biofeedback by using galvanic skin response (GSR) together with modern computer technology to detect the response of the built-mind-spirit body to a large array of stress indicators (Valverde 2015). Galvanic skin response is one measurable quantity generated involuntarily by the body. It's well known as the basis for the polygraph, or lie detector. The theory behind is that a user sweats more when stressed, and that telling a lie is stressful (Valverde 2011).

The brain and muscles generate small electrical signals that can be picked up by electrodes strapped to the body (Valverde 2011). Neuro biofeedback is based on electroencephalographic (EEG) measurements taken from the frontal cortex of the brain. This EEG information is presented to the user who then tries to consciously change their internal reactions to modify their brainwave state (Valverde 2015). Our brain works primarily with bioelectrical energy. Although the power of electricity that handles our neurons is low (measured in mill volts), this power processes, manage, distribute and use vast amounts of information and generates multiple answers (almost infinite in possibilities). So by using micro electricity, we can conclude that the brain is a machine of low frequencies. The first types of brain frequencies that were discovered were the "alpha" and "theta". Later, these findings were complemented by research in the range frequencies captured by the electroencephalograph (Valverde 2015). Each type of wave results in a different neuropsychological state. That is, our mind, our body and our physical and physiological activity are completely different in each of these states or frequencies. The most common consciousness are wakefulness and sleep; however, changes in expressing both cerebral and psycho states change according to conscious or subconscious feelings of each person are distinguished. These changes are directly related to the electrical activity of the brain. This activity can be measured by the number of oscillations per second (Hz) that are linked to different states of consciousness in the brain: our brain only perceives a limited range of frequencies indispensable to operate with ease in this three-dimensional medium. 20 to 20,000 vibrations per second are perceptible by our ears, the colors perceived by our eyes range from red to violet (although extending beyond, up and down), all possible smells and tastes (which are also vibrations) and the endless textures that we can distinguish with our skin. But the brain is not only receiver but also is sends vibrations. It has been proven thanks to the EEG that the brain emits waves of varying intensity and frequency depending on the mental state of the person being observed (Valverde 2015). These waves are classified according to table 1.

As table 1 indicates, beta brain waves can be associated with stress and anxiety while alpha waves are associated with calmness and relaxation.

*Table 1. Types of Brainwaves (Valverde 2015).*

| Types of Brain Waves | States of Consciousness |
|---|---|
| BETA WAVES: 14 Hz to 30 Hz | This type of waves is recorded when the person is awake in a state of normal activity. Correspond to states of conscious attention, anxiety, surprise, fear, stress. |
| GAMMA WAVES: 25 and 100 Hz | They express pathological conditions of maximum tension, excitement and the individual enters a state of STRESS in which the coordination of ideas and normal physical activity are seriously altered. |
| ALPHA WAVES: 8 Hz to 13 Hz | Relaxation and rest, calm, reflective state. Reduction of bodily sensations. The subconscious begins to emerge: Abstraction, suggestibility. Assimilation of the study. Ease of visualization of mental images. |
| THETA WAVES: 3.5 Hz to 7 Hz | During sleep or in deep meditation, autogenous training, hypnosis, yoga (whenever the formations of the subconscious act). The state stimulates creative inspiration. Considered a state for maximum capacity of learning. Fantasy, imagination. Hypnagogic images. |
| DELTA WAVES: 1 Hz to 3 Hz | It arises mainly in the states of deep sleep and unconsciousness. Very rarely can be experienced being awake unless with a very hard training (Yoga, Meditation, Zen, Hypnosis, Self-hypnosis) or with a synchronizer of hemispheres. It corresponds to deep sleep, hypnotic trance, REM sleep. It corresponds to sleep without dream, trance, deep hypnosis. Delta waves are very important in the healing process and strengthening the immune system. |

## NeuroIS

During the past decade, increasingly more scholars from the social and economic sciences and from computer science have started to use methods and tools from Neuroscience. This development is expected to result in a better theoretical understanding of human behavior such as decision making. Moreover, using Neuroscience methods and tools may contribute to the design and development of innovative information systems as demonstrated. (Hevner 2014).

Physiological reactions of humans in IS contexts (e.g., human interaction with computers) are usually measured by sensors placed on the body surface, even though the bodily reaction actually occurs "in" the body. The unit of signal frequency used is Hertz (Hz). The HZ is equivalent to cycles per second (Riedl, Davis, & Hevner, 2014).

Over the past decade, many scholars from various disciplines of social, economic science, computer science have started to pay particular attention to methods used and tools in neuroscience, to measure and conduct research in their respective fields (Riedl, Davis, & Hevner, 2014). In this vein, scholars in the field of Information Systems, have also incorporated on how to incorporate the neuroscience tools and measurement methods, in order to understand the human behavior by directly getting the results from the brain of human body.

Scholars in Information Systems have introduced the concept of NeuroIS into the IS literature (Dimoka et al., 2010; Dimoka, Pavlou, & Davis, 2007). The base of this concept of NeuroIS is to use neuroscience and neurophysiological methods, tools and theories to better understand, design, develop, and use of information communication technologies (ICT) in the society (Riedl et al., 2014).

Traditionally, IS researchers conduct data collection from various means and methods, notably from surveys, lab experiments, interviews, secondary data collection, ethnography, and many more methods (Dimoka et al., 2010; Dimoka et al., 2007). Considering that these methods of data collection are indeed useful, and have contributed importantly on the advancement of this field (IS research), asking directly the brain, and not the person opens an entirely new era of data collections, which is not biased, interpreted, and does not interfere with the subjectivity of human being. In other words, these methods, by means of directly asking the brain (data directly collected), tools offer unbiased measurements of decision-making, cognitive, emotional and social processes (Dimoka et al., 2010; Dimoka et al., 2007).

Moreover, one of the keys figures of neurological data collection is the advantage of continuous real-time measurement that allows collecting data continuously (Dimoka et al., 2010). In addition, this type of data collection, enables a level of precision, on a given period of time, permitting powerful time-series analysis and comparison (Loos et al., 2010). Applications of these types of data collection have been tested and conducted on various processes, for example on decision-making processes, understanding emotional processes (by capturing pleasure, enjoyment, displeasure, happiness, sadness, anxiety, sadness, disgust and etc.), understanding social processes (by capturing series of feelings, such as trust/distrust, cooperation/competition and etc.) and many more.

There are numerous opportunities provided by NeuroIS tools and its measurements in IS. According to Dimoka et al., (2010), these opportunities are illustrated as of the followings: 1) localize the various brain areas associated with IS constructs (neural correlates of IS constructs) and link them to the cognitive neuroscience literature to map IS constructs into specific brain areas, learn about the functionality of these brain areas, and better understand the nature and dimentionality of IS constructs. 2) Capture hidden (automatic and unconscious) mental processes (e.g. habits, ethics, deep emotions) that are difficult or even impossible to measure with existing measurement methods and tools. 3) Complement existing source of data with brain imaging data that can provide objective responses that are not subject to measurement biases (e.g., subjectivity bias, social desirability bias, common method bias). 4) Identify antecedents of IS constructs by examining how brain areas are activated in response to IT stimuli (e.g., designs, systems, websites) that intend to enhance certain outcomes (use behaviours, productivity). 5) Test consequences of IS constructs by showing whether, how, and why brain activation that is associated with certain IS constructs can predict certain behaviours (e.g., system use, online purchasing). 6) Infer causal relationships among IS constructs by examining the temporal order of brain activations (timing of brain activity) stimulated by common IT stimulus that activates two or more IS constructs. 7) Challenge IS assumptions by identifying differences between existing IS relationships and the brain's underlying functionality, thus helping to build IS theories that correspond to the brain's functionality.

There are numerous tools in NeuroIS which enable to the point measurements. These tools, according to Dimoka et al. (Dimoka et al., 2010; Riedl et al., 2014) are categorized under neurophysiological tools and focus measurement tools. The examples are these tools are Eye Tracking, Skin Conductance Response (SCR), Facial Electromyography (eEMG), Electrocardiogram (EKG), Functional Magnetic Resonance Imaging (fMRI), Positron Emission Tomography (PET), and many more (Dimoka et al., 2010). As mentioned above, there are various advantageous of using these devices in order to conduct the research directly from the brain (body) of human. However, these devices are very expensive, and require extensive laboratory settings. Moreover, these experiments are conducted in artificial settings, and scholars might have validity concerns about whether neurophysiological data captured are the construct that they are intended to measure (Dimoka et al., 2010; Dimoka et al., 2007).

## The Pop-Jordanov and Pop-Jordanova Quantum Consciousness Model

In the quantum approach to consciousness model, the brain elementary constituents are not the neurons and the other cells (which cannot be considered as quantum objects), but, in analogy with the quantum field theory approach to living matter (Del Giudice et al. 1985), they have been identified (Jibu & Yasue, 1995) with the vibrational electric dipole field of the water molecules and other biomolecules present in the brain, and with the NG bosons (called the dipole wave quanta) generated in the breakdown of the rotational symmetry of the electrical dipoles.

The description of the observed non-locality of brain functions, especially of memory storing and recalling, was the main goal of the quantum brain model proposed in the 1967 by Ricciardi and Umezawa (Ricciardi and Umezawa 1967). This model is based on the Quantum Field Theory of many body systems and its main ingredient is the mechanism of spontaneous breakdown of symmetry. Spontaneous symmetry breaking is a spontaneous process of symmetry breaking, by which a physical system in a symmetrical state ends up in an asymmetrical state.

In Quantum Field Theory the spontaneous breakdown of symmetry occurs when the dynamical equations are invariant under some group, say G, of continuous transformations, but the minimum energy state (the ground state or vacuum) of the system is not invariant under the full group G. When this occurs, the vacuum is an ordered state and massless particles (the Nambu-Goldstone bosons (NG) also called collective modes) propagating over the whole system are dynamically generated and are the carriers of the ordering information (long range correlations): order manifests itself as a global, macroscopic property which is dynamically generated at the microscopic quantum level (Vitiello 2003).

According to the model, memory recording is achieved under the action of external stimuli producing the breakdown of the continuous phase symmetry. In the quantum model of brain, it is thus imported all the machinery of the spontaneous breakdown of symmetry. The information storage function is thus represented by the coding of the ground state (the lowest energy state, or vacuum) through the coherent condensation of dipole wave quanta collective modes (Stuart et al. 1978). The non-locality of the memory is therefore derived as a dynamical feature rather than as a property of specific neural circuits, which would be critically damaged by destructive actions or by single neuron death or deficiency.

According to Pop-Jordanov & Pop-Jordanova (2010), based on their initial assumptions, the present quantum approaches to consciousness can be separated into four groups:

- Quantum emission probabilities (Eccles, 1986), where the two-way mental-neural interaction (with the electric/magnetic fields as a link) is supposed to be realized in a manner analogous to probability fields in quantum mechanics.
- Photon-corticon interaction (Jibu & Yasue, 1995), where consciousness was reduced to the creation and annihilation dynamics of photons (as quanta of an electromagnetic field) and corticons (as quanta of a rotational field of water dipoles) mechanics.
- Objective reduction in microtubules (Hameroff, 1998; Penrose & Hameroff, 1995), where quantum coherence occurs by exciting quasicrystalline water molecules as dipoles buried in microtubules.
- Virtual photons (Romijn, 2002), where the fleeting patterns of electric and magnetic fields, substituted by virtual photons, encode for conscious experiences.

Reviewing these approaches it can be inferred that, although being mainly conceptual and lacking numerical results, practically all of them have identified electric field and cortical dipoles as crucial elements of neural-mental correlation. With this in mind, the Pop-Jordanov and Pop-Jordanova Quantum Consciousness Model (2010) applies a field-dipole approach as a starting assumption.

## Quantum Transitions Model

The transitions between the states of dipole water molecules as quantum rotators interacting with the time-dependent electric field have been studied recently, both analytically and numerically (Pop-Jordanov & Pop-Jordanova 2010). The corresponding nonstationary Schrödinger equation is not solvable analytically and it is too complicated for abinitio numerical calculation. Applying the adiabatic approach from the theory of atomic collisions, Pop-Jordanov & Pop-Jordanova (2010) proposes the solution in the following form:

$$\psi\left(\hat{d},t\right) = \varphi_a\left(\hat{d}, F\left(wt\right)\right) e^{-\frac{i}{h}\int\limits^{t} E_\alpha\left(F(wt)\right)dt}.$$

Where F is the electric field, $\hat{d}$. is the direction of direction of the dipole vector, while $\varphi_a$. are the eigenfunctions of the stationary Schrödinger equation. Adiabatic approximation requires the signal frequency to be much less than rotational frequency W rot$=10^{13}$ Hz, which is obviously fulfilled in the case of EEG frequency (Pop-Jordanov & Pop-Jordanova 2010). The periodic variation of the electric field F = F0 sin(t) leads to transitions with exponential probabilities as indicated in the formula below:

$$P_{ab} = e^{\frac{2C_{ab}F0}{F0w}}.$$

Where $a$ and $b$ are sets of quantum numbers specifying the initial and the final state of the system, while $Cab$ is a parameter that depends on physical characteristics of the system (magnitude of the dipole and its moment of inertia). Thus, the probability of transition from one to another quantum energy state appears to be independent of the amplitude of the periodic external field, i.e., this mechanism is related to transition of information content rather than energy (Pop-Jordanov & Pop-Jordanova 2010).

the case of a system of N dipoles, each energy level splits into N sublevels (because of interaction between di-poles) with the distance between sublevels being approximately N-times smaller. Hence, the probability of transitions for such a system is (Pop-Jordanov P-Jordanova 2010).

$$P_{ab} = e^{\frac{2C_{ab}}{Nw}}.$$

## The Correlation of the Quantum Transitions With Consciousness Level

Examine the eventual correlation of the transition probability $P_{ab}$ with e probability of mental/neural excitations related to consciousness level (arousal), it is of interest to analyze the variation of $P_{ab}$ with the spectral variable $f = w/2\pi$ for a neuron with $N = 10^{12}$ dipole molecules. This indicates that the arousal sensitivity to EEG frequency may be correlated to the transition probability variation for a system of quantum dipoles in the cortical electric field. The obtained theoretical result, suggesting the correlation of consciousness level with quantum transition probabilities, seems to be reasonable, since wakefulness can be conceived as a general activation, tonic state, and non-focused readiness to change the state, here identified as the probability of transitions between quantum states (Pop-Jordanov & Pop-Jordanova, 2009).

The basic dependence of mental arousal on EEG frequency, established empirically by Pop-Jordanov & Pop-Jordanova, (2005), is summarized in Figure 1 and establishes the level of consciousness that ranges from deep sleep, drowsy, relax, alert, anxiety and peak performance.

A possible objection could be that mental acts cannot be reduced to one neuron. However, since only synchronized neurons of neuronal assemblies contribute to EEG, the relevant frequency is just the one-neuron (representative) frequency we

*Figure 1. Mental arousal (Pop-Jordanov & Pop-Jordanova 2005)*

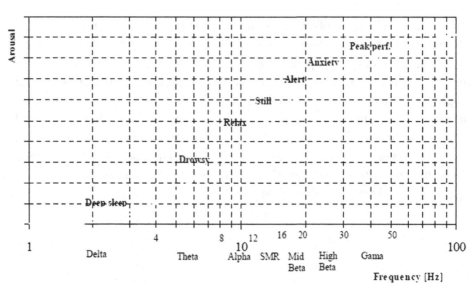

are dealing with, when considering the consciousness level. The obtained formula connecting arousal (*A*) and field frequency (*f*) may be rewritten in the form:

$$P_{ab} = A = 2^{-\frac{f_e}{f}}$$

Where the equilibrium frequency $f_e$ actually corresponds to the dominant frequency with eyes closed, known to be age dependent – ranging from around 6 Hz to around 10 Hz, for children and adults, respectively (Thompson & Thompson, 2003).

The variable *f*, related to the dominant frequency band, can be identified as a spectrum weighted mean frequency(Pop-Jordanov & Pop-Jordanova, 2005). Characterizing the EEG spectrum, it may serve as a quantitative indicator of the general brain activation, and it is term as "brainrate" (in analogue to e.g. heart-rate). As such, it can contribute to the gross, initial assessment, not substituting the subtle, differential investigations of disorders corresponding to the same general level of arousal.

Being defined as the mean frequency of brain oscillations weighted over the all bands of the EEG potential (or power) spectrum, the brain-rate (*fb*) may be calculated as:

$$\cdot f_b = \sum_i f_i P_i = \sum_i f_i \frac{V_i}{V}$$

With

$$V = \sum_i V_i$$

where the index *i* denotes the frequency band (for delta $i = 1$, for theta $i = 2$, etc.) and *Vi* is the corresponding mean amplitude of the electric potential. Following the standard five-band classification, one has $f_i = 2, 6, 10, 14$ and 18, respectively.

## Quantitative Electroencephalography

EEG technology generates raw data, this data can be broken into different frequencies (alpha, theta, etc) by using Fourier analysis. The Fourier analysis decomposes the EEG time series into a voltage by frequency spectral graph commonly called the "power spectrum", with power being the square of the EEG magnitude, and magnitude being the integral average of the amplitude of the EEG signal, measured from(+) peak-to-(-)peak), across the time sampled, or epoch. The epoch length determines the frequency resolution of the Fourier, with a 1-second epoch providing a 1 Hz resolution (plus/minus 0.5 Hz resolution), and a 4-second epoch providing ¼ Hz, or plus/minus 0.125 Hz resolution (Kececi & Degirmenci 2008). The Fourier equation to transform time dependent raw date can be defined by the equation below:

$$X\left(f\right) = \int_{-\infty}^{\infty} x\left(t\right) e^{-i2\pi ft} dt$$

## ARCHITECTURE

The proposed architecture is mainly to support usability testing for a selected learning management system. Usability testing helps to determine how people use systems and where they may encounter difficulty of use (Valverde 2011).

Dumas and Redish (1999) identify five tasks must be completed for a usability test:

1. Define goals and concerns.
2. Determine who your test participants are.
3. Select, organize, and create test scenarios.
4. Determine to measure usability.
5. Prepare test materials.

In the first step of a usability test, goals are identified from the task analysis and quantitative usability goals for the LMS used for the study. For the second step, a sample of user should be selected. In the third step, test scenarios should be designed to detect potential usability problems. Test scenarios are normally prepared based on the HCI designer's experiences on what the user will do with the product (Valverde 2011).

Test scenarios should identity the activities to perform the tasks. The test case should number each task to complete it and provide and a description for each task that is clear enough for the user to perform it. Each task should show the time it will take and the high-level instructions and procedures required to complete the task (Valverde 2011).

The fourth step of defining usability tests requires determining usability measures performance and subjective measures. Performance measures are quantitative measures of specific actions and behaviours that are observed during the test. The subjects performing the usability test will be wearing a EEG device as indicate in figure 2 in order to measure computer anxiety. The Quantum NeuroIS acquires de EEG signal and applies a Fourier analysis in order to brake the data into different frequencies (alpha, theta, etc) (figure 2). The different levels of power of the different frequencies is used to calculate a bit rate that is related to the dominant frequency band in the brain as an indicator of the main level of consciousness (Pop-Jordanov & Pop-Jordanova, 2005). The quantum level of arousal sensitivity is calculated based on the bit rate, this level of arousal is correlated to the consciousness level given its quantum transition probabilities (Pop-Jordanov & Pop-Jordanova, 2009). The brain rate and arousal level are used to establish a particular level of consciousness (deep sleep, drowsy, relax, alert, anxiety and peak performance) as indicated in figure 1.

The time taken to perform each task and task will be recorded as part of the usability test with a video camera that is part of the NeuroIS. This will help the researcher to log each time a user exhibits a certain behaviour during the test, like expressing frustration with a criterion for performance measures (Valverde 2011). The task time and actions are linked to a particular level of consciousness calculated by the NeuroIS and recorded in a permanent storage for further analysis (figure 2).

The collected data from the NeuroIS are a video that records the different activities required to complete a set of tasks associated with a consciousness level that is intended to measure Computer Anxiety. It is expected that there is a linear relation between Computer Anxiety and Ease of Use and Computer Anxiety and Computer Self-Efficacy. The NeuroIS can produce two regression models with the collected data. The first regression will have Ease of Use as a dependent variable and Computer Anxiety as the independent variable. The model can be prepared with the Computer Anxiety measurements in terms of the different level of consciousness. The Ease of Use data that will be used for the regression model will be the log for the behaviour during the test with a four-point scale that evaluates the task from positive to negative ease of use (figure 2).

A second regression model will be produced with Computer Self-Efficacy (CSE) as dependent variable and Computer Anxiety as the independent variable. The CSE data will be computed by calculating the difference between the time taken to perform a task and the expected time to complete the task for each test. A lower CSE factor means a more efficient task while a higher factor means a less efficient task (figure 2).

Figure 3 shows a prototype of the Quantum NeuroIS, the figure shows an image capturing the video recording of the user interacting with the LMS at a particular time on the top right. The first graph on the top displays the raw data collected from the EEG by displaying amplitude in time. The second graph is displaying the Power Spectrum of the raw data signal displaying the concentration of power over the different frequencies, the graph at the bottom displays the Gamma, Beta, Alpha, Theta and Delta signals that are the result of the Fourier analysis.

*Figure 2. Quantum NeuroIS data analytics architecture*

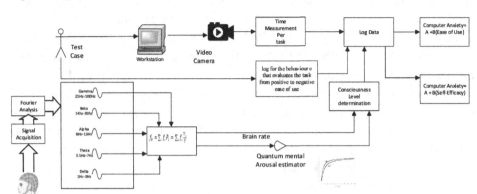

*Figure 3. Quantum NeuroIS Prototype*

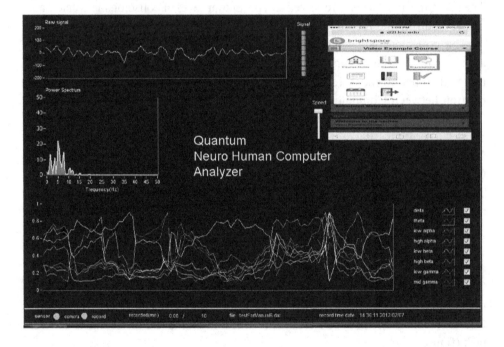

## Test Results

A test was conducted with the prototype, an online course given at Concordia University in Introduction to Information Technology was used for the pilot test. Five users followed a usability test protocol for usability for about 15 minutes by using an EEG device and raw data was recorded for all the sessions. Raw data was used to calculate dominant frequencies and arousal rates and videos were recorded for the sessions. The average of these results for the five students are given in Figure 4 and 5.

Figure 4 shows that dominant frequencies ranges from 18 Hz (Beta state) to 2 Hz (Delta state). It seems that some parts of the course caused stress and there were jumps of frequencies that go from very calm to stress. Videos need to be examined and change of frequencies would help to detect the areas that cause stress to users.

Figure 5 shows arousal rates. Arousal rates go from 0 to 1. A sudden jump in the arousal indicates a sudden change of state of consciousness that can indicate problems of with the usability. Videos would need to be examined in order to detect the tasks that generated sudden changes of states as possible indication of problems with usability.

## CONCLUSION

The proposed NeuroIS is based on a quantum approach to measure consciousness proposed by Pop-Jordanov & Pop-Jordanova (2010), this model captures the levels of anxiety of the user from very relaxed to very stressed. An architecture with the different required components for the NeuroIS and the mathematics to make it work were identified. A software prototype with a possible interface was developed in order to show the feasibility of this architecture. A test with five students was performed in order to show the feasibility of the architecture and use in detecting problems with usability. The NeuroIS provides a tool for the measurement of computer anxiety can help to improve the usability of an LMS. The main advantage of the NeuroIS is that it does not use surveys for data collection and instead uses direct

*Figure 4. Dominant frequency*

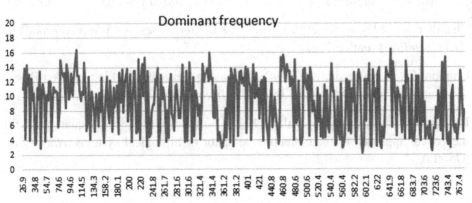

*Figure 5. Arousal*

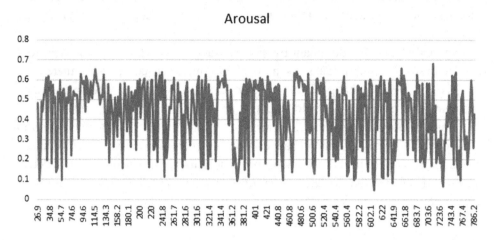

brain wave measurements from the user's brain. Future research should focus on the development of a software based on the proposed architecture for the validation of this design including the implementation of different usability tests for several LMS. In general, the research shows the potential of quantum consciousness research in the development of computer evaluation systems, quantum consciousness models can not only measure state of consciousness but also mental arousals that can detect changes of these states of consciousness. This type of models could have many other applications including NeuroIS for marketing and financial applications and any type of application that can benefit the with the measurement of consciousness and anxiety levels.

## REFERENCES

Ackroyd, S., & Hughes, J. A. (1981). *Data Collection in Context*. Longman.

Chandler, K., & Hyatt, K. (2002). *Customer-Centered Design: A New Approach to Web Usability*. Prentice-Hall.

Condon, C., & Valverde, R. (2014). Increasing Critical Thinking in Web-Based Graduate Management Courses. *Journal of Information Technology Education*, 13.

Del Giudice, E., Doglia, S., Milani, M., & Vitiello, G. (1985). A quantum field theoretical approach to the collective behavior of biological systems. *Nucl Phys*, 375-400.

Dimoka, A., Banker, R. D., Benbasat, I., Davis, F. D., Dennis, A. R., Gefen, D., & Pavlou, P. A. (2010). On the use of neurophysiological tools in IS research: Developing a research agenda for NeuroIS. *Management Information Systems Quarterly*, *36*(3), 679–702.

Dimoka, A., Pavlou, P. A., & Davis, F. D. (2007). Neuro-IS: The potential of cognitive neuroscience for information systems research. *Proceedings of the 28th International Conference on Information Systems*.

Dimoka, A., Pavlou, P. A., & Davis, F. D. (2011). Research commentary-NeuroIS: The potential of cognitive neuroscience for information systems research. *Information Systems Research*, *22*(4), 687–702. doi:10.1287/isre.1100.0284

Dumas, J. S., & Redish, J. C. (1999). *A Practical Guide to Usability Testing*. Portland, OR: Intellect Books.

Eccles, J. C. (1986). Do mental events cause neural events analogously to the probability fields of quantum mechanics? *Proceedings of the Royal Society of London. Series B, Biological Sciences*, *227*(1249), 411–428. doi:10.1098/rspb.1986.0031 PMID:2873576

Hameroff, S. (1998). *Quantum computation in brain microtubules? The Penrose-Hameroff'Orch OR'model of consciousness*. Philosophical Transactions-Royal Society of London Series A Mathematical Physical and Engineering Sciences.

Jibu, M., & Yasue, K. (1995). Quantum brain dynamics: An introduction. Amsterdam: John Benjamins.

Kak, S. (1995). On quantum neural computing. *Information Sciences*, *83*(3-4), 143–160. doi:10.1016/0020-0255(94)00095-S

Kalbach, J. (2007). *Designing Web Navigation*. O'Reilly Publications.

Kececi, H., & Degirmenci, Y. (2008). Quantitative EEG and cognitive evoked potentials in anemia. *Neurophysiologie Clinique. Clinical Neurophysiology*, *38*(2), 137–143. doi:10.1016/j.neucli.2008.01.004 PMID:18423335

Loos, P., Riedl, R., Müller-Putz, G. R., Vom Brocke, J., Davis, F. D., Banker, R. D., & Léger, P.-M. (2010). NeuroIS: Neuroscientific approaches in the investigation and development of information systems. *Business & Information Systems Engineering*, *2*(6), 395–401. doi:10.1007/s12599-010-0130-8

Masuyama, N., Loo, C. K., Seera, M., & Kubota, N. (2017). Quantum-Inspired Multidirectional Associative Memory With a Self-Convergent Iterative Learning. *IEEE Transactions on Neural Networks and Learning Systems*, 1–11. doi:10.1109/TNNLS.2017.2653114 PMID:28182559

Pedersen, M. K., Skyum, B., Heck, R., Müller, R., Bason, M., Lieberoth, A., & Sherson, J. F. (2016). Virtual learning environment for interactive engagement with advanced quantum mechanics. *Physical Review Physics Education Research*, *12*(1), 013102. doi:10.1103/PhysRevPhysEducRes.12.013102

Pop-Jordanov, J., & Pop-Jordanova, N. (2010). Quantum transition probabilities and the level of consciousness. *Journal of Psychophysiology*, *24*(2), 136–140. doi:10.1027/0269-8803/a000025

Pop-Jordanova, N., & Pop-Jordanov, J. (2005). Spectrum-weighted EEG frequency ("brain-rate") as a quantitative indicator of mental arousal. *Prilozi Makedonska Akademija na Naukite i Umetnostite*, *26*(2), 35–42. PMID:16400227

Popper, K. (2004). The Logic of Scientific Discovery (2nd ed.). Routledge, Taylor & Francis. (originally published 1959)

Ricciardi, L. M., & Umezawa, H. (1967). Brain physics and many-body problems. *Kibernetik*, *4*(2), 44–48. doi:10.1007/BF00292170 PMID:5617419

Riedl, R., Davis, F. D., & Hevner, A. R. (2014). Towards a NeuroIS research methodology: Intensifying the discussion on methods, tools, and measurement. *Journal of the Association for Information Systems*, *15*(10), I.

Saadé, R. G., & Kira, D. (2009). Computer anxiety in e-learning: The effect of computer self-efficacy. *Journal of Information Technology Education*, *8*(1), 177–191. doi:10.28945/166

Schuld, M., & Petruccione, F. (2014). *The quest for a Quantum Neural Network*. QNN Research.

Schuld, M., Sinayskiy, I., & Petruccione, F. (2014). The quest for a quantum neural network. *Quantum Information Processing*, *13*(11), 2567–2586. doi:10.1007/s11128-014-0809-8

Stuart, C. I. J., Takahashi, Y., & Umezawa, H. (1978). On the stability and non-local properties of memory. *Journal of Theoretical Biology*, *71*(4), 605–618. doi:10.1016/0022-5193(78)90327-2 PMID:661325

Thompson, M., & Thompson, L. (2003). *The neurofeedback book: An introduction to basic concepts in applied psycho-physiology.* Wheat Ridge, CO: Association for Applied Psychophysiology & Biofeedback.

Valverde, R. (2011). *Principles of Human Computer Interaction Design: HCI Design.* LAP Lambert Academic Publishing.

Valverde, R. (2015). Neurotechnology as a Tool for Inducing and Measuring Altered States of Consciousness in Transpersonal Psychotherapy. *NeuroQuantology: An Interdisciplinary Journal of Neuroscience and Quantum Physics, 13*(4). doi:10.14704/nq.2015.13.4.870

Venkatesh, V., & Davis, F. D. (2000). A theoretical extension of the technology acceptance model: Four longitudinal field studies. *Management Science, 46*(2), 186–204. doi:10.1287/mnsc.46.2.186.11926

Vitiello, G. (2003). Quantum dissipation and information: A route to consciousness modeling. *NeuroQuantology: An Interdisciplinary Journal of Neuroscience and Quantum Physics, 1*(2).

Wang, J., Yan, N., Liu, H., Liu, M., & Tai, C. (2007). Brain-computer interfaces based on attention and complex mental tasks. *Digital Human Modeling,* 467-473.

Yasue, K., Jibu, M., Misawa, T., & Zambrini, J. C. (1988). Stochastic neurodynamics. *Annals of the Institute of Statistical Mathematics, 40*(1), 41–59. doi:10.1007/BF00053954

# Compilation of References

Abraham, Nath, & Mahanti. (2011). Hybrid intelligent systems for stock market analysis. In *Computational science*. Springer-Verlag.

Ackroyd, S., & Hughes, J. A. (1981). *Data Collection in Context*. Longman.

Alattar, A. M. (2003). Reversible Watermark Using Difference Expansion of Triplets. *Proc. of the International Conference on Image Processing, (ICIP 2003)*, 501-504. doi:10.1109/ICIP.2003.1247008

Alattar, A. M. (2004). Reversible Watermark Using Difference Expansion of Quads. *Proceedings of the IEEE International Conference on Acoustics, Speech, and Signal Processing, 3*, 377–380.

Ali, R. (2017). Quantum Computing in Big Data, Computer and Information Technology (CIT). *IEEE International Conference*. Doi:10.1109/CIT.2016.79

Al-Nabhani, Jalab, Wahid, & Noor. (2015). Robust watermarking algorithm for digital images using discrete wavelet and probabilistic neural network. *Journal of King Saud University – Computer and Information Sciences, 27*, 393-401.

Alonso-Weber, J. M., Sesmero, M. P., & Sanchis, A. (2014). Combining additive input noise annealing and pattern transformations for improved handwritten character recognition. Elsevier.

Al-Rabadi, A. N. (2004). New classes of Kronecker-based reversible decision trees and their group-theoretic representation. *Proceedings of the International Workshop on Spectral Methods and Multirate Signal Processing (SMMSP)*, 233–243.

Alves de Lima, D., & Correa Victorino, A. (2016). A hybrid controller for vision-based navigation of autonomous vehicles in urban environments. *IEEE Transactions on Intelligent Transportation Systems, 17*(8), 2310–2323. doi:10.1109/TITS.2016.2519329

Amelio, A., & Pizzuti, C. (2013). A Genetic Algorithm for Color Image Segmentation. In A. I. Esparcia-Alc'azar (Eds.), *EvoApplications, LNCS 7835* (pp. 314–323). Verlag Berlin Heidelberg. doi:10.1007/978-3-642-37192-9_32

Anh, N. T. L., Kim, S. H., Yang, H. J., & Lee, G. S. (2013). Color Image Segmentation using Morphological Gradient based Active Contour Model. *International Journal of Innovative Computing, Information, & Control, 9*(11), 4471–7784.

Araujo, Oliveira, & Meira. (2012). *A Hybrid Model for S&P500 Index Forecasting*. Springer Berlin Heidelberg.

Araujo, T., Nedjah, N., & Mourelle, L. (2008). Quantum-Inspired Evolutionary State Assignment for Synchronous Finite State Machines. *Journal of Universal Computer Science, 14*(15), 2532–2548.

Arumugadevi, S., & Seenivasagam, V. (2016). Color Image Segmentation Using Feedforward Neural Networks with FCM. *International Journal of Automation and Computing, 13*(5), 491–500. doi:10.1007/s11633-016-0975-5

Ayerdi, B., & Grana Romay, M. (2016). Hyperspectral image analysis by spectral-spatial processing and anticipative hybrid extreme rotation forest classification. *IEEE Transactions on Geoscience and Remote Sensing, 54*(5), 2627–2639. doi:10.1109/TGRS.2015.2503886

Aytekin, C., Kiranyaz, S., & Gabbouj, M. (2013). Quantum Mechanics in Computer Vision: Automatic Object Extraction. *Proc. ICIP 2013*, 2489–2493. doi:10.1109/ICIP.2013.6738513

Bakhshi, M., Feizi-Derakhshi, M., & Zafarani, E. (2012). Review and Comparison between Clustering Algorithms with Duplicate Entities Detection Purpose. *International Journal of Computer Science & Emerging Technologies, 3*(3), 108-114.

Baldi, P. (2012). Autoencoders, Unsupervised Learning, and Deep Architectures. *JMLR Workshop and Conference Proceedings, 27*, 37–50.

Bandyopadhyay, S. (2005). Satellite image classification using genetically guided fuzzy clustering with spatial information. *International Journal of Remote Sensing, 26*(3), 579–593. doi:10.1080/01431160512331316432

Barman, P. C., & Miah, S. (2011, December). MRI Image Segmentation Using Level Set Method and Implement An Medical Diagnosis System. *Computer Science & Engineering International Journal (Toronto, Ont.), 1*(5).

Baser, F., & Apaydin, A. (2015). Hybrid fuzzy support vector regression analysis. *Journal of Intelligent & Fuzzy Systems, 28*(5), 2037–2045. doi:10.3233/IFS-141482

Basu, A., Sinha Roy, S., & Chattopadhayay, A. (2016). Implementation of a Spatial Domain Salient Region Based Digital Image Watermarking Scheme. *Int. Conf. Research in Computational Intelligence and Communication Networks*, 269-272. doi:10.1109/ICRCICN.2016.7813669

Basu, A., Sinha Roy, S., & Sarkar, S. (2015). FPGA Implementation of Saliency Based Watermarking Framework. *6th Int. Conf. on Computers and Devices for Communication*.

Behraman, E. (1994). *A quantum dot neural network*. *Proc. Workshop on Physics of Computation*, 22–24.

Bennett, C. H. (1973). Logical reversibility of Computation. *IBM Journal of Research and Development, 17*(6), 525–532. doi:10.1147/rd.176.0525

Bezdek, J. C. (1981). *Pattern Recognition with Fuzzy Objective Function Algorithms*. New York: Plenum. doi:10.1007/978-1-4757-0450-1

Bhattacharyaa, S. (2011). A Brief Survey of Color Image Preprocessing and Segmentation Techniques. *Journal of Pattern Recognition Research*, *1*(1), 120–129. doi:10.13176/11.191

Bhattacharyya, S., & Dutta, P. (Eds.). (2013). Handbook of Research on Computational Intelligence for Engineering, Science, and Business (vol. 1). IGI Global.

Bhattacharyya, S., Dutta, P., Chakraborty, S., Chakraborty, R., & Dey, S. (2010). Determination of Optimal Threshold of a Gray-level Image Using a Quantum Inspired Genetic Algorithm with Interference Based on a Random Map Model. *Proceedings of 2010 IEEE International Conference on Computational Intelligence and Computing Research*, 422-425.

Bhattacharyya, S., Pal, P., & Bhowmick, S. (2014). A Quantum Multilayer Self Organizing Neural Network For Object Extraction From A Noisy Background. *Proceedings of 4th IEEE International Conference On Communication System and Network Technologies (CSNT-2014)*, 512-517. doi:10.1109/CSNT.2014.108

Bhattacharyya, S., Pal, P., & Bhowmick, S. (2014). Binary Image Denoising Using a Quantum Multilayer Self Organizing Neural Network. *Applied Soft Computing, 24*, 717-729. doi:.2014.08.02710.1016/j.asoc

Bhattacharyya, S., Pal, P., & Bhowmick, S. (2015). A Quantum Parallel Self Organizing Neural Network (QPSONN) For Pure Color Object Extraction From A Noisy Background. *Proceedings of 5th IEEE International Conference On Communication System and Network Technologies (CSNT-2015)*, 1129-1135. Doi:10.1109/CSNT.2015.55

Bhattacharyya, S., & Dey, S. (2011). An Efficient Quantum Inspired Genetic Algorithm with Chaotic Map Model based Interference and Fuzzy Objective Function for Gray Level Image Thresholding. *Proceedings of 2011, International Conference on Computational Intelligence and Communication Systems*, 121-125. doi:10.1109/CICN.2011.24

Bhattacharyya, S., Dutta, P., Maulik, U., & Nandi, P. K. (2007). Multilevel Activation Functions For True Color Image Segmentation Using a Self Supervised Parallel Self Organizing Neural Network (PSONN) Architecture: A Comparative Study; World Academy of Science, Engineering and Technology International Journal of Computer, Electrical, Automation. *Control and Information Engineering Vol, 1*(:8), 2007.

Bhattacharyya, S., Dutta, P., Maulik, U., & Nandi, P. K. (2007). Multilevel Activations For True Color Image Segmentation Using a Self Supervised Parallel Self Organizing Neural Network (PSONN) Architecture: A Comparative Study. *International Journal of Computer, Electrical, Automation, Control and Information Engineering*, *1*(8).

Bhattacharyya, S., Maulik, U., & Dutta, P. (2010). Multilevel Image Segmentation with Adaptive Image Context Based Thresholding. *Applied Soft Computing*, *11*(1), 946–962. doi:10.1016/j.asoc.2010.01.015

Bhattacharyya, S., Pal, P., & Bhowmick, S. (2014). Binary Image Denoising Using a Quantum Multilayer Self Organizing Neural Network. *Applied Soft Computing, 24*, 717–729. doi:10.1016/j. asoc.2014.08.027

Blais, A., Huang, R-S, Wallraff, A., Girvin, S.M., & Schoelkopf, R.J. (2004). Cavity quantum electrodynamics for superconducting electrical circuits: An architecture for quantum computation. *Phys. Rev., 69.*

Blumenstein, M., & Verma, B. (1998). An artificial neural network based segmentation algorithm for off-line handwriting recognition. *Proceedings of the Second International Conference on Computational Intelligence and Multimedia Applications.*

Bonci, A., Leo, T., & Longhi, S. (2005). A Bayesian approach to the Hough transform for line detection. *IEEE Trans. Systems Man Cybernet., Part A. Syst. Humans, 35*(6), 945–955. doi:10.1109/ TSMCA.2005.853481

Bora, D. J., & Gupta, A. K. (2014). A Novel Approach Towards Clustering Based Image Segmentation. *International Journal of Emerging Science and Engineering, 2*(11).

Bora, D. J., & Gupta, A.K. (2014). A Comparative study Between Fuzzy Clustering Algorithm and Hard Clustering Algorithm. *International Journal of Computer Trends and Technology, 10*(2), 108-113.

Borsotti, M., Campadelli, P., & Schettini, R. (1998). Quantitative evaluation of color image segmentation results. *Pattern Recognition Letters, 19*(8), 741–747. doi:10.1016/S0167-8655(98)00052-X

Boskovitz, V., & Guterman, H. (2002). An adaptive neuro-fuzzy system for automatic image segmentation and edge detection. *IEEE Transactions on Fuzzy Systems, 10*(2), 247-262. doi:10.1109/91.995125

Bouchain, D. (2007). *Character Recognition Using Convolutional Neural Networks.* Seminar Statistical Learning Theory University of Ulm, Germany Institute for Neural Information Processing.

Bouchiat, V., Vion, D., Joyez, P., Esteve, D., & Devoret, M. H. (1998). Quantum coherence with a single Cooper pair. *Physica Scripta. T, 76*(1), 165–170. doi:10.1238/Physica.Topical.076a00165

Calinski, T., & Harabasz, J. (1974). A dendrite method for cluster analysis. *Communications in Statistics, 3*(1), 1–27.

Celik, M. U., Sharma, G., Saber, E., & Tekalp, A. M. (2002). Hierarchical watermarking for secure image authentication with localization. *IEEE Transactions on Image Processing, 11*(6), 585–595. doi:10.1109/TIP.2002.1014990 PMID:18244657

Celik, M. U., Sharma, G., Tekalp, A. M., & Saber, E. (2005). Lossless generalized-LSB data embedding. *IEEE Transactions on Image Processing, 14*(2), 253–266. doi:10.1109/ TIP.2004.840686 PMID:15700530

Chaabane, S. B., Bouchouicha, M., & Fnaiech, F. (2015). *A Hybrid Technique for Color Image Segmentation: Application to the Fire Forest Images. International Journal of Scientific Engineering and Research.*

Chakraborty, D., Sarkar, A., & Maulik, U. (2016). A New isotropic locality improved kernel for pattern classifications in remote sensing imagery. *Spatial Statistics*, *17*, 71–82. doi:10.1016/j.spasta.2016.04.003

Chandler, D. L. (2016). *A new quantum approach to big data.* MIT News Office.

Chandler, K., & Hyatt, K. (2002). *Customer-Centered Design: A New Approach to Web Usability.* Prentice-Hall.

Chaumont, M., & Puech, W. (2009). A High Capacity Reversible Watermarking Scheme. *Visual Communications and Image Processing, Electronic Imaging.*

Cheng, J. L., Feng, D. H., & Liu, F. (2006). *Immune Optimization Computation, Learn and Recognition.* Beijing: Science Press.

Chen, M., & Ludwig, S. A. (2017). *Color Image Segmentation Using Fuzzy C-Regression Model.* Advances in Fuzzy Systems.

Chi, Z., Wu, J., & Yan, H. (1995). Handwritten numeral recognition using self-organizing maps and fuzzy rules. *Pattern Recognition*, *28*(1), 59–66. doi:10.1016/0031-3203(94)00085-Z

Church, G. M., Tavazoie, S., Hughes, J. D., Campbell, M. J., & Cho, R. J. (1999). Analysis of temporal gene expression pro?les, clustering by simulated annealing and determining optimal number of clusters. *Nature Genetics*, *22*(3), 281–285. doi:10.1038/10343 PMID:10391217

Condon, C., & Valverde, R. (2014). Increasing Critical Thinking in Web-Based Graduate Management Courses. *Journal of Information Technology Education*, 13.

*Congalton & Green. (1999). Assessing the accuracy of classifications of remotely sensed data: Principles and practices.* Boca Raton, FL: Lewis Publications.

Cruz, A. V. A., Vellatco, M. M. B., & Pacheco, M. A. C. (1998). Quantum inspired evolutionary algorithm for numerical optimization. Academic Press.

Das, D., & Mukhopadhyay, S. (2015). *A Pixel Based Segmentation Scheme for Fingerprint Images; Information Systems Design and Intelligent Applications. In Advances in Intelligent Systems and Computing* (Vol. 340, pp. 439–448). New Delhi: Springer; doi:10.1007/978-81-322-2247-7_45

Dasgupta, S., Papadimitriou, C. H., & Vazirani, U. V. (2006). *Algorithms.* McGraw-Hill Education.

Das, S., & De, S. (2016). Multilevel Color Image segmentation using Modified Genetic Algorithm (MfGA) inspired Fuzzy C-Means Clustering. *Second International Conference on Research and Computational Intelligence and Communication Networks (ICRCICN)*, 1, 78-83. doi:10.1109/ICRCICN.2016.7813635

Davies & Bouldin. (1979). A Cluster Separation Measure. *IEEE Transactions on Pattern Analysis and Machine Intelligence, 1*(2), 224–227.

Davies, D., & Bouldin, D. (1979). A cluster separation measure. *IEEE PAMI, 1*(2), 224–227. doi:10.1109/TPAMI.1979.4766909 PMID:21868852

De, S., & Bhattacharyya, S. (2015). Color Magnetic Resonance Brain Image Segmentation by ParaOptiMUSIG Activation Function: An Application. *Hybrid Soft Computing Approaches, 611*, 185-214.

De, S., Bhattacharyya, S., Chakraborty, S., Sarkar, B. N., Prabhakar, P. K., & Bose, S. (2012). Gray Scale Image Segmentation by NSGA-II Based OptiMUSIG Activation Function. *CSNT '12 Proceedings of the 2012 International Conference on Communication Systems and Network Technologies*, 104-108.

Del Giudice, E., Doglia, S., Milani, M., & Vitiello, G. (1985). A quantum field theoretical approach to the collective behavior of biological systems. *Nucl Phys*, 375-400.

Dembele, D., & Kastner, P. (2003). Fuzzy c-means method for clustering microarray data. *Bioinformatics (Oxford, England), 19*(8), 973–980. doi:10.1093/bioinformatics/btg119 PMID:12761060

Denchev, V. S., Ding, N., Vishwanathan, S., & Neven, H. (2012). Robust classification with adiabatic quantum optimization. *Proceedings of the 29 th International Conference on Machine Learning*, 1-8.

Denis, Dubois, Dub'e, & Desrochers. (2016). Blended power management strategy using pattern recognition for a plugin hybrid electric vehicle. *Int. J. Intelligent Transportation Systems Research, 14*(2), 101–114. doi:10.1007/s13177-014-0106-z

De, S., Bhattacharyya, S., & Chakraborty, S. (2010). True color image segmentation by an optimized multilevel activation function. *IEEE International Conference on Computational Intelligence and Computing Research*, 545-548. doi:10.1109/ICCIC.2010.5705833

De, S., Bhattacharyya, S., & Chakraborty, S. (2012). Color image segmentation using parallel OptiMUSIG activation function. *Appl. Soft Comp. J., 12*(10), 3228–3236. doi:10.1016/j.asoc.2012.05.011

De, S., Bhattacharyya, S., & Chakraborty, S. (2013). Color Image Segmentation by NSGA-II based ParaOptiMUSIG Activation Function. *IEEE International Conference on Machine Intelligence Research and Advancement*, 105 - 109. doi:10.1109/ICMIRA.2013.27

De, S., Bhattacharyya, S., & Dutta, P. (2010). Efficient grey-level image segmentation using an optimized MUSIG (OptiMUSIG) activation function. *International Journal of Parallel, Emergent and Distributed Systems, 26*(1), 1–39.

Deutsch, D., & Jozsa, R. (1992). Rapid Solution of Problems by Quantum Computation. *Royal Society of London Proceedings Series, 439*(1907), 553–558.

Deutsch, D. (1985). Quantum Theory, the Church-Turing Principle and the Universal Quantum Computer. *Proceedings of the Royal Society of London, A400*(1818), 97–117. doi:10.1098/rspa.1985.0070

Devi, H. K. A. (2006). Thresholding: A Pixel-Level Image Processing Methodology Preprocessing Technique for an OCR System for the Brahmi Script. *Ancient Asia., 1*, 161–165. doi:10.5334/aa.06113

Devireddy, S., & AppaRao, S. (2005). Hand Written Character Recognition Using Back Propagation Network. *Journal of Theoretical and Applied Information Technology*, 257-269.

Dey, S., Bhattacharyya, S., & Maulik, U. (2013). Chaotic Map Model based Interference Employed in Quantum Inspired Genetic Algorithm to Determine the Optimum Gray Level Image Thresholding. *Global Trends in Intelligent Computing Research and Development*, 68-110.

Dey, S., Bhattacharyya, S., & Maulik, U. (2013a). Quantum Inspired Meta-heuristic Algorithms for Multi-level Thresholding for True Colour Images. *Proceedings of IEEE INDICON, 1*–6.

Dey, S., Bhattacharyya, S., & Maulik, U. (2014a). Quantum Inspired Automatic Clustering for Multilevel Image Thresholding. *Proceedings of International Conference On Computational Intelligence and Communication Networks (ICCICN 2014)*, 247– 251.

Dey, S., Bhattacharyya, S., & Maulik, U. (2014b). Quantum Behaved Multi-objective PSO and ACO Optimization for Multi-level Thresholding. *Proceedings of International Conference On Computational Intelligence and Communication Networks (ICCICN 2014)*, 242– 246.

Dey, S., Bhattacharyya, S., & Maulik, U. (2014c). New Quantum Inspired Tabu Search for Multilevel Colour Image Thresholding. *Proceedings of 8th International Conference On Computing for Sustainable Global Development (INDIACom-2014)*, 311–316.

Dey, S., Bhattacharyya, S., & Maulik, U. (2015). Quantum Behaved Swarm Intelligent Techniques for Image Analysis: A Detailed Survey. In Handbook on Research on Swarm Intelligence in Engineering. IGI Global.

Dey, S., Bhattacharyya, S., & Maulik, U. (2016a). Quantum Inspired Multi-objective SA for Bi-level Image Thresholding. In Quantum Inspired Computational Intelligence: Research and Applications. Morgan Kaufmann.

Dey, S., Bhattacharyya, S., & Maulik, U. (2016b). Optimum Gray Level Image Thresholding using a Quantum Inspired Genetic Algorithm. In Handbook of Advanced Research on Hybrid Intelligent Techniques and Applications. IGI Global.

Dey, S., Saha, I., Bhattacharyya, S., & Maulik, U. (2013b). New Quantum Inspired Meta- heuristic Methods for Multi-level Thresholding. *Proceedings of 2013 International Conference on Advances in Computing, Communications and Informatics (ICACCI)*, 1236-1240.

Dey, S., Bhattacharyya, S., & Maulik, U. (2013). Quantum inspired meta-heuristic algorithms for multi-level thresholding for true colour images. *2013 Annual IEEE Conference on India Conference (INDICON)*, 1-6. doi:10.1109/INDCON.2013.6726024

Dey, S., Bhattacharyya, S., & Maulik, U. (2014). New quantum inspired tabu search for multi-level colour image thresholding. *2014 IEEE International Conference on Computing for Sustainable Global Development (INDIACom)*, 311-316. doi:10.1109/IndiaCom.2014.6828150

Dey, S., Bhattacharyya, S., & Maulik, U. (2014). Quantum inspired genetic algorithm and particle swarm optimization using chaotic map model based interference for gray level Image thresholding. *Swarm and Evolutionary Computation*, *15*, 38–57. doi:10.1016/j.swevo.2013.11.002

Dey, S., Bhattacharyya, S., & Maulik, U. (2016). New quantum inspired meta-heuristic techniques for multi-level colour image thresholding. *Applied Soft Computing*, *46*, 677–702. doi:10.1016/j.asoc.2015.09.042

Dey, S., Bhattacharyya, S., & Maulik, U. (2017). Efficient quantum inspired meta-heuristics for multi-level true colour image thresholding. *Applied Soft Computing*, *56*, 472–513.

Dey, S., Saha, I., Bhattacharyya, S., & Maulik, U. (2014). Multi-level Thresholding using Quantum Inspired Meta-heuristics. *Knowledge-Based Systems*, *67*, 373–400. doi:10.1016/j.knosys.2014.04.006

Dhar, M. (1994). Cardinality of Fuzzy Sets: An Overview. *International Journal of Energy, Information and Communications, 4*(1).

Dimoka, A., Banker, R. D., Benbasat, I., Davis, F. D., Dennis, A. R., Gefen, D., & Pavlou, P. A. (2010). On the use of neurophysiological tools in IS research: Developing a research agenda for NeuroIS. *Management Information Systems Quarterly*, *36*(3), 679–702.

Dimoka, A., Pavlou, P. A., & Davis, F. D. (2007). Neuro-IS: The potential of cognitive neuroscience for information systems research. *Proceedings of the 28th International Conference on Information Systems*.

Dimoka, A., Pavlou, P. A., & Davis, F. D. (2011). Research commentary-NeuroIS: The potential of cognitive neuroscience for information systems research. *Information Systems Research*, *22*(4), 687–702. doi:10.1287/isre.1100.0284

Dineshkumar, R., & Suganthi, J. (2015). Sanskrit Character Recognition System using Neural Network. *Indian Journal of Science and Technology*, *8*(1), 65–69. doi:10.17485/ijst/2015/v8i1/52878

Dong, M. L., Dian, H. W., & Jie, L. (2012). A novel robust blind watermarking algorithm based on wavelet and Fractional Fourier Transform. *IEEE 14th International Conference on Communication Technology*.

Dong, D., Chen, C., Li, H., & Tarn, T.-J. (2008). Quantum Inspired Reinforcement. *IEEE Transactions on Systems, Man, and Cybernetics. Part B, Cybernetics*, *38*(5), 1207–1220. doi:10.1109/TSMCB.2008.925743

Dong, G., & Xie, M. (2005). Color Clustering and Learning for Image Segmentation Based on Neural Networks. *IEEE Transactions on Neural Networks*, *16*(4), 925–936. doi:10.1109/TNN.2005.849822 PMID:16121733

Dorigo, M., Maniezzo, V., & Colorni, A. (1996). The ant system: Optimization by a colony of cooperating agents, *IEEE Trans. Syst. Man Cybernet. – Part B*, *26*(1), 29–41. doi:10.1109/3477.484436 PMID:18263004

Dubey, S., Gupta, Y. K., & Soni, D. (2016). Comparative Study of Various Segmentation Techniques with their Effective Parameters. *International Journal of Innovative Research in Computer and Communication Engineering, 4*(10).

Dueck, G. W., & Maslov, D. (2003). Reversible function synthesis with minimum garbage outputs. *Proceedings of the 6th International Symposium on Representations and Methodology of Future Computing Technologies (RM 2003)*, 154–161.

Dumas, J. S., & Redish, J. C. (1999). *A Practical Guide to Usability Testing*. Portland, OR: Intellect Books.

Dunjko, V., Taylor, J. M., & Briegel, H. J. (2016). Quantum-Enhanced Machined Learning. *Physics Review Letters, 117*(13).

Dunn, J. (1974). Well separated clusters and optimal fuzzy partitions. *Journal of Cybernetics, 4*(1), 95–104. doi:10.1080/01969727408546059

Dunn, J. C. (1973). A Fuzzy Relative of the ISODATA Process and Its Use in Detecting Compact Well-Separated Clusters. *Journal of Cybernetics, 3*(3), 32–57. doi:10.1080/01969727308546046

Durr, C., & Hoyer, P. (1999). *A quantum algorithm for finding the minimum.* arXiv:quant-ph/9607014

Eccles, J. C. (1986). Do mental events cause neural events analogously to the probability fields of quantum mechanics? *Proceedings of the Royal Society of London. Series B, Biological Sciences, 227*(1249), 411–428. doi:10.1098/rspb.1986.0031 PMID:2873576

Emery, O. (1958). Des filigranes du papier. *Bulletin de l'Association technique de l'industrie papetiere, 6*, 185–188.

Engilbrecht, A. P. (2007). *Computational Intelligence: An Introduction* (2nd ed.). John Wiley. doi:10.1002/9780470512517

Ezhov, A. A. (2001). Pattern Recognition with Quantum Neural Networks. Proc. Advances in Pattern Recognition ICAPR:2001, 60–71.

Ezhov, A., & Ventura, D. (2000). Quantum neural networks. In N. Kasabov (Ed.), Future directions for intelligent systems and information science (pp. 213–234). Academic Press. doi:10.1007/978-3-7908-1856-7_11

Fakharzadeh & Khosravi. (2015). A hybrid method for solving fuzzy semi-infinite linear programming problems. *Journal of Intelligent & Fuzzy Systems, 28*(2), 879–884.

Fakhrzad, M. B., & Rahdar, M. A. (2016). Optimization of hybrid robot control system using artificial hormones and fuzzy logic. *Journal of Intelligent & Fuzzy Systems, 30*(3), 1403–1410. doi:10.3233/IFS-152053

Fallahpur, M., & Sedaaghi, M. H. (2007). High capacity lossless data hiding based on histogram modification. *IEICE Electronics Express, 4*(7), 205–210. doi:10.1587/elex.4.205

Feynman, R. (1982). Simulating physics with computers. *International Journal of Theoretical Physics, 21*(6/7), 467–488. doi:10.1007/BF02650179

Feynman, R. (1986). Quantum mechanical computers. *Foundations of Physics, 16*(6), 507–531. doi:10.1007/BF01886518

Feynman, R. P., Leighton, R. B., & Sands, M. (1965). *The Feynman Lectures on Physics* (Vol. 3). Addison-Wesley Publishing Company.

Fridrich, J. J., Goljan, M., & Du, R. (2001). Detecting LSB steganography in color, and gray-scale images. *IEEE MultiMedia, 8*(4), 22–28. doi:10.1109/93.959097

Fridrich, J. J., Goljan, M., & Du, R. (2001a). Invertible authentication. *Security and Watermarking of Multimedia Contents III. Proceedings of the Society for Photo-Instrumentation Engineers*, (1): 197–208. doi:10.1117/12.435400

Fridrich, J. J., Goljan, M., & Du, R. (2002). Lossless data embedding: New paradigm in digital watermarking. *EURASIP Journal on Applied Signal Processing, 2002*(2), 185–196. doi:10.1155/S1110865702000537

T. Friedrich, F. Neumann, & A. M. Sutton (Eds.). (2016). Intelligent on-line energy management system for plug-in hybrid electric vehicles based on evolutionary algorithm. In *Genetic and Evolutionary Computation Conference, GECCO 2016* (pp. 167–168). ACM.

Ganzha, L. M. (Ed.). (2014). The influence of using fractal analysis in hybrid mlp model for short-term forecast of closing prices on warsaw stock exchange. In Proceedings of the 2014 Federated Conference on Computer Science and Information Systems *(vol. 2*, pp. 111–118). IEEE.

Gao, T., & Gu, Q. (2007). Reversible Image Authentication Based on Combination of Reversible and LSB Algorithm. *Proc. IEEE, Computational Intelligence and Security Workshops (CISW 07)*, 636-639. doi:10.1109/CISW.2007.4425576

Gatos, B., Pratikakis, I., & Perantonis, S. J. (2006). Hybrid off-line cursive handwriting word recognition. *Proceedings of 18th international conference on pattern recognition (ICPR'06)*, 2, 998–1002. doi:10.1109/ICPR.2006.644

Ghosh, A., Pal, N. R., & Pal, S. K. (1993). Self organization for object extraction using a multilayer neural network and fuzziness measures. *IEEE Transactions on Fuzzy Systems, 1*(1), 54–68.

Ghosh, A., Pal, N. R., & Pal, S. K. (1993). Self organization for object extraction using a multilayer neural network and fuzziness measures. *IEEE Transactions on Fuzzy Systems, 1*(1), 54–68. doi:10.1109/TFUZZ.1993.390285

Goel. (2010). Land Cover Feature Extraction using Hybrid Swarm Intelligence Techniques - A Remote Sensing Perspective. *ACEEE Int. J. on Signal and Image Processing*, 14–16.

Goldberg, D. E. (1989). *Genetic Algorithm in Search Optimization and Machine Learning*. New York: Addison-Wesley.

Goljan, M., Fridrich, J. J., & Du, R. (2001). Distortion-free data embedding for images. LNCS, 2137, 27–41.

Gonzalez & Woods. (1992). Digital image processing. Addison Wesley.

Gonzalez, R. C., & Woods, R. E. (2002). *Digital image processing*. Upper Saddle River, NJ: Prentice Hall.

Goyal, R., & Kumar, N. (2014). LSB Based Digital Watermarking Technique. *International Journal of Application or Innovation in Engineering & Management*, *3*(9), 15–18.

Grover, L. (1996). A fast quantum mechanical algorithm for database search. *Proceedings of 28th ACM symposium on Theory of Computing*, 212–219. doi:10.1145/237814.237866

Guijarro-Berdiñas, B., Alonso-Betanzos, A., & Fontenla-Romero, O. (2002). Intelligent analysis and pattern recognition in cardiotocographic signals using a tightly coupled hybrid system. *Artificial Intelligence*, *136*(1), 1–27. doi:10.1016/S0004-3702(01)00163-1

Gui, X., Li, X., & Yang, B. (2014, May). A high capacity reversible data hiding scheme based on generalized prediction-error expansion and adaptive embedding. *Signal Processing*, *98*, 370–380. doi:10.1016/j.sigpro.2013.12.005

Gupta, Goel, & Aggarwal. (2013). A hybrid biogeography based heuristic for the mirrored traveling tournament problem. In *Sixth International Conference on Contemporary Computing* (pp. 325–330). IEEE.

Halkidi, M., Batistakis, Y., & Vazirgiannis, M. (2001). On clustering validation techniques. *Journal of Intelligent Information Systems*, *17*(2-3), 107–145. doi:10.1023/A:1012801612483

Hameroff, S. (1998). *Quantum computation in brain microtubules? The Penrose-Hameroff'Orch OR'model of consciousness*. Philosophical Transactions-Royal Society of London Series A Mathematical Physical and Engineering Sciences.

Hamidreza, Omair, & Swamy. (2016). Multiplicative Watermark Decoder in Contourlet Domain Using the Normal Inverse Gaussian Distribution. *IEEE Transactions on Multimedia, 18*(2), 19-207.

Han, K. H., & Kim, J. H. (2000). Genetic quantum algorithm and its application to combinatorial optimization problem. *Proceedings of the 2000 Congress on Evolutionary Computation*, *2*, 1354–1360. doi:10.1109/CEC.2000.870809

Han, K. H., & Kim, J. H. (2001). Analysis of Quantum-Inspired Evolutionary Algorithm. *Proceedings of the 2001 International Conference on Artificial Intelligence*, 727–730.

Han, K., & Kim, J. (2002). Quantum-Inspired Evolutionary Algorithm for a Class Combinational Optimization. *IEEE Transactions on Evolutionary Computation*, 6(6), 580–593. doi:10.1109/TEVC.2002.804320

Hanmandlu, M., & Ramana Murthy, O. V. (2007). Fuzzy model based recognition of handwritten numerals. Pattern Recognition, 40, 1840 – 1854.

Hannachi, M. S., & Hirota, K. (2005). Fuzzy set representation of quantum logic (1-valued) automata. *International symposium on computational intelligence and intelligent informatics*, 14-16.

Hao-Tang, C., Wen-Jyi, H., & Chau-Jern, C. (2015). Digital Hologram Authentication Using a Hadamard- Based Reversible Fragile Watermarking Algorithm. *Journal of Display Technology*, 11(2), 193–203. doi:10.1109/JDT.2014.2367528

Harrabi, R., & Braiek, E. B. (2014). Color image segmentation using a modified Fuzzy C-Means technique and different color spaces: Application in the breast cancer cells images. *2014 1st International Conference on Advanced Technologies for Signal and Image Processing (ATSIP)*, 231-236.

Hey, T. (1999). Quantum computing: An introduction. Computing & Control Engineering Journal, 10, 105–112.

Hinterding, R. (1999). Representation, constraint satisfaction and the knapsack problem. *Proceedings of 2008 Congress on Evolutionary Computation*, 2, 1286–1292. doi:10.1109/CEC.1999.782591

Hirohisa, H. (2002). A data embedding method using BPCS principle with new complexity measures. *Proc. of Pacific Rim Workshop on Digital Steganography*, 30-47.

*Hollander & Wolfe. (1999). Nonparametric statistical methods* (2nd ed.). Wiley.

Hong, L., Di, X., Rui, Z., Yushu, Z., & Sen, B. (2016). Robust and hierarchical watermarking of encrypted images based on Compressive Sensing. *Journal of Signal Processing: Image Communication*, 45, 41–51.

Hong, W., & Chen, T. S. (2012). A Novel Data Embedding Method Using Adaptive Pixel Pair Matching. *IEEE Transactions on Information Forensics and Security*, 7(1), 176–184. doi:10.1109/TIFS.2011.2155062

Honsinger, C. W., Jones, P., Rabbani, M., & Stoffel, J. C. (2001). *Lossless recovery of an original image containing embedded data*. US Patent Application, 6 278 791.

Hoon, de Imoto, Nolan, & Miyano. (2004). Open source clustering software. *Bioinformatics (Oxford, England)*, 20(9), 1453–1454. PMID:14871861

Hopfield, J. J. (1984, May). Neurons with graded response have collective computational properties like those of two-state neurons. *Proceedings of the National Academy of Sciences of the United States of America*, 81(10), 3088–3092. doi:10.1073/pnas.81.10.3088 PMID:6587342

Huang, Y., Huang, K., Tao, D., & Tan, T. (2011). Enhanced Biologically Inspired Model for Object Recognition. *IEEE Transactions on Systems, Man, and Cybernetics*, *41*(6), 1668–1680. doi:10.1109/TSMCB.2011.2158418 PMID:21768049

Hwai-Tsu, H., & Ling-Yuan, H. (2016). A mixed modulation scheme for blind image watermarking. *International Journal of Electronics and Communications*, *70*(2), 172–178. doi:10.1016/j. aeue.2015.11.003

Jacobsen. (1998). A generic architecture for hybrid intelligent systems. *Proceedings of the IEEE Fuzzy Systems*.

Jain, A. K., Murty, M. N., & Flynn, P. J. (1999). Data clustering: A review. *ACM Computing Surveys*, *31*(3), 264–323. doi:10.1145/331499.331504

Jaseena & John. (2011). Text Watermarking using Combined Image and Text for Authentication and Protection. *International Journal of Computer Applications, 20*(4).

Jibu, M., & Yasue, K. (1995). Quantum brain dynamics: An introduction. Amsterdam: John Benjamins.

Juergen, S. (2005). *Digital Watermarking for Digital Media*. IGI.

Kak, S. (1995). On quantum neural computing. *Information Sciences*, *83*(3-4), 143–160. doi:10.1016/0020-0255(94)00095-S

Kalbach, J. (2007). *Designing Web Navigation*. O'Reilly Publications.

Kallel, M., Lapayre, J. C., & Bouhlel, M. S. (2007). A multiple watermarking scheme for medical image in the spatial domain. *Graphics. Vision and Image Processing Journal*, *7*(1), 37–42.

Kalra, K., Goswami, A. K., & Gupta, R. (2013). A comparative study of supervised image classification algorithms for satellite images. *International Journal of Electrical, Electronics and Data Communication, 1*(10).

Kamstra, L., & Heijmans, H. J. (2005). Reversible data embedding into images using wavelet techniques and sorting. *IEEE Transactions on Image Processing*, *14*(12), 2082–2090. doi:10.1109/TIP.2005.859373 PMID:16370461

Kang, S.D., Park, S.S., Shin, Y.G., Yoo, H.W., & Jang, D.S. (2008). Image Segmentation using Statistical approach via Perception-based Color Information. *International Journal of Computer Science and Network Security, 8*(4).

Kapur, J. N., Sahoo, P., & Wong, A. K. C. (1980). A new method for gray-level picture thresholding using the entropy of the histogram. *Computer Vision Graphics and Image Processing*, *29*(3), 273–285.

Kasabov & Song. (2001). *Denfis: Dynamic evolving neural-fuzzy inference system and its application for time-series prediction*. Academic Press.

Kawaguchi, E., & Eason, R. O. (1998). Principle and Applications of BPCS Steganography. *Proc. of SPIE, Multimedia Systems and Applications, 3528*, 464–473.

Kececi, H., & Degirmenci, Y. (2008). Quantitative EEG and cognitive evoked potentials in anemia. *Neurophysiologie Clinique. Clinical Neurophysiology, 38*(2), 137–143. doi:10.1016/j.neucli.2008.01.004 PMID:18423335

Khandare, S., & Shrawankar, U. (2015). Image bit depth plane digital watermarking for secured classified image data transmission. *Procedia Computer Science, 78*, 698–705. doi:10.1016/j.procs.2016.02.119

Kharittha, T., Pipat, S., & Thumrongrat, A. (2015). Digital Image Watermarking based on Regularized Filter. *14th IAPR International Conference on Machine Vision Applications.*

Khemaja. (2016). Using a knapsack mo del to optimize continuous building of a hybrid intelligent tutoring system: Application information technology professionals. *International Journal of Human Capital and Information Technology Professionals, 7*(2), 1–18. doi:10.4018/IJHCITP.2016040101

Kim, H. J., Sachnev, V., Shi, Y. Q., Nam, J., & Choo, H. G. (2008). A Novel Difference Expansion Transform for Reversible Data Embedding. *IEEE Transactions on Information Forensics and Security, 3*(3), 456–465. doi:10.1109/TIFS.2008.924600

Kim, K. S., Lee, M. J., Lee, H. Y., & Lee, H. K. (2009). Reversible data hiding exploiting spatial correlation between sub-sampled images. *Pattern Recognition, 42*(11), 3083–3096. doi:10.1016/j.patcog.2009.04.004

Kim, M., & Ramakrishna, R. S. (2005). New indices for cluster validity assessment. *Pattern Recognition Letters, 26*(15), 2353–2363. doi:10.1016/j.patrec.2005.04.007

Kim, Y., Kim, J., & Han, K. (2006) Quantum-inspired Multiobjective Evolutionary Algorithm for Multiobjective 0/1 Knapsack Problems. *Proceedings of 2006 IEEE Congress on Evolutionary Computation, Sheraton Vancouver Wall Centre Hotel*, 16–21.

Koch, J., Yu, T. M., Gambetta, J., Houck, A. A., Schuster, D. I., Majer, J., ... Schoelkopf, R. J. (2007). Charge-insensitive qubit design derived from the Cooper pair box. *Physical Review A., 76*(042319), 1–19.

Konar, D., Bhattachrayya, S., Das, S., & Panigrahi, B. K. (2015). A quantum bi- directional self-organizing neural network (QBDSONN) for binary image denoising. *Proc. ICACCI*, 54-68. doi:10.1109/ICACCI.2015.7275780

Konar, D., Bhattachrayya, S., Panigrahi, B. K., & Nakamatsu, K. (2016). Quantum bidirectional self-organizing neural network (QBDSONN) architecture for binary object extraction from a noisy perspective. *Applied Soft Computing, 46*, 731–752. doi:10.1016/j.asoc.2015.12.040

Kreinovich, V., Kohout, L. J., & Kim, E. (2008). "Square root of Not": A major difference between fuzzy und quantum logics. *Annual meeting of the North American fuzzy information processing society*, 1-5. doi:10.1109/NAFIPS.2008.4531327

Krishna, R. V. V., & Kumar, S. S. (2015). Color Image Segmentation using Soft Rough Fuzzy-C-Means Clustering and SMO Support Vector Machine. *An International Journal on Signal & Image Processing, 6*(5), 49. doi:10.5121/sipij.2015.6504

Kulkarni, N. (2012). Color Thresholding Method for Image Segmentation of Natural Images, *I.J. Image. Graphics and Signal Processing, 1*(1), 28–34. doi:10.5815/ijigsp.2012.01.04

Kumar, S., & Singh, S. K. (2016). Hybrid BFO and PSO swarm intelligence approach for biometric feature optimization. *International Journal of Swarm Intelligence Research, 7*(2), 36–62. doi:10.4018/IJSIR.2016040103

Kundu, Y. H., & Chen, M. (2002). Alternatives to variable duration HMM in handwriting recognition. *IEEE Transactions on Pattern Analysis and Machine Intelligence, 20*(11), 1275–1280. doi:10.1109/34.730561

Kutter, M. (1999). *Digital Watermarking: Hiding Information in Images* (PhD thesis). Swiss Federal Institute of Technology, Lausanne, Switzerland.

Kutter, M., & Petitcolas, F. A. P. (2000). A fair benchmark for image watermarking systems. *Journal of Electronic Imaging, 9*(4), 445–455. doi:10.1117/1.1287594

L´opez-Garc'ia, Onieva, Osaba, Masegosa, & Perallos. (2016). A hybrid metho d for short-term tra c congestion forecasting using genetic algorithms and cross entropy. *IEEE Transactions on Intelligent Transportation Systems, 17*(2), 557–569. doi:10.1109/TITS.2015.2491365

Laguna, M., & Marti, R. (2002). Neural network prediction in a system for optimizing simulations. *IIE Transactions, 34*(3), 273–282. doi:10.1080/07408170208928869

Lalitha, N. V., & Rao, S. (2013). DWT - Arnold Transform based audio watermarking. *IEEE Asia Pacific Conference on Postgraduate Research in Microelectronics and Electronics*. doi:.2013.6731204 doi:10.1109/PrimeAsia

Landauer, R. (1961). Irreversibility and heat generation in the computing process. *IBM Journal of Research and Development, 5*(3), 183–191. doi:10.1147/rd.53.0183

Lee, J., Huang, X., & Zhu, Q. (2010). Decomposing Fredkin Gate into Simple Reversible Elements with Memory. *International Journal of Digital Content Technology and its Applications, 4*(5).

Lee, S., Yoo, C. D., & Kalker, T. (2007). Reversible Image Watermarking Based on Integer-to-Integer Wavelet Transform. *IEEE Transactions on Information Forensics and Security, 2*(3), 321–330. doi:10.1109/TIFS.2007.905146

Li, C. P., & Li, S. Y. (2008). Learning algorithm and application of quantum BP neural networks based on universal quantum gates. *Journal of Systems Engineering and Electronics, 19*(1), 167–174. doi:10.1016/S1004-4132(08)60063-8

Lin, Wang, Liu, Han, & Lu. (2016). Hybrid multigranulation rough sets of variable precision based on tolerance. *Journal of Intelligent & Fuzzy Systems, 31*(2), 717–725.

Lin, P.-L. (2001). Oblivious Digital Watermarking Scheme with Blob-Oriented and Modular-Arithmetic- Based Spatial-Domain Mechanism. *Journal of Visual Communication and Image Representation*, *12*(2), 136–151. doi:10.1006/jvci.2000.0454

Lior & Maimon. (2005). *Clustering methods. Data mining and knowledge discovery handbook.* Springer US.

Liu, J., & Yang, Y. H. (1994). Multi-resolution color image segmentation. *IEEE Transactions on Pattern Analysis and Machine Intelligence*, *16*(7), 689–700. doi:10.1109/34.297949

Liu, N., Amin, P., Ambalavanan, A., & Subbalakshmi, K. P. (2006). An Overview of Digital Watermarking. In *Multimedia Security Technologies for Digital Rights Management*. Academic Press. doi:10.1016/B978-012369476-8/50009-9

Li, Y., Feng, S., Zhang, X., & Jiao, L. (2014). SAR image segmentation based on quantum-inspired multiobjective evolutionary clustering algorithm. *Information Processing Letters*, *114*(6), 287–293. doi:10.1016/j.ipl.2013.12.010

Loos, P., Riedl, R., Müller-Putz, G. R., Vom Brocke, J., Davis, F. D., Banker, R. D., & Léger, P.-M. (2010). NeuroIS: Neuroscientific approaches in the investigation and development of information systems. *Business & Information Systems Engineering*, *2*(6), 395–401. doi:10.1007/s12599-010-0130-8

Lukac, M., Perkowski, M., Goi, H., Pivtoraiko, M., Yu, C. H., Chung, K., ... Kim, Y.-D. (2003). Evolutionary approach to quantum and reversible circuits synthesis. *Artificial Intelligence Review*, *20*(3–4), 361–417. doi:10.1023/B:AIRE.0000006605.86111.79

Lukac, M., Pivtoraiko, M., Mishchenko, A., & Perkowski, M. (2002). Automated synthesis of generalized reversible cascades using genetic algorithms. *5th International Workshop on Boolean Problems*, 33–45.

Maitra, A., & Parashar, P. (2005). *Hadamard type operations for qubits.* arXiv:quant-ph/0505068v1

Maity, S. P., Kundu, M. K., & Seba, M. (2009). Dual Purpose FWT Domain Spread Spectrum Image Watermarking in Real-Time. *Computers & Electrical Engineering*, *35*(2), 415–433. doi:. compeleceng.2008.06.00310.1016/j

Majumdar, S., Das, T. S., & Sarkar, S. K. (2011). DWT and SVD based Image Watermarking Scheme using Noise Visibility and Contrast Sensitivity. *Int. Conf. on Recent Trends in Information Technology*, 938-942. doi:10.1109/ICRTIT.2011.5972409

Manish, T. W., Keshao, D. K., & Mahendra, P. D. (2015). Document Image Segmentation using Region Based Methods. *International Journal of Computing Science and Information Technology*, *3*(3). Retrieved from http://ijcsit.org

Mao, X., Zhang, Y., Hu, Y., & Binjie, S. (2009). Color Image Segmentation Method Based on Region Growing and Ant Colony Clustering. *Intelligent Systems, GCIS*, *09*. doi:10.1109/GCIS.2009.344

Mashford, J., Davis, P., & Rahilly, M. (2007). Pixel-Based Color Image Segmentation Using Support Vector Machine for Automatic Pipe Inspection. *Australasian Joint Conference on Artificial Intelligence: AI 2007: Advances in Artificial Intelligence*, 739-743.

Maslov, D., & Dueck, G. W. (2003). Garbage in reversible designs of multiple output functions. *Proceedings of the 6th International Symposium on Representations and Methodology of Future Computing Technologies (RM 2003)*, 162–170.

Maslov, D., Dueck, G. W., & Miller, D. M. (2005). Synthesis of Fredkin-Toffoli reversible networks. *IEEE Transactions on Very Large Scale Integration (VLSI) Systems*, *13*(6), 765–769. doi:10.1109/TVLSI.2005.844284

Masulli, F., & Palm, G¨. (Eds.). (2012). A hybrid model for s&p500 index forecasting. In *Lecture Notes in Computer Science: Vol. 7553. Artificial Neural Networks and Machine Learning* (pp. 573–581). Springer.

Masuyama, N., Loo, C. K., Seera, M., & Kubota, N. (2017). Quantum-Inspired Multidirectional Associative Memory With a Self-Convergent Iterative Learning. *IEEE Transactions on Neural Networks and Learning Systems*, 1–11. doi:10.1109/TNNLS.2017.2653114 PMID:28182559

Matan, O. (1990). Handwritten Character Recognition Using Neural Network Architecture. *Proceedings of the 4th USPS Advanced Technology Conference*, 1003-1011.

Matsuda, S. (1993). Quantum neurons and their implications. Proceedings of international joint conference on neural networks, 2, 1610–1613.

Matsui, N., Takai, M., & Nishimura, H. (2000). A network model based onqubit-like neuroncorresponding to quantum circuit. *Inst. Electr. Inform. Commun. Jpn. (Part III: Fundam. Electr. Sci)*, *83*(10), 67–73.

Maulik & Sarkar. (2012). E cient parallel algorithm for pixel classification in remote sensing imagery. *GeoInformatica*, *16*(2), 391–407. doi:10.1007/s10707-011-0136-5

Maulik, Mukhopadhyay, & Bandyopadhyay. (2009). Combining Pareto-Optimal Clusters using Supervised Learning for Identifying Coexpressed Genes. *BMC Bioinformatics*, *10*, 27. doi:10.1186/1471-2105-10-27 PMID:19154590

Maulik, U., & Bandyopadhyay, S. (2002). Performance evaluation of some clustering algorithms and validity indices. *IEEE PAMI*, *24*(12), 1650–1654. doi:10.1109/TPAMI.2002.1114856

Mayers, D. (1998). *Unconditional Security in Quantum Cryptography*. quant-ph/9802025

Mcmohan, D. (2008). *Quantum computing explained*. Hoboken, NJ: John Wiley & Sons, Inc.

Mcmohan, D. (2008). *Quantum Computing Explained*. Hoboken, NJ: John Wiley & Sons, Inc.

Megalingam, R. K., Nair, M. M., Srikumar, R., Balasubramanian, V. K., & Sarma, V. S. V. (2010). Performance Comparison of Novel, Robust Spatial Domain Digital Image Watermarking with the Conventional Frequency Domain Watermarking Techniques. *International Conference on Signal Acquisition and Processing*. doi:10.1109/ICSAP.2010.79

Mekhmoukh, A., & Mokrani, K. (2015). Improved Fuzzy C-Means based Particle Swarm Optimization (PSO) initialization and outlier rejection with level set methods for MR brain image segmentation. *Computer Methods and Programs in Biomedicine*, *122*(2), 266–281. doi:10.1016/j.cmpb.2015.08.001 PMID:26299609

Meng Q & Gong C (2010). Web information classifying and navigation based on neural network. *2nd international conference on signal processing systems, 2*, V2-431-V2-433.

Meng, Q., & Gong, C. (2010). Web information classifying and navigation based on neural network. *2nd Int. Conf. on signal processing systems, 2*, V2-431-V2-433.

Menon, P. S., & Ritwik, M. (2014). A Comprehensive but not Complicated Survey on Quantum Computing. *2014 International Conference on Future Information Engineering, 10*, 144 – 152. doi:10.1016/j.ieri.2014.09.069

Miller, D. M. (2002). Spectral and two-place decomposition techniques in reversible logic. *Proceedings of the IEEE Midwest Symposium on Circuits and Systems (MWSCAS 02)*, II 493–II 496. doi:10.1109/MWSCAS.2002.1186906

Miller, D. M., Maslov, D., & Dueck, G. W. (2003). A transformation based algorithm for reversible logic synthesis. *Proceedings of the Design Automation Conference*, 318–323. doi:10.1145/775832.775915

Mintzer, F., Braudaway, G. W., & Yeung, M. M. (1997). Effective and ineffective digital watermarks. *Proceedings - International Conference on Image Processing, 3*, 9–12.

Mishra, D., Bose, I., De, U. C., & Pradhan, B. (2014). A Multilevel Image Thresholding Using Particle Swarm Optimization. *International Journal of Engineering and Technology, 6*(2), 1204-1211.

Mislav, G., Kresimir, D., & Mohammed, G. (2009). *Recent Advances in Multimedia Signal Processing and Communications*. Springer Science & Business Media.

Mohanty, S. P. (1999). *Digital Watermarking: A Tutorial Review*. Retrieved from http://www.csee.usf.edu accessed

Mohanty, S. P., Parthasarathy, G., Elias, K., & Nishikanta, P. (2006). A Novel Invisible Color Image Watermarking Scheme using Image Adaptive Watermark Creation and Robust Insertion-Extraction. *Proceeding of the 8th IEEE International Symposium on Multimedia (ISM '06)*. doi:10.1109/ISM.2006.7

Mu, D., Guan, Z., & Zhang, H. (2013). *Learning Algorithm and Application of Quantum Neural Networks with Quantum Weights* (Vol. 5). IJCTE.

Mu, D., Guan, Z., & Zhang, H. (2013). Learning Algorithm and Application of Quantum Neural Networks with Quantum Weights. *IJCTE, 5*, 788–792. doi:10.7763/IJCTE.2013.V5.797

Mukherjee, D. P., Maitra, S., & Acton, S. T. (2004). Spatial domain digital watermarking of multimedia objects for buyer authentication. *IEEE Transactions on Multimedia, 6*(1), 1–15. doi:10.1109/TMM.2003.819759

Muthukrishnan, A. (1999). *Classical and Quantum Logic Gates: An Introduction to Quantum Computing.* Quantum Information Seminar, Rochester Center for Quantum Information.

Naik, D., & Shahet, P. (2014). A Review on Image Segmentation Clustering Algorithms. *International Journal of Computer Science and Information Technologies, 5*(3).

Nebti, S. (2013). Bio-Inspired Algorithms for Color Image Segmentation. *International Journal of Computers and Applications, 73*(18).

Nehi, H. M., & Keikha, A. (2016). TOPSIS and choquet integral hybrid technique for solving MAGDM problems with interval type-2 fuzzy numbers. *Journal of Intelligent & Fuzzy Systems, 30*(3), 1301–1310. doi:10.3233/IFS-152044

Nielsen, M. A., & Chuang, I. L. (2002). *Quantum Computation and Quantum Information.* Cambridge University Press.

Nielson, M. A., & Chung, I. L. (2000). *Quantum computation and quantum information.* Cambridge University Press.

Ni, Z., Shi, W. Q., Ansari, N., Su, W., Sun, Q., & Lin, X. (2008). Robust Lossless Image Data Hiding Designed for Semi-Fragile Image Authentication. *IEEE Transactions on Circuits and Systems for Video Technology, 18*(4), 497–509. doi:10.1109/TCSVT.2008.918761

Ni, Z., Shi, Y. Q., Ansari, N., & Su, W. (2003). Reversible data hiding. *Proc. of the 2003 Int. Symposium on Circuits and Systems (ISCAS 2003), 2*, 912-915.

Ni, Z., Shi, Y. Q., Ansari, N., & Su, W. (2006). Reversible data hiding. *IEEE Transactions on Circuits and Systems for Video Technology, 16*(3), 354–362. doi:10.1109/TCSVT.2006.869964

Ono, M., Han, S., Fujiyoshi, M., & Kiya, H. (2009). A location map-free reversible data hiding method for specific area embedding. *IEICE Electronics Express, 6*(8), 483–489. doi:10.1587/elex.6.483

Pal, P., Bhattacharyya, S., & Mani, A. (2016). Pure Color Object Extraction from a Noisy State using Quantum Version Parallel Self Organizing Neural Network. *International Journal of Computers and Applications,* 164-186. 10.1080/1206212X.2016.1237164

Pal, N. R., & Pal, S. K. (1993). A Review on Image Segmentation Techniques. *Pattern Recognition, 26*(9), 1277–1294. doi:10.1016/0031-3203(93)90135-J

Pan, M., Yan, J., Tu, Q., & Jiang, C. (2015). Fuzzy control and wavelet transform-based energy management strategy design of a hybrid tracked bulldozer. *Journal of Intelligent & Fuzzy Systems, 29*(6), 2565–2574. doi:10.3233/IFS-151959

Pantofaru, C., & Hebert, M. (2005). *A Comparison of Image Segmentation Algorithms, CMU-RI-TR-05-40, September 1, 2005.* Pittsburgh, PA: The Robotics Institute, Carnegie Mellon University.

Pappas, T. E. (1992). An adaptive clustering algorithm for image segmentation. *INEE Trans. On Signal Processing, 40*(4), 901–914. doi:10.1109/78.127962

Park, Lee, & Lee. (2015). Hybrid filter based on neural networks for removing quantum noise in low-dose medical x-ray CT images. *Int. J. Fuzzy Logic and Intelligent Systems, 15*(2).

Parpinelli, R., Lopes, H., & Freitas, A. (2002). Data mining with an ant colony optimization algorithm. *IEEE Transactions on Evolutionary Computation, 6*(4), 321–332. doi:10.1109/TEVC.2002.802452

Patra, J. C., Phua, J. E., & Rajan, D. (2010). DCT domain watermarking scheme using Chinese Remainder Theorem for image authentication. *IEEE International Conference on Multimedia and Expo.* doi:10.1109/ICME.2010.5583326

Pedersen, M. K., Skyum, B., Heck, R., Müller, R., Bason, M., Lieberoth, A., & Sherson, J. F. (2016). Virtual learning environment for interactive engagement with advanced quantum mechanics. *Physical Review Physics Education Research, 12*(1), 013102. doi:10.1103/PhysRevPhysEducRes.12.013102

Perkowski, M., Jozwiak, L., & Kerntopf, P. (2001). A general decomposition for reversible logic. *Proceedings of the 5th International Workshop on Applications of Reed-Muller Expansion in Circuit Design (Reed-Muller'01),* 119–138.

Perus, M., & Ecimovic, P. (1998). Memory and pattern recognition in associative neural networks. *International Journal of Applied Science and Computation, 4,* 283–310.

Perus, M., & Ecimovic, P. (1998). Memory and pattern recognition in associative neural networks. *International Journal of Applied Science and Computation, 4,* 283–310.

Pop-Jordanova, N., & Pop-Jordanov, J. (2005). Spectrum-weighted EEG frequency ("brain-rate") as a quantitative indicator of mental arousal. *Prilozi Makedonska Akademija na Naukite i Umetnostite, 26*(2), 35–42. PMID:16400227

Pop-Jordanov, J., & Pop-Jordanova, N. (2010). Quantum transition probabilities and the level of consciousness. *Journal of Psychophysiology, 24*(2), 136–140. doi:10.1027/0269-8803/a000025

Popper, K. (2004). The Logic of Scientific Discovery (2nd ed.). Routledge, Taylor & Francis. (originally published 1959)

Preetha, M. M. S. J., Suresh, L. P., & Bosco, M. J. (2015). Cuckoo Search Based Color Image Segmentation Using Seeded Region Growing. In C. Kamalakannan, L. Suresh, S. Dash, & B. Panigrahi (Eds.), Power Electronics and Renewable Energy Systems (Vol. 326). New Delhi: Academic Press. doi:10.1007/978-81-322-2119-7_154

Purushothaman, G., & Karayiannis, N. B. (2006). On the capacity of feed forward neural networks for fuzzy classification, J. *Applied Functional Analysis, 1*, 9–32.

Pyllkkanen, P., & Pylkko, P. (1995). New directions in cognitive science. *Proc. the International Symposium*, 77-89.

Rabbani, Farrokhi-asl, & Rafiei. (2016). A hybrid genetic algorithm for waste collection problem by heterogeneous eet of vehicles with multiple separated compartments. *Journal of Intelligent & Fuzzy Systems, 30*(3), 1817–1830. doi:10.3233/IFS-151893

Rahman, H., & Islam, R. (2013). Segmentation of color image using adaptive thresholding and masking with watershed algorithm. *2013 International Conference on Informatics, Electronics & Vision (ICIEV)*. doi:10.1109/ICIEV.2013.6572557

Rahman, M., Akhand, M. A. H., Islam, S., & Shill, P. S. (2005). *Bangla Handwritten Character Recognition using Convolutional Neural Network*. I.J. Image, Graphics and Signal Processing.

Ramani, K., Prasad, E. V., & Varadarajan, S. (2007). Steganography using BPCS to the Integer Wavelet Transformed image. *International Journal of Computer Science and Network Security, 7*(7), 293–302.

Raouzaiou, Tsapatsoulis, Tzouvaras, Stamou, & Kollias. (2002). A hybrid intelligent system for facial expression recognition. *Proceedings of the European Symposium on Intelligent Technologies, Hybrid Systems and their implementation on Smart Adaptive Systems*.

Reiffel, E., & Polak, W. (2000). *An Introduction to Quantum Computing for Non-Physicists*. arxive.org.quant-ph/9809016v2.

Ricciardi, L. M., & Umezawa, H. (1967). Brain physics and many-body problems. *Kibernetik, 4*(2), 44–48. doi:10.1007/BF00292170 PMID:5617419

Riedl, R., Davis, F. D., & Hevner, A. R. (2014). Towards a NeuroIS research methodology: Intensifying the discussion on methods, tools, and measurement. *Journal of the Association for Information Systems, 15*(10), I.

Rigatos, G. G., & Rzafestas, S. G. (2006). Quantum learning for neural associative memories. *Fuzzy Sets and Systems, 157*(13), 1797–1813. doi:10.1016/j.fss.2006.02.012

Ross, T.J., & Ross, T. (1995). *Fuzzy Logic with Engineering Applications*. McGraw Hill College Div.

Rousseeuw, P. (1987). Silhouettes: A graphical aid to the interpretation and validation of cluster analysis. *Journal of Computational and Applied Mathematics, 20*(1), 53–65. doi:10.1016/0377-0427(87)90125-7

Saadé, R. G., & Kira, D. (2009). Computer anxiety in e-learning: The effect of computer self-efficacy. *Journal of Information Technology Education, 8*(1), 177–191. doi:10.28945/166

Saha, I., Maulik, U., & Plewczynski, D. (2011). A new multi-objective technique for differential fuzzy clustering. *Applied Soft Computing, 11*(2), 2765–2776. doi:10.1016/j.asoc.2010.11.007

Saini, S., & Arora, K. (2014). A Study Analysis on the Different Image Segmentation Techniques. *International Journal of Information & Computation Technology, 4*(14), 1445-1452.

Salman, N. (2006, April). Image Segmentation Based on Watershed and Edge Detection Techniques. *The International Arab Journal of Information Technology, 3*(2).

Samadiani, N., & Hassanpour, H. (2005). *A neural network based approach for recognizing Multi-font printed English characters*. Academic Press.

Samadiani, N., & Hassanpour, H. (2015). *A neural network based approach for recognizing Multi font printed English characters*. Academic Press.

Sarkar & Das. (2015). *Remote sensing image classification using Fuzzy PSO hybrid approach*. IGI-Global.

Sayood, K. (2006). Introduction to data compression. *Morgan Kaufmann Series in Multimedia Information and Systems, Elsevier, 3E*, 183–217.

Scarlat & Maracine. (2015). The hybrid intelligent systems design using grey systems theory. *Grey Systems: T&A, 5*(2), 194–205.

Schuld, M., & Petruccione, F. (2014). *The quest for a Quantum Neural Network*. QNN Research.

Schuld, M., Sinayskiy, I., & Petruccione, F. (2014). The quest for a quantum neural network. *Quantum Information Processing, 13*(11), 2567–2586. doi:10.1007/s11128-014-0809-8

Shafee, F. (2007). Neural networks with quantum gated nodes. *Engineering Applications of Artificial Intelligence, 20*(4), 429–437. doi:10.1016/j.engappai.2006.09.004

Shah & Adhyaru. (2016). Hjb solution-based optimal control of hybrid dynamical systems using multiple linearized model. *Control and Intelligent Systems, 44*(2).

Shah, P. (2015). A DWT-SVD Based Digital Watermarking Technique for Copyright Protection. *International Conference on Electrical, Electronics, Signals, Communication and Optimization.* doi:10.1109/EESCO.2015.7253806

Sharma, V. C. (2015). A Review: PDE based Segmentation Method and Color Models. *SSRG International Journal of Computer Science and Engineering.* Retrieved from www.internationaljournalssrg.org

Sharma, S. (1996). *Applied multivariate techniques*. New York: John Wiley & Sons, Inc.

Shelke, S., & Shaila, A. (2011). A Multistage Handwritten Marathi Compound character recognition scheme using Neural Networks and Wavelet Features. *International Journal of Signal Processing, Image Processing and Pattern Recognition, 4*.

Shende, V. V., Prasad, A. K., Markov, I. L., & Hayes, J. P. (2002). Reversible logic circuit synthesis. *Proceedings of the International Conference on Computer Aided Design*, 125–132.

Shinde, A., & Kagalkar, R. (2015). Sign Language to Text and Vice Versa Recognition using Computer Vision in Marathi. *International Journal of Computers and Applications*, 23–28.

ShorP. (1998). *Quantum computing.* Available: http://east.camel.math.ca/ EMIS/ journals/ DMJDMV/ xvolicm/ 00/Shor.MAN.html

Shor, P. W. (1994). Algorithms for Quantum Computation: Discrete Logarithms and Factoring. *Proc. 35th Annual Symposium on the Foundation of Computer Science*, 20-22. doi:10.1109/ SFCS.1994.365700

Sin, B.-K., & Ha, J.-Y. (1999). Network-Based Approach to Online Cursive Script Recognition. *IEEE Transactions on Systems, Man, and Cybernetics. Part B, Cybernetics*, *29*(2), 321–328. doi:10.1109/3477.752808 PMID:18252307

Singh, K. K., & Singh, A. (2010). A Study of Image Segmentation Algorithms For Different Types Of Images. *International Journal of Computer Science Issues, 7*(5).

Singh, Maurya, Singh, & Singh. (2012). Analysis of remote sensed data using hybrid intelligence system: a case study of Bhopal region. *Proceedings of National Conference on Future Aspects of Artificial intelligence in Industrial Automation (NCFAAIIA 2012)*, 26–31.

Singla, Jarial, & Mittal. (2015). An analytical study of the remote sensing image classification using swarm intelligence techniques. *International Journal for Research in Applied Science and Engineering Technology*, *3*(6), 492–497.

Sinha Roy, S., Saha, S., & Basu, A. (2015). Generic Testing Architecture for Digital Watermarking. *Proc. FRCCD-2015*, 50-58.

Smith III. (1971). Two-dimensional formal languages and pattern recogni-tion by cellular automata. *Proceedings of IEEE Conference Record of 12th Annual Symposium on Switching and Automata Theory*.

Song, W., Hou, J., & Li, Z. (2008). SVD and pseudorandom circular chain based watermarking for image authentication. *Journal of Beijing Jiaotong University*, *32*(2), 71–75.

Spang, R. (2003). Diagnostic signatures from microarrays, a bioinformatics concept for personalized medicine. *BIOSILICO*, *1*(2), 64–68. doi:10.1016/S1478-5382(03)02329-1

Stach, J., & Alattar, A. M. (2004). A High Capacity Invertible Data Hiding Algorithm using a Generalized Reversible Integer Transform. *IS&T / SPIE's 16th International Symposium on Electronic Imaging*, *5306*, 386-396.

Stuart, C. I. J., Takahashi, Y., & Umezawa, H. (1978). On the stability and non-local properties of memory. *Journal of Theoretical Biology, 71*(4), 605–618. doi:10.1016/0022-5193(78)90327-2 PMID:661325

Suetens P., Verbeeck R., Delaere D., Nuyts J., & Bijnens B. (1991). Model-Based Image Segmentation: Methods and Applications. *AIME, 91*, 3-24. DOI: .10.1007/978-3-642-48650-0_1

Sup, J., & Hao, S. (2009). Research of fuzzy neural network model based on quantum clustering. *2nd international workshop on knowledge discovery and data mining*, 133-136.

Sur, A., Sagar, S. S., Pal, R., Mitra, P., & Mukhopadhyay, J. (2009). A New Image Watermarking Scheme using Saliency Based Visual Attention Model. *Proceedings of IEEE Annual India Conference*. doi:10.1109/INDCON.2009.5409402

Talbi, H., Draa, A., & Batouche, M. (2004). A New Quantum-Inspired Genetic Algorithm for Solving the Travelling Salesman Problem. *2004 IEEE International Conference on Industrial Technology, 3*, 1192-1197.

Talbi, H., Batouche, M., & Draa, A. (2007). A Qantum - Inspired Evolutionary Algorithm for Multi-objective Image Segmentation, International Journal of Mathematical. *Physical and Engineering Sciences, 1*(7), 109–114.

Talbi, H., Draa, A., & Batouche, M. (2004). A New Quantum-Inspired Genetic Algorithm for Solving the Travelling Salesman Problem. *Proceedings of IEEE International Conference on Industrial Technology (ICIT'04), 3*, 1192–1197 doi:10.1109/ICIT.2004.1490730

Talbi, H., Draa, A., & Batouche, M. (2006). A Novel Quantum-Inspired Evolutionary Algorithm for Multi-Sensor Image Registration. *The International Arab Journal of Information Technology, 3*(1), 9–15.

Tanaka, K., Nakamura, Y., & Matsui, K. (1990). Embedding secret information into a dithered multilevel image. *Proc. IEEE Military Communications Conference*. doi:10.1109/MILCOM.1990.117416

Tan, P.-N., Steinbach, M., & Kumar, V. (2005). *Introduction to Data Mining*. Addison-Wesley Longman, Inc.

Tao, W., Jin, H., & Zhang, Y. (2007). Color Image Segmentation Based on Mean Shift and Normalized Cuts. *IEEE Transactions on Systems, Man, and Cybernetics, Part B (Cybernetics), 37*(5), 1382 – 1389. doi: 10.1109/TSMCB.2007.902249

Tavakkoli-Moghaddam, R., Sadri, S., Pourmohammad-Zia, N., & Mohammadi, M. (2015). A hybrid fuzzy approach for the closed-loop supply chain network design under uncertainty. *Journal of Intelligent & Fuzzy Systems, 28*(6), 2811–2826. doi:10.3233/IFS-151561

Tavazoie, Hughes, Campbell, Cho, & Church. (2001). Systematic determination of genetic network architecture. *Bioinformatics (Oxford, England), 17*, 405–414. PMID:11331234

Teh & Lim. (2006). *A Hybrid Intelligent System and Its Application to Fault Detection and Diagnosis*. Springer.

Test images. (n.d.). Available: http://www.math.tau.ac.il/~turkel/images.html.(Accessed on 15-Jan-2007)

The USC-SIPI Image Database. (n.d.). Retrieved from http://sipi.usc.edu/database/database.php?volume=misc

Thodi, D. M., & Rodriguez, J. J. (2004). Reversible watermarking by prediction-error expansion. *Proceedings - IEEE Southwest Symposium on Image Analysis and Interpretation, 6*, 21–25.

Thodi, D. M., & Rodriguez, J. J. (2007). Expansion Embedding Techniques for Reversible Watermarking. *IEEE Transactions on Image Processing, 16*(3), 721–730. doi:10.1109/TIP.2006.891046 PMID:17357732

Thompson, M., & Thompson, L. (2003). *The neurofeedback book: An introduction to basic concepts in applied psycho-physiology*. Wheat Ridge, CO: Association for Applied Psychophysiology & Biofeedback.

Tian, J. (2002). Reversible watermarking by difference expansion. *Proc. of Workshop on Multimedia and Security: Authentication, Secrecy, and Steganalysis*, 19-22.

Tirkel, A. Z., Rankin, G. A., Van Schyndel, R. M., Ho, W. J., Mee, N. R. A., & Osborne, C. F. (1993). *Electronic Water Mark. Digital Image Computing: Techniques and Applications 1993*. Macquarie University.

Tomoyuki, H., Takuma, A., & Bunpei, I. (2007). An analytic word recognition algorithm using a posteriori probability. *Proceedings of the 9th international conference on document analysis and recognition, 2*, 669–673.

Tsai, C., Chiang, H., Fan, K., & Chung, C. (2005, November). Reversible data hiding and lossless reconstruction of binary images using pair-wise logical computation mechanism. *Pattern Recognition, 38*(11), 1993–2006. doi:10.1016/j.patcog.2005.03.001

Valverde, R. (2011). *Principles of Human Computer Interaction Design: HCI Design*. LAP Lambert Academic Publishing.

Valverde, R. (2015). Neurotechnology as a Tool for Inducing and Measuring Altered States of Consciousness in Transpersonal Psychotherapy. *NeuroQuantology: An Interdisciplinary Journal of Neuroscience and Quantum Physics, 13*(4). doi:10.14704/nq.2015.13.4.870

Vamanan, R. (2015). Quantum computing for big data analysis. *Indian Journal of Science, 14*(43), 98–104.

Venkatesh, V., & Davis, F. D. (2000). A theoretical extension of the technology acceptance model: Four longitudinal field studies. *Management Science, 46*(2), 186–204. doi:10.1287/mnsc.46.2.186.11926

Ventura, D., & Martinez, T. R. (2000). Quantum associative memory. *Information Science, 124*(1-4), 237–296. doi:10.1016/S0020-0255(99)00101-2

Verma, M., & Yadav, P. (2013). Capacity and Security analysis of watermark image truly imperceptible. *Int. Journal of Advanced Research in Computer and Communication Engineering, 2*(7), 2913–2917.

Verma, O. P., Hanmandlu, M., Susan, S., Kulkarni, M., & Jain, P. K. (2011). A Simple Single Seeded Region Growing Algorithm for Color Image Segmentation using Adaptive Thresholding. *2011 International Conference on Communication Systems and Network Technologies (CSNT).* doi:10.1109/CSNT.2011.107

Vijay Patil, V., & Shimpi, S. (2011). Handwritten English Character Recognition using Neural Network. *Journal of Elixir Comp. Sci. &Engg, 41*, 5587–5591.

Villar, Chira, Sedano, Gonz´alez, & Trejo. (2015). A hybrid intelligent recognition system for the early detection of strokes. *Integrated Computer-Aided Engineering, 22*(3), 215–227.

Vitiello, G. (2003). Quantum dissipation and information: A route to consciousness modeling. *NeuroQuantology: An Interdisciplinary Journal of Neuroscience and Quantum Physics, 1*(2).

Vlachopiannts, G., & Lee, K. Y. (2008). Quantum-inspired evolutionary algorithm for real and reactive power systems. *IEEE Transactions on Power Systems, 23*(4), 1627-1636.

Vlachopiannts, S. G., & Lee, K. Y. (2008). Quantum-inspired evolutionary algorithm for real and reactive power systems. *Power Systems. IEEE Transactions on, 23*(4), 1627–1636.

Vleeschouwer, C. D., Delaigle, J. F., & Macq, B. (2003). Circular interpretation of bijective transformations in lossless watermarking for media asset management. *IEEE Transactions on Multimedia, 5*(1), 97–105. doi:10.1109/TMM.2003.809729

Wang, J., Yan, N., Liu, H., Liu, M., & Tai, C. (2007). Brain-computer interfaces based on attention and complex mental tasks. *Digital Human Modeling*, 467-473.

Weiner, J., & Mirkes, K. (1972). *Watermarking.* Appleton, WI: The Institute of Paper Chemistry.

Wille, R., Le, H. M., Dueck, G. W., & Grobe, D. (2008). Quantified synthesis of reversible logic. Design, Automation and Test in Europe (DATE 08), 1015–1020.

Wioletta, W., & Ogiela, M. R. (2016). Digital images authentication scheme based on bimodal biometric watermarking in an independent domain. *Journal of Visual Communication and Image Representation, 38*, 1–10. doi:10.1016/j.jvcir.2016.02.006

Wittek, P. (2014). *Quantum Machine Learning: What Quantum Computing Means to Data Mining.* Academic Press.

Wolfram, S. (1983). Statistical mechanics of cellular automata. *Reviews of Modern Physics, 55*(3), 601–644. doi:10.1103/RevModPhys.55.601

Wolfram, S. (1986). Cryptography with cellular automata. *Lecture Notes in Computer Science, 218*, 429–432. doi:10.1007/3-540-39799-X_32

Wong, M. L. D., Lau, S. I. J., Chong, N. S., & Sim, K. Y. (2013). A Salient Region Watermarking Scheme for Digital Mammogram Authentication. *International Journal of Innovation, Management and Technology, 4*(2), 228–232.

Wujie, Z., Lu, Y., Zhongpeng, W., Mingwei, W., Ting, L., & Lihui, S. (2016). Binocular visual characteristicsbased fragile watermarking schemefor tamper detection in stereoscopic images. *International Journal of Electronics and Communications, 70*(1), 77–84. doi:10.1016/j. aeue.2015.10.006

Xhafa, Kolodziej, Barolli, Kolici, Miho, & Takizawa. (2011). Evaluation of hybridization of GA and TS algorithms for independent batch scheduling in computational grids. In *2011 International Conference on P2P, Parallel, Grid, Cloud and Internet Computing* (pp. 148–155). IEEE Computer Society.

Xiang-yang, W., Yu-nan, L., Shuo, L., Hong-ying, Y., Pan-pan, N., & Yan, Z. (2015). A new robust digital watermarking using local polar harmonic transform. *Journal of Computers and Electrical Engineering, 46*, 403–418. doi:10.1016/j.compeleceng.2015.04.001

Xie, X. L., & Beni, G. (1991). A validity measure for fuzzy clustering. *IEEE PAMI, 13*(8), 841–847. doi:10.1109/34.85677

Xu, Olman, & Xu. (1999). Clustering gene expression data using a graph theoretic approach, an application of minimum spanning trees. *Bioinformatics (Oxford, England), 17*, 309–318.

Xuan, G., Yao, Q., Yang, C., Gao, J., Chai, P., Shi, Y. Q., & Ni, Z. (2006). Lossless Data Hiding Using Histogram Shifting Method Based on Integer Wavelets. *5th Int. Workshop on Digital Watermarking (IWDW 2006), LNCS 4283*, p. 323-332. doi:10.1007/11922841_26

Xuan, G., Shi, Y. Q., Ni, Z. C., Chen, J., Yang, C., Zhen, Y., & Zheng, J. (2004). High capacity lossless data hiding based on integer wavelet transform. *Proceedings of IEEE 2004 International Symposium on Circuits and Systems, 2*, 29-32.

Xuan, G., Shi, Y. Q., Yang, C., Zheng, Y., Zou, D., & Chai, P. (2005). Lossless data hiding using integer wavelet transform and threshold embedding technique. *IEEE Int. Conf. on Multimedia and Expo (ICME05)*. doi:10.1109/ICME.2005.1521722

Xuan, G., Zhu, J., Chen, J., Shi, Y. Q., Ni, Z., & Su, W. (2002). Distortionless Data Hiding Based on Integer Wavelet Transform. *Electronics Letters, 38*(Dec), 1646–1648. doi:10.1049/el:20021131

Xu, H., Wanga, J., & Kim, H. J. (2010). Near-Optimal Solution to Pair Wise LSB Matching Via an Immune Programming Strategy. *Information Sciences, 180*(8), 1201–1217. doi:10.1016/j. ins.2009.12.027

Yang, C. H. (2008). Inverted pattern approach to improve image quality of information hiding by LSB substitution. *Pattern Recognition, 41*(8), 2674–2683. doi:10.1016/j.patcog.2008.01.019

Yang, J., Yan, X., & Yao, B. (2012). Character Feature Extraction Method based on Integrated Neural Network. *AASRI Procedia*, *3*, 197–202. doi:10.1016/j.aasri.2012.11.033

Yang, Y., Sun, X., Yang, H., Li, C., & Xiao, R. (2009). A Contrast-Sensitive Reversible Visible Image Watermarking Technique. *IEEE Transactions on Circuits and Systems for Video Technology*, *19*(5), 656–667. doi:10.1109/TCSVT.2009.2017401

Yaqub, M. K., & Jaber, A. (2006). Reversible watermarking using modified difference expansion. *Int. Journal of Computing and Information Sciences*, *4*(3), 134–142.

Yasue, K., Jibu, M., Misawa, T., & Zambrini, J. C. (1988). Stochastic neurodynamics. *Annals of the Institute of Statistical Mathematics*, *40*(1), 41–59. doi:10.1007/BF00053954

Yogamangalam, R., & Karthikeyan, B. (2013). Segmentation Techniques Comparison in Image Processing. *International Journal of Engineering and Technology, 5.*

Zadeh, L. A. (1965). Fuzzy sets. *Information and Control*, *8*(3), 338–353. doi:10.1016/S0019-9958(65)90241-X

Zhang, G. (2011). Quantum-inspired evolutionary algorithms: A survey and empirical study. *Journal of Heuristics*, *17*(3), 303–351. doi:10.1007/s10732-010-9136-0

Zhang, H., Fritts, J., & Goldman, S. (2004). An entropy-based objective evaluation method for image segmentation. *Proceedings of SPIE Storage and Retrieval Methods and Applications for Multimedia.*

Zhao, Y., & Karypis, G. (2002). Evaluation of hierarchical clustering algorithms for document datasets. *Procedings of CIKM*, 515–524.

Zhao, Z., Zheng, S., & Shang, J. (2007). A study of cognitive radio decision engine based on quantum genetic algorithm. *Wuli Xuebao*, *56*, 6760–6766.

Zhou, S., Chen, Q., & Wang, X. (2010). Deep quantum networks for classification. *20th International conference on international conference on pattern recognition*, 2885–2888.

# Index

## A

ant colony optimization 16, 27, 29, 34, 39, 41, 53, 184
artificial intelligence 1, 23, 28, 181

## B

back-propagation algorithm 263-265, 269, 272-273
big data 15, 23, 279

## C

cellular automata 178-180, 189, 193, 205-206, 212
cluster 4, 22, 27-29, 35-39, 41, 43-44, 47, 54, 56, 58-60, 67-68, 94, 153, 196, 202-204, 212, 215
cluster validity index 41, 44, 54
clustering 13, 15, 27-29, 35, 39, 41, 44, 47, 53-56, 58-59, 88, 94, 108, 151, 153, 179-180, 195, 198, 202-203, 206, 212, 214, 220-221
computational intelligence 2, 5, 12, 16, 26
context sensitive 141, 143-144, 174, 244, 246, 253
context sensitive threshold 174
Correlation Coefficient 65-66

## D

digital image watermarking 95, 101, 116, 129

## E

EEG 277-280, 284, 289-294
empirical measures 65

## F

FCM 13, 55-59, 67-68, 70-71, 78, 84-90, 94, 178, 180, 193, 195-196, 198-200, 204, 207

## G

genetic algorithm 2, 55-57, 59-60, 64, 67, 70, 88, 94, 108, 183-184, 216
gray scale image 56, 143-146, 154, 161, 164, 174, 223

## H

handwritten character recognition 262-265, 271-272
hardware 95-96, 100, 103, 105, 108, 118, 126, 129, 184

## I

imperceptibility 95-96, 100-102, 114, 126, 129, 131

## K

K-Means algorithm 21, 153, 195-196, 199, 203, 212

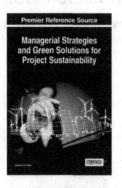

# Information Resources Management Association

Advancing the Concepts & Practices of Information Resources Management in Modern Organizations

# Become an IRMA Member

Members of the **Information Resources Management Association (IRMA)** understand the importance of community within their field of study. The Information Resources Management Association is an ideal venue through which professionals, students, and academicians can convene and share the latest industry innovations and scholarly research that is changing the field of information science and technology. Become a member today and enjoy the benefits of membership as well as the opportunity to collaborate and network with fellow experts in the field.

## IRMA Membership Benefits:

- **One FREE Journal Subscription**
- **30% Off Additional Journal Subscriptions**
- **20% Off Book Purchases**
- Updates on the latest events and research on Information Resources Management through the IRMA-L listserv.
- Updates on new open access and downloadable content added to Research IRM.
- A copy of the Information Technology Management Newsletter twice a year.
- A certificate of membership.

## IRMA Membership $195

Scan code or visit **irma-international.org** and begin by selecting your free journal subscription.

Membership is good for one full year.

Printed in the United States
By Bookmasters